The Boundaries between Us

The Boundaries between Us

*Natives and Newcomers along the Frontiers of the
Old Northwest Territory, 1750–1850*

EDITED BY DANIEL P. BARR

The Kent State University Press

KENT, OHIO

© 2006 by The Kent State University Press, Kent, Ohio 44242
All rights reserved
Library of Congress Catalog Card Number 2005016600
ISBN-10: 0-87338-844-5
ISBN-13: 978-0-87338-844-3
Manufactured in the United States of America

10 09 08 07 06   5 4 3 2 1

LIBRARY OF CONGRESS CATALOGING-IN-PUBLICATION DATA

The boundaries between us : Natives and newcomers along the frontiers of the Old
Northwest Territory, 1750–1850 / edited by Daniel P. Barr
    p.   cm.
Includes bibliographical references and index.
ISBN-13: 978-0-87338-844-3 (pbk. : alk. paper) ∞
ISBN-10: 0-87338-844-5 (pbk. : alk. paper) ∞
 1. Indians of North America—First contact with Europeans—Ohio River Valley.
2. Indians of North America—Land tenure—Ohio River Valley.   3. Indians of North
America—Ohio River Valley—Government relations.   4. Frontier and pioneer
life—Ohio River Valley.   5. Whites—Ohio River Valley—Relations with Indians.
6. Ohio River Valley—Race relations.   7. Ohio River Valley—Politics and
government.   I. Barr, Daniel P., 1971–
    E78.O4B58   2005
    977'.02—dc22   2005016600

British Library Cataloging-in-Publication data are available.

Contents

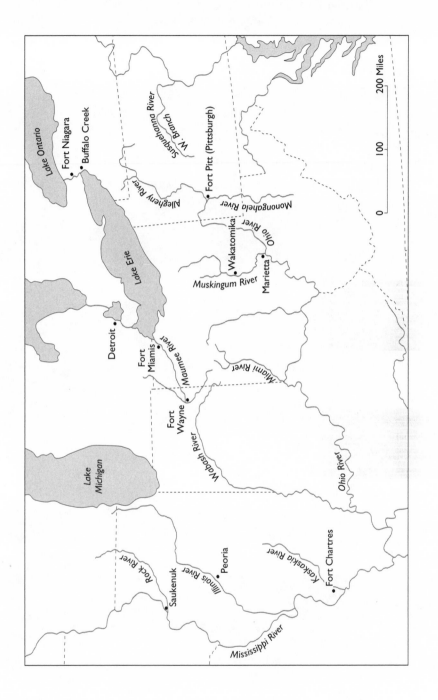

Introduction: Fluid Boundaries and Negotiated Identities

Intersection, Accommodation, and Conflict on an Evolving Frontier

The settlement history of the United States' first national frontier, the Old Northwest Territory, is rich with compelling drama and captivating characters, especially when focused on the interaction between native peoples and Euro-American newcomers. One can hardly envision this aspect of the region's early history without bringing to mind Tecumseh or Black Hawk, William Henry Harrison or Anthony Wayne, while images of Indian warriors stalking Arthur St. Clair's doomed army in the Ohio wilderness contrast with visions of American pioneers successfully establishing themselves upon the fields and prairies of Indiana and Illinois. Yet outside of these familiar stories and comfortable understandings of Indians and white settlers in the Old Northwest Territory, there is much that remains unexplored, understudied, or misunderstood about cultural interaction and accommodation. Such sentiment was raised, in part, by historians Andrew Cayton and Peter Onuf, whose 1990 interpretive work *The Midwest and the Nation: Rethinking the History of an American Region* critiqued the existing body of scholarship on the Old Northwest Territory. Cayton and Onuf asserted their intention to "encourage historians to think about the region in more systematic ways than they have in the past . . . [and] to suggest that the Old Northwest was more than a generic frontier or a cultural crossroads." They hoped to excite historians into a vast reexamination of the Old Northwest Territory and the states it eventually became, a process that began with the meetings of native inhabitants and newcomers. Moreover, this conceptual call-to-arms underscored an understanding that the Old Northwest Territory occupies a fundamental place in the early history of American westward expansion. Here for the new American nation came the first great challenge of the West, to manage and control not only its claimed territory, but also the diverse peoples—Indian and white—whose lives, ambitions, and futures were tied to the region. The region thus served as a primer for the larger process of contact, conquest, and colonialism that would unfold as the United States expanded westward.[1]

The Old Northwest Territory was fertile ground for conflict, accommodation, resistance, and adaptation, and it thus remains fertile ground for historical inquiry. A generation of new studies has reopened the ground in the Old Northwest in an effort to advance our understandings of the region, its diverse peoples, and their significance in the larger realm of American history.[2] Much of recent scholarship pertaining to the Old Northwest Territory derives its focus from significant trends that emerged in early American historiography over the past few decades. Among the most vibrant have been the (now-not-so) "'New' Indian history" and the growing number of studies that focus on the eastern frontiers of North America. The New Indian history grew in large part from the efforts of a specialized group of historians, generally dubbed ethnohistorians, who eschewed longstanding but worn out themes of American Indian victimization and helplessness in favor of agency, in the process offering compelling new insights into the diverse ways that native peoples influenced, shaped, and participated in American history. While the body of work in this field is broad, much of the best scholarship has addressed early American history, where the meeting of diffuse cultures was so crucial. Scholars such as Colin Calloway, Richard White, R. David Edmunds, and James Axtell, among many others, have declined to settle for viewing Indian history through the old lens of interpretation—the simplistic, often redundant tale of the violent clash between Indian nations and the Anglo-Americans who dispossessed them, a tired interpretive vehicle driven most often by the monolithic theme of inevitable conquest—and instead focused their vision on the complicated interrelationships that grew out of the diverse meetings, intersections, and conflicts between natives and newcomers along the frontiers of early America. As a consequence, they have opened intriguing new avenues for investigation into what Colin Calloway has termed "New Worlds for All."[3]

Concurrently, albeit somewhat younger than the New Indian scholarship, there have been transforming studies of the importance of frontier settlement in early American history. Focused on the eastern frontiers of North America, which in truth stretch geographically from the Atlantic seashore to the Mississippi River (though the eastern frontier is too often referred to simply as the colonial backcountry), these works, like those of New Indian history, move beyond familiar historical models—namely the seemingly linear evolution of the transplanted British communities along the Atlantic coast into the United States—and instead attribute great importance to the intersection of Indians, westward moving colonists, and empires in midland North America.

Here, on the fluid frontiers of early America, historians have found patterns of interaction, cooperation, competition, and conflict that established important precedents and left lasting legacies for the future westward expansion of what would become the United States, offering interesting new avenues of exploration for Frederick Jackson Turner's much maligned but incredibly resilient notion that the frontier experience shaped American culture.[4]

Most importantly, there has been a trend to blend these two methodologies into a singular approach, as both the New Indian history and eastern frontier studies share a common understanding that the significance of cultural interaction is more often found in the meeting than in the end result. Perhaps no singular study has done more to advance this understanding than *The Middle Ground: Indians, Empires, and Republics in the Great Lakes Region, 1650–1815,* Richard White's vastly influential take on the intersection of diverse cultures, interests, and aspirations in what would eventually become the Old Northwest Territory. White argued that "on the middle ground diverse peoples adjust their differences through what amounts to a process of creative, and often expedient misunderstandings." Here natives and newcomers came together in the spirit of accommodation, appealing to each others' cultural values, always, however, with an eye toward advancing their own interests. Moreover, White demonstrated that to truly understand the meeting of natives and newcomers in this region, historians must examine events at the local or village level. Only by looking there can we come to an understanding of how Indians and Euro-Americans strove to create a world that might include everyone.[5]

In the wake of *The Middle Ground* have come several recent studies that build upon, interpret, and in some cases recast White's model of frontier and cultural interaction. These studies engage both the middle ground as an interpretive model and the influence that White's interpretation has had upon scholars studying cultural interaction, tacitly—if not overtly—examining where the concept of the middle ground failed, floundered, or persevered. Recent works by Daniel Richter and Jane Merritt, for example, have demonstrated that the development of racial hatred among both natives and newcomers occurred earlier and was more widespread than White acknowledges.[6] White certainly allows for this concept, but he sees it primarily as a phenomenon that arises in the wake of the American Revolution, arguing that in the years following the Revolution "the common world yielded to a frontier over which people crossed only to shed blood."[7] Yet emerging scholarship, including several of the essays in this collection, is demonstrating that real forms of accommodation existed between natives and newcomers in the Old Northwest region long after the creation of the United States. These may have been limited to prominent individuals or particular localities, but the concept of the middle ground did not necessarily die away entirely.

The Boundaries between Us seeks to engage and expand on these ideas and methodologies while asking new questions about the relationships between natives and newcomers, both ahead of and behind the frontiers of Euro-American settlement in the Old Northwest Territory. Gathering together eleven original essays, it examines the sociocultural contexts in which natives and newcomers lived, traded, negotiated, interacted, and fought. Together they created a landscape of fluid boundaries and negotiated identities, a rapidly changing world where the possibility for accommodation or conflict ebbed and flowed within the context of local circumstances and individual choices. Examples of this shifting world come from a broad geographic range of what can be considered the Old Northwest Territory, originating in the upper Ohio River valley of what is now western Pennsylvania, stretching west to the Illinois-Iowa border, and encapsulating many points in between. The temporal journey is expansive as well, ranging from the years just prior to the Seven Years' War, moving through the Early Republic, and eventually coming to rest in the Indian Removal Era of the 1830s and 1840s. Together the essays offer a broad historical perspective on a century of contact, interaction, conflict, and displacement that aspires to offer new avenues of inquiry for unfolding discussions in the history of the Old Northwest Territory, as well as the history of early America, the eastern frontier, and cultural interaction between native peoples and newcomers.

The essays are arranged chronologically and spatially, with the first four essays investigating the interaction of natives and newcomers within the context of the imperial struggle to control the interior of North America prior to the creation of the United States. Beginning in the mid-eighteenth century in the Ohio Country—widely defined here as stretching from the forks of the Ohio River to the Illinois Valley—these essays focus primarily on native reactions to colonialism and imperial reactions to native resistance. Here, indeed, a new world was created for all, one that demanded change on the part of both natives and newcomers while presenting challenges that both struggled to meet as they alternately traded, negotiated, and fought with one another.

In the opening essay, "The Shawnees and the English: Captives and War," distinguished historian Ian K. Steele reexamines the relationship between the Ohio Shawnees, British authorities, and American colonists during the era of the Seven Years' War in North America. His account focuses on the circumstances surrounding the incarceration of six Shawnee warriors in 1753 by colonial authorities in South Carolina, an imprisonment that precipitated the destruction of pro-British sympathies among the Shawnees, prompted their alliance with the French during the Seven Years' War, and caused lingering bitterness toward Americans that again led to violence during Pontiac's Rebellion in 1763. In tracing this little-known episode in Shawnee history, Steele offers a thought-provoking analysis of the differing cultural understandings of captivity, stressing the role that misconceptions and failed negotiations played in the onset of war. He concludes that the Anglo-American demands for the return of white captives as a condition of peace at war's end constituted a serious "grievance of honor" for the Shawnees, a perceived decline of status so severe that it brought about new political and diplomatic orientations within Shawnee society, which in turn forged the militant stance that dominated Shawnee-American relations through the War of 1812.

Similarly, my offering, "'This Land Is Ours and Not Yours': The Western Delawares and the Seven Years' War in the Upper Ohio Valley," addresses the motivations and actions of the western Delaware Indians, those living along the present-day Pennsylvania-Ohio border, before and during the Seven Years' War. Like the Shawnees in Steele's account, I find that the western Delawares' decision for war was specific to their own experiences, which included strong recollections of earlier removals from Pennsylvania, the failure of negotiation to preserve their land rights in the upper Ohio Valley, and a militant determination not to become migrants again. Emboldened by their past experiences, these Delawares launched a systematic campaign designed to achieve not victory over the enemy's military forces on the battlefield, but rather the subjugation of the settler population in the Pennsylvania backcountry in order to force a negotiated political settlement that would assure their territorial integrity against the advancing tide of colonial settlement. At first unwilling, and then unable to defend their borders, colonial officials in Pennsylvania eventually settled, agreeing to a treaty that, at least in spirit, satisfied western Delaware demands.

On the heels of the Seven Years' War, David Dixon uncovers the broad roots of native unity during the 1763 Indian uprising in the Ohio Country in "'We Speak as One People': Native Unity and the Pontiac Indian Uprising." Disputing interpretations that too narrowly afford the Ottawa chief Pontiac a primal role in fomenting unified native resistance, Dixon explains native unity during the uprising through the anthropological model of ethnogenesis—the process of cultural reinvention practiced by native groups who, facing great pressure and stress from advancing Anglo-American colonialism, reorient their societies and cultures in an effort to stave off elimination. He finds that it was chiefly their desire to retain and reinvigorate traditional lifeways and preserve their cultural integrity that led diverse native groups in the Ohio Country to forge the unanimity necessary to launch a Pan-Indian uprising against the British and their American colonialists.

In the years following the Seven Years' War, Matthew C. Ward argues, the British Army and the Ohio Indians developed an unusually close social and economic relationship, centered on the British Army's attempts to protect the

Indians from aggressive American colonial settlers. In "'The Indians Our Real Friends': The British Army and the Ohio Indians," Ward demonstrates that most British officers, and many enlisted men, sympathized with the plight of the Indians of the Northwest, instead blaming interloping colonial traders and settlers for causing the contention that had marked the region over the previous decade. In discussing the British Army's role in overcoming that tension, Ward illuminates a compelling dichotomy faced by the army in the Old Northwest: on one hand, the British Army existed as a force of mediation and direction between Indians and colonists, especially in matters of trade and commerce; on the other hand, the army had to keep the two cultures separate, especially where territory and land issues were at stake, in order to preserve peace. The British Army thus had the difficult, if not impossible, task of bridging certain boundaries between cultures while also keeping others firmly in place. Viewed within the context of this dilemma, Ward offers a clearer understanding of the pitfalls of British frontier policy and the inability of the army to successfully integrate its bifurcated duty assignment along the Old Northwest frontier.

The remaining seven essays address the Old Northwest Territory after the formation of the American nation. They illuminate specific individuals, episodes, and developments within the complex struggle for control of the region during the formative years of the Early Republic, including the military, economic, social, and conceptual layers of the contest for the region. From the end of the American Revolution through the height of the Indian Removal Era, the Old Northwest housed continued tensions between native peoples and newcomers. During these turbulent and expansive decades, however, the struggle took new forms as American settlement and development intensified and the American government sought to consolidate its hegemony over the region. As had occurred during the imperial contest for the Midwest, native peoples met these challenges in diffuse ways, particular to their own needs and circumstances. The essays in this section move beyond familiar accounts of the Northwest Indian wars and Tecumseh, and instead illuminate some of the ways in which natives and newcomers addressed one another away from the battlefield.

Lisa Brooks's essay begins this process, looking beyond the violence that often accompanied Indian efforts to preserve their lands in the Northwest, instead exploring the important ways in which native traditions and political philosophy guided the struggle for autonomy. In "Two Paths to Peace: Competing Visions of Native Space in the Old Northwest," she explores the competing visions of Mohawk leader Joseph Brant and Stockbridge Mahican leader Hendrick Aupaumut regarding peace and the preservation of native space in the Old Northwest Territory in the decade after the American Revolution.

Brant, advocating a traditional Iroquoian concept known as "the Dish with
One Spoon," argued for the creation of an Indian Confederation in the Northwest, a unified polity that could speak with one voice and successfully negotiate favorable terms with the newly formed United States. Aupaumut also
desired union, but he strove to reintegrate his Mahican people into a position
of importance vis-à-vis the Indians of the region by brokering a treaty with
the United States government. It was his hope that his dispossessed people
might hang their "kettle" alongside a "common pot" for all Northwest tribes,
finding both a new home and a new meaning for their disrupted lives. Both
leaders ultimately sought the same goals—union and self-preservation—
but by dissecting and analyzing their differing approaches and self-interests,
Brooks advances our understanding of how native peoples conceived and
constructed that most elusive of creations—unity.

In "'A Superior Civilization': Appropriation, Negotiation, and Interaction
in the Northwest Territory," Frazer Dorian McGlinchey takes a somewhat different tack, addressing the landscape of the Old Northwest and the hopes and
aspirations that American newcomers had for its development. His analysis
focuses on Marietta, Ohio, the first official settlement in the region formally
defined as the Northwest Territory by the United States government. Here the
associates of the Ohio Company planned to erect an atypical settlement, a
gleaming example of the magnificent civilization to which the new American
nation could aspire. As McGlinchey relates, the plans of the Marietta settlers
had little use for the former native inhabitants of the region, yet they struggled to imprint their vision for the landscape over the tangible and physical
reminders that the land once boasted a formidable native presence. And when
native resistance again flared during the Northwest Indian wars of the 1790s,
their vision for the landscape eroded beneath practical demands for defense
and security. Despite their best efforts, the Marietta settlers struggled to create
their "superior civilization" in a landscape that did not yet allow for a world
without Indians.

The social and cultural boundaries separating natives and newcomers in
northeastern Indiana is the subject of Donald H. Gaff's essay, "Three Men
from Three Rivers: Navigating between Native and American Identity in the
Old Northwest Territory." Taking material culture as his cue, Gaff brings an
anthropologist's eye to studying the clothing, homes, and possessions of three
prominent Miami Indian leaders, Little Turtle, Jean Baptiste Richardville, and
William Wells. By studying their material habits and creature comforts, Gaff
demonstrates the porous nature of the boundaries separating native and
American identity in the Old Northwest Territory, especially when applied to
influential and important individuals. As he points out, the lives of these three
prominent men reveal the fluidity of the frontier in this portion of the Old

Northwest, where cultural and societal barriers were transparent enough to
allow Little Turtle, Richardville, and Wells to actively involve themselves on
both sides of the cultural divide as it pleased them. By relating their activities
along the Old Northwest frontier, Gaff offers a compelling case that it is still
eminently useful, where possible, to understand cultural assimilation in terms
of individuals, rather than tightly confining our historical inquiries in that
arena to the broader categories of tribes and ethnicities.

Few events along the frontiers of the Old Northwest Territory generated
the level of tension between natives and newcomers as did murder, both
of whites by Indians and of Indians by whites. In "Negotiating Law on the
Frontier: Responses to Cross-Cultural Homicide in Illinois," Bruce P. Smith
examines the seldom addressed ways in which Americans and native peoples
engaged the law in response to the murder of one of their own by the other.
Noting that there is scant extant scholarship devoted to the study of murder in
the Old Northwest Territory, Smith employs case studies to demonstrate that
native peoples were capable, at least in certain instances, of engaging American law and using American legal institutions for their own ends. As such,
the legal system on the Old Northwest frontier remained a *de facto* middle
ground, and the law remained a place where natives and newcomers could engage one another on relatively equal footing, long after other forms of cultural
mediation had been subjugated.

Phyllis Gernhardt's essay, "'Justice and Public Policy': Indian Trade, Treaties, and Removal from Northern Indiana," scrutinizes the route by which
treaties signed by the Potawatomis and the Miamis forced these Indian nations into economic entrapment. Crucial to this process were self-serving
American Indian traders, merchants, and businessmen whose livelihood depended on maintaining a native presence in the region. As Gernhardt relates,
these traders became intricately involved in American Indian policy. Recognizing the traders' intimate contacts with native society, the United States
government relied on these merchants' abilities to influence the native inhabitants at treaty negotiations, and in particular, the government manipulated
the Indians' financial obligations and debts to the traders as a means to secure
native land cessions. Yet the formula did not always produce a favorable equa-
tion. From their central place of influence, the Indian traders of northern
Indiana often put themselves ahead of both Indians and the federal government, playing both sides against the other to assure that they stood to reap the
greatest benefit from the removal process. Gernhardt's essay is a wonderful
departure point for greater study of the role that private citizens played in
bringing about Indian removal in the Old Northwest.

Ginette Aley explores the surprising and often ironic influence of the
transportation revolution on federal Indian policy in the Old Northwest Ter-

ritory during the first half of the nineteenth century. Seeking to shed light on how the transportation revolution affected native-newcomer relations, her essay, "Bringing About the Dawn: Agriculture, Internal Improvements, Indian Policy, and Euro-American Hegemony in the Old Northwest," charts an intriguing course along the parallel streams of internal improvement and Indian removal. In her analysis, the construction of canals and the establishment of market-based agriculture represented the finalization of American dominion over the land. Yet it is the process, more than the result, that merits attention in Aley's careful handling of events. Utilizing Indiana as her litmus test, she makes a clear case for understanding the internal improvement movement, subject as it was to both national and local machinations, as an important determinant in native-newcomer relations and the formulation of the Indian Removal policy as a desired federal objective in the Old Northwest Territory. Of particular interest is the impact that improved transportation had on the ability of native peoples to retain any presence in the emerging landscape of the region, as the proposed routes of canals and roads transformed formerly undesirable land—territory often relegated to Indians in treaties—into highly coveted space that resulted in refocused efforts to remove all Indians even further to margins of territorial society and space.

The leadership of Keokuk, a contemporary and sometimes adversary of Black Hawk, is the subject of Thomas J. Lappas's essay, "'A Perfect Apollo': Keokuk and Sac Leadership during the Removal Era." Examining Keokuk not from the vantage point of a cross-cultural mediator but rather as a traditional leader of native peoples, Lappas concludes that Keokuk's adherence to the requirements of native society led him to seek peace and accommodation with the United States government, in contrast to his more celebrated counterpart Black Hawk. Consciously avoiding the path of military resistance, Keokuk nonetheless achieved a remarkable level of success in securing rights and privileges for his people from the United States government. The key to his success, Lappas concludes, was his ability to don the familiar roles of a traditional Sac leader, appeasing his home constituency while at the same time playing the role of warrior and military leader, which seemed necessary in order to gain concessions from the Americans. With feet firmly planted in two worlds, Keokuk steered his people through the dangerous Removal Era, affording them at least the possibility of new life west of the Mississippi River.

Collectively the essays presented in *The Boundaries between Us* narrate the rich history of cultural convergence and conflict that marked the struggle for resources, land, and ultimately the future of the Old Northwest. The authors do not attempt to present a unified interpretation of the many dimensions of this struggle, rather they focus on both specific and general topics, revisit and reinterpret well-known events and actors, and underscore how cultural, political, and ideological maxims shaped the interaction between natives and newcomers in the Old Northwest Territory. None of the essays collected here make pretense to being the definitive account of the region's history, rather they hope to come at the integrated story of cooperation, competition, and conflict from fresh and interesting angles, and ultimately to help spur more inquiry into the subject. Like all useful history, the essays hope to spawn, as well as answer, questions about the past, reminding us that we yet have much to learn.

Finally, a brief word about the rationale behind the title: *The Boundaries between Us* is a reflection of the ways in which natives and newcomers organized their interactions with one another in the Old Northwest Territory. Like so many zones of intercultural contact, Indians and Euro-Americans in the Old Northwest understood their relationship with each other in terms of boundaries. Euro-Americans had clearly held definitions of political borders and their place in society, but native peoples also increasingly came to understand the value of a political boundary, as when Indian representatives at a 1793 treaty meeting with the United States asserted, "We shall be persuaded that you mean to do us justice if you agree that the Ohio shall remain the boundary line between us, and if you do not consent thereto, our meeting will be altogether necessary."[8] Their worlds were aligned around political boundaries: the Proclamation Line of 1763, the Fort Stanwix Treaty Line of 1768, the border established by the Treaty of Greenville in 1795, among many others. But the title also refers to a more subtle usage of the term boundary within a cultural lexicon, as an amorphous, negotiated construct that meant different things to different people on individual, societal, or even emotional levels. Definitions of such boundaries were not found on treaties but in the beliefs, motivations, and hopes of the people and their home cultures. This, as much as any other factor, perhaps accounts for the great diversity of interaction between natives and newcomers in the Old Northwest Territory.

NOTES

1. Andrew R. L. Cayton and Peter S. Onuf, *The Midwest and the Nation: Rethinking the History of an American Region* (Bloomington: Indiana Univ. Press, 1990), xii.

2. The following list of scholarship pertaining to the Old Northwest is, admittedly, only a selective representation of the literature available. It is limited to selected works that have appeared since Cayton and Onuf's call-to-arms in 1990. See, for example, Walter Dunn, *Opening New Markets: The British Army and the Old Northwest* (Westport, Conn.: Praeger, 2002); Milo Milton Quaife, *Chicago and the Old Northwest, 1763–1835: A Study of the Evolution of the Northwestern Frontier* (Urbana: Univ. of Illinois Press, 2001); David Curtis Scaggs and Larry L. Nelson, eds., *The Sixty Years' War for the Great Lakes,*

1754–1814 (East Lansing: Michigan State Univ. Press, 2001); Nicole Etcheson, *The Emerging Midwest: Upland Southerners and the Political Culture of the Old Northwest, 1787–1861* (Bloomington: Indiana Univ. Press, 1996); and Susan E. Gray, *The Yankee West: Community Life on the Michigan Frontier* (Chapel Hill: Univ. of North Carolina Press, 1996). See also numerous titles in Indiana University Press's History of the Trans-Appalachian Frontier series, including Douglas R. Hurt, *The Ohio Frontier: Crucible of the Old Northwest* (1996); Andrew R. L. Cayton, *Frontier Indiana* (1996); James E. Davis, *Frontier Illinois* (1998); and Mark Wyman, *The Wisconsin Frontier* (1998).

3. The wonderful variety of compelling work relating to the New Indian history of early America is far too vast to list here. However, for starters, see Colin G. Calloway, *The American Revolution in Indian Country: Crisis and Diversity in Native American Communities* (New York: Cambridge Univ. Press, 1995), and *New Worlds for All: Indians, Europeans, and the Remaking of Early America* (Baltimore, Md.: Johns Hopkins Univ. Press, 1997); Richard White, *The Middle Ground: Indians, Empires, and Republics in the Great Lakes Region, 1650–1815* (New York: Cambridge Univ. Press, 1991); R. David Edmunds, *The Potawatomis: Keepers of the Fire* (Norman: Univ. of Oklahoma Press, 1978), and *Tecumseh and the Quest for Indian Leadership* (Boston, Mass.: Little, Brown, 1984); and James Axtell, *After Columbus: Essays in the Ethnohistory of Colonial North America* (New York: Oxford Univ. Press, 1989), *Beyond 1492: Cultural Encounters in Colonial North America* (New York: Oxford Univ. Press, 1992), and *Natives and Newcomers: The Cultural Origins of North America* (New York: Oxford Univ. Press, 2001).

4. Like the New Indian history, the emerging body of studies focusing on the eastern frontiers of North America is expansive. Among the more compelling are Stephen Aron, *How the West Was Lost: The Transformation of Kentucky from Daniel Boone to Henry Clay* (Baltimore, Md.: Johns Hopkins Univ. Press, 1996); Eric Hinderaker, *Elusive Empires: Constructing Colonialism in the Ohio Valley, 1673–1800* (New York: Cambridge Univ. Press, 1997); David Colin Crass, ed., *The Southern Colonial Backcountry: Interdisciplinary Perspectives on Frontier Communities* (Knoxville: Univ. of Tennessee Press, 1998); and Andrew R. L. Cayton and Fredericka Teute, eds., *Contact Points: American Frontiers from the Mohawk Valley to the Mississippi, 1750–1830* (Chapel Hill: Univ. of North Carolina Press, 1998). In addition, a recent overview has much to offer; see Eric Hinderaker and Peter C. Macall, *At the Edge of Empire: The Backcountry in British North America* (Baltimore, Md.: Johns Hopkins Univ. Press, 2003).

5. White, The *Middle Ground*, x.

6. Daniel K. Richter, *Facing East from Indian Country: A Native History of Early America* (Cambridge, Mass.: Harvard Univ. Press, 2001), 189–236; and Jane T. Merritt, *At the Crossroads: Indians and Empires on a Mid-Atlantic Frontier, 1700–1763* (Chapel Hill: Univ. of North Carolina Press, 2003), 235–307. White painted such a masterful picture of the potential and possibility represented by accommodation in *The Middle Ground* that there has been a tendency to overemphasize that aspect of cultural interaction on the early American frontier.

7. White, The *Middle Ground*, 456.

8. Indian Representatives, "Proposal to Maintain Indian Lands, 1793," in Colin G. Calloway, ed., *The World Turned Upside Down: Indian Voices from Early America* (Boston, Mass.: Bedford, 1994), 183.

1

The Shawnees and the English

Captives and War, 1753–1765

IAN K. STEELE

For a quarter of a millennium, the Ohio Shawnees were maligned and misunderstood participants in the Seven Years' War. They were seen as bloodthirsty opportunists who accepted French inducements to commence war against the English in 1754, with whom they fought with demonic cruelty. Then, in making peace, they were known "for their deceit and perfidy, paying little or no regard to their word and most solemn engagements," as Robert Rogers claimed in 1765.[1] These self-serving claims need to be reexamined to provide a more balanced account of the Shawnees. One particularly fruitful way of reviewing them comes through the study of Shawnee captivities. Despite all the scholarly attention to surviving white captivity narratives, as culturally defining popular literature or even as cultural "liberation" for white women, there has been little general analysis of the experiences of Shawnee captives or any understanding of the persisting Shawnee views of captivity in the face of growing English rigidity on the subject. The Shawnees' decision to engage in the Seven Years' War, their conduct in the war, and their prolonged and unfinished route to peace are more comprehensible if captives are seen as central.[2]

Although the Shawnees' road to war against the English had preconditions in land disputes and personal grievances, it was unintentionally triggered in Wakatomika (Waketummaky, Lapitchuna, Upper Shawnee Town) on the Muskingum River in April of 1753, when thirteen warriors undertook an arduous, risky, and time-honored quest to raid the distant Catawbas for prisoners and scalps. The intent was to weaken and humiliate a traditional enemy, replace specific war casualties, and enhance the reputations of the captors. Even as it began, this particular raid had at least one additional purpose. The

1

Iroquois Confederacy, with British colonial encouragement, had claimed a dubious authority over the Shawnees during the previous decade. The Iroquois had finally made a tentative peace with the British-allied Catawbas in 1751, and the pro-British Shawnees of Wakatomika were challenging the Iroquois overlordship by launching this highly visible attack on the Catawbas in the spring of 1753.[3]

This Shawnee raid was destined to become a fiasco with serious consequences. The party set off equipped with horses and several prized rifled guns, evidences of cultural adaptability, status, and prosperity. The expedition was also accompanied by its leader's medicine bundle, which included a belt of black wampum, sacred buffalo hair "prisoner ties" for anticipated captives, and silver bracelets and a silver cross. This mix of traditional and alien accouterments suggests the hybridity of these Shawnees, who were long familiar with Europeans. The leader was Itawachcomequa, "the Pride," who once had attacked Pennsylvanian traders along the Allegheny River but more recently had become a prominent pro-English chief whom one Shawnee spokesman called "a noted Man among the Shawonese, a great Warrior and a true Friend to the English." Staying "out of the Way, and by the Heads of the Rivers" the group reportedly lost their way in the Appalachian Mountains and seven of them turned back, including two who had become lame and two others who agreed to see them safely home. The remaining six persevered in their quest. "After we had marched a very long Way, not knowing the Path, we found ourselves in the white People's Country. The white People told us that if we should be taken, we should be carried Prisoners to Charles Town."[4]

These Shawnees later indicated that they understood English quite well, but they did not know how dangerous the South Carolina frontier had become. A series of incidents had prompted a panic in 1751 that caused mutually antagonistic South Carolinians and Cherokees to migrate or fortify. South Carolinians continued to be witnesses, and occasionally victims, of raiding bands of Caughnawaga Iroquois and various poorly identified "Northern Indians," thought to have been encouraged by the increasingly belligerent French. In April 1753, South Carolina's veteran governor, James Glen, issued a proclamation offering £100 to anyone who captured or killed Indians involved in a recent murder. The proclamation also offered £50 to those who captured or killed any "other Northern Indians who shall come into our Settlements after the Expiration of Three Months, unless such Indians shall have in their Company some white Man, and be coming down on any Business or Message to this Government." To counter the northern Indians, the nervous South Carolina government offered identical rewards for Indians taken dead or alive, and bounty hunters could be expected to kill Indian strangers, who would then pose no threat to either the lives or the explanations of their "captors." Itawachcomequa and his band had entered very dangerous territory.[5]

Responding to reports of suspicious strangers, thirty South Carolina militiamen surrounded the six Ohio Shawnees in a farmhouse near the Salkehatchie River in the southeastern corner of the colony. Surprisingly, the Shawnees agreed to surrender their weapons and be conducted to the governor "under the Care and Protection of a Party of our Militia, rather than as Prisoners of War, that they may go without Fear," as Lt. Gov. William Bull explained in sending them on to Governor Glen in Charles Town. Bull added, "I have treated them kindly, for which they seem very thankful, and told them they are a going to hear your Excellency's Talk." The non-violent capture of well-armed warriors by white militiamen was extraordinary, especially since Indian warriors abhorred incarceration, seldom surrendered to whites, and were rarely taken as captives.[6]

Might Shawnee captives fare well in peacetime if they understood some English, surrendered without inflicting any casualties, were supported by a lieutenant governor's sympathetic letter, and arrived during Governor Glen's declared three-month period of grace? The initial reception in Charles Town was certainly not encouraging. On June 18, 1753, the *South Carolina Gazette* printed an article that stated the hope that other militia would act similarly and "soon clear the Country of these French and Northern Indians that have for some Years past infested this Province," an item that was widely reprinted in the British colonies. Governor Glen immediately ordered the Shawnees to be jailed and then, together with his Council, grilled the prisoners individually, accusing them of murder and of contradicting each other. Once an adequate translator was found, the Council heard Itawachcomequa say, "I am a Friend to all the People here. I am a Shavanah and loyal to the English."[7]

The clearest statement of the warriors' purpose was offered by the youngest Shawnee, a teen captured with his father and initially interrogated with him as well. The youth admitted that they came to capture Catawba prisoners but had taken none, and he insisted that white people had promised the Shawnees freedom if they went to talk with the governor. Another Shawnee prisoner reported that the entire war party was drunk when it set out and some had turned back when they sobered. Others gave various accounts of their purpose, including a visit to "Shartier's [sic] people," a Shawnee band said to include 185 warriors and their families who, several years earlier, had followed *métis* Peter Chartier in migrating from the Ohio to join the Upper Creeks.[8]

Strangers, even those captured during peacetime, seemed easier to exploit than to set free. The South Carolina governor and council, admitting that "there are [sic] not any positive Proof that they had actually killed any of our People," nonetheless kept the Shawnees in jail, underestimating or disregarding how much Indians detested imprisonment. When a Catawba chief gloated about the sickly look of his jailed Shawnee enemies, the governor insisted that the prisoners were being treated well. Nonetheless, he voiced concern to the Commons House of Assembly two weeks later: "I should be sorry that any of them should die in Prison, [and] I think the sooner we get rid of them, the better." Glen did not hesitate to authorize imprisonment of the Shawnees, but his insistence on good treatment of the imprisoned was a badge of his civility. It was only the prospect of a captive dying in jail that raised serious concern.[9]

Glen and his council decided to send two of the Shawnees home, accompanied by letters to the lieutenant governors of Virginia and Pennsylvania, Robert Dinwiddie and James Hamilton, that made clear that the other four Shawnees had become hostages who would be released when headmen of their tribe came to Charles Town and gave assurances for the future good behavior of their people. The South Carolina Commons House balked even at sending these two back, "till the People of the Nation to whom they shall belong shall restore such Slaves as they have taken in this Province and carried away Captives into their Country." Finally, after the Shawnees had been imprisoned for nearly four months, Glen personally decided to send two of the captives home by way of Pennsylvania. Glen's calculations now included his assembly's demand that the Shawnee tribe return all "our friendly Indians or Mustee Slaves," noting with surprise that northern raiders were carrying off "such of our Slaves as had the least Tincture of Indian Blood in them." Hamilton was asked to call Shawnee headmen down to Philadelphia or to send "some proper Person" to the Ohio Country with the two returnees to explain the terms under which the other four would be released. Six disarmed Shawnees had become prisoners without being charged; four of them were now held as involuntary hostages by a British colonial government willing to act on the widely shared assumption that one alien could be punished for the behavior of inadequately identified others.[10]

News of their brethren's capture had reached the Ohio Shawnees within two months. While they seldom made an effort to recover warriors captured in battle, they regarded this entrapment and incarceration in peacetime as outrageous.[11] That September, at conferences with evasive Virginians and Pennsylvanians at Winchester and Carlisle, respectively, Ohio Shawnees and Delawares asked both those governments to intervene to secure the release of the six captives. The Ohio Iroquois leader Scarouady, who regarded the raid, the imprisonments, and the diplomatic petitions as embarrassing violations of the Iroquois diplomatic overlordship that he embodied, had to be restrained from going to Charles Town himself to retrieve those he regarded as errant Shawnee subordinates. Dinwiddie and Hamilton had written Glen about the captives, with Hamilton noting that they were "the Flower of their Nation for Courage and Activity," very pro-English, and much needed in Ohio Country during the developing confrontation with the French.[12]

A week after the two hostages had left Charles Town for Philadelphia, three of the four detained Shawnees escaped from the Charles Town watch house "by cutting out one of the Iron Barrs [sic] of a Window, and bending two others." The South Carolina council admitted that "through the Negligence of the Centinel [they] escaped out of the Prison, and as they have not been retaken, have, as we suppose, bent their Course to their own Country." Glen did not give up so easily, pressing Creek chiefs to help in recovering the escaped hostages. He again insisted that the prisoners had been treated well, that they were given good beef and corn or bread every day and rum "very often," and he claimed to be puzzled that three had decided to escape. Conflicting accounts of the escape can be reconciled if it is presumed that Itawachcomequa died during the escape, either in jail or in the woods. Glen likely projected his own values when he claimed that the one Shawnee hostage remaining in custody, who may have been ill, "thought it dishonorable to go and still continues here."[13]

The two Shawnees originally returned by Glen arrived in Philadelphia in mid-November of 1753. After a month-long delay due to "a bloody Flux" that afflicted one of them, they were escorted home by John Patten, a Pennsylvanian Indian trader recently returned from captivity in the Ohio Country and in France. Patten's assignment was to see these Shawnees safely through Pennsylvania to the frontier town of Carlisle, then pick up the colony's leading frontier diplomats and translators, Andrew Montour and George Croghan, at the latter's station at Aughwick. Hamilton envisaged that, once this party had crossed the Allegheny Mountains, it would proceed to Shannopintown at the forks of the Ohio River to find the Six Nations chiefs Scarouady and Tanaghrisson. These Iroquois leaders were to receive Hamilton's formal message and a validating string of wampum, and then the whole party was expected to proceed down the Ohio to Lower Shawnee Town at the mouth of the Scioto River. Once there, Scarouady and Tanaghrisson would conduct a meeting with the principal Shawnee leaders, conveying the messages of Glen and Hamilton with appropriate dignity. Then the Iroquois and British would release the two healthy and reclothed Shawnee captives to their grateful people, who would acknowledge the supposed power of the Iroquois-British covenant chain and would confirm their own loyalty at that crucial time.[14]

Behind this proposed public drama, Hamilton's secret instructions to Patten called for him to measure the road from Carlisle to Shannopintown carefully to see if this increasingly contested site was within Pennsylvania.

Since reliable information concerning the Ohio Country had become scarce in the months since the French had expelled all Pennsylvanian traders, Hamilton also instructed Patten to observe the numbers, arms, and loyalties of the Mingos (migrants from the Iroquois Confederacy), Delawares, Shawnees, Wyandots, and Miamis; discover what the French and the Virginians had been doing in the region; and, even more discreetly, investigate George Croghan's management of substantial presents sent to the natives by the governments of both Virginia and Pennsylvania.[15]

Hamilton's expectations met deflating reality when Patten and the two Shawnees finally caught up with Croghan and Montour at Shannopintown in mid-January 1754. Croghan had just learned that George Washington's quixotic mission to warn the French away from the upper Ohio Valley had failed, and that the new French Fort Le Boeuf on the upper Allegheny River was soundly built, fully provisioned, and, even in winter manned by about one hundred soldiers and fifty workmen. It was expected that the French would build another fort in the spring at Logstown, the diplomatic and trading center of the region. Patten and his enlarged party thus proceeded less than triumphantly and only as far as Logstown, where Shawnee warriors seized Croghan and Montour, on whose heads the French had fixed a good price. Upon recognizing their two returning kin, the Shawnees released Croghan and Montour, evidently in an exchange. Croghan understated: "The Shawonese had been Very uneasy about those Men that were in Prison, and had not those Men been released it might have been of very ill consequence at this time." Putting the best face on a diplomatic disaster, he insisted that though all the Shawnees were too drunk for serious talks, they "seem'd all overjoyed, and I believe will prove true to their Alliance." The next day a party of seventeen Canadian soldiers camped nearby and promptly captured John Patten while he was spying on them. Tanaghrisson, the Iroquois "Half King," stormed into the commander's tent and gained the inept spy's release.[16]

In Croghan's version, nothing could be done for the next ten days because the Indians were drunk. Then the French apparently concluded their inebriating visit with a one-day council, distributed presents, and called on the locals to stand aside while their French "Father" dealt with the English, whom "he will not suffer to live or tread on this River Ohio." Patten's group had spent twelve frustrating days in Logstown before they could finally attempt their formal ceremony to return the two captive Shawnee warriors. Croghan delivered the official messages and heard a soothing formal response from Tanaghrisson on behalf of the silent Shawnees and Delawares.[17]

The most revealing speech of this week-long council was the formal reply, intended for Dinwiddie and Hamilton, accompanied by a belt and eight strings of wampum for emphasis, and supposedly signed by seven Iroquois and Delaware chiefs.[18] The chiefs endorsed the general messages received from the governors, with the pointed exception of a suspicious addition, doubtless by Croghan and Patten, demanding land grants for traders such as themselves whose goods had earlier been stolen. It is noteworthy that no Shawnees signed this letter, though the Delawares' signatures indicate that declining to do so was not simply diplomatic deference to the Iroquois. It is more noteworthy that this reply did not thank the governors for the return of the two Shawnees, did not reciprocate by returning any captives, and did not pledge any legation to Charles Town or indicate acceptance of any restraint on private raiding into the Carolinas. Croghan copied his translation of this surprisingly frank speech into his journal. By now news of the escape of the other hostages would have arrived, bringing angering details and clearly invalidating Glen's bargain even if the two other returnees were not considered simply as exchanged for the captured Croghan and Montour.[19]

Montour and Patten returned to Philadelphia immediately, bringing Croghan's journal as well as Patten's diary. Both records were read to the Pennsylvania Council, who decided to transcribe and preserve only Croghan's account. They liked Patten's calculation of the distance from Carlisle to Shannopintown, which would upset the Quaker assemblymen by indicating that the disputed forks of the Ohio were within Pennsylvania's grant, and they asked him to prepare a supporting map. However, when Patten appeared before the Pennsylvania Assembly with that map, he was dismissed as an amateur by Quakers who did not want to know that the impending French initiative would invade Pennsylvanian territory. Patten's diary, probably a frank account of a failed diplomatic mission, promptly disappeared.[20]

The capture and return of the Shawnees had proven a diplomatic disaster. Governor Glen had angered the Shawnees without gaining assurances or returned slaves. Glen, now supported by his assembly, sent the last Shawnee hostage homeward by sea the following spring; he was reportedly with George Washington's force in June 1754. Once again a captive was apparently being used in an unsuccessful attempt to lure the Shawnees to a conference. Neither Hamilton nor Pennsylvania gained much from involvement in this affair. The two returned Shawnees were, in effect, exchanged for Croghan and Montour, and there was little Shawnee gratitude. English attempts to exploit the detainees had created a Shawnee grievance at a particularly dangerous time, and it was a grievance of honor that could not easily be addressed by diplomacy.[21]

This bungled hostage-taking may also have triggered the Shawnees' diplomatic revolution of 1754, which initiated decades of intermittent war with British Americans. The two Shawnees who had escaped alive from Charles Town jail had made their way home and turned their kin against the English, while the French helped them spread a rumor that the last two captive-hostages were dead. On New Year's Day of 1755, a very surprised Joseph-Gaspard Chaussegros de Léry, the Canadian lieutenant in charge of the Lake Erie outpost of Chatakoin, received a letter announcing the Shawnees' war against the English. His Huron courier explained over a drink that the Shawnees had reacted to the escapees' account by declaring perpetual war against the English, and they had even opened negotiations with the Hurons.[22]

Lieutenant Léry was surprised because this Shawnee declaration of war reversed a decade-long trend in Ohio Shawnees' diplomacy. Only a single Shawnee had attended the Lancaster treaty of 1744, at a time when the Pennsylvanian government regarded them as tending toward the French interest. Métis trader Peter Chartier had reinforced that view the next summer when he and some four hundred Shawnees (including Itawachcomequa) robbed two prominent Pennsylvanian traders. However, after Chartier and a substantial pro-French Shawnee faction had migrated southward to join the Creek, the remaining Ohio Shawnees had become active in the anti-French "Mutiny of 1747" and confirmed a Shawnee-Pennsylvania alliance at Lancaster and Logstown the next year.[23] The Shawnees had threatened the heralds of Céloron de Blainville's expedition in Lower Shawnee Town in 1749, and the French retaliated by killing one Shawnee the next year and holding three others captive in Fort Miami for nearly four months. By 1752 the French governor of Louisiana had become suspicious of the Shawnees and had hoped that their anti-European attitude could be channeled toward the English. Early in 1752 several Ohio Shawnee chiefs had assured Hamilton that they were about to attack the French in support of their Miami neighbors.[24]

Even as late as September 1754 a Shawnee spokesman thanked Hamilton for "procuring the Discharge of some of the Shawanese, who had been Prisoners in Carolina, and our kind Treatment of them in their Return, and Goodness in sending them back to their Nation." With his brother and brother-in-law in attendance to receive condolence gifts, a Shawnee delegation even claimed that Itawachcomequa's death would not cause a breach with the English, though he was much lamented, "and the most High knows how he came to his End."[25]

While one Shawnee faction was reassuring the English in September 1754, another was attacking them at Buffalo Creek on South Carolina's Broad River. Marquis Duquesne, New France's governor, claimed that it took persistent French chiding to prompt the Shawnees to seek revenge for the Charles Town captivity, and they had finally attacked and sent prisoners, scalps, and a war belt to neighboring tribes. While the Carolinians could not initially identify the attackers in what they called the unprovoked "Buffalo Creek Massacre," the Cherokees reported that the raiders had been Shawnees and Nottoways. The raiders killed sixteen recently established settlers and thirteen others went missing. It was likely the same raiding party, on their way home through the Cumberland Gap, who killed three men at Holston's River, on land that the Shawnees and other tribes had long claimed.[26]

American Indians repeatedly insisted that it was the captivity in Charles Town that provoked the Shawnees to war, and the English were expected to find that explanation adequate. Shawnee warrior Wauntaupenny, captured by a Cherokee war party in 1757 and interrogated by Pennsylvanian officers at Fort Lyttleton, said that the Shawnees and Delawares attacked the English "by Reason of their People's being taken and imprisoned by the white People in Carolina." Succomabe, a Chickasaw refugee who had lived with the Shawnees for about three years before being captured along with Wauntaupenny, was interrogated separately. Though the Shawnees had been at peace when Succomabe had joined them, "some time after he came to them, they concluded on a War, & the Reason whereof was, Some of the Shawonese were taken in Carolina and put in Prison."[27]

Six Nations spokesmen repeated the same argument. A Mohawk sachem, Little Abraham, told the Pennsylvanian authorities, at a conference that same year at Lancaster Court House where no Shawnees were present, that the Shawnees had a single war grievance:

A Party of Shawaneese who was going to War against their Enemies in their way thro Carolina called at a house not suspecting any harm as they were amongst their Friends, a number of the Inhabitants rose & took them Prisoners on Account of some Mischief that was done there, about that time[,] suspecting them to be the People that had done the Mischief and carried them to Charles Town & put them in Prison, where the Chief Man called the Pride died. The Relations of these People were much exasperated against you our Brethren the English on Account of the ill treatment you gave their Friends & have been continually spiriting up their Nations to take Revenge.[28]

Little Abraham urged the Pennsylvanians to "do justice" but did not specify how. Instead he emphasized Delaware land grievances, which had obvious solutions from which the Iroquois could benefit directly. At the crucial Easton Peace Conference of October 1758, the Oneida orator Thomas King returned to the same theme, reminding the English that "you gave the first Offence; For in Time of Profound Peace, some of the Shawanese passing through South Carolina to go to War with the[ir] Enemies, were taken up and put in Prison . . . and one who was an Head Man of that Nation, lost his Life, and the others were severely used." He then recounted that the Shawnees, encouraged by the French, lured young Delaware warriors to help them avenge the death.

The Ohio Seneca chief Ackowanothio elaborated further on the same incident, blaming French priests for seducing the Shawnees to that side, but admitting that this had been possible only because of their "being wrong'd in Carolina, and Imprisoned, and had their Chief hanged or put to death in a cruel manner." Ackowanothio also agreed that the Shawnees were the initiators who convinced the Delawares to join them in a revenge that became "the French and Indian War."[29]

Whatever the Indians claimed, the Charles Town captivity never became part of either French or English descriptions of the coming of the Seven Years' War. Most French participants who eventually published accounts of the war had arrived in North America after 1754 and made no mention of the Shawnee captives. Richard Waddington's magisterial *La Guerre de Sept Ans* starts its detailed discussion of the American aspects of the war in 1756, and Guy Frégault's standard *La Guerre de la Conquête* makes no mention of the Shawnee captives.[30] Quaker leaders, who could not comprehend the intensity of the Shawnees' grievance, sought in vain for some unfair Virginia or Pennsylvania land transaction that they could help renegotiate or reverse. Charles Thomson, Quaker scribe to Delaware chief Teedyuscung, focused overwhelmingly on Delaware grievances in his 1759 *An Inquiry into the Causes of the Alienation of the Delaware and Shawanese Indians from the British Interest*. He mentioned the Charles Town captivity of the Shawnees only in passing and in his concluding list of grievances, where he noted "the Imprisonment of the Shawnee Warriors in Carolina, where the principal Man died."[31]

Early British and American histories were predictably determined to blame the French for starting a world war and had no room for the embarrassing and unconvincing story of the Shawnee captives. The incident was not part of the war's causes in the books by William Smith, John Almon, John Entick, or Thomas Mante.[32] In 1765 Robert Rogers offered his bold lie: "The ... Shawanees are remarked for their deceit and perfidy, paying little or no regard to their word and most solemn engagements," twisting the origin of the conflict, however plausible he might have seemed concerning peacemaking.[33] By 1855 the lone surviving version of the Shawnee captivity had become garbled and framed in racial condescension; Quaker missionary Henry Harvey recorded the imprisonment as being in North Carolina and occurring about 1755, during a "time of peace, when their chief man died in prison, and as this was to them a grievous act, after so long a time of peace, it is not to be expected, considering the nature of an Indian, anything short of restitution or revenge would ever satisfy them."[34] Francis Parkman would eventually echo Rogers, describing the "Shawanoes" as fickle, opportunistic, and easily seduced by the French, though Parkman allowed that "neglect and ill usage" drove Britain's Shawnee and Delaware allies into the hands of the French.

Francis Jennings indicated vaguely that by 1755 the British government re-garded Glen as a bungler of Indian diplomacy. Recent scholarly works by Richard White and Michael McConnell mention the Charles Town captivity, but no European writer then or since has been willing to accept the native understanding of this trigger for the Shawnees' involvement in the war.[35]

Did the Shawnee captivity of 1753 help shape their very long Seven Years' War, especially in their taking, treatment, and return of captives? The Charles Town captivities prompted retaliation in the Buffalo Creek Massacre, which opened the Shawnees' war in September 1754, but the Shawnees readily shifted their attacks on the English from the Carolinas to the closer Virginia frontier. The struggle between the Shawnees and the Virginians became self-reinforcing and continued spasmodically for six decades. While more study is needed on this antagonism, it is clear that the Shawnees killed or captured more Virginians than other colonials between 1754 and 1765, and the Shaw-nees cooperated with the French most fully when the French targets were Vir-ginian.

Compared to other Indian attackers on the Allegheny frontiers during this period, including their very close Delaware allies, the Shawnees seem to have captured more and killed fewer.[36] Such apparent differences could be due to relatively poor British colonial identification of Shawnee attackers or to the survival of detailed lists of captives still held by the Shawnees late in 1765, including some who were not initially captured by them. The Shawnees also tended to limit their participation in extended campaigns organized by the French. In such sustained operations, a warrior could take scalps with-out encumbering further action, but they could take prisoners only at the end of the campaign. The Shawnees' separate and parallel war of revenge against the English was larger and lasted much longer than any contribution the tribe made to French-backed multiracial expeditions. These attacks were usually single-strike surprise raids, with terrifying beginnings that were quickly shifted to the very different tactics needed to take and keep healthy captives.[37]

In clearly identified Shawnee attacks, very few children under sixteen were killed compared to the number captured (of 103 captured children, nine were killed), despite the fact that crying children assisted pursuers in locating war parties hurrying their captives westward. Four times as many women over sixteen were captured by the Shawnees than were killed (of twenty-eight captured, seven were killed), suggesting that those who did not fight back were less likely to be killed. In addition, captive women could produce more food than they consumed, even if they did not become integrated members of the village.[38] Because adult men predominated in the armies, militias, and as white frontier laborers, men were nearly twice as likely as women to be victims of attacking Shawnees. Adult men were more likely to be killed than were women. Whether or not the Shawnees were deliberately seeking multi-racial demographic growth, their captives were those less likely to resist and more likely to adjust to life in a native community. The Shawnees' choice of captives does not suggest that they regarded the capture and adoption of prisoners as a fate worse than death, or as anything like being incarcerated in a jail. Although all captives were not adopted, and those who were not lived harder lives, there is evidence of full acceptance and eventual prominence for numerous captives within Shawnee society. It is particularly revealing that the Shawnees' propensity for taking captives was not eroded by years of war in which their English-speaking enemies took no Shawnee prisoners at all. The endless English talk about exchanging prisoners was entirely hypocritical.[39]

There were very few confirmed instances of Shawnees torturing colonial captives before 1765 and much evidence that the Shawnees intended to as-similate most of their captives. Peter Lewney's widely reprinted account of the horrid torture, death, and cannibalizing of a Virginia militiaman named Cole was an exception that deserves scrutiny. Some two hundred Indians and twenty-six Canadians had attacked Ephraim Vause's Fort in June 1756, a joint expedition with European objectives, tactics, scale of losses, and concluding diplomacy. Shawnees and Miamis, and possibly Wyandots and Potawatomis, had been with the Canadians, led by the experienced woodland diplomat and commander of Fort Miami, François-Marie Picoté de Belestre. At least thirty-two Indians were reported killed in the eight-hour firefight that preceded the burning of this stockaded house and the surrender of nine militiamen and their families. At least one severely wounded defender was executed, without torture, after the surrender, in keeping with a practice that the Indians con-sidered a realistic and merciful necessity and their opponents saw as a bar-baric violation of surrender terms. After a division of the surviving defenders among the victorious, the Shawnee warriors and their captives headed for Lower Shawnee Town, and one elderly captive who could not keep up was killed without torture on the way. Days later, before reaching the town where the fate of the captives would be decided by prominent matrons, warriors re-portedly tortured, killed, and consumed parts of militiaman Cole. It is not known whether this had been a ritual revenge for exceptionally high Shaw-nee losses to a handful of defenders, a savage response to something Cole had done or said after capture, or an impromptu act of barbarity initiated by angry and vengeful fighting men. Fellow captive Peter Lewney was not tor-tured. In fact he was treated well in captivity and escaped the following year to tell what remains the sole surviving version of Cole's fate, a horror story promptly widely reprinted to stiffen the backbone of English and colonials in a war going badly, and to counter the rather subversive published stories of good treatment told by others who had escaped from Shawnee and Delaware captivity.[40]

Very few escaped from Shawnee captivity. Only one captive, a young man taken in the Buffalo Creek Massacre, is reported to have escaped on the way to the Ohio Shawnee villages. Pursuit of a retreating party of warriors and their captives always put the latter at very grave risk, as it would in any martial situation, and no captives of the Shawnees are known to have been recovered that way. An attack on a settlement where captives were held was equally rash, though the Cherokees did conduct one successful raid to free captives from a Shawnee village in 1765. Because these villages were about two hundred miles west of Fort Pitt, escape from there was difficult. Adult male captives were reportedly allowed only three charges of ammunition when hunting from Shawnee villages, to deter escape attempts; nonetheless, fourteen of the twenty who escaped from Shawnee towns were adult males. Regular captured soldiers needed a witness to prove that they escaped and were not merely deserters, a potentially fatal accusation; soldiers tended to come back in pairs. Pairs also appealed to women escaping from Shawnee towns. Ann Mullin and Lany Pussey made the attempt but were captured by Onondaga while on their way home and spent an additional eleven months in Shawnee hands. Mary Draper Ingles and Mrs. Bingamin barely survived on nuts and berries during their harrowing forty-day escape, by the end of which the latter was threatening the former with cannibalism.[41]

The Shawnees gave few of their captives as diplomatic gifts to Indian allies or the French, and they did not routinely sell captives to the French or to those British American families, religious groups, or governments who sought to ransom captives. The Shawnees also firmly refused to surrender captives without payment; such transfers were traditionally compensation that admitted guilt for serious tribal or intertribal crimes. Consequently, numerous young whites lived with Shawnee families through two wars, and those families became increasingly averse to losing their adoptees. As Pontiac's Rebellion ended, the Shawnees also acquired captives from Indian neighbors who were making their peace with the British, neighbors who could then, without the humiliation of surrendering captives, attest that they had absolutely no English remaining with them.[42]

The return of all captives eventually became not an attending consequence of a peace that had been concluded but the central precondition for Shawnees' peace talks with colonial and British negotiators. For Pennsylvanians, the return of captives had been the only objective for which their fractured polity could unite, and the return of all captives had been a feature of Pennsylvanian negotiations with the Delawares from as early as the spring of 1756. Six Nations intermediaries and advisors seem to have readily favored English insistence on the return of prisoners, recognizing that this would humiliate the Delawares and Shawnees who had rebelled against their Iroquois over-lords in going to war against the British.[43]

British soldier-negotiators, led by Col. Henry Bouquet, were not initially preoccupied with captives but eventually learned the value of returned cap-tives as a humiliating mark of submission and as a clear sign that the peace had been "ratified" beyond the immediate circle of negotiators. When pru-dent, the British military certainly ignored the issue of returning captives, as they did at the crucial Easton Conference of October 1758 or at Fort Pitt that December, when Bouquet reportedly told Delaware chief Custaloga:

> I do not speak to you about the English prisoners you have adopted as your relatives and incorporated into your families. I only hope that, when peace is made, you will be willing to return those of advanced age, who would be in your way, or of very little use to you. As for the young children, who are pretty and able to serve you, I will not be angry if they stay among you.[44]

After the fall of Canada, however, the British demand for the return of all prisoners became more insistent, and Shawnee negotiators felt forced to make promises that they could not fulfill. By the summer of 1761 a frustrated Henry Bouquet proposed a ban on trade with the Shawnees until they re-turned their captives and stopped stealing horses. At precisely the same time, deputy superintendent of Indian affairs George Croghan was openly buying captives despite General Amherst's ban on all "presents," and Croghan urged that the resistant Shawnees not be pressed to return any more prisoners. Shawnee spokesman Red Hawk [Miskapalathy] exploited Croghan's concili-atory views and brought nothing but promises to a major conference at Lan-caster in August of 1762. Five months later Red Hawk and two other Shawnee chiefs came to Fort Pitt to return two women and a child who had become part of their own families, again disappointing British expectations. Although the Shawnees brought in five more captives as late as June 1763, negotiations evaporated with the outbreak of Pontiac's Rebellion.[45]

There had been a truce, but no peace, between the Shawnees and the British between 1760 and 1763. Shawnee raids had been suspended, and ac-commodating sachems had brought in a few of their own captives, but the British came to believe that wider tribal assent to peace would be indicated only when all those holding captives returned them, and that clearly had not happened. For their part, the Shawnees and other Ohio Indian leaders had recognized that, besides fomenting severe internal disruption, surrendering more adoptees would completely destroy the Indian negotiating position. As long as the English-speaking people wanted their captives back unharmed, there was a chance to negotiate a British withdrawal from the Ohio, or at least to forestall renewed British hostilities that would endanger those captives who had become such an English preoccupation.[46]

Although the Shawnees were peripheral players in Pontiac's Rebellion, they and their allies understood the value the British had come to attach to captives. Despite the deadly violence that accompanied the initial destruction of minor military forts, one prisoner was taken for every three people killed in Pontiac's Rebellion, compared to fewer than one for every four killed in the raids of the years 1756 to 1758. The Shawnees were clearly identified as involved in killing or capturing 37 individuals between 1763 and 1765, and of these 14 are known to have been killed. Despite this minor role in Pontiac's Rebellion, the Shawnees remained a major enemy of the British primarily because of the captives they still held from the previous war. As early as September 1763, Bouquet mapped an invasion of the Ohio that targeted Wakatomika. The next spring Bouquet drafted terms of a peace to be imposed on the Ohio tribes, including: "That they deliver up all the white men, they have amongst them, either as Prisoners or adopted, and the last to be absolutely insisted on, whether they themselves consent to it or not, as they [and some Frenchmen living with the Shawanese] have been very active against us." Bouquet's proposal also included requiring Indian leaders to become voluntary hostages until all conditions of the settlement were fulfilled.[47]

When Bouquet's fifteen-hundred-man expedition invaded the Ohio in October of 1764, they proceeded to within a day's march of Wakatomika, and Bouquet demanded the return of all English, French, and blacks, and all their children of whatever ages, living amongst the Indians. Bouquet's messenger-interpreter bearing these harsh terms was none other than David Owens, a former army deserter who had recently murdered his Shawnee wife and relatives, claimed a bounty on their five scalps, and apparently escaped retribution from either society.[48] The Shawnees, Delawares, and Mingos were given twelve days to bring in their captives, and the Shawnees predictably proved the most resistant. When Big Wolf and eight other Shawnees finally arrived with eight captives, a disappointed Bouquet demanded that the Shawnees "deliver every drop of White blood in your Nation." A few days later, after the Delawares had brought in more captives, Bouquet threatened to attack the "hauty [sic] Shawnees." Although Red Hawk promptly sent Bouquet some stolen horses and an encouraging letter carried by a released captive, Bouquet admitted, "I don't know what measures I shall be Obliged to take with that Insolent Nation."[49]

After more harsh threats on both sides, including a Shawnee threat to kill all their captives, the Shawnees finally joined in the sad and poignant climax that split multiracial families and attempted to impose racial segregation.

Promising a hundred more captives still held in Lower Shawnee Town, the Shawnees delivered what may have been as few as twenty-two captives in 1764. Many of these were bound and forced to come; some promptly escaped back to their Shawnee families, and some were forcibly returned to the English as often as three times. While some colonial families were tearfully reunited in this process, others could not be, and many multiracial families were simply broken apart. For all the cross-cultural knowledge shared by captives who became translators, brokers, traders, warriors, and wives, in colonial or Shawnee society, the invading Europeans were forcefully delineating the boundaries between the cultures.[50]

As at Charles Town eleven years before, the British again held six Shawnee hostages who were to ensure compliance. These hostages, including chiefs Red Hawk and Cornstalk, were initially held in Fort Pitt, where they were apparently threatened by onlookers and taunted with scalps. These hostages were to ensure the truce, the delivery of the remaining captives, and Shawnees' negotiation of peace through Sir William Johnson the next spring. This time all six Shawnee hostages escaped, though one was killed and scalped in the woods near Fort Pitt. Bouquet demanded new hostages, though he considered this diplomatically dangerous death as a murder in peacetime and sought, unsuccessfully, civilian prosecution of the killer.[51]

Although the Shawnees brought 9 frostbitten captives to Fort Pitt in January 1765 and 44 more in May, the Shawnees definitely did not return all of their captives. The Shawnees smoked a peace pipe at Johnson Hall that July, despite the recent murders of 9 Shawnees by Virginian "Augusta boys." Yet Shawnee spokesman Benavissica was unconvincing both in disavowing those Shawnee hostages who had escaped from Fort Pitt and in claiming, "as for the Prisoners we really believe they are all at present remitted." Yet Johnson needed to end an embarrassing Indian war, so his negotiation with the Shawnees merely left them to return the remainder of their captives in their own good time. Although these numbers are very tentative, the Shawnees are thought to have taken some 285 live captives between 1753 and 1765. Only 135 had returned by 1765, and four more would be returned between 1767 and 1771. Forty-six captives are known to have lived out their lives among the Shawnees, and the fate of about 100 others remains unknown.[52]

The Ohio Shawnees certainly did not come out of the 1765 negotiations as firm British allies. Some Shawnees had visited Fort Chartres and New Orleans in the spring of 1765, claiming continuing Shawnee support for the French. Prominent among these Shawnees was Charlot Kaské, whose German father had married a Shawnee and who himself had married a British captive, with whom he had a family. Kaské had been a close ally of Pontiac but completely rejected the peace; he became influential among the pro-French Illinois and eventually migrated west of the Mississippi. Other Ohio Shawnees talked of renewing their war against the British as early as 1766. They were furious when the British bought Shawnee hunting grounds from the Iroquois at the Treaty of Stanwix in 1768 and were thereafter thought to be constructing an intertribal anti-British alliance. Dunmore's War, in which Wakatomika was completely destroyed and Shawnee hunting grounds in Kentucky appropriated, was another violent episode, but by no means the final one.[53]

Although they had included factions for and against the English, the Shawnees had acquired much to resent since that naive party of warriors had gone from Wakatomika to Charles Town in 1753. The Shawnees would go on to fight the "Long Knives" in the American Revolution, again in that decade of war that ended at Fallen Timbers in 1794, and again under Tecumseh. Although they did not cause those sixty years of intermittent war, the captivities of 1753 had triggered a reversal in Shawnee diplomacy and launched violence that was reinforced for generations. The Ohio Indian commitment to the Seven Years' War had begun with an obvious and serious Shawnee grievance of honor. The Shawnees tended to take more captives than other combatants and were known to keep them longer; the English, who took no Shawnee captives, eventually made a race-based return of all captives an unenforceable prerequisite of peace, and there was no genuine peace between 1760 and 1763 or after 1765. The Shawnee escape of 1753 had destroyed one dictated solution and a similar escape in 1765 had destroyed another. To recognize the importance of this long-forgotten initial grievance in the Shawnees' decision for war is to challenge enduring misunderstandings of their character and motives, to suggest that they had a war of their own—fought with Delaware and French assistance—and to appreciate the prominent place of captivity in the origin, conduct, and conclusion of this colonial frontier conflict.[54]

NOTES

1. Robert Rogers, *A Concise Account of North America: Containing a Description of the Several British Colonies on that Continent* (London: J. Millan, 1765), 237.

2. Recent studies include Linda Colley, *Captives: Britain, Empire and the World, 1600–1850* (New York: Pantheon, 2002); John Demos, *The Unredeemed Captive: A Family Story from Early America* (New York: Knopf, 1994); Alden T. Vaughan and Daniel K. Richter, "Crossing the Cultural Divide: Indians and New Englanders, 1605–1763," *American Antiquarian Society Proceedings* 90 (1980): 23–99; and James Axtell, "The White Indians of Colonial America," *William and Mary Quarterly* 32 (1975): 55–88 [hereafter cited as *WMQ*]. For captives along Allegheny frontiers, see Matthew C. Ward, "La Guerre Sauvage: The Seven Years' War on the Virginia and Pennsylvania Frontier" (Ph.D. Diss., The College of William and Mary, 1992); and "Redeeming Captives: Pennsylvania Cap-

tives among the Ohio Indians, 1755–1765," *Pennsylvania Magazine of History and Biography* 125 (2001): 161–89. On gender, see Carroll Smith-Rosenberg, "Captured Subjects/ Savage Others: Violently Engendering the New American," *Gender and History* 5 (1993): 177–95; and June Namias, *White Captives: Gender and Ethnicity on the American Frontier* (Chapel Hill: Univ. of North Carolina Press, 1992).

3. Dwight L. Smith, "Shawnee Captivity Ethnohistory," *Ethnohistory* 2 (1955): 29–57; Vernon Kinietz and Erminie W. Voegelin, eds., *Shawnee Traditions: C. C. Trowbridge's Account* (Ann Arbor: Univ. of Michigan Press, 1939), viii–x, 11–12; James H. Merrell, *The Indians' New World: Catawbas and Their Neighbors from European Contact through the Era of Removal* (Chapel Hill: Univ. of North Carolina Press, 1989), 40–41, 118–19, 135; Merrell, "Their Very Bones Shall Fight: The Catawba-Iroquois Wars," in Daniel K. Richter and James H. Merrell, eds., *Beyond the Covenant Chain: The Iroquois and Their Neighbors in Indian North America, 1600–1800* (Syracuse, N.Y.: Syracuse Univ. Press, 1987), 115–33.

4. William L. McDowell Jr., ed., *Colonial Records of South Carolina: Documents Relating to Indian Affairs, May 21, 1750–August 7, 1754* (Columbia: South Carolina Archives Department, 1958–70), 422–29, 432–33 [hereafter cited as *SCDIA*]; *South Carolina Gazette*, June 18, 1753; Samuel Hazard, ed., *Colonial Records of Pennsylvania, 1683–1790*, 16 vols. (Philadelphia, Pa.: T. Fenn, 1851–53), 6:153, 160 [hereafter cited as *CRP*]; "Conrad Weiser's Journal of a Tour of the Ohio, Aug. 11–Oct. 2, 1748," in Reuben Gold Thwaites, ed., *Early Western Travels, 1748–1846*, 32 vols. (Cleveland, Ohio: A. H. Clark, 1904–7), 1:32; Richard White, *The Middle Ground: Indians, Empires, and Republics in the Great Lakes Region, 1650–1815* (New York: Cambridge Univ. Press, 1991), 190–92, 243.

In 1753 Itawachcomequa married the sister of Lepechkewe, called "the Young King." See *CRP* 6:153, 160; Charles A. Hanna, *The Wilderness Trail*, 2 vols. (New York: Putnam's, 1911), 1:232, 280–81, 287–88, 309, 311, 325, 331; 2:139, 159; E. B. O'Callaghan, ed., *Documents Relative to the Colonial History of the State of New York, Procured in Holland, England, and France*, 15 vols. (Albany, N.Y.: Weed, Parsons, 1857), 10:20 [hereafter cited as *NYCD*]; Wilber Jacobs, ed., *The Appalachian Indian Frontier: The Edmund Atkin Report and Plan of 1755* (Lincoln: Univ. of Nebraska Press, 1954), 65; Francis Jennings, *The Ambiguous Iroquois Empire: The Covenant Chain Confederation of Indian Tribes with English Colonies, from Its Beginnings to the Lancaster Treaty of 1744* (New York: Norton, 1984), 269–70; James H. Merrell, *Into the American Woods: Negotiators on the Pennsylvania Frontier* (New York: Norton, 1999), 73–75. See also Francis Jennings, "Bisaillon (Bezellon, Bizaillon), Peter," in *Dictionary of Canadian Biography*, 14 vols. (Toronto: Univ. of Toronto Press, 1966–1991), 3:65–66 [hereafter cited as *DCB*]; Michael N. McConnell, *A Country Between: The Upper Ohio Valley and Its Peoples, 1724–1774* (Lincoln: Univ. of Nebraska Press, 1992), 53–54.

5. Gregory Evans Dowd, "The Panic of 1751: The Significance of Rumors on the South Carolina–Cherokee Frontier," *WMQ* 53 (1996): 527–60; *South Carolina Gazette*, April 18, May 28, June 12, 1753; McDowell, ed., *SCDIA*, 414–20. Glen offered a full defense of the proclamation to the Board of Trade in his letter of June 25, 1753, but did not report anything of the Shawnee captives in his letters during the next year; Colonial Office Records, Class 5 Papers, Records Office of Great Britain, Kew, England, 5/374, 150–53 [hereafter cited as PRO/CO]. On Glen, see W. Stitt Robinson, *James Glen, From Scottish Provost to Royal Governor of South Carolina* (Westport, Conn.: Greenwood, 1996).

6. McDowell, ed., *SCDIA,* 421; *South Carolina Gazette,* June 18, 1753. For eight Mohawks held in irons at Quebec in December 1748, see Jon Parmenter, "At the Woods' Edge: Iroquois Foreign Relations, 1727–1768" (Ph.D. Diss., Univ. of Michigan, 1999), 227–33, 250; *NYCD,* 10:144.

7. *South Carolina Gazette,* June 18, 1753; reprinted in *Pennsylvania Gazette,* July 26, 1753; *New York Mercury,* July 30, 1753. Indeed, Edmund Atkin, former South Carolina Councillor later to become superintendent of Indian affairs for the southern frontier, considered the Ohio Shawnees to be firm allies of the British. McDowell, ed., *SCDIA,* 422; Jacobs, ed., *The Edmund Atkin Report,* xviii–xx, 41, 43.

8. Jacobs, ed., *The Edmund Atkin Report,* 43; McDowell, ed., *SCDIA,* 421–27, 433. James Adair claimed that he led a party of Catawbas to apprehend Chartier in 1747; see Adair's *History of the American Indians,* ed. Samuel Cole Williams (New York: Argonaut, 1966), 4n1.

9. McDowell, ed., *SCDIA,* 456. Execution was regarded as more acceptable; see Jan Grabonski, "French Criminal Justice and Indians in Montreal, 1670–1760," *Ethnohistory* 43 (1996): 405–29.

10. J. H. Easterby, ed., *Colonial Records of South Carolina: Journals of the Commons House of Assembly,* 14 vols. (Columbia: Historical Commission of South Carolina, 1951–89), 12:xxiii–xxiv, 291–92, 297, 301; McDowell, ed., *SCDIA,* 457–58; Glen to Hamilton, October 3 and 12, 1753, *CRP,* 5:462–64, 699–700.

11. For Shawnee threats of war against the Miami for wrongful capture of a woman and boy in 1751, see William M. Darlington, ed., *Christopher Gist's Journals* (Pittsburgh, Pa.: J. R. Weldin, 1893), 46; Lawrence H. Keeley, *War before Civilization* (New York: Oxford Univ. Press, 1996), 85–88; Theda Perdue, *Slavery and the Evolution of Cherokee Society, 1540–1866* (Knoxville: Univ. of Tennessee Press, 1979), 6.

12. Hamilton to Glen, October 30, 1753, *CRP,* Dinwiddie to Glen, October 26, 1753; McDowell, ed., *SCDIA,* 466–67; Leonard W. Labaree, ed., *The Papers of Benjamin Franklin,* 32 vols. (New Haven, Conn.: Yale Univ. Press, 1959–96), 5:105–6; Francis Jennings, *Empire of Fortune: Crowns, Colonies and Tribes in the Seven Years' War in America* (New York: Norton, 1988), 57–59.

13. McDowell, ed., *SCDIA,* 464–65, 468; John Sullivan, ed., *The Papers of Sir William Johnson,* 14 vols. (Albany: Univ. of the State of New York, 1921–65), 9:755 [hereafter cited as *SWJP*]; *New York Mercury,* July 30, 1753; *South Carolina Gazette,* October 29, 1753.

14. *South Carolina Gazette,* October 29, 1753; McDowell, ed., *SCDIA,* 467–68; *CRP,* 5:698–700, 704; Howard N. Eavenson, *Map Maker and Indian Traders: An Account of John Patten, Trader, Arctic Explorer, and Map Maker* (Pittsburgh, Pa.: Univ. of Pittsburgh Press, 1949); *Pennsylvania Archives,* 9 ser., 138 vols. (Philadelphia: State Printer of Pennsylvania, 1852–56, 1875–1949), 1st ser., 2:209–10.

15. Hamilton to Glen, December 6, 1753, McDowell, ed., *SCDIA,* 471; *CRP,* 5:704–9; Eavenson, *Map Maker,* 154–55.

16. "Croghan's Journal, 1754," *CRP,* 5:732, and Thwaites, *Early Western Travels,* 1:74–75; Fernand Grenier, ed., *Papiers Contrecoeur et autres documents concernant le conflit anglo-français sur l'Ohio de 1745 à 1756* (Ottawa, Can.: Presses Universitaires Laval, 1952), 99–101, 128; Eavenson, *Map Maker,* 52–61; Hanna, *Wilderness Trail,* 2:3; William A. Hunter, *Forts on the Pennsylvania Frontier, 1753–1758* (Harrisburg: Pennsylvania Historical and

Museum Commission, 1960), 35, 103. On the French commander Michel Maray de la Chauvignerie, see *DCB*, 2:126, 625; 3:101, 320, 401, 614.

17. Grenier, ed., *Papiers Contrecoeur,* 99–101, 128; *CRP,* 5:734.

18. There has been some confusion about whether Newcomer (Netawatwees), who signed, was a Delaware or a Shawnee, but he was definitely the former. See John W. Jordan, ed., "Journal of James Kenny, 1761–1763," *Pennsylvania Magazine of History and Biography* 37 (1913): 187; Franklin D. Dexter, ed., *Diary of David McClure, Doctor of Divinity, 1748–1820* (New York: Knickerbocker, 1899), 61; British Library (London, England), Additional Manuscripts, MSS 21655, fol. 251; Earl P. Olmstead, *Blackcoats among the Delaware* (Kent, Ohio: Kent State Univ. Press, 1991), 10; Gregory Evans Dowd, *A Spirited Resistance: The North American Indian Struggle for Unity, 1745–1815* (Baltimore, Md.: Johns Hopkins Univ. Press, 1991), 68–69.

19. *CRP,* 5:734; Hanna, *Wilderness Trail,* 1:360, 375; Nicholas B. Wainwright, *George Croghan, Wilderness Diplomat* (Chapel Hill: Univ. of North Carolina Press, 1959), 57–60.

20. Eavenson, *Map Maker,* 52–70; *CRP,* 5:730–35, 750–51, 760–63.

21. Washington to Dinwiddie, June 10, 1754, W. W. Abbot, ed., *The Papers of George Washington, Colonial Series,* 10 vols. (Charlottesville: Univ. Press of Virginia, 1983–95), 1:133.

22. "Journal de Joseph-Gaspard Chaussegros de Léry, Lieutenant des troupes, 1754–1755," in *Rapport de l'Archivists de la Province de Québec pour 1927–1928* (Québec, Can.: Proulx, 1928), 409–10; *DCB,* 4:145–47.

23. Randolph C. Downes, *Council Fires on the Upper Ohio* (Pittsburgh, Pa.: Univ. of Pittsburgh Press, 1940), 39–41; Merrell, *Into the American Woods,* 73–75; White, *Middle Ground,* 190–92; Jennings, "Bisaillon," *DCB,* 3:65–66.

24. *CRP,* 5:482–84, 496–98, 568–71; Vaudreuil to Macarty, April 27, 1752, in Theodore C. Pease and Ernestine Jenison, eds., *Illinois on the Eve of the Seven Years' War* (Springfield, Ill.: Trustees of the State Historical Library, 1940), 597. See also ibid., 362–65, 773; Joseph-Pierre de Bonnécamps, "Relation du Voyage de la Belle Rivière faite en 1749, sous les ordres de M. de Céloron," in Reuben Gold Thwaites, ed., *Jesuit Relations and Allied Documents,* 73 vols. (Cleveland, Ohio: Burrows, 1896–1901), 69:170–71.

25. Pease and Jenison, eds., *Illinois on the Eve of the Seven Years' War,* 597; *CRP,* 5:568–71.

26. "Votes of the Assembly," *Pennsylvania Archives,* 8th ser., 5:4,120, 4,145–49 (quotation on 4,148); *CRP,* 6:150–60 (quotation on 153); Grenier, ed., *Papiers Contrecoeur,* 222–23, 266, 289; H. R. Casgrain, ed., *Extraits des Archives des Ministères da la Marine et de la Guerre à Paris* (Quebec, Can.: L. J. Demers, 1890), 9–10; *South Carolina Gazette,* October 17, 1754; McDowell, ed., *SCDIA,* 23, 79; William Preston Papers, Lyman C. Draper Manuscript Collection, Historical Society of Wisconsin, Division of Archives and Manuscripts, University of Wisconsin, Madison, Wisconsin [hereafter cited as DMC], Ser. QQ, 1:83; A. A. Lambling, ed., *The Baptismal Register of Fort Duquesne* (Pittsburgh, Pa.: Myers, Shinkle, 1885), 56–57.

27. *CRP,* 7:531–32.

28. *SWJP,* 9:755; *CRP,* 7:540.

29. *CRP,* 8:197–98; *Pennsylvania Archives,* 1st ser., 3:147, 548–50.

30. The major French chroniclers of the war, Bougainville, Desandrouins, Malartic, and Pouchot, all arrived in North America in 1755. See Richard Waddington, *La Guerre de*

Sept Ans, 5 vols. (Paris: Firmin, 1899–1907), especially 1:217. Frégault's book (Montreal, Can.: Fides, 1955) was translated by Margaret M. Cameron as *Canada: The War of the Conquest* (Toronto, Can.: Univ. of Toronto Press, 1969).

31. Charles Thomson, *Hopewell Friends History 1734–1934, Frederick County, Virginia* (Strasburg, Va.: Shenandoah, 1936), 113–25. See also Thomson, *An Inquiry into the Causes of the Alienation of the Delaware and Shawanese Indians from the British Interest* (London: J. Wilke, 1759), 77, 81.

32. Smith, *Review;* John Almon, *An Impartial History of the Late War: Deduced from the Committing of Hostilities in 1749, to the Signing of the Definitive Treaty of Peace in 1763* (London: 1763); John Entick, *General History of the Late War, Containing Its Rise, Progress, and Event in Europe, Asia, Africa, and America* (London: E. and C. Dilly, 1764–66); Thomas Mante, *The History of the Late War in North America and the Islands of the West Indies* (London: W. Strahan and T. Cadell, 1772). George Bancroft also said nothing of the incident and dismissed the Shawnees: "So desolate was the wilderness, that a vagabond tribe could wander undisturbed from Cumberland River to the Alabama, from the headwaters of the Santee to the Susquehannah [*sic*]." See Bancroft, *History of the United States of America,* Centenary Edition, 6 vols. (Boston, Mass.: Little, Brown, 1879), 2:327.

33. Rogers, *A Concise Account,* 237.

34. Henry Harvey, *History of the Shawnee Indians from the Years 1681 to 1854, Inclusive* (Cincinnati, Ohio: E. Morgan, 1855), 85. Thomas Wildcat Alford, self-described keeper of Shawnee history, made no mention of the incident in *Civilization and the Story of the Absentee Shawnees* (Norman: Univ. of Oklahoma Press, 1979).

35. Francis Parkman, *Montcalm and Wolfe,* 3 vols. (Boston, Mass.: Little, Brown, 1905), 2:14; Jennings, *Empire of Fortune,* 147–48; White, *Middle Ground,* 243–44; McConnell, *A Country Between,* 120.

36. The following estimates are from a provisional and incomplete database of persons reported as captured, killed, or missing by all parties on Allegheny frontiers between 1745 and 1765. All surviving newspapers of New York, Pennsylvania, Maryland, Virginia, and South Carolina have been studied and checked against other sources. Major unpublished sources include Admiralty, Amherst, and Virginia Papers in the Public Record Office, the Abercromby, Amherst, and Stonehouse Manuscripts in the Huntington Library; the Bouquet Papers in the British Library; and DMC. Major printed document collections include *NYCD; Illinois on the Eve of the Seven Years' War; CRP; Pennsylvania Archives; The Papers of George Washington;* and *SWJP.* The captivity narratives of Mary Draper Ingles, Robert Kirk, Peter Lewney, Jacob Persinger, and John Slover (cited below) were also employed. Of the 409 reported victims of Shawnee attacks, 129 (31.5 percent) are known to have been killed either immediately or within five days of capture. The Delawares killed 53 percent of their 347 known victims, and all Indian attackers killed an estimated 69 percent of some 1,215 victims.

37. For French complaints see Grenier, ed., *Papiers Contrecoeur,* 364–67. On the debatable role of Shawnees against Braddock, see C. A. Weslager, *The Delaware Indians, a History* (New Brunswick, N.J.: Rutgers Univ. Press, 1972), 224; "Kenny Journal," 183; and Beverly W. Bond Jr., ed., "The Captivity of Charles Stuart, 1755–1757," *Mississippi Valley Historical Review* 13 (1926–1927): 63. The major attacks were Williams Fort (March 7), Vause's fort (June 25), and Fort Granville (August 31) in 1756; and those at South Branch (April 27) and Fort Seybert (April 28) in 1758. The Shawnees also participated in the de-

feat of Maj. James Grant's expedition in September 1758 and the last French raid from Fort Duquesne two months later.

38. For Hannah Dennis's six years with the Shawnees, and escape, see Chester Raymond Young, "The Effects of the French and Indian War on Civilian Life in the Frontier Counties of Virginia, 1754–1763" (Ph.D. Diss., Vanderbilt Univ., 1969), 133–35; James B. Finley, *Life among the Indians* (Cincinnati, Ohio: Hitchcock and Walden, 1857), 45–47; and Joseph Waddell, *Annals of Augusta County, Virginia*, 2 vols. (Richmond, Va.: Ellis Jones, 1886), 1:111. For the intriguing case of Margaret Moore, who married Blue Jacket, see John Sugden, *Blue Jacket, Warrior of the Shawnees* (Lincoln: Univ. of Nebraska Press, 2000), 3, 255; and Joshua Antrim, *The History of Champaign and Logan Counties* (Bellefontaine, Ohio: Press Printing, 1872), 327–28.

39. Charlot Kaské's wife was a captive, as was Blue Jacket's. Captive boys who grew up to be Shawnee warriors included John Ward and George Brown. Norman J. Heard, *White into Red: A Study of the Assimilation of White Persons Captured by Indians* (Metuchen, N.J.: Scarecrow, 1973), 120; Ward, "La Guerre Sauvage," 361.

40. *Pennsylvania Gazette*, July 28, 1757, reprinted in *New York Mercury*, August 1, 1757, in *London Chronicle* (*Universal Evening Post*), September 6–8, 1757; Milo M. Quaife, ed., "Captivity of Peter Looney," *Mississippi Valley Historical Review* 15 (1928): 95–96; reprinted in *Mississippi Valley Historical Review*, 15 (1928): 95–96. Captain and self-styled Maj. John Smith was in charge of the defense; PRO/CO, 30/8/95, 214–15; Loudon Papers, Henry Huntington Library, San Marino, Calif., 4,791, 4,807, 4,925, 5,452, 5,658. See also William Preston Papers, DMC, Ser. QQ, 1:131–35; and *Shawnee Traditions*, 19–21, 53–54. The torture was reported in Robert Kirk, *The Memoirs and Adventures of Robert Kirk, Late of the Royal Highland Regiment* (Limerick, Ire.: J. Ferrar, 1770), 7–11, 38–40 (likely apocryphal).

Montcalm and Bougainville both heard reports of cannibalism in the Ohio Valley and made light of them. Bougainville's remark that the Delawares and Shawnees "have eaten an English officer whose pallor and plumpness tempted them" may refer to Cole. See Edward P. Hamilton, ed., *Adventure in the Wilderness: The American Journals of Louis Antoine de Bougainville, 1756–1760* (Norman: Univ. of Oklahoma Press, 1964), 114; and Waddington, *La Guerre de Sept Ans*, 1:228.

A brief and rather humane captivity among the Delawares was published as *A Narrative of the Sufferings and Surprizing Deliverances of William and Elizabeth Fleming*, by William Fleming (Boston, Mass.: Green and Russell, 1756), with accounts in the *New York Mercury* of March 8 and 15, 1756. The story of Mary Draper Ingles' escape from fellow captive Mrs. Bingamin, who had her own cannibalistic intents, was first published in the *New York Mercury* of February 16, 1756.

41. The Cherokee recovered all five of their captives; see *Pennsylvania Gazette*, June 6 and 13, 1765. A Catawba war party recovered an unidentified prisoner in a fight in the spring of 1757; *Pennsylvania Gazette*, May 19, 1757. At the strategically successful attack on Kittaning, September 8–9, 1756, Pennsylvania forces killed fourteen Delawares, lost thirty-three killed, and recovered only seven captives. The Delawares killed only one of their captives, Mrs. Alexander McAllister, who was recaptured after being "rescued." See William A. Hunter, "Victory at Kittanning," *Pennsylvania History* 23 (1956): 376–407. Escaping soldiers were Martin Barrowelly and John Hogan; David Owens and Robert Kirk. See Huntington Library, Loudoun Papers, 3,758, and Abercromby Papers, 659; *Pennsyl-*

vania Gazette, August 19, 1756, September 28, 1758, October 19, 1758; *CRP,* 8:561–62; Kirk, *Memoirs,* 5–40; and *Pennsylvania Gazette,* March 17, 1763, on Mullin and Pussey. On Mary Ingles, compare the accounts in Roberta Ingles Steele and Andrew Lewis Ingles, eds., *The Story of Mary Draper Ingles and Son Thomas Ingles, as Told by John Ingles Sr.* (Radford, Va.: Commonwealth, 1969) and Mary Rodd Furbee, *Shawnee Captive: The Story of Mary Draper Ingles* (Greensboro, N.C.: Morgan Reynolds, 2001) with *New York Mercury,* January 16, February 16, and March 1, 1756. On Hannah Dennis's solo escape, see Young, "The Effects of the French and Indian War on Civilian Life," 133–35.

42. Smith, "Shawnee Captivity Ethnohistory," 36–37; *Shawnee Traditions,* 13–14. On gifts, see Quaife, ed., "Captivity of Peter Looney," 95–96; James Everett Seaver, ed., *A Narrative of the Life of Mrs. Mary Jemison* (Canandaigua, N.Y.: J. D. Bemis, 1824); "The Narrative of John Slover," in Archibald Louden, ed., *A Selection, of Some of the Most Interesting Narratives of Outrages, Committed by the Indians, in Their Wars, with the White People,* 2 vols. (Carlisle, Pa.: A. Louden, 1808–11), 1:17–32. See also *Pennsylvania Gazette,* November 13, 1755; *New York Mercury,* November 17, 1755; Sylvester K. Stevens, Donald H. Kent, and Autumn L. Leonard, eds., *The Papers of Henry Bouquet,* 6 vols. (Harrisburg: Pennsylvania Museum and Historical Commission, 1951–94), 6:89 [hereafter cited as *PHB*]. On ransom, see Christian Frederick Post, "Two journals of Western Tours . . . [July–Sept. 1758; Oct. 1758–Jan. 1759]," in Thwaites, *Early Western Travels,* 1:287; "Kenny Journal," 172.

43. *CRP,* 7:97–110, 137–41.

44. *PHB,* 2:626; Sylvester K. Stevens and Donald H. Kent, eds., *Wilderness Chronicles of Northwestern Pennsylvania* (Harrisburg: Pennsylvania Historical Commission, 1941), 134–38; Stephen F. Auth, *The Ten Years' War: Indian-White Relations in Pennsylvania, 1755–1765* (New York: Garland, 1989), 58, 123–24; "Kenny Journal," 423.

45. British Library, Additional Manuscripts, MSS 21638:244, 248, MSS 21655:177–79; *SWJP,* 3:210–17, 10:317–18; *Minutes of Conferences Held at Lancaster in August 1762* (Philadelphia, Pa.: B. Franklin and D. Hall, 1763), 12–13. Ecuyer reported that two women and two children had been returned, and the "presents" given in exchange were valued at thirty Pennsylvania Indians. See *PHB,* 6:139–41, 156n1; British Library, Additional Manuscripts, MSS 21634, fol. 207. A Shawnee party had given William Johnson two prisoners and a scalp at a meeting in Detroit in December 1761. See *SWJP,* 10:328, 546–48; "Kenny Journal," 194.

46. *SWJP,* 3:550; 10:317–18; White, *The Middle Ground,* 261–63.

47. *PHB,* 6:416–17, 532–33, 538–40. Bouquet was remembering the spying, deceptions, and robberies blamed on adoptees; see *PHB,* 514–16, 522–26, 534, 540–41, 586, 663.

48. Bouquet admitted to Gage that the demand for all the children of white women that Indians had was his own; see *PHB,* 6:706. On Owens, see Loudon, *A Selection,* 2:166; Hanna, *Wilderness Trail,* 2:386; Stephen Brumwell, *Redcoats: The British Soldier in the Americas, 1755–1763* (New York: Cambridge Univ. Press, 2001), 175. On the terms, see William Smith, *An Historical Account of the Expedition against the Ohio Indians, in the Year 1764, under the Command of Henry Bouquet Esq.* (Philadelphia, Pa.: T. Jefferies, 1766), 15–16; and *PHB,* 6:674.

49. *PHB,* 6:681–82, 684, 687–89, 697–99. For Shawnee resistance, see John McCullough, *A Narrative of the Captivity of John McCullough, Esq.* in Louden, *A Selection,* 1:252–302, esp. 284–85.

50. Bouquet claimed that the "obstinate Shawnee" still had 150 prisoners, and there was a named list of 84 still in Shawnee towns. See British Library, Additional Manuscripts, MSS 21655, fol. 251; *PHB*, 6:709; Stevens, *Wilderness Chronicles*, 289–90; Smith, *An Historical Account*, 26–29; Jacob Persinger, *The Life of Jacob Persinger* (Sturgeon, Mo.: Moody and McMichael, 1861).

51. *PHB*, 6:738–39, 746. The hostages were Mesquepalathy (Red Hawk), Ewechonmey (the Wrestler), Keightque, Tamimabuck (Corn Stalk), Wapekapa (White Legs), and Weighthakina. See Huntington Library, Huntington Manuscripts, San Marino, Calif., 569:37–38. Both Red Hawk and Cornstalk would be murdered while held hostage once again in Fort Randolph in 1777. See Colin G. Calloway, *The American Revolution in Indian Country: Crisis and Diversity in Native American Communities* (New York: Cambridge Univ. Press, 1995), 167.

52. *PHB*, 6:751–54; Smith, *An Historical Account*, 34–35; *NYCD*, 7:750–58; *SWJP*, 11:720–21, 823, 831. There were eighty-eight named captives still in Lower Shawnee Town alone late in November 1764. See British Library, Additional Manuscripts, MSS 21655, fol. 296. Ten Shawnees, given a pass by an Augusta county magistrate to travel through Virginia, were attacked, and nine of them were killed. See *Pennsylvania Archives*, 1st ser., 4:218.

53. *NYCD*, 10:1,157–60; White, *Middle Ground*, 301–5; Dowd, *Spirited Resistance*, 42; Michael N. McConnell, "Peoples In Between: The Iroquois and the Ohio Indians, 1720–1768," in Richter and Merrell, eds., *Beyond the Covenant Chain*, 93–112.

55. Calloway, *The American Revolution in Indian Country*, 158–81; John Sugden, *Tecumseh* (New York, Henry Holt, 1997), and *Blue Jacket*.

2

"This Land Is Ours and Not Yours"

The Western Delawares and the Seven Years' War
in the Upper Ohio Valley, 1755–1758

Daniel P. Barr

On September 7, 1732, Delaware Indians living along the Tulpehocken Creek ceded to the Pennsylvania colonial government the Lebanon Valley, a fertile district that today encompasses the region between Harrisburg and Reading. The cession was the capstone of a process that had been under way for more than a decade, whereby the Delaware Indian nation had diffused tension with westward-moving colonists by vacating contested regions after negotiating a peaceful transfer of disputed lands. After the cession of the Lebanon Valley, many Tulpehocken Delawares migrated to the upper Ohio Valley in an effort to avoid future complications with British colonists over territory. Yet within a generation, those that removed to the upper Ohio, identified herein as the western Delawares, again found themselves in occupation of sharply contested ground. On this occasion, however, the western Delawares would break with past precedent, refuse to abandon their lands, and, along with other native peoples from the upper Ohio, wage a war against the British and their colonists designed to secure recognition of their political and diplomatic goals.[1]

The war launched by the upper Ohio Indians in 1755 was an important component of the Seven Years' War in North America. Accordingly, the conflict has been afforded an increasing amount of scholarly attention in recent years. Yet the western Delawares' role in this story remains underdeveloped and misunderstood. Too often they have been downplayed as pawns of the French or overshadowed by the actions of their eastern cousins along the Susquehanna River. Moreover, while the western Delawares were closely linked with other native peoples living in the upper Ohio Valley, primarily the Shawnees and Mingos (a group of separatist Iroquois peoples who were mostly

Senecas), the border war initiated by the western Delawares in 1755 was not necessarily the product of united Indian action, but rather it represented a cumulative reaction to past traumas, a violent response to their past removal experiences manifested in a militant determination not to become migrants again.[2]

The western Delawares were among a number of native peoples displaced by English colonization of the mid-Atlantic seaboard in the late seventeenth century. As eastern Pennsylvania rapidly filled with poor European newcomers seeking land, many Delawares, Shawnees, and Mingos moved west during the first half of the eighteenth century and settled alongside the numerous rivers and streams of the upper Ohio River watershed. Like the Tulpehocken Creek Delawares, these native groups chose mediation over conflict, agreeing to remove themselves westward in exchange for peace and relative security from further land pressures. They soon discovered, however, that they had not completely escaped the reach of European colonists.

French traders had been active in the Ohio Country since at least 1680, following Robert Chevalier de La Salle's voyage of discovery down the Ohio River, and they moved as far eastward as the Ohio forks in their pursuit of furs. Similarly, American colonial traders from New York and Pennsylvania had entered into lucrative trade arrangements with the native residents of the region in the late seventeenth century. The American traders, particularly those from Pennsylvania, soon outnumbered their French rivals, who lamented in 1730 that "the English are found scattered as far as the sea." The role played by these peddlers, trappers, hunters, and adventurers, often lumped together under the generic name Indian trader, transcended the economic boundaries of trade. They were the advance agents of colonial westward expansion. Through economic interaction with the native peoples, the traders opened inroads into the trans-Appalachian west that heightened the awareness of their eastern colonial brethren to the latent possibilities of the region, particularly to the potential profits to be realized in land acquisition. Thanks in no small part to the activities of the traders, land speculators in Virginia, most visibly represented by the union of economic resources and political power known as the Ohio Company, began moving to secure possession of land in the upper Ohio Valley by any means necessary.[3]

Thus the western Delawares once again found themselves crowded by Anglo-American pressures for land and trade. It was not a welcome development. In the early 1740s a Pennsylvania fur trader observed a curious ritual during a visit to a Delaware village near the intersection of the Allegheny and Monongahela rivers, in the vicinity of present-day Pittsburgh. Thomas Kinton watched in amazement as the village's inhabitants killed an unwelcome intruder that they discovered lurking in their village—a rat. While the extermination of the rodent seemed commonplace enough to Kinton, the reaction of the Delawares to the rat's presence in their village struck the trader as extraordinary. Many of the Indians "seemed concerned" over the appearance of the rat and its potential significance. These "antiants," as the trader called them, approached Kinton and sternly informed him that "the French or English should not get that land [the Allegheny River basin] from them, the same prediction being made by their grandfathers on finding a rat on [the] Delaware [River] before the white people came there." For the western Delawares, the presence of rats and bees, or "English flies" as many eastern woodlands Indians referred to them, were telling portents of impending troubles, as they were well-known products of the ecological changes wrought upon the environment by the advancing tide of white settlement. For the natives, it was an ominous sign that a struggle for power was about to ensue.[4]

Despite the increased pressures from land developers and traders, war was not the western Delawares' first course of action, rather it came after traditional forms of mediation had failed. From 1744 to 1754 western Delaware negotiators engaged in a sustained diplomatic effort to secure recognition of their territorial autonomy in the upper Ohio Valley. During councils and meetings in Pennsylvania and Virginia, they delineated a clear political policy that welcomed trade but strongly opposed settlement or land acquisition. Yet the claims against their territory only increased as Pennsylvanians and Virginians alike schemed to deprive the western Delawares of their lands. Land speculators in Virginia and merchant firms in Pennsylvania, motivated by the region's tremendous potential for economic development, gradually intertwined trade agreements with land contracts, pointing to Iroquois-brokered treaties that jeopardized the western Delawares' territorial integrity. Angered by the pressure brought to bear upon their lands by Pennsylvania traders and Virginia speculators, and reminiscent of their earlier migrations from the east, the western Delawares intensified their determination to maintain their place in the upper Ohio Valley.[5] Moreover, the western Delawares' diplomatic agenda was severely complicated by the French, who forcefully asserted their claims to the upper Ohio Valley in an attempt to impose control over the Indians and drive out all competitors for native trade.

During the summer of 1752 a large force of French-allied Indians and Canadian militia sacked Pickawillany, a large Piankashaw Indian village in central Ohio. Foreshadowing the horror to come, the French and their Indian allies killed the Piankashaw's pro-British leader, Memeskia, along with several Pennsylvania traders discovered in the village. While the brief engagements at Jumonville Glenn and Fort Necessity in 1754 are traditionally associated with the opening phases of the Seven Years' War in North America, the French attack on the pro-British village of Pickawillany marked the true beginning of the conflict. The attack came about in part because of the intrusion of Anglo-American traders into French commercial enclaves during the 1740s, but it was the struggle between Pennsylvania traders and the Ohio Company of Virginia to exercise power over the upper Ohio Valley that convinced the French to act in earnest. The raid at Pickawillany revealed only a fraction of their resolve. In early 1753 two thousand French-Canadians and their Indian allies descended upon the upper Ohio, building a string of forts along the Allegheny River and forcefully asserting their political and economic control over the region.[6]

The French invasion presented a direct threat to the western Delawares' territorial security. By establishing a formidable military presence in the upper Ohio Valley, the French clearly violated native sovereignty. The French invasion also contained potentially disastrous economic implications for the native inhabitants of the upper Ohio Valley. In 1754 the French captured the forks of the Ohio River and then beat back an attempt to retake the forks by Virginia militia units under George Washington. The French victory at Fort Necessity not only secured French control of the Ohio forks but also destroyed important trade networks as the majority of British traders fled from the region. The French proved eager to fill the void but only if native leaders agreed to discontinue relations with the British colonists. If they refused, the French promised to drive them out of the upper Ohio Valley. Some upper Ohio Indians readily allied themselves with the French, while others, wary of engaging their people alongside any European imperial power, adopted a more cautious approach.[7]

Although the British colonists' land hunger had caused many western Delaware leaders to reevaluate their relationship with their neighbors, most were not yet inclined to seek accommodation with the French. From a political standpoint, the French represented a more immediate threat than the American colonists. The French had invaded the Delawares' homeland and now threatened to expel them if they didn't comply with French demands. Moreover, the French offered few economic advantages, as French trade goods generally were more expensive and of a lesser quality than those of the American colonial traders. Such considerations left western Delaware leaders in a difficult position, wedged between economic and political constraints. Lacking a clear path to advantage, they decided to play a middle course and continue negotiations with both sides, although they directed the majority of their diplomatic efforts toward the American colonials and their British masters. During the fall of 1754 western Delaware leaders, along with representatives of other upper Ohio tribes, traveled to western Virginia to meet with Virginia provincial officials. Delaware negotiators sought clarification of American and British intentions regarding the French, and, more importantly, they hoped to discover whether the French invasion might provide bargaining leverage they could manipulate in their campaign to preserve their upper Ohio homeland. What they found surprised them. The Americans, greatly dismayed by Washington's defeat at Fort Necessity, refused to make any effort to dislodge the French from the upper Ohio Valley and instead encouraged the Indians to take matters into their own hands. This posture struck a cord with the western Delawares, who, according to British Indian agents, now believed "the English [were] afraid of the French." If the colonists truly were afraid of the French, western Delaware leaders must have wondered whether they could use that fear to secure formal recognition of their territorial autonomy.[8]

When word reached the upper Ohio Valley that the British government had dispatched a formidable army to dislodge the French from the Ohio forks, the western Delawares decided to put their theory to the test. In June 1755 a Delaware military delegation traveled to Cumberland, Maryland, to negotiate an alliance with the British commander, Maj. Gen. Edward Braddock. The Delaware war captain Shingas offered his people's support in the British campaign against the French, but the negotiations, and any chance for an alliance, soured when Shingas inquired of Braddock what was to become of the upper Ohio lands after the French were driven from Fort Duquesne. The general promptly replied that "no savage shall inherit the land," instead declaring that the upper Ohio Valley would be incorporated into the colonies. An outraged Shingas led his warriors out of camp but not before angrily announcing that "if they [the Indians] might not have liberty to live on the land, they would not fight for it." At least not on the side of the British.[9]

Following the encounter with Braddock, many upper Ohio Indians allied themselves with the French. But western Delaware leaders, wary of engaging their people on the losing side of the upcoming confrontation, restrained their warriors and adopted a more cautious approach. Although they chose to wait and watch, the fear that Braddock's army would force their removal from the upper Ohio region made further negotiation with the British unlikely. It also caused some western Delawares to openly speak of forming an alliance with the French. The French alliance was by no means a popular option, but at least the French had betrayed no intention to seize Indian land where, as native leaders recalled, Braddock had "looked upon us as Dogs . . . [and] never appeared pleased with us." They soon resigned themselves to the realization that the land aggression shown by the British and their American colonists must be deterred, and Delaware leaders gradually reached the conclusion that no amount of negotiation could achieve that design. Thus the western Delawares, along with a large number of Shawnees and a scattering of other tribes along the upper Ohio, allied themselves with the French. As

Shingas explained, "We the Delawares of Ohio do declare war against the English. We have been their friends many years but now have taken up the hatchet against them, and we will never make it up with them whilst there is an Englishman alive."[10]

For the western Delawares, the decision to make war was part of a focused attempt to use force as means of achieving political concessions that had eluded their diplomatic efforts. The fear of becoming migrants again, coupled with the weakness of British arms demonstrated by Braddock's crushing defeat, eventually led the western Delawares to abandon their traditional practice of diplomacy in favor of violence. Since the British and their colonists were unwilling to recognize the western Delawares' territorial autonomy via treaty, the Delawares decided to obtain recognition through war. Throughout the three-and-a-half-year war that ensued, the western Delawares held to this singular objective. While freedom from Iroquois suzerainty may have slightly influenced the decision for war, this was no more than a secondary motivation, as Iroquois control of the Indians living in the upper Ohio Valley was much weaker than their influence over the Indians living along the Susquehanna River in central Pennsylvania. Nor were French military objectives particularly relevant. Numerous Indian peoples cooperated closely with the French during the Seven Years' War, including Caughnawaga Iroquois, Ottawas, Potawatomis, Wyandots, and Miamis from the Great Lakes, and Shawnees and Mingos from the Ohio Country. But these tribes comprised only a small portion of the Indians involved in the conflict along the Pennsylvania and Virginia frontiers. The bulk of the fighting here was done by the western Delawares, later joined by their cousins living along the Susquehanna. For the western Delawares, the French alliance was one of mutual convenience: the Delawares needed French weapons and trade, while the French needed Delaware warriors to secure their grasp on the Ohio forks. The western Delawares fought for their own ends, however, which did not always coincide with French objectives, rendering French participation in their campaigns for the most part limited and advisory.[11]

In the purest sense then, for the western Delawares the conflict was a border war. Their objective, learned from dealing with both the British and the Iroquois, was to use war as a leveraging tool to obtain the political concessions that diplomacy had failed to produce. To accomplish their goal they targeted the frontier population of Pennsylvania and Virginia. The strategy hinged on the ability of Delaware warriors to unleash such terror and suffering upon the colonial backcountry that the frontier population would call upon their provincial leaders to make peace with the Indians, which the western Delawares would not accept without a guarantee of native territorial autonomy within the upper Ohio Valley. It was a sound strategy, one that their new French allies wholeheartedly supported. The governor of New France, Pierre François Rigaud de Vaudreuil, believed that France's best chance for victory in North America was to take the war into the homes of the American colonials. "Nothing is more calculated to disgust the people of those colonies," Vaudreuil reasoned, "and to make them desire the return of peace." The French garrison at Fort Duquesne thus eagerly provided Delaware warriors with weapons and ammunition and encouraged them to attack the frontier settlements.[12]

Putting this strategy into effect on the ground level was the work of western Delaware war chiefs, including noted military leaders Shingas and Captain Jacobs. The warriors focused on weaknesses prevalent in the colonial border country, where thinly populated villages and individual farms dominated the landscape. Large plantations or densely populated settlements were few and far between. In addition, forts or well-defended homesteads were almost non-existent, often leaving backcountry settlers no place of refuge from an attack. Throughout the border war, Delaware warriors used this isolation to their advantage while waging a war of terror against the frontier populace. A cursory reading of the attacks gives the impression that the raids were random and arbitrary, but closer investigation reveals a sophisticated level of organization. Larger war parties, sometimes in excess of fifty warriors and occasionally accompanied by French advisers, attacked denser settlements or military targets, including forts. Such attacks usually occurred during the planting or harvesting season, when stronger settlements were vulnerable because the male inhabitants were out in the fields, leaving women, children, and the elderly to look after defense. Shingas's warriors destroyed Fort Granville in Cumberland Country, Pennsylvania, in this manner during July 1756. The majority of the raids during the border war, however, involved smaller groups of warriors, often numbering less than twenty Indians. These far-ranging war parties typically bypassed the few large settlements and forts in favor of attacking an isolated farm or homestead, where they engaged in a sort of lightning warfare. Delaware raiders struck quickly and without warning, killed or captured as many inhabitants as possible, burned the buildings, and withdrew before retaliation could be organized.[13]

Shingas personally engaged in all types of attacks, often on the same raid. In October and November 1755, he led an exceptionally large war party, numbering more than 150 warriors, across the mountains to attack the Pennsylvania and Virginia frontiers. His band fell upon the region around Fort Cumberland, killing nearly 100 people in the settlements along Patterson's Creek. The Delawares then crossed into Cumberland County, Pennsylvania, where Shingas divided his warriors into smaller parties and launched several simultaneous attacks throughout the countryside. They sacked numerous communities in the area, along with many outlying farms. Two-thirds of the inhabitants of the Juniata Valley fled their homes for the safety of the east during the raid, leaving one official to declare that "I am of opinion this county will be lead [left] dissolute without inhabitant[s]."[14]

Speed and surprise were the key elements of the Indians' success. Yet their tactics also demonstrated a merger of traditional native warfare practices with new techniques learned from their European adversaries. On the one hand, Indian warriors waged a traditional native war of plunder. Hundreds of women and children were taken as captives, farms and homesteads were looted and ransacked, and livestock were stolen and taken back to the upper Ohio Valley. On the other hand, tradition was mediated by the incorporation of European concepts of war. One particularly important change was the adoption of the European emphasis placed on killing the enemy. As Indian warriors took prisoners and plunder, they simultaneously killed nearly every male colonist they encountered, often going out of their way to escalate the body count. Moreover, the Indians also employed terror tactics long associated with the type of psychological warfare Europeans waged against Indians. The bodies of dead settlers often were mutilated and then left prominently displayed for the other residents to view. At Penn's Creek in October 1755, Delaware warriors purposefully burned the lower half of a man in fire and then arranged the body in a sitting position with two tomahawks protruding from his head. A woman was found with her breasts cut off and propped up by a long stake that had been driven through her body. While mutilation was not uncommon in eastern woodland warfare practices, these actions were inconsistent with the Indians' traditionally ritualistic forms of torture. These mutilations were part of a psychological terror campaign designed to intimidate and dishearten their opponents, not at all unlike the English colonists' mounting of Metacom's head on a pike in Plymouth Colony following King Philip's War.[15]

If the objective of the attacks was to create a level of suffering and fear so great that the frontier population would pressure their colonial governments to make peace with the Indians, the western Delawares achieved a remarkable level of success. Neither Pennsylvania nor Virginia provincial authorities were able to adequately defend their frontiers against Indian warriors who, according to one observer, "lurk in the woods until they have an opportunity of surprising unguarded settlers." The border war thus devastated the backwoods settlements of Pennsylvania and Virginia. Terror and paranoia gripped entire communities as residents feared to venture out of their homes or tend to their fields. After an attack on Vause's Fort in Augusta County, Virginia, in 1756, a local official lamented that it was impossible "to describe the confusion and disorder [of] the poor people." Another beleaguered victim, who had just experienced a raid, informed his father that "I'm in so much horror and confusion I scarce know what I am writing." In both colonies, backcountry inhabitants fled by the thousands as the frontier rapidly retreated eastward under the strain of the border war. In 1756 the Pennsylvania assembly learned that a thirty-mile-wide swath of land stretching from the headwaters of the Potomac River to the upper Delaware River "[had] been entirely deserted . . . [and] the houses and improvements reduced to ashes." A similar situation existed in Virginia, where the populations of the western counties dropped significantly as settlers fled up to one hundred or more miles east to escape the attacks. During the height of the raids in 1756, a French officer at Fort Duquesne bragged to his superiors that Delaware raiding parties could travel two hundred miles to the east through abandoned settlements without finding a single inhabitant.[16]

Yet somehow the bleeding had to be stopped. The displaced border population demanded protection, and to some backcountry inhabitants, it mattered little whether that security came from the French, the British, or their own colonial governments. Reports indicated that some backcountry inhabitants were "capitulating and coming to terms with the French and Indians" in order to save their homes and farms. The majority of the afflicted frontier population undoubtedly remained loyal to Britain and their respective colonies, but their calls for the provincial governments to protect them became deafening. The frontier inhabitants "are quitting their habitations and crowding into the more settled parts of the province," an exasperated Robert Morris told the Pennsylvania assembly, "which in their turn will become the frontier if some stop is not speedily put to the cruel ravages of these bloody invaders."[17]

The governments of Pennsylvania and Virginia struggled to manage the onslaught. Provincial authorities recognized the severity of the situation but seemed incapable of stopping the raids. Political divisions in the provincial legislatures handicapped efforts to facilitate frontier defense as the border war divided men of power and influence who could not agree on how best to respond to the western Delawares' aggression. Divided internally, they lost control of not only the upper Ohio Valley but also the significantly larger backcountry region between the Ohio Country and the more established eastern settlements. On those occasions when action did occur, the results were rarely as desired. Both Pennsylvania and Virginia raised regiments and constructed fortifications to defend their frontiers, but neither had any meaningful impact on the conflict. Offensive campaigns also proved impotent, as western Delaware warriors eluded or defeated ranger units sent to intercept them and openly attacked thinly garrisoned stockades and forts. Even the one notable exception, Col. John Armstrong's surprise assault on the western Delaware village of Kittanning in 1756, failed to produce tangible results. The war leader Captain Jacobs died during the assault—burned alive in his lodge after refusing to surrender—but the majority of the Delawares, Shingas included, escaped. The failure to capture or kill Shingas, who had a $700 bounty on his head, rendered Armstrong's raid a political failure as the Pennsylvanians failed to eliminate one of the main tormentors of their frontier populace.

The raid was also a military failure. The Pennsylvanians suffered more than three times as many casualties as the Indians by the time the campaign had concluded, and while the raid served to displace many Delawares further west to the Kuskuskies towns on the Beaver River, the destruction of Kittanning had little tangible effect on the war. Indeed, in reprisal for Armstrong's attack, Delaware raids against the Pennsylvania frontier increased in 1757. Thus despite the attack on Kittanning, the western Delawares continued to dictate the pace and character of the war, and it seemed there was little that the colonists could do to alter the arrangement.[18]

Much of their dilemma stemmed from the unpreparedness of the provincial governments to meet the challenges posed by the border war. Pennsylvania had no laws providing for the raising of troops or even for the formation of militia for defense, and Quaker pacifists in the assembly seemed unlikely to enact any, regardless of the state of the frontier. Virginia had militia, but managing the troops was taxing. Militia from different sections of the colony refused to serve outside of their immediate counties, their officers citing the need to protect their families and look after agricultural pursuits. Moreover, no consensus existed in the House of Burgesses regarding the deployment of the militia. Backcountry representatives clamored for deployment along the frontier, but the tidewater planter elite opposed sending militia units to the border settlements because it might interfere with the militia's traditional responsibilities, most notably the maintenance of order among the slave population. Planters feared the militia's absence could provide the impetus for slave insurrections, especially after rumors surfaced of a slave uprising in Lancaster County. Despite the widespread suffering along the frontier, Virginia governor Robert Dinwiddie acknowledged that "we dare not venture to part with any of our white men any distance, as we must have a watchful eye over our Negro slaves."[19]

Handicapped by these restrictions, the few efforts the provincial governments took to defend their frontiers were largely unsuccessful. The Virginia House of Burgesses outfitted a provincial military regiment to defend its borders, and the Quakers in Pennsylvania begrudgingly allowed the formation of a provincial army in 1756, but neither was an effective fighting force. Both remained undermanned during the war, primarily because few residents of either colony were willing to lay their lives on the line to secure possession of a remote frontier region. Colonists living in the established parts of either colony sympathized with their frontier brethren, but few were anxious to fight a war against a determined foe such as the western Delawares when it appeared that only land speculators and other elites stood to gain from victory. Most volunteers who turned out to fill the provincial regiments came from the lesser elements of society—landless tenants, poor artisans, debtors, recent immigrants, or in some cases, indentured servants—who enlisted not out of patriotic zeal or a desire to assist their beleaguered border brethren but because paid military service represented an improvement, however diminutive, over their present condition.[20]

The manpower shortages prevented both provincial governments from retaliating directly against the western Delawares; instead they adopted a defensive posture. Both the Pennsylvania assembly and the Virginia House of Burgesses placed their faith in the erection of forts along the border, believing they would provide a barrier against the raids. The multitude of structures built between 1756 and 1758 varied greatly in design and form. There were a few substantial earth and log forts, such as Fort Augusta on the Susquehanna River, but most were small wooden county forts or individual private forts, which were little more than a stockaded homestead. Their irregularity, together with flaws in the provincial leaders' strategy, made the forts ineffective. Colonial authorities in Pennsylvania and Virginia believed Indian raiders would be obligated to deal with the forts before attacking the settlements, a European doctrine of warfare that mattered little to native warriors. Western Delaware war parties generally bypassed the posts in favor of an easier target, although they just as often assailed the smaller forts, setting fire to the wooden structures or starving the garrison into submission. During the first half of 1756 Delaware war parties assaulted nine forts along the Virginia frontier, destroyed five of them, and killed or captured nearly three hundred Virginians. The attacks were so successful that George Washington, in charge of his colony's border defenses, advocated abandoning Fort Cumberland, the largest Virginia fort, in favor of taking up a defensive position further east.[21]

Frontiersmen turned soldiers garrisoned most of the forts. There were too few provincial soldiers to man the posts, forcing the frontier folk to look after their own defense. Left to their own devices, these part-time troops, dubbed rangers, patrolled the regions between forts in an effort to intercept Delaware war parties before they could reach the settlements. Their success rate was poor. Very seldom did the rangers actually intercept an incoming war party before it hit its mark. "Skulking Indians keep around us every day," reported a Pennsylvania ranger leader. "[We] discover their fresh tracks but cannot come up with them." The rangers' inability to acquire accurate information concerning the location and movement of the Indians severely limited their effectiveness. Moreover, the frontier posts were too distant from one another to allow for effective coverage by the patrols, especially along the Virginia frontier. "They [the Delawares] pass and repass to destroy the inhabitants," explained Adam Stephen, commander at Fort Cumberland. "As this insulting behavior escapes without impunity, it increases their insolence and demonstrates that forts, without sufficient number of men to defend them and scour the country about, are a useless burden to the province."[22]

The inadequacy of these defensive measures lay firmly in the failure of the Pennsylvania and Virginia provincial governments to garner widespread support from their constituent populations or the British colonial administration. Although the shortage of manpower was the greatest problem facing either colony during the border war, British military commanders, focused on the campaigns in northern New York, offered little assistance, leaving Pennsylvania and Virginia without succor. As provincial leaders grew increasingly desperate to end the carnage, they resorted to desperate measures. In 1756 both colonies offered bounties for Indian scalps. Officials believed the bounties would attract otherwise apathetic colonists to participate in frontier defense by appealing to their own self-interest. Anyone could cash in a bounty, regardless of enlistment in the provincial regiments or the militia, and the terms were generous. The Pennsylvania assembly set bounties of $130 for every adult male Indian scalp and $50 for every adult female Indian scalp. The scalps of prominent Indian war leaders brought even larger bounties, with Shingas's valued at $700. The bounties, like most other measures adopted by the provincial governments during the border war, were ineffective. Scores of adventurers and frontiersmen volunteered to "hunt" hostile Indians and collect the rewards, but they failed to lessen the intensity of Indian raids. More importantly, the scalp bounties did not distinguish between differing Indian peoples, with the exception of the Iroquois, making all other Indians potential targets regardless of their political alignment. Bounty hunters, free to attack friendly or neutral Indians, often chose easier targets than marauding war parties. The indiscriminate killing only intensified native resolve. In 1758 newly appointed Virginia governor Francis Fauquier repealed his colony's bounty law, citing its propensity "to produce bad consequences by setting our people on to kill Indians whether friends or enemies." It came too late to prevent the scalping of friendly Cherokee and Catawba Indians in southwest Virginia, precipitating an additional border conflict that further strained the colony's precariously thin resources.[23]

Colonial defense efforts thus failed miserably during the border war, as the western Delawares seemed able to strike at anytime and anyplace without warning. And as intended, terror and paranoia gripped entire frontier communities, where residents were reluctant to venture outside of their homes or tend to their fields lest they be caught unaware by "Shingas the terrible" and his warriors. The settlers' fears were firmly rooted in the reality of their suffering. During the three years of the border war as many as two thousand colonists were killed or captured during the raids, with thousands of uncounted others driven from their homes. At their apex, when the eastern Delawares joined the border war, the raids had penetrated deep into eastern Virginia and Pennsylvania, at one point reaching as far east as the settlement at Reading, only forty miles from Philadelphia.[24]

Perhaps more importantly, the Delaware raids and the inability of the provincial governments to prevent them had left the frontier population angry. For the backcountry people targeted by the Indians, there seemed to be no escape from their torment. They could not run, they could not hide, and they could not make it stop. Thousands of people, displaced from their homes and forced into refugee camps in the east, wanted either protection or retaliation. The failure of both intensified their rage, which was increasingly directed against their elected provincial leaders. In an early expression of the parochial mentality that would take root along the western colonial frontier, many backcountry residents blamed their suffering on "the negligence and insensibility of the administration, to whose inactivity there are so many sacrifices." Twice their rage boiled over into a state of near-rebellion in Pennsylvania. During the fall of 1755 a mob of nearly seven hundred people descended on Philadelphia and demanded protection for their families. In April 1756 residents of Cumberland County gathered to make a second march on Philadelphia, although they eventually disbanded before reaching the city. Their unhappiness underscored the inability of provincial authorities to bring relief from the raids. The mounting popular pressure, coupled with the total failure of provincial military efforts, finally forced the colonial governments of Pennsylvania and Virginia to seek a negotiated settlement that would end the war.[25]

The negotiation process began with the eastern Delawares in 1756 but reached the upper Ohio Valley by early 1758. Two factors helped spur its advance. British general John Forbes had brought an army to Pennsylvania in preparation of making an attack against Fort Duquesne, and the general preferred to fight the French without also engaging the upper Ohio Indians. In addition, deteriorating economic conditions among the western Delawares left some native leaders equally desirous for peace and the reopening of trade. The western Delawares, much like the American colonists they fought, had suffered greatly during the border war. British military successes in the northeast had obliterated French supply lines and brought the western Indian trade to a standstill. The steady decline in the supply of trade goods from Canada had undermined the western Delawares' ability to provide for themselves and

in turn strained their alliance with the French. By early 1758 the French could
barely supply their own western posts—Fort Duquesne was "almost starved
with hunger" and could no longer provide the Indians with supplies or provisions. Adding to the Indians' difficulties was the sporadic absence, injury, and
deaths of their warriors, which disrupted their seasonal hunting practices and
decreased their agricultural production. Declining trade opportunities combined with the interruption of traditional socioeconomic patterns to severely
curtail the normal rhythms of native life, leaving many western Delaware
communities in duress.[26]

But these factors alone were not sufficient to guarantee peace, which could
only last if British provincial officials took steps to alleviate the grievances of
the upper Ohio Indians. While these considerations differed from tribe to
tribe, the centerpiece of any peace agreement with the western Delawares remained a treaty guarantee of their territorial autonomy in the upper Ohio
Valley. Yet British provincial officials and Indian agents remained hesitant
to give up their interest in upper Ohio lands, a fact not lost on Shingas or
other western Delaware leaders. Still, in July 1758 two western Delaware negotiators, Pisquetomen and Keekyuscung, traveled to Philadelphia to discuss
the prospect of peace. General Forbes, overseeing the commencement of the
army's march toward the Ohio forks, instructed Pennsylvania governor William Denny to make every effort to secure the Indians' friendship. The Delaware negotiators seemed receptive. They informed the governor that their
people "were sorry that they had gone to war against the English" and hoped
to reinstate their old alliances, to which the governor ceremoniously replied
that they "held the peace belt, . . . [and] every offense that has been passed
shall be forgot forever." However, no formal peace agreement was reached
as Pisquetomen and Keekyuscung had no authority to make such arrangements. Instead, they agreed to return to their villages and appraise other
upper Ohio Indian leaders of their dealings in Philadelphia.[27]

A Moravian preacher named Christian Frederick Post accompanied the
two Delaware diplomats as Forbes' representative in the peace process. He
was a good choice for the assignment. Post, a Prussian-born religious prose-
lytizer, had spent nearly ten years among the Susquehanna Delawares, spoke
their language fluently, and had twice married Delaware women. However, in
the upper Ohio Valley he entered a native world fraught with political division and uncertainty. Post quickly discovered that some western Delaware
leaders did not support coming to terms with the British or the colonists. A
peace faction under Delaware headman Tamaqua, the brother of Shingas, had
gained some influence, but many Delawares believed peace to be but a precursor to the seizure of their lands by the colonists. As Shingas informed Post:

We have great reason to believe you intend to drive us away and settle the country, or else why do you come to fight in the land that God has given us? . . . It is clear that you white people are the cause of this war; Why do not you and the French fight in the old country, and on the sea? Why do you come to fight in our land? That makes everybody believe you want to take the land from us by force and settle it.

Post replied that the British army intended "only to drive the French away," but he could not overcome native apprehension about the loss of their lands. If peace was the end objective, native leaders questioned, then "what makes you come with such a large body of men and make such large roads into our country?"[28]

The precariousness of the peace negotiations was further underscored by western Delaware participation in two attacks against advanced elements of Forbes' army during the fall of 1758. In October, under intense pressure from General Forbes to end Indian hostilities, provincial representatives finally relented and opened a treaty council at Easton, Pennsylvania, to address Indian grievances, including western Delaware territorial concerns. Through an Iroquois-brokered agreement, the colonists agreed to drop all claims to upper Ohio lands and promised to rekindle the "first old council fire" at Philadelphia, renewing "the old and first treaties of friendship" between the colony and the Delaware nation. This gesture represented the culmination of the political aims that guided the Delawares' war effort, the political recognition of their autonomous territorial integrity. With this guarantee the western Delaware diplomat Pisquetomen agreed to peace. After lengthy discussion Shingas also agreed to accept the peace agreement and promised not to interfere when Forbes's army attacked Fort Duquesne. The war leader also agreed to personally carry news of the cessation of hostilities to the other Indian nations of the region, whom they believed would honor the terms of the treaty. Final confirmation of the agreement came the following year at Fort Pitt, where Delaware spokesman Tamaqua reminded the British, "the land is ours and not yours." Yet even this came with a warning. Another Delaware negotiator, Keekyuscung, informed the British that "All the nations [of the upper Ohio] had jointly agreed to defend their hunting place at Allegheny, and suffer nobody to settle there . . . if they [the English] stayed and settled there, all the nations would be against them and it would be a great war and never come to peace again."[29]

That warning proved prophetic. In the years following the Easton accord, colonial settlers renewed their pursuit of upper Ohio lands and British officials attempted to subjugate the upper Ohio Indians. The resulting tensions helped to ignite the unified Indian uprising of 1763–1764, generally known as Pontiac's Rebellion. But the course of these subsequent events should not diminish the success of the western Delawares' military and political strategies during the border war of 1755–1758. Through warfare rather than their traditional practice of negotiation, the Delawares gained the concessions they sought. This formula for success would be replicated on subsequent frontiers of the Old Northwest, albeit with less success, by native leaders ranging from Blue Jacket to Little Turtle to Tecumseh, all of whom tacitly if not overtly sought to emulate the western Delawares' model of achieving their political goals through warfare rather than negotiation. The primary difference between these later endeavors and that of western Delawares during the border war was proximity. Later native military efforts, unable to sufficiently take war into the homes of American settlers or bring destruction to consolidated American territory, were defeated on the battlefield, in the process losing their lands, their lives, and their independence. Only the western Delawares, by terrorizing and intimidating civilians and noncombatants along the colonial frontier, in the process avoiding a decisive standoff on the field of battle, secured any measure of success, even if it was only temporary.

NOTES

1. *Pennsylvania Archives,* 9 ser., 138 vols. (Philadelphia: State Printer of Pennsylvania, 1852–56, 1875–1949), 1st ser., 1:330–33; C. A. Weslager, *The Delaware Indians: A History* (New Brunswick, N.J.: Rutgers Univ. Press, 1972), 184–85.

2. See Michael N. McConnell, *A Country Between: The Upper Ohio Valley and Its Peoples, 1724–1774* (Lincoln: Univ. of Nebraska Press, 1992); Matthew C. Ward, "La Guerre Sauvage: The Seven Years' War on the Virginia and Pennsylvania Frontier" (Ph.D. Diss., The College of William and Mary, 1992); and Ward, "Fighting the Old Women: Indian Strategy on the Virginia and Pennsylvania Frontier, 1754–1758," *Virginia Magazine of History and Biography* 103 (1995): 297–320.

3. French official quoted in Lawrence Henry Gipson, *The British Empire before the American Revolution,* 15 vols. (New York: Knopf, 1958–70), 4:166; William A. Hunter, "Traders on the Ohio: 1730," *Western Pennsylvania Historical Magazine* 35 (1972): 85–89. For Indian migrations to the Upper Ohio, see Francis Jennings, *The Ambiguous Iroquois Empire: The Covenant Chain Confederation of Indian Tribes with English Colonies, from Its Beginnings to the Lancaster Treaty of 1744* (New York: Norton, 1984), 221–375; McConnell, *A Country Between,* 5–46; and Paul A. W. Wallace, *Indians in Pennsylvania,* rev. ed. (Harrisburg: Pennsylvania Historical and Museum Commission, 1993), 108–41. For a corollary to the Indian trader or explorer as "cultural geographer" in the trans–Mississippi west, see Robert M. Utley, *A Life Wild and Perilous: Mountain Men and the Paths to the Pacific* (New York: Henry Holt, 1997).

4. John W. Jordan, ed., "Journal of James Kenny, 1761–1763," *Pennsylvania Magazine of History and Biography* 37 (1913): 45; James P. McClure, "The Ends of the American Earth: Pittsburgh and the Upper Ohio Valley to 1795," (Ph.D. Diss., Univ. of Michigan, 1983), 3–6.

5. Weslager, *Delaware Indians*, 173–220; McConnell, *A Country Between*, 61–112.

6. Gipson, *The British Empire in North America*, 4:269–73; Donald H. Kent, *The French Invasion of Western Pennsylvania, 1753* (Harrisburg: Pennsylvania Historical and Museum Commission, 1954), 43–44; Francis Jennings, *Empire of Fortune: Crowns, Colonies and Tribes in the Seven Years' War in America* (New York: Norton, 1988), 50–52.

7. McConnell, *A Country Between*, 119–21; Ward, "Fighting the Old Women," 300–301.

8. Samuel Hazard, ed., *Colonial Records of Pennsylvania, 1683–1790*, 16 vols. (Philadelphia, Pa.: T. Fenn, 1851–53), 6:140 [hereafter cited as *CRP*]; Ward, "La Guerre Sauvage," 65–66.

9. *CRP*, 6:398–99; Beverly W. Bond Jr., ed., "The Captivity of Charles Stuart, 1755–1757," *Mississippi Valley Historical Review* 13 (1926–27): 63–64.

10. *CRP*, 6:588–89, 659, 683; Bond, ed., "Captivity of Charles Stuart," 63–64; McConnell, *A Country Between*, 119–21; Ward, "Fighting the Old Women," 300–301.

11. Weslager, *Delaware Indians*, 230–31; McConnell, *A Country Between*, 120–21.

12. Pierre François Riguad de Vaudreuil de Cavagnial to Jean Baptiste de Machault d'Arnouville, June 8, 1756, E. B. O'Callaghan, ed., *Documents Relative to the Colonial History of the State of New York, Procured in Holland, England, and France*, 15 vols. (Albany, N.Y.: Weed, Parsons, 1857), 10:413 [hereafter cited as *NYCD*]; Matthew C. Ward, "Fighting the Old Women," 299–300.

13. Ward, "Fighting the Old Women," 308–9. Reports of the differing types of Indian raids are found throughout vols. 6–7 of the *CRP* as well as the May–June 1756 issues of the *Pennsylvania Gazette*. Also see Ward, "La Guerre Savage," 175–251; and C. Hale Sipe, *The Indian Wars of Pennsylvania*, 2nd ed. (Harrisburg, Pa.: Telegraph, 1931; repr., Lewisburg, Pa.: Wennawoods, 1994), esp. 230–303.

14. Adam Stephen to George Washington, October 4, 1755, W. W. Abbot, ed., *The Papers of George Washington, Colonial Series*, 10 vols. (Charlottesville: Univ. Press of Virginia, 1983–95), 2:72–73; John Potter to Richard Peters, November 3, 1755, *CRP*, 6:673–74; John Armstrong to Robert Morris, November 2, 1755, ibid., 6:676.

15. *Pennsylvania Archives*, 1st ser., 3:633; Sipe, *Indian Wars of Pennsylvania*, 204–16.

16. Edward Biddle to his father, *CRP*, 6:705; Council minutes, December 29, 1755, ibid., 6:767–68; Memorandum, July 1756, William Preston Papers, Lyman C. Draper Manuscript Collection, Historical Society of Wisconsin, Division of Archives and Manuscripts, University of Wisconsin, Madison, Wisconsin [hereafter cited as DMC], Ser. QQ, 1:132; Abstract of dispatches from America, August 30, 1756, *NYCD*, 10:486. For a comprehensive assessment of the abandonment of the Pennsylvania and Virginia frontiers, see Chester Raymond Young, "The Effects of the French and Indian War on Civilian Life in the Frontier Counties of Virginia, 1754–1763" (Ph.D. Diss., Vanderbilt Univ., 1969); and Ward, "La Guerre Sauvage."

17. Robert Dinwiddie to Robert Morris, October 31, 1775, R. A., Brock, ed., *The Official Records of Robert Dinwiddie, Lieutenant-Governor of the Colony of Virginia, 1751–1758*,

2 vols. (Richmond: Virginia Historical Society, 1883–1884), 2:259; Dinwiddie to William Shirley, October 18, 1755, ibid., 2:244; Robert Morris to the Pennsylvania Assembly, November 5, 1755, *CRP*, 6:676–77; George Washington to Robert Dinwiddie, April 24, 1756, Abbot, ed., *Papers of George Washington*, 3:46.

18. *CRP*, 6:676–77, 767–68; 7:257–63; *Pennsylvania Gazette*, September 23, 1756; Timothy Alden, ed., "An Account of the Captivity of Hugh Gibson among the Delaware Indians," *Collections of the Massachusetts Historical Society*, 3rd ser. (Boston, Mass.: American Stationer's, 1837), 4:143; William A. Hunter, "Victory at Kittanning," *Pennsylvania History* 23 (1956): 376–407; James P. Myers, "Pennsylvania's Awakening: The Kittanning Raid of 1756," *Pennsylvania History* 66 (1999): 399–420. Some historians (Hunter, "Victory at Kittanning," 405–7; McConnell, *A Country Between*, 126) have argued that the destruction of Kittanning severely impeded future Delaware raiding and led to the rise of a peace faction under Shingas's brother, Tamaqua. However, reports from the Pennsylvania frontier indicate that raiding did not sharply decline in the wake of Armstrong's campaign but rather intensified. See *CRP*, 7:302, 356, 399, 459–60, 506–7, 619, 632, 735, 757, 762.

19. Robert Dinwiddie to Lord Loudon, August 9, 1756, Brock, ed., *Records of Dinwiddie*, 2:474; James Titus, *The Old Dominion at War: Society, Politics, and Warfare in Late Colonial Virginia* (Columbia: Univ. of South Carolina Press, 1991), 74–76. The House of Burgesses underscored this fear in August 1755 when it ruled that the governor or commander of its military forces could not force the militia to move more than five miles beyond the established boundaries of Virginia. See William Waller Henning, ed., *The Statutes at Large: Being a Collection of All the Laws of Virginia*, 18 vols. (Richmond, Va.: Samuel Pleasants, 1809–23), 6:548 [hereafter cited as *Virginia Statutes at Large*].

20. Titus, *Old Dominion at War*, 80–88; R. S. Stephenson, "Pennsylvania Provincial Soldiers in the Seven Years' War," *Pennsylvania History* 62 (1995): 196–212; Matthew C. Ward, "An Army of Servants: The Pennsylvania Regiment during the Seven Years' War," *Pennsylvania Magazine of History and Biography* 119 (1995): 75–93. For a dissenting view, which argues that the Virginia Regiment's makeup was consistent with the diverse nature of Virginian society during the late colonial era, see John Ferling, "Soldiers for Virginia: Who Served in the French and Indian War?" *Virginia Magazine of History and Biography* 94 (1986): 307–28.

21. George Washington to Robert Dinwiddie, August 4, 1756, Abbot, ed., *Papers of George Washington*, 3:312–16; Dinwiddie to Washington, August 19, 1756, Brock, ed., *Records of Dinwiddie*, 2:480–81; Louis M. Waddell, "Defending the Long Perimeter: Forts on the Pennsylvania, Maryland, and Virginia Frontier, 1755–1765," *Pennsylvania History* 62 (1995): 185–88; Matthew C. Ward, "The European Method of Warring Is Not Practiced Here: The Failure of British Military Policy in the Ohio Valley, 1755–1759," *War in History* 4 (1997): 258–60. For a detailed examination of the forts constructed by Pennsylvania during this period, see William A. Hunter, *Forts on the Pennsylvania Frontier, 1753–1758* (Harrisburg: Pennsylvania Historical and Museum Commission, 1960), 214–543.

22. James Hyndshaw to Conrad Weiser, May 31, 1757, Weiser Correspondence, Penn Manuscripts, Official Correspondence, Historical Society of Pennsylvania, Special Collections Research Library, Philadelphia, Pennsylvania [hereafter cited as HSP]; George Washington to John Robinson, April 24, 1756, Abbot, ed., *Papers of George Washington*, 3:48; Adam Stephen to George Washington, August 1, 1756, ibid., 3:310; Washington to

John McNeill, August 12, 1756, ibid., 3:343; Washington to Lord Loudon, January 1757, ibid., 4:82; Waddell, "Defending the Long Perimeter," 184–85.

23. Council minutes, April 8 and 10, 1756, *CRP,* 7:74–76, 78–79; Proclamation, April 14, 1756, ibid., 7:88–90; *Pennsylvania Gazette,* January 1, 1756; Francis Fauquier to William Henry Lyttleton, October 13, 1758, George Reese, ed., *The Official Papers of Francis Fauquier, Lieutenant Governor of Virginia, 1758–1768,* 3 vols. (Charlottesville: Univ. Press of Virginia, 1980–83), 1:89; Fauquier to the Board of Trade, January 5, 1759, ibid., 1:146; Henry J. Young, "A Note on Scalp Bounties in Pennsylvania," *Pennsylvania History* 24 (1957): 208–11; McConnell, *A Country Between,* 123–24.

24. Memorandum, July 1756, William Preston Papers, DMC, Ser. QQ, 1:132; Edward Biddle to his father, *CRP,* 6:705; Ward, "Fighting the Old Women," 313–18. The figures presented here are based on the excellent quantitative study compiled by Matthew C. Ward in Appendix C of "La Guerre Sauvage," 418–55. Ward offers an exhaustive examination of nearly every existent report of Indian raids along the Pennsylvania and Virginia frontier for this period to arrive at a total of 1,217 killed and 755 captured, including at least 89 women and 250 children. As Ward points out, these figures likely represent a low-end estimate of the actual numbers killed or taken prisoner because the surviving records are incomplete.

25. Penn MSS: Indian Affairs, HSP, 2:52; *Pennsylvania Gazette,* April 15, 1756; *Pennsylvania Archives,* 4th ser., 2:552; Ward, "Fighting the Old Women," 318.

26. Israel Pemberton to Joseph Morris, July 30, 1757, Pemberton Papers, Etting Collection, HSP, 12:50; John Forbes to James Abercromby, June 27 and July 9, 1758, Alfred Proctor James, ed., The *Writings of General John Forbes Relating to His Service in North America* (Menasha, Wis.: Collegiate, 1938), 126–28, 134–40; Abercromby to Forbes, July 23, 1754, ibid., 140; Journal of Frederick Post's Journey to Wyoming, *CRP,* 8:145; Jennings, *Empire of Fortune,* 253–81, 323–48; McConnell, *A Country Between,* 128–30; Fred Anderson, *Crucible of War: The Seven Years' War and the Fate of Empire in British North America, 1754–1766* (New York: Knopf, 2000), 164–65, 269–70.

27. Council minutes, March 15, 1758, *CRP,* 8:32–35; Journal of Frederick Post's Journey to Wyoming, ibid., 8:144; McConnell, *A Country Between,* 129–30.

28. *CRP,* 8:32–35, 144; Journal of Christian Frederick Post in Reuben Gold Thwaites, ed., *Early Western Travels, 1748–1846,* 32 vols. (Cleveland, Ohio: A. H. Clark, 1904–7), 1:213–14, 240; Richard White, *The Middle Ground: Indians, Empires, and Republics in the Great Lakes Region, 1650–1815* (New York: Cambridge Univ. Press, 1991), 250–52; McConnell, *A Country Between,* 130–31; James H. Merrell, *Into the American Woods: Negotiators on the Pennsylvania Frontier* (New York: Norton, 1999), 242–49; Anderson, *Crucible of War,* 270–71.

29. Sylvester K. Stevens, Donald H. Kent, and Autumn L. Leonard, eds., *The Papers of Henry Bouquet,* 6 vols. (Harrisburg: Pennsylvania Museum and Historical Commission, 1951–94), 2:428–29, 460–62, 499–504, 517–21, 552, 555–56, 560; *CRP,* 8:205–7; Journal of Christian Frederick Post in Thwaites, ed., *Early Western Travels,* 1:253–78; McConnell, *A Country Between,* 133–35.

3

"We Speak as One People"

Native Unity and the Pontiac Indian Uprising

David Dixon

In the mid–nineteenth century Americans embraced an ideology that summoned them to expand their moral virtues and political institutions across the continent. The public eagerly heralded testaments supporting this notion of "Manifest Destiny" and insisted that any impediments to progress and civilization must be swept aside. It was during this time that New England historian Francis Parkman introduced *The Conspiracy of Pontiac and the Indian War after the Conquest of Canada,* an epic narrative concerning the Woodland Indian conflict that erupted in the aftermath of the Seven Years' War in America. In this classic account, Parkman places the Ottawa leader, Pontiac, as the central figure who magically orchestrates a powerful and united Pan-Indian Confederation intent on eliminating Anglo-American presence west of the Appalachian Mountains. Parkman could not have picked a better story to relate to an American public bursting with a sense of its own destiny to expand from the Atlantic to the Pacific.

As Parkman's tale develops, the English are almost overwhelmed by a cunning and loutish foe who will stop at nothing to halt the progress of civilization. The Indians are whipped into a frenzy by the charismatic leadership of Chief Pontiac, who artfully organizes a confederation of all the tribes of the Northeast. The English, who have no ill designs other than to raise their crops and families in the austere wilderness, are completely caught off guard as the Indian horde rolls over the forts that are situated along the frontier to protect them. Only Forts Detroit and Pitt are able to withstand the ferocious onslaught. Though outnumbered, the garrisons at these two beleaguered outposts somehow manage to hold out against the barbaric menace that surrounds them. Through courage and determination the British and Americans finally prevail and defeat the bloodthirsty Indians. In this compelling and dramatic chronicle Parkman provides his readers with an instructive lesson: in the end civilization will always triumph over savagery.

Since it first appeared in 1851, *The Conspiracy of Pontiac* has gone through numerous editions and reprints. Its popularity is largely due to the author's ability to simply tell a good story. While Parkman glorified the nation's struggle to conquer a hostile wilderness, he also keenly grasped the concept that nothing can be more appealing than a sweeping epic narrative that draws the reader into the story. The acclaim that Parkman has received over the years underscores his mastery in composing narrative history.[1]

It took nearly one hundred years for historians to begin to raise questions regarding Parkman's methodology and interpretation of events. In an obscure 1943 article that appeared in *The Papers of the Bibliographic Society of America*, historian Howard Peckham suggests that Parkman had missed, ignored, or fabricated crucial evidence while composing his epistle on the Indian conflict that became known as Pontiac's Uprising. Further, Peckham insisted that Parkman's interpretation was seriously flawed by elevating Pontiac to the position of sole inspiration and authority during the Indian war. Peckham's own research indicated that the chief's leadership role was limited to a few Indian villages around Detroit and his insubstantial influence among several neighboring nations such as the Chippewas and Potawatomis. In fact, Peckham made clear that Pontiac's leadership among his own people was frequently challenged by other chiefs such as Wasson, a Chippewa leader, who also maintained considerable power over the tribes that besieged Detroit. Even a fledgling Erie chief chastised Pontiac during the siege, stating, "Thou hast begun the war ill-advisedly and art now in a rage at not having been able to take the English fort."[2]

In recent years many other historians have taken up the challenge of exploring the relationship between Europeans and native peoples in early America, and in doing so they have continually exposed Francis Parkman's flawed research and called into question his interpretations and motives. These works tend to diminish Pontiac's role as the creator of a great Pan-Indian Confederation. Instead these historians point out that the nations residing in the Great Lakes region and upper Ohio River valley had already achieved a sense of unification fostered by mutual political, social, and economic concerns. Many of these scholars further insist that the alliance hinged on a powerful religious movement that was embraced by the Indian nations living on the frontier.[3] In order to fully understand and assess these recent interpretations, it is important to review Indian efforts to unify in the years preceding Pontiac's Uprising. It is also essential to evaluate how British officials may have contributed to the growing confederation and what efforts, if any, they took to prevent the alliance. Lastly, it is critical to ascertain the level of cooperation and unity among the tribes during the conflict in order to gauge the strength of their efforts.

In 1748 Pennsylvania's Indian agent and interpreter, Conrad Weiser, visited the Indian village of Logstown, an important trading community along the Ohio River. In the town he found 789 warriors, including representatives from the Delawares, Wyandots, Shawnees, Hurons, and Mahicans. Also present were Mohawks, Oneidas, Onondagas, Cayugas, and Senecas—tribes identified as members of the powerful Iroquois Confederacy. During his negotiations with the Indians Weiser took particular note of the fact that they identified themselves as "all one People." In particular, the Iroquois representatives insisted that they spoke "in behalf of all the Indians of Ohio."[4]

What Weiser witnessed at Logstown was the product of nearly one hundred years of destabilization that had infected the region known as the Ohio Country—a land roughly bordered by Lake Erie to the north, the Allegheny Mountains to the east, the Ohio River to the south, and the Miami River to the west. As early as 1656 the Iroquois had swooped down on the Erie Indians living in this area and all but annihilated them. In efforts to replenish their dwindling population, gain advantages in trade with the Europeans, and establish barriers against white encroachment, the League of Five Nations, as the five tribes of the Iroquois Confederacy were sometimes called, devastated and displaced other Indians throughout what was to become the colony of Pennsylvania. In the aftermath of these so-called Beaver Wars, the Iroquois claimed the Ohio Country and much of Pennsylvania as part of their domain. Some members of the confederacy, such as the Senecas, chose to stay in the Ohio Country and were later joined with other Iroquoian speaking people. This polyglot eventually lost the connection with its own tribes and clans and became known as the Mingos.[5]

Later, as the English became more numerous and began occupying the Delaware River valley in eastern Pennsylvania, more Indians moved to the Ohio Country. The Lenapes, known to the British as the Delawares, vacated most of their land in the east and settled into a new environment along the Susquehanna River valley. From there, small bands and entire communities left the valley and trekked across the mountains to join the "people on the other side" in the Allegheny River valley region.[6] Presumably these movements were accomplished with the acquiescence of the Iroquois Confederacy, who claimed the land. Perhaps the largest migration of Delawares into the Ohio Country came about as a result of the 1737 "Walking Purchase." This land transaction took place when the Penn family desired more property along the upper Delaware River valley. The practice of purchasing land from the Indians had begun with Pennsylvania's founder, William Penn, who would then sell the land to prospective European immigrants. With the rapid advance of settlement beyond Philadelphia, the Penn heirs needed to acquire the remaining Delaware land located north of the City of Brotherly Love. To accomplish this transaction, Thomas Penn instructed his provincial secretary, James Logan, to arrange yet another land purchase from the Delawares. When the natives refused to sell, Logan requested that the Iroquois intercede and force the Delawares to relocate. The provincial secretary was well aware of the influence that the League of Five Nations claimed over subordinate tribes residing in Pennsylvania. For their part, the Iroquois were interested in furthering ties with the English in Pennsylvania and agreed to assist Logan. As a result, the Iroquois sent a delegation to the Delaware villages to compel their removal. Eventually, the land transaction was completed when Englishmen marked off the boundaries by walking a day and a half. This so-called Walking Purchase served to terminate all Indian claims to land in the Delaware River valley. The dispossessed tribesmen, filled with bitterness and resentment toward both the English and the Iroquois, begrudgingly moved west into the Susquehanna River valley. Many others went even further, across the mountains into the Ohio Country.[7]

The Senecas, Mingos, and Delawares were not the only Indian nations that occupied the land beyond the Appalachians. Other refugees migrated into the region in the early part of the eighteenth century. The Shawnees, who other tribes often called "wanderers," established a trading community along the Allegheny River in 1734. Other Shawnee people settled at villages such as Sewickley Town, near the winding river that the Indians called Youghiogheny, and Keckenepaulin's Town, which was located west of Laurel Ridge at the mouth of what would later be known as Loyalhanna Creek.[8]

Soon other native peoples came to the Ohio Country. Mahicans arrived in small numbers from the Hudson River and Wyandots came from the west and settled near the Delaware village of Kuskuski, along the river that the Indians referred to as Shenango. Miamis (also known as Twightwees), Neutral Hurons, Ottawas, and Piankashaws could also be found in the region as they participated in a spirited intertribal trade network. As more and more native people entered the Ohio Country, they learned not only to coexist but also to forge a collective identity. They had all arrived on the Allegheny Plateau as refugees of sorts, escaping the pressure of European colonization or taking advantage of a new land rich in resources. They chiefly desired to recapture their traditional and familiar ways of life and preserve their cultural integrity, which was being threatened by the close proximity to the whites that lived east of the mountains. In the process, these people reinvented themselves, exchanging and sharing cultural mores. Anthropologists have come to define this particular form of acculturation as ethnogenesis—a process of cultural re-creation associated "with tribal societies that face advancing colonialism and are forced to change or perish."[9]

The collective identity that the Ohio Country Indians came to embrace was further facilitated by political exigencies emanating from the Iroquois Confederation in New York. Wishing to maintain close supervision over the Indian nations inhabiting the region, the League of Five Nations placed vice-regents, known to the English as "half kings" among the Ohio Country natives. The Iroquois council believed that their vice-regents could arbitrate intertribal quarrels, serve as spokesmen for the various tribes, and quell any dissent from Iroquois hegemony. This situation would have worked well if the half kings had remained loyal to the New York council. Over time, however, these vice-regents identified more with the interests of their charges than with the dictates of the League of Five Nations. This became evident in 1747 when Pennsylvania's new provincial secretary, Richard Peters, attempted to enlist the support of the Iroquois to drive French traders from the upper Ohio River valley. When the league council proclaimed a stance of neutrality in the conflict between Great Britain and France, Peters decided to appeal directly to the Ohio Country nations. This diplomatic initiative was fraught with a considerable degree of uncertainty and danger for it tended to represent a breach in protocol. Since the Walking Purchase, officials from the Quaker colony had found it beneficial to treat solely with the League of Five Nations from their council fire at Onondaga in New York. The Pennsylvanians had learned that it was problematic to deal with diverse local tribes. By negotiating with the Onondaga council, the Pennsylvania officials added weight to Iroquois claims of dominance over other tribes and simplified the diplomatic process. Nonetheless, when the Iroquois refused to support Peters in his efforts to push the French from western lands, he decided to bypass the Five Nations and seek aid from the Ohio Country tribes.[10]

In November the Oneida leader Monacatootha, along with a delegation of other Indians from across the mountains, arrived outside Philadelphia to discuss an alliance against the French. Monacatootha was a vice-regent who believed his role was to serve the interests of the Ohio natives, despite the fact that those interests could be at odds with the wishes of New York Iroquois. He informed Secretary Peters that the Ohio Indians were no longer bound to the dictates of the league council. The Oneida chief said, "The old men at the Fire at Onondaga are unwilling to come into the War so the Young Indians, the Warriors, and Captains consulted together and resolved to take up the English Hatchet against the will of their old People, and to lay their old People aside as of no use but in time of Peace."[11] Monacatootha believed that for too long the Indians living along the Ohio and its tributaries had allowed others to dictate their fate. They now seemed determined to make their own arrangements with the English by initiating a new Ohio council, autonomous from the fire at Onondaga. Richard Peters warmly embraced this Ohio delegation and loaded the Indians down with presents to take back to their villages. In bypassing the Iroquois and directly providing the Ohio Indians with gifts, Peters invigorated the growth of unity among the Ohio Country nations. They recognized that the Pennsylvanians believed them to be powerful enough to act on their own accord without seeking approval from the Iroquois.

Despite Peters' attempt to thwart their occupation of the upper Ohio River valley, the French seized the initiative by moving into the region with military force. This action precipitated the Great War for Empire between the two rival European powers of Great Britain and France. Initially, the Ohio Country Indians resolved to stand aside in the conflict. After British defeats at Fort Necessity in 1754 and General Braddock's debacle at the Monongahela the following year, however, the Indians cast off their stance of neutrality and joined with the French. Their motivations stemmed from the fact that they had become desperately dependent upon European trade goods that only the French could now supply. In addition, the decision to ally with the French once again demonstrated their autonomy from the Iroquois council, since the League of Five Nations had once again proclaimed neutrality in the conflict. By asserting their independence, the Ohio tribes hoped that Pennsylvania and other colonies would be forced to negotiate directly with them. The Indians believed this was the only way they could hope to preserve their lands.

The war also brought the Ohio Country people into closer contact and cooperation with the Great Lakes Indian nations. A handful of Senecas and Delawares fought alongside the Ottawas, Hurons, Chippewas, and Potawatomis at Braddock's defeat. They helped the Great Lakes warrior repel an attack against Fort Duquesne led by Maj. James Grant and his Highland forces in 1758; and Ohio Country Indians also participated with the French and their other native allies in the failed attempt to relieve Fort Niagara in 1759. Without question, the shared experience of war facilitated growing ties between all the Indian nations west of the Appalachian Mountains.[12]

Like the Ohio Country people, the Indians that inhabited the environment surrounding the Great Lakes arrived as refugees, driven westward by the ferocity of the Iroquois Beaver Wars. In the wake of this Native American diaspora, people who had enjoyed close relationships in earlier times became dispersed and scattered. This was likely the case with the Ottawas, Potawatomis, and Chippewas who, according to tribal legend, were once regarded as one people.[13] These Algonquian-speaking people were not the only victims of Iroquois conquest. Other Iroquoian nations such as the Hurons and Neutrals fled south and west from the wrath of the powerful New York Confederation. All of these Indians emerged from the struggle in the land that the

French referred to as the *pays d'en haut,* or "Upper Country." Here, the
refugees formed new associations within polyglot communities that eventually spread from the Detroit River in the east to the western shores of Lake
Michigan. Also, like the Delaware, Shawnee, and Mingo inhabitants of the Allegheny plateau, national identity among these Great Lakes people became
blurred and subordinated to new political and social organizations that centered on various villages and extended communities. Unlike the Ohio Country natives, however, these coaptations were fostered by the introduction of a
new power broker that entered the Upper Country—the French.[14]

The French had established important trade links with the Hurons and
Neutrals early in the colonial period. When these people were driven westward by the Iroquois, the French fur traders had no recourse but to follow. In
the Upper Country the traders encountered the Ottawas, who became important middlemen in the thriving barter system. The Ottawas, in turn, brought
other nations such as the Potawatomis, Miamis, Mascoutens, and Winnebagos
into closer contact with the French. As the Indian newcomers to the pays d'en
haut struggled to form new relationships with each other, the French found
themselves serving as mediators in intertribal and regional disputes between
the various refugee communities. They also assisted the Indians in fending off
assaults from the powerful Iroquois Confederation by encouraging alliances
among the Indian nations. Eventually the French organized their own attacks
against the Five Nations, which devastated the tribes and forced them to accept a negotiated peace in 1701. As a result of this extraordinary role, the Great
Lakes people came to regard the French as Onontio, an Iroquois word ren-
dered by the Algonquians to represent father.[15]

With peace restored between the Iroquois and the people of the Great
Lakes, the French became more entrenched in the region, building a string of
forts to protect their vital interests in the pays d'en haut and to bridge the gap
between colonial possessions in Canada and the lower Mississippi River valley. In 1691 they constructed Fort Saint Joseph, situated near the southern end
of Lake Michigan. A decade later the French soldier Antoine de la Mothe
Cadillac established another military post called Fort Pontchartrain, located
along what is now known as the Detroit River. In 1715 another post, Fort
Michilimackinac, helped secure the vital Straits of Mackinac between Lakes
Michigan and Huron. Two years later the French erected Fort La Baye along
the Green Bay in present-day Wisconsin. Like other such establishments, La
Baye was occupied by a small militia garrison, fur traders, and Jesuit missionaries intent on converting the Indians who were settled nearby. With the
Great Lakes in seemingly firm control, the French began to establish other
military posts to protect the access route from Quebec to New Orleans. In
1719 work commenced on Fort Ouiatenon along the banks of the Wabash, a

river that wound its way to the Lower Ohio and thence to the Mississippi.[16] With the construction of all these posts, France was able to secure its claims to the Great Lakes, protect the line of communication between Canada and Louisiana, and establish a viable trade relationship with the natives in the region. For the French, trade represented the cement that held together their alliances with the Indians. The relationship between the French and numerous Indian people who occupied the Upper Country flourished without interruption until Anglo fur traders began to penetrate the region in the 1740s.

Unable to compete with the British in the fur trade, the French recognized that their system of alliances with the tribes would be compromised. The Indians who occupied both the Ohio Country and the Great Lakes became seduced by the lower trade prices and superior quality of goods offered by enterprising Anglo traders such as Irishman George Croghan, who ventured as far west as the Cuyahoga River, just a little south of Lake Erie, in the autumn of 1744. Here he exchanged his assortment of trade goods for furs collected by Senecas living in the region. The French commandant at Fort Pontchartrain along the Detroit River, Céloron de Blainville, became greatly alarmed over the presence of English traders on the Cuyahoga. He urged the Ottawas and Miamis to drive Croghan and any other Englishmen in the region back across the mountains. The Indians, however, refused to give up their new trading partners.

Just like the French, who had used trade to foster important links with the Great Lakes people, the English adopted a strategy to win over the Indian nations. The Shawnees asked their Oneida vice-regent, Monacatootha, to intercede on their behalf in order to join in the "Chain of Friendship" with Pennsylvania. In addition, an important Piankashaw chief, Memeskia, moved his village away from French influence along the Maumee River to a new site at the headwaters of the Miami River called Pickawillany. From here he urged other tribes south of Lake Erie to join with the English.[17]

By the end of 1747 it appeared that French influence in the west was waning. George Croghan and other English traders were engaged in lively and profitable commerce with natives as far west as the gates of the French fort at Detroit, and there seemed little that their rivals could do to prevent such an exchange. The Provincial Council of Pennsylvania took note of the fact that "Great quantities of Goods were vended in the Towns of the Twightwees [Miamis] at their own pressing Instances. Several Nations Twightwees, Picts, Tawas [Ottawas], Piankkishaws, and Owendats [Wyandots or Hurons] entered into an Intimate Friendship with the scattered tribes of Shawanese Delawares and Six Nation Indians [Iroquois Confederacy] and pressing to enter into an Alliance they were on the recommendation of the Six Nations Shawness and Delawares admitted in the summer of 1748."[18]

The reference to a 1748 alliance stems from a treaty held at Lancaster in 1748 whereby the Miami Indians joined with the Delawares, Shawnees, and Iroquois in a "Great Chain of Friendship" with the English. This compact, also known as the Covenant Chain, was organized under the leadership of the Iroquois Confederation who presumed to represent the interests of all the tribes that belonged to the alliance. In essence, English diplomacy was working to bring about formal unification between Great Lakes peoples and the Ohio Country nations. This seemed reasonable at the time, since it was the expressed goal of the English colonies to draw the western tribes away from French influence. Also, it served to streamline the diplomatic process since the English could negotiate solely with the Iroquois, who claimed hegemony over the tribes who had entered into the Covenant Chain. In the end, however, the English would come to regret their efforts to draw the tribes together.

Since the French could not dissuade the Indians from trading with the English, they determined to drive Croghan and the other traders from the region by military force. On June 21, 1752, a war party of 250 Ottawas, Chippewas, and Potawatomis, led by a multiracial French colonial officer named Charles Langlade, swooped down on the Miami trading village of Pickawillany. The French launched this raid to counter the growing influence of the Piankashaw leader Memeskia, who had abandoned the French in favor of an alliance with the British. French colonial authorities recognized that if some action was not taken their link between Canada and Louisiana might be severed. A small group of British traders were captured during the attack and carried off to the French outpost at Detroit. Memeskia was also captured, and, while his followers looked on, the Ottawas killed him, boiled his body, and ate it. The new governor in Canada, the Marquis Duquesne, praised Charles Langlade for his zeal and bravery. In a letter to a French minister, Duquesne asserted that "I hope that this blow, taken with the total pillage that the English have sustained on this occasion, will deter them from coming to carry on trade in our lands."[19]

France's military initiative west of the Appalachians continued the following year when they began to construct a chain of forts in the upper Ohio River valley. This action precipitated the French and Indian War that drew the Great Lakes and Ohio Country warriors into nearly a decade of conflict on the frontier. Early French victories over the British prompted the Indian nations to ally themselves with Onontio. While the Great Lakes tribes fought to support their French fathers, the Ohio Country warriors struggled to break the yoke of Iroquois authority and gain recognition from the English of their independence and sovereignty over their homeland. When the English began to gain the upper hand in the contest, the Ottawas, Potawatomis, and Chippewas were forced to retreat with their French allies to their Great Lakes sanctuaries at Detroit, Michilimackinac, and Ouiatenon. The Ohio Country natives, however, fared much better when they managed to wring concessions from the English that guaranteed them sovereignty over the upper Ohio River valley.[20]

Although the tribes of the Great Lakes and those of the Ohio Country had participated in the war for different reasons, the conflict had further served to bring about closer and stronger ties between the Indians. As French military forces began their withdrawal from the region, the Indians were left alone to contend with the Redcoats. For their part, the Great Lakes peoples were hopeful that the British would build a relationship with them similar to that which they had enjoyed with the French. But the Ohio natives were insistent that the Anglos adhere to their promises and withdraw their troops back across the mountains. Both groups quickly realized that the British had no intention of meeting these goals. They also recognized that their newfound unity offered the only hope of preserving their lands and maintaining their sovereignty.

Shortly after the French abandoned their outpost at the forks of the Ohio River, the British began the construction of their own stronghold—Fort Pitt, an elaborate complex covering some seventeen acres at the triangular confluence. Whenever Indian delegations complained of the overt augmentation, British civil and military officials offered continuous reassurances that they did not intend to remain in the land beyond the mountains. At a conference in Philadelphia with Iroquois and Delaware chiefs in the spring of 1759, Pennsylvania governor William Denny instructed an interpreter to inform them that "the French have told the Indians that the English intend to cheat them of the Land on the Ohio, and settle it for themselves, but this he assures you is false." Again at Fort Pitt that summer, George Croghan, speaking as an Indian agent for the crown, assured a large assembly of Ohio and Great Lakes tribes that, once the French were finally driven away, the British "will depart your Country after securing our Trade with you and our Brethren to the Westward."[21] Despite these promises, the Delawares, Shawnees, and others looked on with suspicion as the fort continued to grow in size.

The British also tried to assure the Great Lakes tribes that they were not intent on conquest. Croghan, who accompanied Maj. Robert Rogers on an expedition to take over the French fort at Detroit, promised a group of Ottawas that they "should enjoy a Free Trade with their Brethren the English, and be protected in Peaceable Possession of their Hunting Country as long as they wou'd adhere to His Majesty's Interest."[22] When Rogers' command finally reached Fort Detroit and assumed formal control over the outpost, Croghan held another conference with the assembled Great Lakes tribes. Once again, the Indian agent promised the Indians free trade and security in their homeland. A Huron chief, speaking on behalf of the other tribes, responded to Croghan's address saying that "All the indians in this Country are Allies to each other and as one People." The Indians agreed to release those captives willing to be repatriated and promised to take hold of the "Ancient Chain of Friendship." The chief warned Croghan, however, that "if ever it be broak it will be on your side, and it is in your Power, as you are an Able People to prevent it for while this Friendship is preserved we shall be a Strong Body of People."[23] Once the British had control over the region, however, the Indians discovered that their promises were hollow.

With the French defeated in North America, British officials in London needed to shift troops and resources to other theaters of operation in the ongoing war. Consequently, the home government directed Maj. Gen. Jeffery Amherst as the commander of North America to retrench on expenses. The general began by eliminating the practice of providing presents to Indian leaders. He further ordered a sharp curtailment in the sale of arms and ammunition to the tribes. This had a devastating effect on the Indians since many of them had become dependent upon firearms for hunting purposes. Lastly, Amherst directed that trade with the tribes be confined to the established military posts. This created considerable hardship since native traders were forced to sometimes travel long distances to conduct business.[24]

Sir William Johnson, the Superintendent of Indian Affairs, vigorously objected to Maj. Gen. Amherst's new policies. In a letter to the secretary of state, Charles Wyndham, the Earl of Egremont, Johnson stated:

> Your Lordship will observe that the Indians are not only very uneasy, but Jealous of our growing power, which the Enemy [the French] (to engage them firmly in their interest) had always told them would prove their ruin, as we should by degrees Surround them on every side, & at length Extirpate them . . . from [the] treatment they receive from us, different from what they have been accustomed to by the French, who spared no labor, or Expence to gain their friendship and Esteem, which alone enabled them to support the War in these parts so long whilst we, as either not thinking of them of sufficient Consequence, or that we had not so much occasion for their assistance not only fell infinitely short of the Enemy in our presents &ca to the Indians, but have of late I am apprehensive been rather premature in our sudden retrenchment of some necessary Expences, to which they have been always accustomed, & which on due consideration I flatter myself your Lordship will be of opinion they should be gradually weaned from, rather than be totally deprived of, as that cannot fail increasing their Jealousy, and adding fuel to their discontent.[25]

Unlike Amherst, who had nothing but contempt for Indians, Johnson was under no delusions regarding their capacity to wage desultory and bloody war on the border. In his mind, the best way to prevent such conflict was by treating the Indians in a fair manner and keeping them supplied with necessities to hunt and carry on other economic activities. Johnson insisted that Amherst's plan would require the remote outposts to be garrisoned by "a verry [sic] large Regular Force at a Monstrous Expence to the Nation." He further maintained that "These Indians conscious of their own Strength and Situation, will, unless kept in the best temper by Us, be easily persuaded to commit depredations on the Traders whose goods are a temptation to the Savages, thus once embarked they will not stop till they have spread Havock over all our frontiers."[26] Therefore Sir William believed that the expense of providing the Indians with a few presents was still cheaper than fighting an Indian war.

The superintendent was not alone in endorsing a policy of extending benevolence to the Indian tribes. George Croghan also believed that a few presents of powder and lead were far cheaper than engaging in an Indian war. "The Indians are a very Jelous peple," Croghan proclaimed, "and they had great Expectations of being Ginerally Supplyed by us & from their poverty & Mercenery Disposition they cant Bear such a Dissapointment." In a letter to Sir William Johnson, Croghan sarcastically noted, "Undoubtedly ye Gineral [Amherst] has his own Rason for Nott allowing any presents or ammunition to be given them, & I wish itt may have its Desired Effect Butt I take this opertunity to acquaint you that I Dread the Event as I know Indians cant long persevere."[27]

Amherst's policies convinced the Indians living in the Ohio Country that the British intended to keep them poor and short on ammunition and to eventually "rub them out." As a result, it would be these people who would make the first overture for war with the Redcoats. In the summer of 1761 a pair of Indian emissaries representing the Indians of the Ohio Country arrived at Fort Detroit bearing war belts for the Great Lakes tribes. The two Senecas, named Kiasutha and Tahaiadoris, called for a council among the nations living near the outpost in order to plan a concerted strike against all the English forts. They believed that they were "ill Treated" as a result of General Amherst's new policies and the British attempts to take away their land. The Seneca diplomats informed the assembled Ottawas, Chippewas, Hurons, and Potawatomis that "the English treat us with much disrespect, & we have the greatest reason to believe by their behavior they intend to cut us off entirely." Incensed by Amherst's policies, the Senecas encouraged all the tribes "from Nova Scotia to the Illinois, to take up the Hatchet against the English." They informed their Great Lakes compatriots that the British "have possessed themselves of our Country, it is now in our power to dispossess them & recover it, if we will embrace the opportunity before they have time to assemble together, & fortify themselves there."[28]

Fortunately for the British, a friendly Indian informed Capt. Donald Campbell, the commandant of Fort Detroit, of the Seneca plot. In turn, Campbell called the local tribes into council and informed them that he was well aware of their designs against the English. He boldly admonished the two Seneca leaders for their behavior, saying, "I advise you with all my heart in the most friendly manner, to return home and ardently recommend it to your Chiefs and those of other Nations in Concert with you to quit their Bad Intentions and live in peace, for if they proceed in their Designs against the English it will terminate in their utter Ruin and Destruction." Tahaiadoris replied "that he would bury all bad thoughts [and] lay aside all thoughts of War and live in peace."[29] Captain Campbell was convinced of the Seneca leader's sincerity and the conference adjourned. In all likelihood, the Indians reasoned that since their plot had been uncovered there was no chance of achieving the element of surprise. The Senecas would bide their time and let the war belts continue circulating among the many western tribes.

Back at his headquarters in New York, General Amherst seemed unconcerned about the Senecas' attempt to foment rebellion against the British. Sometime later, in a letter to Sir William Johnson, Amherst disclosed that the intended uprising "never gave me a Moments Concern, as I know their incapacity of attempting anything serious, and that if they were rash enough to venture upon any Designs, I had it in my power not only to frustrate them, but to punish the Delinquents with Entire Destruction, which I am firmly resolved on whenever any of them give me cause."[30]

Other individuals, more intimately familiar with Indian affairs, did not take the Seneca Plot so lightly. Indian agent George Croghan spelled out the Indians' grievances in his diary:

> The Six Nations [Iroquois] look on themselves to be ill Treated by the English General [Amherst], and in particular the Sinicas . . . they say since the English has Conquered the french they insult the Sinicas, and won't let them travel thro' their own Country, they are forbid the Communication [along the Niagara portage]. Traders are not suffered to go amongst them, Powder and Lead is prohibited being sold to them, and the General is giving away their Country to be settled, which the King of England Promised to secure for their use, these steps they say appears to them as if the English had a mind to Cut them off the face of the Earth.[31]

Even before word of the Seneca Plot reached his fortified estate in the Mohawk Valley, Sir William Johnson sensed something was awry. In a letter to
General Amherst the superintendent stated that he was "verry apprehensive
that something not right is brewing, and that verry privately among them. I
do not only mean the Six Nations, I fear it is too generall. Whatever it be, I
shall endeavour to find it out if possible."[32] Sir William's plan to discern the
temper of the various tribes involved traveling to Detroit and holding a grand
council among them. By this time, Johnson had learned of the Seneca attempt to enlist the Great Lakes tribes in a war against the English. On his way
to Detroit he paused at Niagara to hold a council with Iroquois chiefs. The Indian Superintendent called the Seneca leaders together and demanded that
they provide an explanation for fomenting such a plot and sending war belts
to the Great Lakes tribes. Following Indian custom, the Seneca leader, Sonajoana, delivered his response the following day, by offering a belt of wampum to Sir William and saying, "what you declared to us yesterday has given
us much uneasiness especially, as we are not only innocent, but entirely ignorant of the whole charge against us. No such Message having been ever to our
knowledge sent by our nation." The chief went on to suggest that the war belts
may have come from their Seneca brethren living in the Ohio Country. Sonajoana's suspicions revealed that the natives living along the Allegheny and
Ohio rivers had, once again, asserted their independence from the Iroquois
Confederacy.

Since 1748, when Conrad Weiser first traveled to the multicultural village
of Logstown, the Indians living in the region had insisted that they spoke as
one people, that they had kindled their own fire in the land beyond the
mountains, and that they did not accept dictates from the Iroquois Confederation. During the late war, Seneca and Mingo warriors had ignored the neutrality of the Five Nations and fought alongside the French. Now in 1761, the
Ohio Country Senecas Kiasutha and Tahaiadoris took yet another step toward sovereignty from their cousins to the north by attempting to initiate a
war without consulting the Iroquois council.[33]

Sir William had always believed that by dealing directly with the New York
Iroquois he could supervise all the tribes regardless of their location. Surely,
no tribe or group of tribes would deny Iroquois leadership. In fact, that is ex-
actly what had happened. Johnson, however, could not accept this new para-
digm. He still believed that the war belts circulating among the Great Lakes
warriors could only travel with the knowledge and acquiescence of the New
York council. Consequently, he denounced Sonajoana and declared that his
"frivolous excuses that the Messengers lived Detached from you, have [no]
Weight with me, being thoroughly convinced that they, or any Tribes of your

Nation would not presume to undertake so dangerous an affair without your Concurrence & approbation." With this admonition, Sir William returned the wampum belt given him by the Senecas, a gesture that indicated that he "paid no regard to what they had said." To prove their innocence, several chiefs insisted on accompanying Sir William to Detroit and addressing the council he planned to hold with the western tribes.[34]

When Sir William arrived at the post along the Detroit River on September 3, 1761, he found George Croghan had already assembled representatives from the Ottawa, Huron, Potawatomi, Chippewa, Miami, Shawnee, and Delaware nations for a grand council. The conference served as the focal point for Sir William Johnson's new initiative in Indian diplomacy. He began by addressing the assembled chiefs with words of condolence for those warriors who had been slain in the war with France. He then asked them to hold fast to the ancient Covenant Chain that bound the English colonies with the native world. In essence, he invited the western tribes to join that chain of friendship with a status equal to that of the Iroquois Confederacy. As one experienced Indian trader later noted, Sir William had in effect "cast off ye Onandago Yoke (of ye Six Nations) from ye Delawares, Shawanas, Wyondots, Picks or Tweetwees, & others to ye Westward which makes those Nations a Separate Power Independent of the Six Nations."[35]

Johnson hoped that his initiative would create jealousy between the Iroquois and the other tribes, which would prevent them from considering an alliance against the British. As he later informed a British officer, "I did all in my power in private conferences to create a misunderstanding between the Six Nations and Western Indians, also between the latter and those of Ohio so as to render them jealous of each other."[36] Johnson then went on to assure the Great Lakes tribes that the English had no desire to possess their lands and promised an increase in the volume of trade and a reduction in the price of goods. The superintendent thus concluded the conference satisfied that he had "left the Western Indians Extremely well Disposed towards the English," and that "unless greatly Irritated thereto they will never break the Peace Established."[37]

Johnson's biggest miscalculation at Detroit was his underestimating the strong ties that already existed between the Great Lakes tribes and those of the Ohio Country. While Johnson worked to "create a misunderstanding between the Six Nations and the Western Indians," his efforts only served to strengthen the bond that already existed between the Ohio and Great Lakes people. In addition, this new autonomy gave the western nations enhanced power and prestige to act independently from the Iroquois.

To further exacerbate the deteriorating relations between the English and the tribes living west of the mountains, militant native leaders across the trans-Appalachian frontier began to embrace a new religious message that called for them to divest themselves of the ways of the whites. The principle proponent of this new religion was a Delaware mystic named Neolin who claimed to have communed with the Master of Life in a vision. The Master of Life admonished Neolin and all other natives saying:

> This land where ye dwell I have made for you and not for others. Whence comes it that ye permit the Whites upon your lands? Can ye not live without them? I know that those whom ye call the children of your Great Father [the French] supply your needs, but if ye were not evil, as ye are, ye could surely do without them. Ye could live as ye did before knowing them,—before those whom ye call your brothers [the English] had come upon your lands. Did ye not live by the bow and arrow? Ye had no need of gun or powder, or anything else, and nevertheless ye caught animals to live upon and to dress yourselves with their skins. But when I saw that ye were given up to evil, I led the wild animals to the depths of the forests so that ye had to depend upon your brothers to feed and shelter you. Ye have only to become good again and do what I wish, and I will send back the animals for your food.[38]

One of the more intriguing aspects of Neolin's vision came when the Master of Life enjoined him from attacking the French. According to the dream, the creator told Neolin, "I do not forbid you to permit among you the children of your Father [the French]; I love them. They know me and pray to me, and I supply their wants and all they give you. But as to those who come to trouble your lands,—drive them out, make war upon them. I do not love them at all; they know me not, and are my enemies, and the enemies of your brothers. Send them back to the lands which I have created for them and let them stay there."[39]

Neolin's preaching spread rapidly throughout the pays d'en haut and Ohio Country. The call for holy war against the British served as the final link between the Great Lakes tribes and the Ohio Country people. Over the years they had found commonality in culture, trade, politics, and warfare. Neolin's prophecy gave them common religious foundations. It is not surprising that Pontiac used Neolin's teachings to inspire the Ottawas, Chippewas, Potawatomis, and Hurons to attack the British garrison at Fort Detroit.

This overview of unification efforts among the Indian nations of the trans-Appalachian west demonstrates that Pontiac did not orchestrate the Pan-Indian Confederation that waged war against the British in 1763. The struggle for unification among the various tribes predates the Ottawa leader by more than one hundred years. This does not, however, detract from Pontiac's role as an inspirational leader during the conflict. Warriors under his influence did manage to seize and destroy four British outposts during the months of May and June 1763—Forts Sandusky, Miami, St. Joseph, and Ouiatenon. It is important to note that Ohio Country warriors had nothing to do with these battlefield victories. Instead, the Delawares, Shawnees, and Mingos worked independently to defeat the Redcoats in the upper Ohio River valley. Some Great Lakes Indians, however, did enter the Ohio Country to assist in the siege of Fort Pitt. During a parley outside the gates of the fort, a Delaware chief hoped to convince the garrison to surrender by informing the British commander, Capt. Simeon Ecuyer, that he was surrounded by "Six different Nations of Indians that are now ready to Attack you."[40] The warriors of the Great Lakes and Ohio Country also achieved a true Pan-Indian alliance during the siege and capture of Fort Presque Isle, along the southeastern shore of Lake Erie. In this attack, Ottawas, Chippewas, and Hurons from Detroit assisted Senecas and Delawares in compelling the surrender of the British garrison.[41]

Although these efforts seem to underscore the apparent strength of the confederation, in reality the coalition was extremely fragile. This was due, in part, to the diffuse nature of Indian leadership. In order to achieve ultimate victory in the conflict, the warriors needed to be directed by a centralized authority. This, however, was completely foreign to the decision making process that existed among most Indian people. The siege of Detroit had been going on for less than a month when a group of Potawatomi chiefs approached the fort to secretly discuss terms for peace with the post commandant, Maj. Henry Gladwin. The Indian leaders confessed that "they were led into the War by Pondiac," to which Gladwin "advised them to disperse & mind to their hunting & planting, for if they persisted it would end in their utter Ruin." This overture by the Potawatomis encouraged other Indians to approach the fort to discuss peace terms. The Hurons, who were under the influence of a Jesuit missionary, entered the post by a secret gate and pledged to Major Gladwin that they were "peacibly inclin'd." The major informed all of these emissaries that "the only thing they could do to convince him of their good intentions wou'd be to give up the rest of their Prisoners and go to their villages and tend to their Corn & hunt."[42]

Pontiac's leadership role at Detroit was further eroded on the last day of May when a party of more than two hundred Chippewas led by the great chief Wasson arrived from Saginaw Bay. The arrival of these Chippewas signaled a change in the leadership dynamic among the Indians. Wasson was an influential warrior-chief with a remarkable ability to unify the various tribes of the Great Lakes region. In addition, the Chippewas now outnumbered the Ottawas around Detroit and were more inclined to take direction from one of their own kinsmen than from Pontiac. With his stature diminished, Pontiac no longer exercised absolute authority over the siege of Detroit.[43]

The Ottawa leaders' greatest embarrassment came in mid-June when a delegation of Chippewas arrived from Michilimackinac. The Indians were led by Kinonchamek, son of the powerful chief Minavavana, whose warriors carried out the successful attack against the British fort at the straits. After locating his camp two and a half miles above Detroit, Kinonchamek received messengers from Pontiac's village. According to one account, the young Chippewa chief treated these diplomats "pretty coldly" and informed them that he would hold a council with Pontiac that afternoon. He then called together some of the local French inhabitants and inquired about the progress of the siege and Pontiac's actions. These French residents informed the Chippewa leader that Pontiac had forcefully requisitioned food and other provisions and threatened them if they were lax in complying. When Kinonchamek finally convened his council, all of the local Indian leaders were present. He opened the conference by boasting of the victory over the British at Michilimackinac, exclaiming, "We have learned at home, my brothers, that you are waging war very differently from us. Like you, we have undertaken to chase the English out of our territory and we have succeeded. And we did it without glutting ourselves with their blood after we had taken them, as you have done; we surprised them while playing a game of lacrosse." Then, addressing himself directly to Pontiac, Kinonchamek chastised the Ottawa leader by saying, "But as for thee, thou hast taken prisoners upon the lake and the river, and after having brought them to thy camp thou hast killed them, and drunk their blood, and eaten their flesh. Is the flesh of men good for food? One eats only the flesh of deer and other animals which the Master of Life has placed on the earth." Continuing his denouncement, Kinonchamek said, "Moreover, in making war upon the English thou hast made war upon the French by killing their stock and devouring their provisions, and if they refuse thee anything thou hast had thy followers pillage them."[44]

After the Chippewa chief finished his tirade against Pontiac, a leader from the nearly extinct Erie nation rose and spoke:

My brothers, we have also fallen upon the English because the Master of Life by one of our brother Delawares told us to do so, but he forbade us to attack our brothers, the French, and thou hast done so. . . . We see well what has obliged thee to do what thou hast done to our brothers, the French: it is because thou hast begun the war ill-advisedly and art now in a rage at not having been able to take the English in the Fort. . . . We desired to come to thy assistance but shall not do so.[45]

Three days later, Kinonchamek and the Chippewas from Michilimackinac broke up their encampment and returned to the straits.

Pontiac's rebuke by the young Chippewa chief and the Erie leader demonstrates that his leadership and authority were far from absolute. As the fortunes of war continued to turn from the Indians in the fall of 1763, the Indian Confederation besieging the fort collapsed and the various tribes dispersed to hunt, harvest their crops, and prepare for the coming winter. The same situation occurred among the Ohio Country warriors at Fort Pitt. When a relief column under the command of Col. Henry Bouquet approached the forks of the Ohio River, many of the allied tribes moved off to ambush the oncoming Redcoats. Not all of the Indians were in favor of continuing the war, however, and a group of Delawares under the leadership of a peace advocate named Tamaqua decided to abandon the siege and return to their village along the Muskingum River.[46] When the other warriors were defeated and driven off by Bouquet's relief force at the Battle of Bushy Run, the Ohio Country coalition retreated to winter hunting grounds. Low on ammunition and provisions, and lacking unanimity to continue the war, the once great confederation of western tribes collapsed the following year, bringing an end to Pontiac's Uprising.[47]

In the years that followed, the Indian nations of the Great Lakes and Ohio Country would again attempt confederation in an effort to preserve their homelands and way of life. While these efforts met with some initial success, they eventually failed to stem the tide of white encroachment. In addition, these attempts did not reach the same level of unification that had been achieved in the years immediately preceding and during Pontiac's Uprising. Francis Parkman, whose research and interpretations have been called into question by modern historians, once proclaimed that Pontiac's Rebellion represented "a fury unparalleled through all past and succeeding years."[48] In that regard, at least, Parkman was right.

NOTES

1. Parkman's place as a historian in the romantic tradition is discussed in Michael McConnell's introduction to the latest reprint of *The Conspiracy of Pontiac and the Indian War after the Conquest of Canada,* 2 vols. (Lincoln: Univ. of Nebraska Press, 1994), vii–xv.

2. Howard H. Peckham, "The Sources and Revisions of Parkman's *Pontiac,*" *Papers of the Bibliographic Society of America* 37 (1943): 298–99; and *Pontiac and the Indian Uprising* (Detroit, Mich.: Wayne State Univ. Press, 1994), 107–10, 187–88, 194–95.

3. For more recent interpretations see Francis Jennings, "A Vanishing Indian: Francis Parkman versus His Sources," *Pennsylvania Magazine of History and Biography* 87 (July

1963): 306–23; Richard White, *The Middle Ground: Indians, Empires, and Republics in the Great Lakes Region, 1650–1815* (New York: Cambridge Univ. Press, 1991); Michael N. Mc-Connell, *A Country Between: The Upper Ohio River Valley and Its People, 1724–1774* (Lincoln: Univ. of Nebraska Press, 1992); Gregory Evans Dowd, *A Spirited Resistance: The North American Indian Struggle for Unity, 1745–1815* (Baltimore, Md.: Johns Hopkins Univ. Press, 1992), and *War under Heaven: Pontiac, the Indian Nations and the British Empire* (Baltimore, Md.: Johns Hopkins Univ. Press, 2002).

4. "Conrad Weiser's Journal of a Tour to the Ohio, August 11–October 2, 1748," in Reuben Gold Thwaites, *Early Western Journals, 1748–1765* (Lewisburg, Pa.: Wennawoods Publishing, 1998), 31, 42.

5. For a thorough explanation of the origins and conduct of the Beaver Wars, readers should consult Daniel K. Richter and James H. Merrell, eds., *Beyond the Covenant Chain: The Iroquois and Their Neighbors in Indian North America, 1600–1800* (New York: Syracuse Univ. Press, 1987), 20–24; William N. Fenton, *The Great Law and the Longhouse: A Political History of the Iroquois Confederacy* (Norman: Univ. of Oklahoma Press, 1998), 229, 244–45; and José António Brandão, *"Your Fyre Shall Burn No More": Iroquois Policy toward New France and Its Native Allies to 1701* (Lincoln: Univ. of Nebraska Press, 1997). For information regarding the origins of the Mingos see Francis Jennings, *Empire of Fortune: Crowns, Colonies and Tribes in the Seven Years' War in America* (New York: Norton, 1988), 26.

6. The word Appalachian means "People on the Other Side" in the Choctaw tongue. See George P. Donehoo, *A History of the Indian Villages and Place Names in Pennsylvania* (Harrisburg, Pa.: Telegraph, 1928; rpr., Lewisburg, Pa.: Wennawoods, 1994), 6–7.

7. The Walking Purchase is discussed in Jennings, *Empire of Fortune*, 25–28.

8. Information on Shawnee migration can be found in McConnell, *A Country Between*, 14–15, 22; C. Hale Sipe, *The Indian Wars of Pennsylvania*, 2nd ed. (Harrisburg, Pa.: Telegraph, 1931; rpr., Lewisburg, Pa.: Wennawoods, 1995), 45–50, 749, 753; and Charles A. Hanna, *The Wilderness Trail, or The Ventures and Adventures of the Pennsylvania Traders on the Allegheny Path*, 2 vols. (New York: Putnam's, 1911), 1:119–60.

9. The forging of a collective identity among the Ohio Country people is a major theme in McConnell's study, *A Country Between*. For information concerning the anthropological term ethnogenesis, see Gary Clayton Anderson, *The Indian Southwest, 1580–1830: Ethnogenesis and Reinvention* (Norman: Univ. of Oklahoma Press, 1999), 3–6, 267–68.

10. The Ohio Country Indians' claim of autonomy from the League of Five Nations is fully discussed in McConnell, *A Country Between*, 69–72; and Jennings, *Empire of Fortune*, 28–30.

11. Samuel Hazard, ed., *Colonial Records of Pennsylvania, 1683–1790*, 16 vols. (Philadelphia, Pa.: T. Fenn, 1851–53), 5:146–47 [hereafter cited as *CRP*].

12. For details on these engagements see Paul E. Kopperman, *Braddock at the Monongahela* (Pittsburgh, Pa.: Univ. of Pittsburgh Press, 1977); Alfred Proctor James and Charles E. Stotz, *Drums in the Forest* (Pittsburgh: Historical Society of Western Pennsylvania, 1958); and Brian Leigh Dunnigan, *Siege—1759: The Campaign against Niagara* (Youngstown, N.Y.: Old Fort Niagara Association, 1996).

13. Some archaeologists suggest that the Potawatomis may have separated from their Chippewa and Ottawa kinsmen prior to the Iroquois Beaver Wars. These scholars

point out that early Potawatomi economic and settlement patterns are more closely associated with a prairie culture than with Ottawa and Chippewa traditions. Regardless, the cataclysmic results of the Beaver Wars further disrupted the political and social patterns of all of these people. See R. David Edmunds, *The Potawatomis: Keepers of the Fire* (Norman: Univ. of Oklahoma Press, 1978), 3–8.

14. Information on the effects of the Beaver Wars among Great Lakes people and their migrations into the *pays d'en haut* can be found in White, *The Middle Ground,* 1–20; and in Edmunds, *Potawatomis,* 4–6.

15. White, *The Middle Ground,* 36. For additional information concerning the French role see Edmunds, *Potawatomis,* 11–15; Helen Hornbeck Tanner, *Atlas of Great Lakes Indian History* (Norman: Univ. of Oklahoma Press, 1986), 31–35; and Fenton, *The Great Law and the Longhouse,* 253, 257–58, 267–68.

16. Information on the establishment and purpose of the French forts in the Great Lakes region can be found in Peckham, *Pontiac and the Indian Uprising,* 8–10; and Parkman, *The Conspiracy of Pontiac,* 1:55.

17. McConnell, *A Country Between,* 72–73; Jennings, *Empire of Fortune,* 29–31.

18. "Detail of Indian Affairs," *Pennsylvania Archives,* 9 ser., 138 vols. (Philadelphia: State Printer of Pennsylvania, 1852–56, 1875–1949), ser. 1, 2:233–34.

19. Hanna, *The Wilderness Trail,* 2:290.

20. The British counteroffensive of 1758 included a campaign against the French stronghold of Fort Duquesne, located at the confluence of the Allegheny and Monongahela rivers. To draw Indian support from the French during this campaign, John Forbes, brigadier general, promised the Delawares, Shawnees, and others that, once the French were defeated, the British would also withdraw across the mountains and leave the Ohio Country as an Indian sanctuary. For information on Forbes's campaign and his desire to draw the Ohio tribes away from the French see Alfred Proctor James, ed., *The Writings of General John Forbes Relating to His Service in North America* (Menasha, Wis.: Collegiate, 1938), 126–28.

21. *CRP,* 8:265–69, 387–92.

22. Nicholas B. Wainwright, ed., "George Croghan's Journal, 1759–1763," *Pennsylvania Magazine of History and Biography* 71 (Oct. 1947): 393–94 [hereafter cited as "Croghan's Journal"].

23. John Sullivan, ed., *The Papers of Sir William Johnson,* 14 vols. (Albany: Univ. of the State of New York, 1921–65), 10:198–206 [hereafter cited as *SWJP*].

24. For an overview of Amherst's policies see David Dixon, *Bushy Run Battlefield* (Mechanicsburg, Pa.: Stackpole, 2003), 13–15.

25. Johnson to Earl of Egremont, May 1762, *SWJP,* 10:461–62.

26. Ibid.

27. Croghan to Sir William Johnson, December 10, 1762, *SWJP,* 3:965.

28. Wainwright, ed., "Croghan's Journal," 409–10; Capt. Donald Campbell to Col. Henry Bouquet, June 16, 1761, Sylvester K. Stevens, Donald H. Kent, and Autumn L. Leonard, eds., *The Papers of Henry Bouquet,* 6 vols. (Harrisburg: Pennsylvania Museum and Historical Commission, 1951–94), 5:556 [hereafter cited as *PHB*]; "Copy of the Conference sent by Capt. Campble At a Council held at the Wiandot Town near Detroit 3d July 1761 by the Deputy's of the six Nations with the Ottawas, Wiandots, Chipeweighs, and Powtewatamis," *SWJP,* 3:450–53.

29. "Report of Indian Council Near Detroit," enclosed with Campbell to Bouquet, July 22, 1761, *PHB*, 5:646–50.

30. Jeffery Amherst to Sir William Johnson, August 9, 1761, *SWJP*, 3:514–16.

31. Wainwright, ed., "Croghan's Journal," 409–10.

32. Sir William Johnson to Jeffery Amherst, June 21, 1761, *SWJP*, 10:291.

33. "Niagara and Detroit Proceedings, July–September, 1761," *SWJP*, 3:460–63.

34. Ibid.

35. Sir William Johnson to Jeffery Amherst, November 5, 1761, *SWJP*, 3:559; John W. Jordan, ed., "Journal of James Kenny, 1761–1763," *Pennsylvania Magazine of History and Biography* 37 (1913): 24.

36. Sir William Johnson to Gen. Thomas Gage, January 12, 1764, *SWJP*, 4:296.

37. Sir William Johnson to Sir Jeffery Amherst, November 5, 1761, *SWJP*, 3:559. An evaluation of Sir William Johnson's diplomatic strategy while at Detroit can be found in Stephen F. Auth, *The Ten Years' War: Indian-White Relations in Pennsylvania, 1755–1765* (New York: Garland, 1989), 151–53.

38. For background information on nativist religious revivals during this time period see Dowd, *A Spirited Resistance*, 33–36; Anthony F. C. Wallace, "New Religions among the Delaware Indians," *Southwest Journal of Anthropology* 12 (1956): 1–21; Charles E. Hunter, "The Delaware Nativist Revival of the Mid-Eighteenth Century," *Ethnohistory* 18 (1971): 39–49; and Gregory Evans Dowd, "Thinking and Believing: Nativism and Unity in the Ages of Pontiac and Tecumseh," *American Indian Quarterly* 16 (1992): 309–36. This version of Neolin's vision comes from an anonymous journal of the siege of Detroit that has generally been credited to a French resident inside the fort named Robert Navarre. Presumably, Navarre attended an Indian council near Detroit where Pontiac related Neolin's teachings to the assembled chiefs and warriors. It is also quite possible that Navarre learned of the contents of Neolin's message from some other person who attended the council. See Milo Milton Quaife, ed., *The Siege of Detroit, 1763* (Chicago: R. R. Donnelley, 1958), 8–15.

39. Quaife, ed., *The Siege of Detroit*, 15–16.

40. "Discourse Between Delawares and Ecuyer, June 24, 1763," *PHB*, 6:261.

41. Dixon, *Bushy Run Battlefield*, 24.

42. Franklin B. Hough, ed., *Diary of the Siege of Detroit in the War with Pontiac* (Albany, N.Y.: J. Munsell, 1860), 22–28; Quaife, ed., *The Siege of Detroit*, 130–32, 135–38.

43. Quaife, ed., *The Siege of Detroit*, 121, 129. For biographical information on Wasson see *Dictionary of Canadian Biography*, 12 vols. (Toronto: Univ. of Toronto Press, 1966–91), 4:761–62.

44. Quaife, ed., *The Siege of Detroit*, 143–44; Peckham, *Pontiac and the Indian Uprising*, 186–87. For information concerning the fall of Fort Michilimackinac see David A. Armour, ed., *Attack at Michilimackinac: Alexander Henry's Travels and Adventures in Canada and the Indian Territories between the Years 1760 and 1764* (Mackinac Island, Mich.: Mackinac State Historical Parks, 1971).

45. Quaife, ed., *The Siege of Detroit*, 144–45.

46. Capt. Simeon Ecuyer to Henry Bouquet, August 5, 1763, *PHB*, 6:341–42.

47. For an overview of the engagement at Bushy Run and the end of Pontiac's Uprising see Dixon, *Bushy Run Battlefield*, 29–41.

48. Parkman, *Conspiracy of Pontiac*, 2:85.

4

"The Indians Our Real Friends"

The British Army and the Ohio Indians, 1758–1772

M ATTHEW C. W ARD

In November 1758 advance units of the British Army occupied the abandoned French post of Fort Duquesne at the forks of the Ohio, renaming the post Fort Pitt. Over the next fourteen years, until its final withdrawal from the region in 1772, the British Army played a major role in shaping relations between the Indians and settlers in the Northwest. During this period many army officers and troops came to echo the view of Gen. John Forbes, who described the Indians as "our real friends." Increasingly the army came to view the Indians of the Northwest as requiring protection from the bands of "lawless Banditti" who roamed the frontier and saw it as their role "to remove these Lawless settlers, and to obtain some satisfaction for the ill treatment the Indians daily complain of." Even Pontiac's Uprising, when Indian warriors destroyed most of the British forts in their midst and launched raids on the colonial frontier, did not in the long term change this view. Many, if not most, army officers and imperial administrators with hindsight viewed the war as the consequence of Gen. Jeffery Amherst's misguided Indian policy and the inevitable outcome of the outrages committed by frontier settlers.[1]

The army played a pivotal role across the Old Northwest in mediating Indian-white relations in this period. Civilian authority in many matters was subordinated to military authority, and the army played a major role in determining Indian as well as military policy. Commanding officers in the forts and posts dotted across the region controlled day-to-day relations with the Indians and in particular regulated the fur trade and the activities of settlers. The role of the army in the Northwest contrasts starkly to its role in the Southeast, on the frontier of Georgia and North and South Carolina. Here a few "Indian officers" were posted in Indian towns to direct Indian affairs. The number of military posts amongst the Southeastern Indians was much fewer, and most of these were quickly abandoned. Consequently, the army's role in shaping and directing Indian affairs was relatively minor.[2]

Historians have often perceived the relationship between the British Army and the Northwestern Indians as fraught with tension: at best the army served to slow the spread of settlers into the region; at worst it participated in genocide as Amherst's instructions to Henry Bouquet "to try to Inoculate the *Indians*, by means of Blankets, as well as to Try every other Method, that can Serve to Extirpate this Execrable Race" seem to surmise. British Army officers are rarely seen as attempting to comprehend the concerns of the alien world of the Northwestern Indians.[3]

Amherst's attitude was not widely echoed amongst officers or the rank and file in the British Army. At a superficial level many troops and commanders did view Indians with a degree of disdain. General Forbes, for instance, complained about their "natural fickle disposition which is not to be got the better off by words nor presents" and wrote that he "dare trust none of the Race of Indians, who are both perfidious and Expencive." However, officers' comments about Indians were often the result of specific frustrations and paled when compared to comments about their own troops and more specifically about colonists and frontiersmen. Forbes described the provincial soldiers as no more than "a gathering from the scum of the worst of people in every Country, who . . . are more infamous cowards, than any other race of mankind." One British officer described the civilian inhabitants of Pittsburgh as "the scum of nature."[4]

Most officers, and increasingly the rank and file, viewed the Indians of the Northwest with sympathy and consideration as they struggled to restrain the actions of frontier settlers. Indeed, following the capture of Fort Duquesne, General Forbes wrote from Fort Pitt to Governor Denny of Pennsylvania that "the Conquest of this Country is of the greatest Consequence to the adjacent Provinces by securing the Indians our real friends for their own advantage." Not only the British but also the Indian inhabitants should benefit from their arrival in the region. He did not see the conquest of the Ohio as opening up the region for settlement, as many colonists did, but rather as an opportunity for the British to extend their protection to the Northwestern Indians and to develop a flourishing trade that would benefit both sides. He begged Amherst to "not think trifflingly of the Indians or their friendship."[5]

Forbes's views were soon picked up by one of his principal officers, Col. Henry Bouquet. Bouquet repeatedly intervened to protect the Northwestern Indians from the activities of Virginia and Pennsylvania frontiersmen who swarmed onto their lands. In particular, he evicted squatters and sought repeatedly to regulate the Indian trade. In repeated conferences at Fort Pitt he sought to reassure the Indians of the security of their lands. When Amherst ordered a halt to all Indian supplies, Bouquet wrote a long missive questioning Amherst's actions, arguing that "at a moderate Expence," a "Fixed Sum" should be "Appropriated Yearly, to be Laid out, in Small Presents to the Warriors, and occasionally to Other Indians for Services Done; and in some Cloaths to be given to such as might be in real Want, through Age or Infirmities." Colonel Bradstreet echoed Bouquet's views, arguing that it was essential for the army to "gain their affections" and enforce "strict Justice, moderation, [and] fair Trade."[6]

General Thomas Gage also held similar views. Throughout his tenure as commander-in-chief he sought to protect the rights of the Indians, a view reflected when he wrote to Lord Hillsborough, "I am of opinion, independent of the Motives of common Justice and Humanity, that the Principles of Interest and Policy should induce us rather to protect than molest them." Such thoughts were even held by the rank and file. Gage wrote that he found "every where that the Soldiers agree perfectly well with the Indians" and added that they saw their role quite clearly as being "to protect them from Injurys."[7]

The view of the British Army of its Indian neighbors in the Northwest was shaped in part by Sir William Johnson, the Superintendent of Indian Affairs for the Northern Department. Johnson took a much more proactive role in shaping Indian policy than his southern counterparts William Atkin and John Stuart. Johnson had few ties with the fur traders who flocked into the region, most of whom he viewed with derision. Instead, he had developed close ties with many army officers. In part this was because Johnson himself held military rank and had served with some distinction during the Seven Years' War. At the siege of Fort Niagara in July 1759, following the death of General Prideaux, he had taken command of the British forces that seized the French post. Because Johnson had such close military ties, he understood military policy better than Atkin and Stuart and felt free to correspond with fellow officers. Yet his role as superintendent and his many years of close relationship with the New York Iroquois allowed him to influence military policy and imperial policy in a manner more understanding of the needs and fears of the Northwestern Indians.[8]

Johnson also relied heavily on his assistant George Croghan. If Johnson had friends and influence in the army and the ministry in Whitehall, Croghan had influence amongst the Indians. His many years as a trader in the Ohio Valley had gained him an intimate knowledge of the Ohio Indians. Samuel Lightfoot, agent of the Quaker "Friendly Association" at Fort Pitt, commented that he had "frequently heard the Indians ask for George Croghan, as a man for whom they have some regard." Although his relationship with Johnson was sometimes stormy, Croghan was able to provide Johnson with much insight into affairs in the Ohio Valley. Together they had a symbiotic relationship that linked Whitehall diplomats, British officers, and Indian headmen.[9]

The relationship of many officers with Whitehall was of crucial importance, because decisions taken in London, by the Board of Trade, the Privy Council, and the secretary of state for the Southern Department, also had a direct impact on the relationship between the British Army and the Ohio Indians. In the years immediately following the conquest of the Ohio Valley, the British government had to weigh several sometimes-conflicting concerns as they considered how to organize their new conquests: how the region was to be governed; how peace with the Indians was to be retained; how many troops should be stationed in the region.[10]

The army and the government did not necessarily agree on policy. Indeed, the army served in many ways to mollify government policy toward the Ohio Indians. For the British government the primary, if not the sole, aim of American policy during the late 1760s and early 1770s was to minimize expenses and maximize income. As the British struggled to meet payments on their massive war debt, western policy had to be subordinated to some degree to economic issues. Lord Hillsborough, for instance, instructed Sir William Johnson in 1770 that "the Service shall be conducted with all the Frugality & Economy that is possible, consistent with the public Safety." Any Indian war on the frontier would naturally involve considerable expense, and it was cheaper to assuage the Indians than to prepare for war. However, while British policy was driven by economy, it does not mean that even in Whitehall administrators did not develop a genuine interest in protecting what they saw as the rights of the Ohio Indians. Indeed, Lord Hillsborough was horrified with proposals that the crown should foster war between the Ohio Indians and the Creeks, Cherokees, and Catawbas, a proposal he saw as "irreconcilable with the Principles of humanity."[11]

As the British Army moved into the Northwest, the first task was to gain Indian consent to its presence. To win their acquiescence the army needed to provide assurances for the security of the Indians' lands and to reopen the fur trade to meet the Indians' needs. However, in both these areas the army faced problems. Having just reoccupied the forks of the Ohio, and with the French still threatening their presence from Detroit, the British continued to occupy all the French posts in the west and even began building new posts such as the fort at Sandusky that had previously been an unprotected trading post.[12]

While occupying the French posts and building new forts, the British Army attempted to convince Indian headmen that it had no long-term ambitions to seize their lands. In the summer of 1760 Brig. Gen. Robert Monckton sent a message to the Ohio headmen promising that he "did not send an Army here against the Indians but against the French, neither did He build Forts in the Indians Country with an Intent to take their Lands from them by Force, but to prevent the French from doing the same." However, Monckton's promises seemed rather empty as the French surrendered Canada and then settlers and hunters poured onto Indian lands in ever larger numbers. Angus McDonald wrote from Fort Burd, on Pennsylvania's frontier, "Here Comes Such Crowds of Hunters out of the Inhabitence as fills those woods at which the Indians seems very much disturbed and say the white people Kills all there [sic] Deer." Along the frontier skirmishes broke out between squatters and Indian warriors. Matters were made even worse because colonial governors, if only by their inaction, seemed to give the squatters and hunters a degree of official sanction. The army had failed very singularly to convince the Indians of the security of their lands.[13]

If the British could not provide the Indians with security for their lands, it might have been possible for a renewal of the fur trade to lessen some of the Indians' concerns. However, the army was not in a position to provide the Indians with any supplies, for the forces on the Ohio were initially desperately short of supplies. The commander at Fort Pitt, Hugh Mercer, begged for "a large quantity of Indian Goods." He added that "the Constant Sollicitations of all our friends obliges me again to repeat it, as a measure equally necessary to gain the Indian Interest, as a Body of Troops is to Secure the Country." Johnson warned Amherst that without a "plentiful & proper Supply of Goods, we shall . . . soon loose all those . . . favorable Dispositions." When trade goods did begin to arrive in the Ohio Valley they were often of poor quality, sold at high prices, and more often than not rum and whisky rather than cloth and metal goods.[14]

The army might have been able to compensate, at least in part, for the problems of the Indian trade by using the traditional diplomatic protocol of gift exchanges to win important allies in the region. However, at the same time that policy in the Ohio Valley required generosity in diplomacy, British imperial policy demanded a new frugality. During the previous years of warfare the British government had run up huge war debts, and now, with peace on the horizon and the French threat receding, the costs of running the empire had to be constrained. As a series of administrations sought to rein in the costs of empire, officers and officials feared that such parsimony would cause tension. Meanwhile, Indian headmen complained that they were "obliged to pay such exorbitant prices, that our hunting is not sufficient to purchase us more cloathing as is necessary to cover us, & our families, indeed, our hunting is not so great as usual—(altho there is more game) through the want of ammunition which we can by no means procure."[15]

The parsimony of Whitehall seriously handicapped the army's capability to conduct effective Indian diplomacy. This capability was further undermined by the lack of any clear government policy toward the west for most of the 1760s. As ministries came and went and as new crises in colonial policy unfolded, so the tide of western policy ebbed and flowed. In May 1763 Charles Wyndham, the Earl of Egremont and secretary of state to the Southern Department responsible for colonial affairs in North America, suggested to the Board of Trade that it adopt a clear policy "of conciliating the Minds of the Indians . . . by protecting their Persons & Property & securing to them all Possessions, Rights and Priviledges they have hitherto enjoyed, and are entitled to, [and] most cautiously guarding against any Invasion or Occupations of their Hunting Lands." After only a brief deliberation, the Board of Trade agreed and concluded that western lands should be specifically reserved "to the Indian Tribes for their hunting Grounds; where no Settlement by planting is intended." The Indians should remain "under the protection of such Military Force, to be kept up in the different Posts & Forts in the Indian Country as may be judged necessary, as well for the Protection of Trade and the good Treatment of the Indians, as the maintenance of Your Majesty's Sovereignty." In October the crown finally issued a formal proclamation forbidding settlements in the west. If the west was to be reserved for Indian hunting grounds and colonial settlements forbidden, who was to restrain frontier settlers? Experience during the Seven Years' War had convinced military and imperial officials alike that the colonies could not be relied upon to maintain posts in the west or in case of emergency to provide troops for the west. The only alternative was to use the British Army. In this manner the army's role in the west was defined.[16]

Post commanders were expected to regulate Indian affairs and to maintain the friendship of local Indians. Before 1763 they were often forced to do this with little assistance. At isolated western posts commanders struggled to find lead and powder for visiting Indian deputations. At Fort Pitt parties of headmen from villages across the Old Northwest would arrive expecting the niceties of diplomatic exchanges, only to be informed that there were no presents available. They often returned home empty-handed, surly, and sullen. At Detroit Donald Campbell was faced by a constant stream of Indians from numerous villages across the Ohio Valley and Great Lakes region demanding food and ammunition, and he fretted to Bouquet, "I am much put to it, how to behave in Indian Affairs." At Fort Niagara William Walters came up with an ingenious partial solution by setting his men to work catching fish for the local Indians to prevent them from starving.[17]

When Amherst forbade the traditional provision of presents and ammunition to visiting Indian deputations, it was the forts' commanders who were forced to face the brunt of Indian displeasure. Many officers begged to be allowed to provide at least a modicum of supplies. Walters informed Johnson that he had had "great numbers of poor Indians at this post this two winters past which I have Supported Chiefly with fish Which costs no Expence. . . . [T]hey Even Collected all the Guts and offel of the fish the Soldiers caught here [and] . . . in compassion I cannot help giving them a Little Support." He confessed to Johnson that he had "some times given them a pound or two of powder with a Little Ball in order to keep them Alive Which I have Don at a very Easy rate, or Else Some of them Must have Starv'd." Indeed, many of the Ohio Indians may have felt some pity for the post commanders and understood the dire straits into which they were placed, for at the start of Pontiac's Uprising many of the commanders in the western posts, although captured by the Indians who seized their posts, were quickly returned to Detroit or Fort Pitt and treated relatively kindly.[18]

During this period day-to-day relations between the army and the neighboring Indian villages were often surprisingly cordial. At many western posts the men played the local Indian men at baggataway, a version of lacrosse, while others engaged in games of a more intimate nature. Indeed, one reason why the smaller posts in the Northwest fell so quickly at the start of Pontiac's Uprising was because the Indians used these ties to surprise the posts. At Michilimackinac a band of Chippewas threw down their baggataway sticks and seized their guns to storm the post. At Fort Miamis the post's commander, Ensign Robert Holmes, received a message from his Indian mistress informing him that she was desperately ill. As he left the post he was ambushed and the Indians broke into the fort.[19]

In the aftermath of Pontiac's Uprising some of the smaller posts, such as Fort Miamis, were never reoccupied. However, from its larger posts such as Detroit and Fort Pitt, the army continued to exercise its influence. Indeed, after the war the role of the army in many areas increased. Pontiac's Uprising made it apparent that Amherst's policy of parsimony and control could not work, and Whitehall sought a new Indian policy. The Board of Trade's "Plan for the future management of Indian affairs," drawn up in July 1765, considered in detail how the west might be administered in the wake of Pontiac's Uprising. The report proposed the establishment of a sophisticated Indian department within the colonies, headed by the superintendent. Below the superintendent would be numerous agents at each western post, who in turn would supervise a range of other officers from commissaries to blacksmiths.[20]

Ultimately, only certain aspects of this plan were put into effect as Whitehall sought ways of financing the policy at a time when the colonies refused to pay the costs of imperial administration; the plan was simply too expensive to be implemented in full. While Whitehall sought to finalize policy, in the

Northwest officers continued to conduct their own Indian diplomacy. On occasion they were even given broad powers to conclude peace with nearby Indian villages. But this latitude of powers brought with it many problems. At several posts officers were accused of overstepping the bounds of their authority. At Michilimackinac Maj. Robert Rogers was accused of abusing his powers by concluding a peace treaty between the Chippewas and the Sioux, his opponents argued, merely to further the interests of a group of traders who had supposedly lined his pockets. Indeed, many of the Michilimackinac traders seem to have been more annoyed by Rogers' influence with the local Indians, which his position gave him, than by any abuse of his military power. At Fort Chartres Col. Edward Cole found his financial accounts rejected by the government, and he was eventually dismissed from his post for his profligate spending on Indian diplomacy. Both Rogers and Cole, as well as many smaller commanders, found that when faced with coordinating Indian diplomacy their best intentions could not always meet the requirements of imperial administrators: simultaneously to ensure peace with the neighboring Indians and to avoid all unusual expenditures; to manage and supervise Indian diplomacy but not to be seen as conducting affairs in their own interest.[21]

If conducting Indian diplomacy proved problematic for British commanders, regulating the fur trade was equally fraught with difficulties. Whitehall desperately hoped that the western trade could boost Britain's customs revenues and help to meet the costs of colonial administration. At the very least, British officials believed that duties on the western fur trade would be able to meet the costs of administering the newly acquired western territories. Thus the government sought to encourage the fur trade. The fur trade also served another purpose: to help maintain a cordial relationship with the Northwestern Indians at little direct cost to the crown. However, officials could not agree on whether the trade should be restricted to army posts or whether traders should be allowed to trade in the Indians' villages. Initially, government policy favored restricting all trade to army posts. Here officers could ensure that traders did not bring large quantities of rum to the Ohio Valley and could mediate complaints about substandard goods and fraudulent weights. Traders were required to produce licenses acquired from the colonial governors; those without licenses would be arrested and their goods seized. At Detroit and Fort Pitt, officers intervened to seize traders' goods when it was discovered they lacked licenses or were using fraudulent weights. However, officers and the posts' commissaries found it impossible to inspect more than a fraction of the traders who poured into the Northwest.[22]

The Indians' main complaints, however, were not concerning fraudulent trade but the wide extent of the liquor trade. Across the Northwest small-scale peddlers tempted Indians to buy their concoctions, often leaving the Indians with little money for the "respectable" traders who brought ammunition, cloth, metal goods, and other day-to-day necessities. Army officers made repeated attempts to stop the illegal transportation of liquor into the west and bemoaned "the vast Quantitys of Rum carried amongst the Indians." British troops were ordered to seize any liquor they found and to arrest the traders concerned. But intercepting the numerous traders who smuggled goods to the Northwest proved all but impossible, and Gage lamented to Hillsborough, "It's so easy for the Traders to smuggle it past the Posts, and the Temptation from the Gain upon that Article so great, that I apprehend a great deal will always be carried up. And an Indian Trader, generally a pretty Lawless Person, would not pay much Regard to Laws So many hundred Miles in the Desarts, where it is difficult to detect him, and will be much more so to convict him." In a final attempt to control the trade, Gage suggested to Johnson that "the Indians should interfere themselves to prevent Quantitys of Spirits being carried into their Villages and hunting Grounds." Johnson was horrified and pointed out that such a policy would allow the Indians to freely plunder the traders under the pretence of searching for liquor.[23]

Even if they could arrest traders, officers were frustrated in their attempts to bring them to trial. Officers could only directly intervene if traders violated regulations within the posts. Outside the posts, the jurisdiction of the army was much more questionable as in times of peace civilians could not be subjected to martial law. Even those traders arrested in army posts required trial in a civil court. As part of its plan for the management of Indian affairs, the Board of Trade had proposed that the Indian superintendents or their agents might act as justices of the peace in the Northwest to hear such cases. This would have allowed fraudsters and other criminals to be brought speedily to trial in the west rather than attempting to try them in eastern courts. For if they did not escape on the journey east, colonial juries proved extremely reluctant to convict anyone who had abused an Indian. In addition, in many colonial courts Indians were forbidden from testifying against white traders. If Indian testimony of fraudulent trade was unacceptable, convicting traders would prove an all but impossible task, and indeed the board's plans specifically called for Indians to be allowed to testify in all civil and criminal cases. The costs of implementing the plan, however, meant that Whitehall prevaricated and traders continued to smuggle liquor into the Northwest and to defraud their Indian customers. Johnson and Gage both repeatedly called for the plan's final and full implementation to allow them to rein in the worst frauds of the traders. But as colonial towns were engulfed in violent protests against the Stamp Act, the thoughts of imperial officials in London were far from the Northwest. Officers were left with little option but to stave the whisky kegs of such traders or to attempt to send them to trial in Quebec.[24]

Even these attempts were hampered as traders protested the feeble attempts of the army to restrict trade to the western posts. Traders from Montreal and Quebec in particular repeatedly petitioned the Board of Trade to deregulate the fur trade and to allow them to travel directly to Indian villages. Eventually Whitehall caved in to their demands, but rather than formally lifting regulations from the fur trade the government instead handed regulation of the Indian trade back to the colonies. Whitehall hoped that the colonies would do their utmost to establish regulations that suited the trading conditions in each area of North America and, more importantly, would have to meet the costs of enforcing any regulations. It was after all, the government believed, in their own interest to retain harmony with the Indians. However, Gage soon informed Hillsborough that "the Views and Opinions of the Provinces are so different upon it, they would not agree upon any plan whatever." The colonies would not regulate the Indian trade, and the army in the future would be unable to restrain all but the worst excesses.[25]

If regulating trade proved a difficult task for the army, protecting the Indians from the atrocities of white settlers and protecting their lands from illegal squatters proved even more difficult. While Pontiac's Uprising may not have dramatically transformed Whitehall's perception of the empire's Indian inhabitants, the war did seem to change the frontier inhabitants' perception of the Indians. Increasingly frontiersmen viewed their Indian neighbors with hatred and anger, and more and more of that hatred dissolved into violence.[26]

In December 1764 a party of fifty-seven frontiersmen from Paxton in Lancaster County, Pennsylvania, popularly celebrated as "The Paxton Boys," rode to nearby Conestoga where they slaughtered six Conestoga Indians. Not content with this action, a larger mob returned a few days later to butcher the survivors who had taken shelter in the county jail. Other frontiersmen actively copied their example. In May 1765 in Augusta County, Virginia, a party of frontiersmen attacked a party of peaceful Cherokees traveling through the Shenandoah Valley. When the local justice of the peace arrested the murderers, a mob, styling themselves "The Augusta Boys," broke into the jail to free their comrades and threatened to march on Williamsburg. Such scenes were repeated up and down the frontier. John Penn wrote to his brother Richard in May 1764 that "the people . . . are . . . Inveterate against the indians . . . [and] the neighbouring Governments are to the full as Inverterate against Indians as we are."[27]

It was not only Indians who had to brave such attacks, but also those who supported them, in particular army units. In March 1765 a wagon train and its military escort carrying gifts and trade goods bound for the Ohio was attacked by a mob of Cumberland County frontiersmen calling themselves the "Black Boys" at Sideling Hill near Fort Loudon in Pennsylvania. The mob looted all the trade goods and forced the escort to flee to the safety of the nearby fort. Benjamin Franklin bemoaned that "our Frontier People are yet greater Barbarians than the Indians, and continue to murder them in time of Peace." Over the following spring and summer Sir William Johnson claimed that at least twenty Indians were murdered on the colonial frontier from New York to Virginia, while Gov. Henry Moore of New York lamented the "violences and murders among the Indians" all along the frontier. The colonial backcountry had become a locus of violence and disorder against all Indians.[28]

By 1767 the Indians of the Northwest, in particular the Shawnees, Delawares, and Hurons, had become alarmed at the increasing cycle of violence. Rumors began to spread of meetings and councils to coordinate opposition. Belts purportedly circulated throughout the Northwest urging all nations to rise up once more against the British. Increasingly nervous officials began to believe in rumors of the creation of a "Pan-Indian confederacy" to resist white settlers. The commanders of the western posts desperately tried to assuage the Indians' concerns, but there was little that they could do to bring the perpetrators of these crimes to justice. Johnson lamented that even when the perpetrators of the murders were well known it was impossible to bring them to trial because the western territories were not covered by the jurisdiction of any courts since they were not included within the bounds of any colony, while under normal circumstances civilians could not be subjected to martial law. All the Indians could do was appeal to the local post commanders for protection.[29]

If murders did take place within colonial jurisdiction, on the frontier of New York, Virginia, or Pennsylvania, it was still all but impossible to convict any of the murderers. For as Gage confided to Shelburne, "it is a Fact that all the People of the Frontiers from Pennsylvania to Virginia inclusive, openly avow, that they will never find a Man guilty of Murther, for killing an Indian. These People must of Course be impannelled upon every Jury, the Law directing the Tryal to be held, where the Fact is committed." Indeed, one murderer openly declared that "he thought it a meritorious act to kill Heathen, wherever they were found," and Johnson believed "this seems to be the opinion of all the common people." Army officers were outraged and Gage concluded that "unless extraordinary Means are used, as well to apprehend and Secure these Lawless People, as to bring them afterwards to condign Punishment, by Removing the Tryals to the Capitals of the Provinces, where the Jurys would be composed of Men more civilized than those of the Frontiers, no Satisfaction can ever be obtained for any Outrages committed upon the Indians."[30]

One of the most notorious murders occurred on the Pennsylvania frontier in February 1768 when Frederick Stump, a German settler, slaughtered six Indians. Stump then attempted to cover his crime by hiding the bodies beneath the frozen river and butchering four possible witnesses, an Indian woman and her three children. The wheels of colonial justice moved slowly, especially for the murderer of an Indian. Johnson fretted to Gage, "I much fear that the Lawless Gentry on the frontiers will render it worse by Screening the Murderer." Eventually Stump was apprehended, but "some of the riotous frontier inhabitants assembled[,] forced the doors & carried him to some place of obscurity." Stump would not face a colonial court. Then, as if to add further insult to injury, colonial authorities moved to stop several Iroquois warriors who were hunting in the region from returning home, "least the News should be too soon propagated." Increasingly the Northwestern Indians saw the military posts as the only locations where they could get protection from frontiersmen questing for their blood. Army officers attempted where possible to arrest criminals and try them either in Canada or by martial law, a policy that foresaw the passage of the Quebec Act in 1774 when most of the Northwest came under the jurisdiction of Quebec and criminals could finally be tried in civil courts.[31]

The principal cause of the rising tide of violence between frontiersmen and Indians were conflicts over Indian lands. White frontiersmen who crossed the Appalachians destroyed the game upon which the Indians depended for their living. In 1762 Henry Bouquet issued orders for post commanders to arrest all hunters they discovered trespassing on Indian lands. It was not, however, frontiersmen hunting on their lands that most angered the Ohio Indians, but the establishment of permanent settlements. As early as 1761 the British Army moved to remove settlers moving onto Indian lands, and the following year Bouquet issued a formal proclamation forbidding settlement west of the Appalachian Mountains under the guise of the need for military security.[32]

In particular, around Redstone Creek and on the Greenbrier River, Virginia settlers established thriving communities on Indian lands. The activities of these settlers received little hindrance from colonial government. Indeed, Virginia's Governor Fauquier in 1767 rather lamely claimed that he "was in the dark as to the Sentiments of the Ministry by having never receivd His Majesty's Royal Proclamation of 7 October 1763." Fauquier's claim left Shelburne aghast, as the governor himself had specifically asked for clarification of the proclamation. Provincial governments found themselves under further pressure from members of the colonial elite, many of whom had bought shares in land speculation companies such as the Ohio Company, Mississippi

Company, or Illinois Company. These companies explored the west and pressured colonial and imperial authorities to issue land grants or even establish new colonies in the Northwest. With popular support for western settlement so widespread, the provincial governors refused to remove settlers from the west. Indeed, even had they wished to do so they had no means with which to act, for the colonies lacked any military force with which to compel the squatters to leave.[33]

With the provincial governments offering little resistance to the expansion of colonial settlements, the army found itself as the last bulwark in defense of Indian lands. The army itself thus took action to remove illegal squatters. In the spring of 1767 Gage ordered the commander at Fort Pitt to warn the settlers at Redstone Creek and on the Cheat River to remove from Indian land. The threats had only limited impact. Some settlers removed but most did not, and even those who removed later returned or were replaced by new squatters. Consequently, in the summer of 1767 a detachment of one hundred men, accompanied by several Indian headmen, marched to Redstone Creek to remove the settlers forcibly. The officers informed the settlers that they would not be able to protect them in case of any Indian assault, while the headmen warned them that it was only with great difficulty that they had so far been able to restrain their men from attacking the settlement. The combination of threats and warnings had some success. Most of the Redstone Creek settlers departed and the troops burned their cabins. However, their departure was only temporary, and within a few months more settlers were pouring west and even establishing settlements on the Ohio River.[34]

The activities of the British Army served in several areas to buttress imperial authority against the encroachments of white settlers. Through their restraining the expansion of white settlement and controlling the liquor trade, army officers gained some trust and respect from Indian headmen. So far did Indian headmen believe that British officers would protect them that following the murder of Pontiac by a Peoria Indian in the summer of 1769, over five hundred Peorias fled to Fort Chartres seeking the army's protection. The army, however, was incapable of fully undertaking the task required of it. The wishes of the imperial administrators in Whitehall to protect the Ohio and Great Lakes Indians from the abuses of white settlers and traders could only have been fulfilled if the Board of Trade's plan for the management of Indian affairs, drafted in 1765, had been put into full effect. Only then could the complex array of commissaries and interpreters, with numerous officers and posts maintained in the Ohio Valley and Great Lakes region, have hoped to have restrained the worst excesses of traders and squatters.[35]

By the late 1760s Whitehall could not contemplate such a vast expense on the western territories, and the government attempted to retrench all expenses. As a result of the Seven Years' War the government's debt had risen to £137 million and the fund required merely to service the debt consumed £5 million of the government's total £8 million budget. It was little wonder then that the administration sought all possible means to both reduce costs and raise revenue. For several years officers had been repeatedly warned to re- duce their expenditures in the west yet still they remained alarmingly high. Gage counseled Shelburne that expenditures "have of late years been every [sic] expensive. The making up of old Quarrells, to conciliate the Affection of Strange Indians, who had great Suspicions of our Intentions, and Jealousy of Power; would Naturaly occasion them to be so: And tho' I hope many Ex- pences before incurred, May now be retrenched, yet I fear those Departments will be always a heavy Charge." In six months Col. Edward Cole, command- ing at Fort Chartres, ran up accounts of over £7,000 for conducting Indian di- plomacy at the post. The following year, in negotiating the Treaty of Fort Stanwix, Sir William Johnson spent over £13,000. There was no sign of those expenses being retrenched.[36]

Finally, in January 1768 the Earl of Hillsborough took control of the newly created American office with responsibility for the North American colonies. Hillsborough believed that the main threat to the British Empire lay not in the interior of North America but in the challenge to British authority in the east. He argued that the proper role for the army was thus maintaining law and order in the seaport towns, not garrisoning the Northwest. The troops would be withdrawn and expenses reduced.[37]

As early as 1766 the army had abandoned several of the smaller posts that secured communication with the Northwest, such as Fort Ligonier in Pennsylvania. In 1768 the army withdrew from several other small posts. Fort Chartres was maintained in case of a war with Spain, and Fort Pitt was main- tained to secure the communication with the Illinois Country. As the threat of war with Spain receded, in the fall of 1772 Fort Chartres and Fort Pitt were both abandoned. By the end of 1772 the army's presence in the Northwest had been reduced to the forts on the Great Lakes at Michilimackinac, Niagara, and Detroit, and a small post at Vincennes on the Wabash. The units withdrawn were posted initially to seaboard cities, where their maintenance was much cheaper and where they could also be used if necessary to restrain the increas- ingly boisterous colonists. Without troops to restrain the colonists' excesses in the west, the British resorted to legislation. In 1774 parliament passed the Quebec Act. The act extended the boundary of Quebec southward, placing the Ohio Valley under Quebec's jurisdiction and extending the ban on settle- ment in the region. The future of the Ohio Valley would now be determined in Canada, where Indian interests might receive a more favorable reception than they would in Williamsburg or Philadelphia. Smugglers, fraudsters, and squatters could now be tried effectively in Canada. However, the outbreak of the Revolutionary War ensured that the Quebec Act would never fully be enforced, and indeed, the act served principally to heighten colonial suspicion and hostility toward Britain.[38]

The army's evacuation of the west was received with mixed feelings by many frontiersmen. Some settlers feared the loss of protection but others saw an opportunity for further expansion of their settlements. With the realization that British authority in the west had collapsed, both Virginia and Pennsylvania scrambled for control of the upper Ohio Valley. Virginia seized the abandoned fortifications at Fort Pitt, renaming them Fort Dunmore in honor of their governor. Meanwhile Pennsylvania countered by extending its civil jurisdiction in the west, creating Westmoreland County and sending agents, surveyors, and even militia into the region. As both colonies squabbled for control civil authority in the region all but disappeared.[39]

The lack of civil authority was matched by a breakdown in relations between settlers and Indians. The liquor trade expanded rapidly as the army's watch over traders disappeared. Rum and whiskey soon became the principal objects of trade in the upper Ohio Valley. The traders' reliance on alcohol increased as the political crisis between the colonies and Great Britain intensified and trade boycotts led to a general shortage of British goods. Not only did trade abuses increase but also did the extent of illegal settlement. Squatters poured into the region, driving Indians from their lands and destroying their hunting grounds. By 1774 perhaps fifty thousand settlers had crossed the Appalachians to settle in the Ohio Valley. Indian headmen sought to turn back this tide of settlement and to maintain the Ohio River as a boundary between white and Indian lands. Indian warriors seeking to protect their lands soon clashed with surveyors and squatters. Following the withdrawal of the army, it was no surprise that violence escalated rapidly. In May 1774 a party of Virginians killed ten Ohio Indians who retaliated by attacking the Pennsylvania frontier. These attacks provided an excuse for the Virginians to launch their own raids into the Ohio Country, culminating in September 1774, when the governor of Virginia, John Murray, the Earl of Dunmore, led a provincial army into the west to chastise the Ohio Indians for their attacks. In a brief but bloody campaign Dunmore "plundered, burnt and murdered without mercy" before withdrawing back across the Ohio River.[40]

Rather than creating peace, however, "Dunmore's War" proved merely a foretaste of future events. The outbreak of the Revolutionary War once more plunged the region into chaos, and for the next half-century the Indians in the Northwest engaged in a desperate and bloody struggle to protect their homelands from American expansion. The British Army now more than ever took on the mantle of the Indians' benefactors, providing them with both military and material support. However, as in the late 1760s and early 1770s, the concerns of Whitehall lay with the British Empire and not with the Indians, as the British sought to contain the new American republic. If necessary, Indian interests would be sacrificed for those of the empire. At the treaty negotiations in Paris in 1783, and in Ghent in 1814, the British pressed to create a protected homeland for the Ohio Indians. But in both cases when it became apparent that diplomats faced intense and insurmountable American opposition, such demands were quietly dropped and the British effectively abandoned their former Indian allies.[41]

The breakdown of order in the Northwest following the withdrawal of the British Army reveals clearly the central importance of the army's presence. From 1758 to 1772 the British Army thus served in many ways to support the Ohio Indians and to restrain the worst excesses of frontiersmen, and commanders came to view the Ohio and Great Lakes Indians in many ways as their friends. Ironically, though, the army's presence also played a vital role in undermining Indian cultural integrity in the west. The army itself had constructed a network of roads and stations to move supplies and troops into the region. These roads could just as easily be used to move settlers and goods. Indeed, Virginia and Pennsylvania squabbled bitterly over the route that Forbes's army was to take to the Ohio in 1758, knowing that the route would serve as a future highway west. As well as protecting the Indians the army forts served as a focus for white settlers who flooded west. Around all the western posts small garrison towns sprang up. The men stationed at the forts required supplies and services. Settlers and sutlers flocked to meet these demands. The towns that sprang up around these posts were a strange mixture of Indian traders, merchants, whores, and army auxiliaries. As early as April 1761 there were 160 houses huddled around Fort Pitt, and the settlement grew rapidly. As Indian headmen traveled to the fort they questioned whether the British "designed to Build another Philadelphia on their Lands."[42]

The presence of these forts also encouraged frontiersmen to establish their own settlements further afield. While army officers might have seen their role as being to evict squatters and illegal settlers whenever they could, these same settlers knew that if another Indian war should break out in the west they could seek protection within the walls of the army's forts. Without the prospect of such protection, many may have thought twice before venturing so far west. The posts also provided markets at which these western settlers could sell their crops, skins, and meats. Indeed, many commanders, struggling to curtail the spiraling expenses of garrisoning the west, welcomed these cheaper goods. Without the market offered by the army, initial settlement may have proceeded at a much slower pace.[43]

The army's presence also served to undermine Indian life in other invidious ways. The western garrisons spread disease. Troops fresh from Europe or the West Indies brought with them smallpox, influenza, typhus, and measles, which swept through the Indian villages of the Northwest. Army officers also served to transform the nature of the Indian economy. Officers hired Indians as hunters and guides. Indian battoemen paddled army supply vessels across the Great Lakes and down the Ohio River. Indian men who served alongside the army returned to their villages with European goods and with a degree of acculturation. By the late 1760s Anglo-American travelers to the region were commenting on the Indians' cattle and pigs and even on their skill in producing butter and cheese.[44]

Between 1758 and 1772 the British Army played a crucial role in directing the relationship between settlers and Indians in the Old Northwest. The army served as an arm of imperial government and sought to restrain the worst excesses of frontier settlers and traders. Officers and men built up sometimes-close relationships with the Indian villagers who lived around their posts. Many if not most of the officers who served in the west quickly came to see the Ohio Indians, in Forbes's words, as "our real friends." However, the army's role was undermined by the instability and frugality of government in Whitehall and by the government's preoccupation with the heightening dispute with the American colonies. Whitehall would not fund the policy requested by military and Indian agents alike and ultimately the decision was taken, in the name of economy, to withdraw the army from the west. The impact of the withdrawal of the British Army reveals clearly the significance of its presence. For no sooner had it withdrawn from the Northwest than the region descended into an orgy of conflict, speculation, and bloodshed.[45]

NOTES

1. John Forbes to Governor Denny, November 26, 1758, Colonial Office Records, Class 5 Papers, Records Office of Great Britain, Kew, England, 5/54:37 [hereafter cited as PRO/CO]; Gage to Governors Penn and Fauquier, December 7, 1767, ibid., 5/86:15–16; Earl of Halifax to Gage, January 14, 1764, Thomas Gage Papers, William L. Clements Library, Ann Arbor, Michigan, English Series, vol. 1.

2. Shelburne to Johnson, December 11, 1766, Clarence Walworth Alvord and Clarence Edwin Carter, eds., *The New Régime, 1765–1767*, vol. 11, *Collections of the Illinois State Historical Library: British Series* (Springfield: Illinois State Historical Library, 1916), 449–451 [hereafter cited as *CISHL*]; Gage to Hillsborough, November 10, 1770, Clarence Edwin Carter, ed., *The Correspondence of General Thomas Gage with the Secretaries of State, 1763–1775*, 2 vols. (New Haven, Conn.: Yale Univ. Press, 1931) 1:276; J. Russell Snapp, *John Stuart and the Struggle for Empire on the Southern Frontier* (Baton Rouge: Univ. of

Louisiana Press, 1996); David H. Corkran, *The Cherokee Frontier: Conflict and Survival, 1740–1762* (Norman: Univ. of Oklahoma Press, 1962); Tom Hatley, *Dividing Paths: Cherokees and South Carolinians through the Revolutionary Era* (New York: Oxford Univ. Press, 1995).

3. [Enclosure] Amherst: Memorandum, Sylvester K. Stevens, Donald H. Kent, and Autumn L. Leonard, eds., *The Papers of Henry Bouquet*, 6 vols. (Harrisburg: Pennsylvania Museum and Historical Commission, 1951–94), 6:315 [hereafter cited as *PHB*]. For a discussion of this episode see Elizabeth A. Fenn, "Biological Warfare in Eighteenth-Century North America: Beyond Jeffery Amherst," *Journal of American History* 86 (1999–2000): 1552–80. For a discussion of Anglo-Indian relations in the Northwest see Michael N. McConnell, *A Country Between: The Upper Ohio Valley and Its Peoples, 1724–1774* (Lincoln: Univ. of Nebraska Press, 1992); Richard White, *The Middle Ground: Indians, Empires, and Republics in the Great Lakes Region, 1650–1815* (New York: Cambridge Univ. Press, 1991); Eric Hinderaker, *Elusive Empires: Constructing Colonialism in the Ohio Valley, 1673–1800* (New York: Cambridge Univ. Press, 1997); James H. Merrell, *Into the American Woods: Negotiators on the Pennsylvania Frontier* (New York: Norton, 1999). For a general discussion of the role of the British Army in America see Daniel J. Beattie, "The Adaptation of the British Army to Wilderness Warfare," in Maarten Ultee, ed., *Adapting to Conditions: War and Society in the Eighteenth Century* (University: Univ. of Alabama Press, 1986), 56–83; Peter Way, "The Cutting Edge of Culture: British Soldiers Encounter Native Americans in the French and Indian War," in Martin Daunton and Rick Halpern, eds., *Empire and Others: British Encounters with Indigenous Peoples, 1600–1850* (Philadelphia: Univ. of Pennsylvania Press, 1999), 123–48.

4. John Forbes to William Pitt, June 17 and September 6, 1758, Alfred Proctor James, ed., *The Writings of General John Forbes Relating to His Service in North America* (Menasha, Wis.: Collegiate, 1938), 117, 205; John Forbes to General Abercromby, September 4, 1758, War Office Papers, 34/44:174, Records Office of Great Britain, Kew, England; Capt. Simeon Ecuyer to Bouquet, April 25, 1763, *PHB*, 6:176–79.

5. Forbes to Denny, November 26, 1758, PRO/CO 5/54:37; Forbes to Amherst, February 7, 1759, War Office Papers, 34/44:204.

6. "Queries from Bouquet with J. Amherst's Answers," January 10–11, 1763, *PHB*, 6:147–48; Colo. Bradstreet's Thoughts upon the Indian Trade, etc., December 4, 1764, PRO/CO 5/65, 3:135–41.

7. Gage to Shelburne, June 13, 1767, Gage to Hillsborough, November 10, 1770, Carter, ed., *Correspondence of Gage*, 1:143, 278.

8. Johnson to Amherst, July 15, 1759, John Sullivan, ed., *The Papers of Sir William Johnson*, 14 vols. (Albany: Univ. of the State of New York, 1921–65), 3:108–10 [hereafter cited as *SWJP*]; James Thomas Flexner, *Mohawk Baronet: Sir William Johnson of New York* (New York: Harper, 1959); Milton W. Hamilton, *Sir William Johnson: Colonial American, 1715–1763* (Port Washington, N.Y.: Kennikat, 1976).

9. Samuel Lightfoot to Israel Pemberton, June 18, 1759, Friendly Association Records, Collection 1250, Haverford College, Quaker Collection, Haverford College, Haverford, Pennsylvania, 3:179; Nicholas B. Wainwright, *George Croghan: Wilderness Diplomat* (Chapel Hill: Univ. of North Carolina Press, 1959); Albert Tangeman Volwiler, *George Croghan and the Westward Movement, 1741–1782* (Cleveland, Ohio: Arthur H. Clark, 1926).

10. Egremont to the Board of Trade, May 5, 1763, PRO/CO 5/65, 1:43–51; Clarence Walworth Alvord, *The Mississippi Valley in British Politics: A Study of the Trade, Land Speculation, and Experiments in Imperialism Culminating in the American Revolution,* 2 vols. (Cleveland, Ohio: Arthur H. Clark, 1917); Jack M. Sosin, *Whitehall and the Wilderness: The Middle West in British Colonial Policy, 1760–1775* (Lincoln: Univ. of Nebraska Press, 1961).

11. Earl of Hillsborough to Sir William Johnson, April 14, 1770, PRO/CO 5/71, 1: 81–82.

12. Bouquet: Orders for Meyer, August 12, 1761, *PHB,* 5:691.

13. McDonald to Bouquet, October 25, 1761, *PHB,* 5:840; Richard Peters to Conrad Weiser, February 21, 1760, Conrad Weiser Correspondence, Historical Society of Pennsylvania, Special Collections Research Library, Philadelphia, Pennsylvania, 2:169: Fauquier to Board of Trade, March 13, 1760, May 7, 1760, PRO/CO 5/1,329:105–10, 145–47; "A Narrative of what hath passed between the King's Generals, Governors etc. and the Indians in relation to Lands," [June 1761], PRO/CO 5/1,330:173–178.

14. Mercer to Forbes, January 8, 1759, *PHB,* 3:26; Johnson to Amherst, February 22, 1759, War Office Papers, 34/39:77–80; Samuel Lightfoot to Israel Pemberton, July 7, 1759, Friendly Association Records, 3:199.

15. Journal of Indian Affairs, March 8–15, 1761, *SWJP,* 10:238.

16. Royal Proclamation, October 7, 1763, Egremont to Board of Trade, May 5, 1763, Board of Trade, Report on Acquisitions in America, June 8, 1763, PRO/CO 5/65, 2:31–41, 46–47, 67; Matthew C. Ward, *Breaking the Backcountry: The Seven Years' War in Pennsylvania and Virginia, 1754–1765* (Pittsburgh, Pa.: Univ. of Pittsburgh Press, 2003).

17. Donald Campbell to Bouquet, May 21, 1761, Edward Ward to Bouquet, June 15, 1762, *PHB,* 5:490–92, 6:95–97; Instructions to Officers at Western Posts, September 16, 1761, William Walters to Johnson, April 5, 1762, *SWJP,* 3:527–28, 10:426–28.

18. William Walters to Johnson, April 5, 1762, *SWJP,* 10:426–28; Amherst to Gage, August 5, 1763, Jeffery Amherst Papers, William L. Clements Library, Ann Arbor, Michigan, vol. 6.

19. Daniel Claus to Johnson, August 6, 1763, Court of Inquiry, July 6, 1763, *SWJP,* 10:731–32, 777–78; Howard H. Peckham, *Pontiac and the Indian Uprising* (Detroit, Mich.: Wayne State Univ. Press, 1947), 160–63.

20. Plan for the Future Management of Indian Affairs [July 1765], PRO/CO 5/65, 3:123–35.

21. Col. Edward Cole to Croghan, December 19, 1767, Johnson to Gage, August 24, 1768, Gage to Shelburne, March 12, 1769, Theodore C. Pease, ed., *Trade and Politics, 1767–1769,* vol. 16, *Collections of the Illinois State Historical Library: British Series* (Springfield: Illinois State Historical Library, 1921), 147–48, 207–12, 383–86; Johnson to Shelburne, October 26, 1767, PRO/CO 5/69:7–8, Memorial of Maj. Robert Rogers, [Nov. 1769], ibid., 5/70:311.

22. Board of Trade Report on Acquisitions in America, June 8, 1763, PRO/CO 5/65, 1:59–78; Johnson to Henry Seymour Conway, June 28, 1765, ibid., 5/66:148–50; Johnson to the Lords of Trade, January 15, 1767, Johnson to Earl of Shelburne, December 16, 1766, ibid., 5/67:266–69, 281–84; Review of the Progressive State of the Trade, Politics and Proceedings of the Indians in the Northern District, November 16, 1767, ibid., 5/68:176–212; Gage to Hillsborough, November 10, 1770, Carter, ed., *Correspondence of Gage,* 1:274–81.

23. Gage to Hillsborough, February 5, 1772, Carter, ed., *Correspondence of Gage*, 1:316–17; Peter C. Mancall, *Deadly Medicine: Indians and Alcohol in Early America* (Ithaca, N.Y.: Cornell Univ. Press, 1995).

24. Plan for the Future Management of Indian Affairs [July 1765], PRO/CO 5/65, 3:125–26; Johnson to Henry Seymour Conway, June 28, 1766, ibid., 5/66:148–50; Gage to Hillsborough, September 8, 1770, Carter, ed., *Correspondence of Gage*, 1:267–70.

25. Gage to Hillsborough, February 5, 1772, Carter, ed., *Correspondence of Gage*, 1:316–17; John Campbell to William Howard, November 9, 1766, PRO/CO 5/85:193–95.

26. Richard Slotkin, *Regeneration through Violence: The Mythology of the American Frontier, 1600–1860* (Middletown, Conn.: Wesleyan Univ. Press, 1973).

27. John Penn to Richard Penn, [May 1764], Penn Manuscripts, Official Correspondence, Historical Society of Pennsylvania, Special Collections Research Library, Philadelphia, Pennsylvania, 9:238; Andrew Lewis to Governor Fauquier, May 9, June 3, 1765, PRO/CO 5/1,331:285–87, 299–301; *CRP*, 9:89–90, 100, 104–5; Thomas Slaughter, *The Whiskey Rebellion: Frontier Epilogue to the American Revolution* (New York: Oxford Univ. Press, 1986), 28–29; James Kirby Martin, "The Return of the Paxton Boys and the Historical State of the Pennsylvania Frontier," *Pennsylvania History* 38 (1971): 117–33.

28. Franklin to Johnson, September 12, 1766, *CISHL*, 11:376–77; Nathaniel McCulloch to George Croghan, March 12, 1765, John Penn to Sir William Johnson, March 21, 1765, *SWJP* 11:635–36, 643–45; Moore to Shelburne, November 11, 1766, E. B. O'Callaghan, ed., *Documents Relative to the Colonial History of the State of New York, Procured in Holland, England, and France*, 15 vols. (Albany, N.Y.: Weed, Parsons, 1857), 11:877 [hereafter cited as *NYCD*]; Johnson to the Board of Trade, August 20, 1766, PRO/CO 5/67:60.

29. Croghan to Gage, January 16, 1767, *CISHL*, 11:487–94; Johnson to the Board of Trade, August 20, 1766, PRO/CO 5/67:60–61.

30. Johnson to the Board of Trade, August 20, 1766, PRO/CO 5/67:60; Gage to Shelburne, October 10, 1767, Carter, ed., *Correspondence of Gage*, 1:151–54.

31. Johnson to Gage, February 18, 1768, Gage to Hillsborough, October 7, 1769, Pease, ed., *Trade and Politics*, 16:171–72, 628–31; Johnson to the Lords of Trade, March 14, 1768, *NYCD*, 8:53–54; Gage to Shelburne, January 30, 1768, Carter, ed., *Correspondence of Gage*, 1:163–64; Merrell, *Into the American Woods*, 304–5; Fauquier to Bouquet, January 17, 1762, *PHB*, 6:39.

32. Robert Monckton to Bouquet, April 5, 1761, Fauquier to Bouquet, January 17, 1762, Bouquet to Maj. James Livingston, February 6, 1762, *PHB*, 5:391–93, 6:39, 43.

33. Shelburne to Stuart, September 17, 1767, May 2, 1768, PRO/CO 5/69:133, 157; Fauquier to Board of Trade, February 13, 1764, ibid., 5/1,330:219–24; Articles of Agreement of the Illinois Company, March 29, 1766, Minutes of the Mississippi Company, May 22, 1767, Johnson to Gage, July 11, 1767, *CISHL*, 11:203–4, 570–72, 582–83; Gage to Shelburne, April 7, 1767, Carter, ed., *Correspondence of Gage*, 1:133–35.

34. Gage to Shelburne, April 29, 1767, August 24, 1767, Carter, ed., *Correspondence of Gage*, 1:137–39, 145–49.

35. Gage to Hillsborough, August 12, 1769, Pease, ed., *Trade and Politics*, 16:576–79.

36. Gage to Shelburne, April 4, 1767, *CISHL*, 11:552–55; Col. Edward Cole to Croghan, October 25, 1767, 16:98–100, ibid., 16:98–100; Sir William Johnson's Account of Expences (Fort Stanwix Treaty), November 1768, PRO/CO 5/87:7; Sosin, *Whitehall and the Wilderness*, 82.

37. Hillsborough to Colonial Governors, July 4, 1768, PRO/CO 5/65:391; Sosin, *Whitehall and the Wilderness*, 166.

38. Gage to Hillsborough, March 4, 1772, October 7, 1772, Hillsborough to Gage, January 22, 1771, Carter, ed., *Correspondence of Gage*, 1:317–20, 334–36, 2:125–26; Hillsborough to Johnson, July 1, 1772, PRO/CO 5/73:154–55; Sosin, *Whitehall and the Wilderness*.

39. McConnell, *A Country Between*, 268–79; R. Douglas Hurt, *The Ohio Frontier: Crucible of the Old Northwest, 1720–1830* (Bloomington: Indiana Univ. Press, 1996), 55–60.

40. Lt. Gov. Henry Hamilton to Gen. Guy Carleton, November 30, 1775, Reuben Gold Thwaites and Louise Phelps Kellog, eds., *The Revolution on the Upper Ohio, 1775–1777* (Port Washington, N.Y.: Kennikat, 1970), 129; Helen Hornbeck Tanner, ed., *Atlas of Great Lakes Indian History* (Norman: Univ. of Oklahoma Press, 1986), 59–61; White, *The Middle Ground*, 342–43, 359–62; Hurt, *The Ohio Frontier*, 55–58; McConnell, *A Country Between*, 275.

41. David Curtis Skaggs and Larry L. Nelson, eds., *Sixty Years' War for the Great Lakes, 1754–1814* (East Lansing: Michigan State Univ. Press, 2001); J. Leitch Wright, *Britain and the American Frontier, 1783–1815* (Athens: Univ. of Georgia Press, 1975); Donald Hickey, *The War of 1812: A Forgotten Conflict* (Urbana: Univ. of Illinois Press, 1990), 238.

42. Forbes to Amherst, January 26, 1759, War Office Papers, 34:198–99; Edward Shippen to Thomas Penn, November 20, 1759, Penn Manuscripts: Official Correspondence, 9:126–28; Bouquet to Stanwix, April 26, 1760, List of House and Inhabitants at Fort Pitt, April 14, 1761, *PHB*, 4:541–43, 5:407–11.

43. Gage to Shelburne, April 7, 1767, Carter, ed., *Correspondence of Gage*, 1:133–35; Gage to Conway, March 28, 1766, *CISHL*, 11:197–202; John Armstrong to Joseph Shippen, August 8, 1769, PRO/CO, 5/87:161–62.

44. Bouquet to Robert Monckton, January 14, 1761, Receipt for Venison at Venango, January 26, 1761, *PHB*, 5:244–46, 269; George Morgan's Journal, September 30–November 1, 1767, Pease, ed., *Trader and Politics*, 16:67–71; Matthew C. Ward, "The Microbes of War: The British Army and Epidemic Disease among the Ohio Indians," in Skaggs and Nelson, eds., *Sixty Years' War for the Great Lakes*, 63–98; Stephen Aron, "'Rights in the Woods' on the Trans-Appalachian Frontier," in *Contact Points: American Frontiers from the Mohawk Valley to the Mississippi, 1750–1830*, ed. Andrew R. L. Cayton and Fredericka J. Teute (Chapel Hill: Univ. of North Carolina Press, 1998), 190.

45. Forbes to Denny, November 26, 1758, PRO/CO 5/54:37.

5

Two Paths to Peace

Competing Visions of Native Space in the Old Northwest

LISA BROOKS

In 1791 the United States government held a meeting with representatives of the Iroquois Confederacy at Newtown Point to gage Iroquois sentiment regarding the prospects for peace between the new American nation and the Western Indians living in the Ohio River valley. At this meeting Oneida speaker Young Peter proclaimed:

> What shall we do, now you have told us the mind of the United States? We have told you that since the peace, we have sent to the Western Nations so many belts of peace as would make a very large heap. Now whatever more shall we do in the matter? Four paths for peace are already made: Brant went in the first path; The Big Gun tried to go in the second; The Stockbridge Indians go in the third; and in the fourth go the Western Army, carrying peace in their hands.[1]

The "peace" to which Young Peter referred was the 1783 treaty between the United States and Great Britain that ended the Revolutionary War. To the astonishment of Britain's Indian allies, they had been left out of the treaty entirely, and the Iroquois Confederacy were charged with transmitting a message to Western Algonquians to lay down the hatchet, without being able to offer any guarantee for their land rights. Rumors spread quickly through the Ohio tributaries that backcountry settlers had resumed their ferocious drive to acquire land in the valley and that the United States claimed to own, by conquest, the full span of the continent to the Mississippi River. The Treaty of Paris left Britain's allies in a precarious position in the changing political space of the continent, with both Indians and settlers embroiled in a whirlwind of frontier violence. Many on both fronts desired a solution that would lead to peace, although settlers and Indians had very different ideas about what that solution should entail.[2]

Young Peter spoke of two paths to peace led by the United States—that of the "Big Gun," Col. Thomas Proctor, and that of the American Army. While Proctor was presenting peace proposals to the Iroquois Confederacy in 1791 at the newly reconfigured confederacy fire at Buffalo Creek in western New York, the army was moving into the Ohio Valley, and the Iroquois received a message from the American commander, Gen. Arthur St. Clair, to join in the military action. Young Peter implied, with more than a hint of irony, that Proctor's mission had failed because the Americans were entangled in contradictory intentions. Seneca leader Red Jacket added, "Your discourse is intermixed with friendship and trouble. When we speak to you, we speak of friendship unmixed. . . . In ancient times, when we made peace, we cleared the path and made it open both ways."[3]

Although wary of American efforts, the Iroquois expressed hope for the peacemaking missions of Mohawk leader Joseph Brant and Stockbridge Mahican leader Hendrick Aupaumut, and they seemed confident that the two paths could be pursued simultaneously. Young Peter told the Americans that "Our minds are still strong for peace. Just before you came from home, we sent off Brant to continue the peace with the Western Indians," and "our nephews . . . are going on the same business with Brant. We hope they also will succeed, and that those nations may be brought to take hold of the chain of friendship with the U.S."[4]

Meanwhile, at the British Fort Niagara just north of Buffalo Creek, Aupaumut and Brant encountered each other for the first time on the path that led to the Western Indian Country. Aupaumut related, "I had the opportunity to talk with Brant but he never say a word to me of his business, and when he saw that these Indians were so friendly & free, he privately calls them together and tell them not to talk or walk with these Yankees." Aupaumut offered to "go with" Brant, but at every turn, according to Aupaumut, Brant "stopped" him from traveling further. He waited for months for the path to clear but finally "set out homewards" and returned to "find my family alive—but my business lay desolate." Brant, Aupaumut related, "advise[d] me never to do anything for the United States, for they are strong & must do everything themselves."[5]

The origin of the confrontation between Joseph Brant and Aupaumut can be found in their shared history and common experience. Although the Mahicans and Mohawks had fought bitterly during the tumultuous Beaver Wars, they shared a longstanding mutual alliance with the British. In service to their English "friends," Aupaumut's grandfather and Brant's clan chief,

Hendrick, had led joint scouting expeditions in the Connecticut River valley during Greylock's (or Dummer's) War. Hendrick's position in his native Mohawk community led him to play an instrumental role in maintaining the Iroquois Confederacy's tradition of diplomacy with the British, while ties through his Mahican father enabled him to strengthen the precarious alliance between these two indigenous nations. Aupaumut, in fact, may have been named for the renowned Mohawk leader. "King" Hendrick was in residence at the elder Aupaumut's village of Stockbridge for a number of years just prior to the younger Aupaumut's birth, which took place only one year after Hendrick was killed in the battle of Lake George. Joseph Brant was present at that battle, as one of Hendrick's youngest recruits.[6]

A generation later Aupaumut and Brant chose opposite sides in the Revolutionary War, but their experience of its aftermath was strikingly similar. John Sullivan's 1779 campaign, the infamous American assault on Iroquoia, devastated Brant's village of Canajoharie, and he subsequently led a movement to relocate his community to Grand River, near Fort Niagara, where Mohawk families had gathered during the war. Aupaumut's participation on the side of the United States did not prevent settlers from taking over his village at Stockbridge in western Massachusetts, and his entire community had recently removed to Oneida.[7] Brant and Aupaumut's actions were thus embedded in a complicated cycle of warfare and alliance between their two nations, a history of friendship between their two "grandfathers," and a shared experience of violent loss and reconstruction. The two paths they took to the Ohio Valley emerged from a geographic, social, and historical space inhabited by both. However, their distinctive visions of peace arose from competing visions of native space, rooted in each man's particular cultural and geographic location.[8]

Brant developed his sweeping vision of the "Common Pot," a native conception of land held in common by all tribes, while camped near the mouth of the Detroit River, where, from fall through mid-winter of 1786, an enormous number of Indians—including "the Five Nations [Iroquois], the Hurons, Delawares, Shawanese, Ottawas, Chippewas, Powtewattimies, Twichtwees, Cherokees, and the Wabash confederates"—gathered in council, "deliberating," in the words of Brant, "the best method we could to form a lasting reconciliation with the thirteen United States." From within these councils an extraordinary document emerged: a communal narrative and proclamation of union, agreed upon by all nations present and written by Brant. The "Speech of the United Indian Nations to the Congress of the United States of America" challenged American claims to ownership of the continent and made it clear that the newly formed nation would have to negotiate directly with the older nations that continued to maintain the space as their own.

While these confederated nations were willing to share space with their American brothers, they were unwilling to share in a European system that constructed them as unequal inhabitants of a colonial environment.[9]

The United Indian Nations opened by expressing disappointment in their exclusion from the treaty between "the King of Great Britain and you," while welcoming the opportunity to negotiate a plan of accommodation on their own terms. They had worked hard to promote a friendship with the Americans "during this time of tranquility" and, in Brant's words,

> We thought we were entering upon a reconciliation and friendship with a set of people born on the same continent as ourselves, certain that the quarrel between us was not of our own making. In the course of our councils, we imagined we hit upon an expedient that would promote a lasting peace between us . . . the first step towards which should, in our opinion, be, that all treaties carried on with the United States, on our parts, should be with the general voice of the whole confederacy, and carried on in the most open manner, without any restraint on either side; and especially as landed matters are often the subject of our councils with you, a matter of great importance and of general concern to us, in this case we hold it indispensably necessary that any cession of our lands should be made in the most public manner, and by the united voice of the confederacy; holding all partial treaties as void and of no effect.

The speech evoked an image of the continent as shared space, suggesting that Americans and Indians both had an investment in the land that birthed them and a responsibility to its future inhabitants. Yet it simultaneously maintained native sovereignty over the Ohio Valley. Insisting that their rights and privileges had been "transmitted to us by our ancestors," the United Indian Nations asserted that the claim of indigenousness was stronger than that of conquest. They held the responsibility for determining the best course of action for the future of their lands.[10]

The cornerstone of the confederation's plan of accommodation was their insistence that the United States deal with the whole, especially in matters of land, a vision firmly grounded in the tradition of "the Dish with One Spoon." Brant later explained this concept to Alexander McKee, a British agent and trader with strong relational and political ties to the Shawnees:

> We have been told that such a part of the country belongs to the Six Nations [Iroquois]. But I am of the opinion that the country belongs to the confederated Indians in common. If we say that such a part of the country belongs to one nation and such a part to another the Union cannot sub-

sist.... Upwards of one hundred years ago a moon of wampum was placed
in this country with four roads leading to the center for the convenience of
the Indians from different quarters to come and settle or hunt here. A dish
with one spoon was likewise put here with the moon of wampum. This
shows that my sentiments respecting the lands are not new.[11]

But the American leadership had a particular and different vision for
the Ohio Valley. If Indians were to remain at all, they would be contained on
small, limited plots, while the bulk of the land would be divided into lots and
sold to settlers to fill the nearly empty national treasury. The United Indian
Nations, however, sought to bolster a much older vision of the valley. The
land itself was held in common, consisting of a network of shifting riverside
villages within a larger shared hunting territory of grasslands and forests, all
fed and connected by the Ohio River and its tributaries, enabling an efficient
and diplomatic utilization of resources. The Dish with One Spoon was a geo-
graphic-social configuration and a political concept that solidified in councils
following the Revolution. The political vision depended on developing and
maintaining unity and unanimity between the many nations that had a stake
in the valley. As Brant told the Western Indians during one of those early
councils, "let there be peace or war, it shall never disunite us, for our interests
are alike, nor should anything ever be done but by the voice of the whole as
we are but one with you."[12]

The United Indian Nations put the blame for continuing violence firmly
on the United States and their attempts to divide the Dish and its inhabitants.
Their speech continued:

> Brothers: We think it is owing to you that the tranquility which, since the
> peace between us, has not lasted.... You kindled your council fires where
> you thought proper, without consulting us, at which you held separate
> treaties, and have entirely neglected our plan of having a general confer-
> ence with the different nations of the confederacy. Had this happened, we
> have reason to believe every thing would now have been settled between us
> in a most friendly manner.[13]

In particular, they referred to the Americans' orchestration of a series of
faulty, forced treaties with individual nations that were often represented by
spurious leaders. The course began at Fort Stanwix, where American emissaries coerced some of the Iroquois leadership into signing a treaty when only
a preliminary council was planned. The commissioners infuriated the Iroquois by taking several men hostage to ensure compliance. When the Americans sent an invitation to the Shawnees to join them at a similar "council"
at "the Mouth of Great Miami," Shawnee leaders chastised the Americans,

saying, "You ought to know this is not the way to make good on lasting peace, to take our Chiefs prisoners, and come with Soldiers at your backs." Calling on the principles of the Dish with One Spoon, they insisted, "We are Unanimous [that] . . . nothing is to be done by us but by general consent, we Act and speak like one Man."[14]

Dismissing the false treaties entirely, the United Indian Nations reiterated their call for an open council between American representatives and the whole confederation. "Notwithstanding the mischief that has happened," they insisted, "we are still sincere in our wishes to have peace and tranquility established between us, earnestly hoping to find the same inclination in you." Renewing their request for a treaty "in the manner we proposed" they suggested, "let us pursue reasonable steps; let us meet half ways, for our mutual convenience; we shall then bring in oblivion the misfortunes that have happened and meet each other on a footing of friendship."

The United Indian Nations proposed a middle ground where they might meet the Americans as equals in political and geographic space, to clear their minds of past violence and to construct a path to mutually agreeable peace. Yet the speech concluded by revealing another facet of the Dish with One Spoon. If the United States rejected their earnest proposals for peace, the Indians would "most assuredly, with our united force, be obliged to defend those rights and privileges which have been transmitted to us by our ancestors." The United Indian Nations' speech forced the American Congress into diplomatic action but also alerted them to the power of the confederation. They instructed Arthur St. Clair, the governor of the Northwest Territory, to answer the call for a treaty but to simultaneously "ascertain who are the head men and warriors of the several tribes, and who have the greatest influence among them; these men you will attach to the US, by every means in your power." Above all, they insisted, "Every exertion must be made to defeat all confederations and combinations among the tribes."[15]

Joseph Brant would not have been surprised by this declaration. He understood most fully the power of divisiveness: the Beaver Wars that had torn apart the tightly knit indigenous networks of the Northeast, the Revolution that had divided the once powerful Iroquois Confederacy, and the current U.S. policy that sought to divide, isolate, and contain Indian communities to enable the colonization of the continent. For more than a decade the Mohawk leader urged "unanimity" above all and worked to maintain the United Indian Nations as "one body" and "one mind" dedicated to sustaining the native space of the Dish with One Spoon.[16]

Writing from his home of New Stockbridge in 1792, after completing a long journey from the Ohio Valley, Aupaumut told American commissioner Timothy Pickering:

When I come to reflect on the path of my ancestors, the friendship and connections they have had with these western tribes, and my own feelings towards them, I conclude that I could acquaint them my best knowledge with regard of the dispositions, desires, and might of the United States, without partiality—and without groundless opinion I could be more useful in that particular embassage than those who have been opposing my undertaking.[17]

Aupaumut claimed a position within indigenous networks that made him uniquely qualified to mediate a peace between the Indians of the Ohio Valley and the United States. He emphasized ancient connections to his Western Algonquian relations and downplayed Brant's opposition by suggesting that the Mahicans' old Mohawk enemies were not to be trusted. He began his first report by relating that when he arrived at Niagara and "found the different nations of the westward," "they rejoiced to see us—and we immediately [began] to speak together as our fathers & forefathers use to do." At every stop along his journey, Aupaumut described the relationship the Mahicans had with each village and the welcome they received on arrival. Aupaumut's vision rested on renewing an old Algonquian network and reasserting a place for Mahicans within it. When his Western relations told him about the confederation "of all who has one [color]" and asked "whether my nation would accept the plan of Union," he responded, "It is a happy thing that we should maintain a Union. But to us it is not a new thing; . . . we must always remind each other how our ancestors did agree on this Subject, that we may never forego that."[18]

At the same time Aupaumut wished to claim a place for his nation in post-Revolution political space, reminding his American brother in the east of Mahican service in the war and the ancient friendship between them. Aupaumut told Pickering, "I, my nation, have always been the friends of the Americans; even from the first day they entered into the covenant of friendship. . . . My blood has been spilt with yours: and to this day my bones lie in the fields with yours." Like Brant, Aupaumut incorporated Americans into his network of relations, yet he called to mind a more intensely corporeal image of shared space—a mixing of bodies through the bloodshed of war and a mingling of bones that would eventually transform into earth.

While the Mahicans had acted as a good brother in defending their American neighbors against the domineering British, the Americans had not fully participated in the relationship of reciprocity:

I lost many lives in your defence: I stood by you in all your troubles. . . . But I had no territory to fight for, nor had I to fight for liberty, for liberty

I always possessed. But friendship, pure friendship, induced me and my nation to join you. But sometimes I feel sorrow, and shame, that some of my great brothers have forgotten me—that all my services and sufferings have been forgotten, and that I—my nation—remain neglected. What are the reasons I cannot say. Perhaps I am too small to be regarded. My friendship however is strong: my friendship I do not forget.[19]

Like the United Indian Nations, Aupaumut insisted that the Mahicans stood on equal ground with Americans, conveying that they cherished their ancient liberty as much as Yankees valued their newfound freedom. He acknowledged that warfare had weakened his nation, but he carefully employed the Algonquian rhetoric of reciprocity between equals rather than requesting patriarchal protection. The Mahicans had come to their brother's defense when he was weak, and the United States had failed to return the favor. Refusing containment within colonial space, Aupaumut also insisted that he did not follow an American road to peace but traveled on the path of his ancestors. When the British commander at Niagara interrogated him, the Mahican leader responded: "I did not come to this Country in order to see you. . . . My business is with my own color, that we might brighten the Chain of friendship which has subsisted between our forefathers." This statement was not merely a ruse for the British. He told Pickering, too, that his mission had originated from the deliberations of his own mind and the councils of his nation. Even if the United States was supplying the means for his journey, the motive was indigenous:

For some time past I have felt a disposition to use my endeavors to effect an accommodation; seeing the Shawanese are my younger brothers, the Miamis my fathers, the Delawares my grandfathers, the Chippewas my grandchildren, and so on: They have always paid great respect to my advice. . . . Brother, my mind is now ripe. I am appointed by my nation: and these are my men who would go with me. I would undertake to visit the Shawanese and the other hostile tribes with a view to persuade them to make peace with the United States.[20]

As Aupaumut's statement implied, Mahicans had traditionally served as mediators and messengers between eastern and western Algonquian groups. Aupaumut related, "It was the business of our forefathers to go around the towns of these nations to renew the agreements between them, and tell them many things which they discover among the white people in the east." The Revolution had divided Stockbridge from its western relations. Too much

time had elapsed between councils of renewal, messages had stopped traveling, and geopolitical alliances had put them on opposite sides of the conflict.
Aupaumut sought to repair this tear in the network and to reclaim the traditional Mahican role by weaving a new relationship between his American
brother to the east and his Algonquian relations in the west. His first task was
to clear the way for communication. [21]

While Aupaumut agreed to advocate for the United States in the Ohio Valley, in serving as a Mahican mediator and messenger he also had a responsibility to relate his relations' perspective to the American leadership. In his 1791
report to Pickering, Aupaumut cleverly centered a narrative of false treaties,
relaying an Algonquian perception of recent history:

> They told me that by the transactions of the big knifes, at the treaty [of]
> McIntosh 6 years ago was the beginning of the displeasure of the Indians—
> that the big knifes did wrong the Indians in taking unlawfully of their best
> hunting grounds. Further they upon my querie tell me that if the big knifes
> [are] willing to restore the hunting grounds to the Indians, they would
> have peace immediately, and further, they say that they would exchange
> lands with them . . . but now, [as] long as they take our lands [in] such [a]
> manner as they have done we will never have peace with them for this rea-
> son. The great Spirit did give us that land and fill it with abundance of wild
> creatures for our living.[22]

Aupaumut, like Brant, pointed to the false treaties as a root cause of the
current violence, calling particular attention to the Fort McIntosh treaty of
1785, which concerned his close relations, the Delawares. As Aupaumut explained to Pickering, the Algonquians were willing to compromise, but the invalid treaties would impose conditions that were not viable in the Ohio Valley
environment. The American leadership, in their ignorance of the social and
geographical landscape, made impossible demands for lands on which the
Western Indians depended for subsistence. Aupaumut also asserted the claim
to indigenousness, quoting the Western Algonquians' statement that this land
was given to them by the "Great Spirit" and suggesting that his relations were
as embedded in the valley as the "wild creatures" on which they relied.[23]

One of the foremost characters in Aupaumut's narrative of false treaties
was Brant. Although critical of Brant's opposition to his mission, Aupaumut
constructed the Mohawk as a praiseworthy leader, implying, perhaps, that
their paths to peace were not so far apart. As he told it, Brant tried to broker
an important compromise preceding the Fort Harmar treaty of 1789, which
followed on the United Indian Nations' speech. Aupaumut related:

Before this, the Western Indians had been displeased with the treaty at Fort McIntosh, by which their land had been taken away. Brant proposed this to them—Whether in order to get those lands back (as they were their best hunting grounds) they would give other lands in exchange? They were pleased with the idea, and told him they would. Then he mentioned a place, where he thought it best to have the line run. To wit—To follow the Muskingum to its head, where it approaches Cayahoga, then to run to the Head of Cayahoga river, & follow it down to its mouth; and that the Indians should relinquish all the land eastward of this line to the United States. This proposition greatly pleased the Western Indians and they asked Brant to assist them in getting that line settled.[24]

Aupaumut referred to Brant's Muskingum Compromise, a proposed boundary between the United States and the Western Indian Country that allowed for the continuance of the Dish with One Spoon and extant colonial settlements. The line represented a compromise between the Ohio River boundary established during the original Fort Stanwix treaty in 1768—which many of the Western Indians wanted to maintain—and the boundaries set by the false treaties—which delineated nearly all of the Ohio Valley as American space. Brant worked diligently to bring the Western nations into "unanimous" agreement, and, as Aupaumut's narrative intimated, he gradually achieved enough support to bring the compromise to the Americans.[25]

The "Address of the Chiefs of the Six Nations & Western Confederacy to Gov. St. Clair," which Brant recorded, stated that the confederation had been working "for several years past, to bring the whole of the Indian Nations of this Country, to agree to come to some terms of peace with the US" and asserted that American "backwardness" had thwarted their efforts. Confronting the false treaties, the address continued:

This is our last and full determination, it being what was agreed upon by the Confederate Indian Nations that were lately Assembled at the Miami River, and . . . differs widely from the Councils held by General Butler, which was only with a few Nations and those not authorized to transact any Business which Concerned the whole. . . . Brother, as it is our wish to live in peace with all men, and . . . to convince the world that it is from our desire to enter into a War without the Greatest reason. Indeed, As the Great Spirit Above has been pleased to place us in this Country, which until the late unhappy War Between great Britain and America we enjoyed peaceably, We look upon ourselves to be Masters and only true proprietors of it, to avoid further trouble we propose to give to the US all the Lands lying on the East side Muskingum.

Brant reasserted the claim to indigenousness and the confederation's determination to maintain the Dish as a whole, both in terms of the land and its inhabitants. If lines were to be drawn, they would do the drawing, as the "only true proprietors," and such lines would concern the boundaries of the Common Pot, not its division into smaller pieces. Indeed, it was their concern for the land and the community it contained that prompted them to offer a generous compromise in order to prevent the valley's destruction by war. Still, in their conclusion, they made clear that the Americans would face the full force of the confederacy if they persisted in claiming sovereignty over the pot. In laying out the parameters of the Muskingum Compromise, they emphasized, "this is the Boundry line . . . which we cannot Exceed."[26]

Aupaumut's journal related the events that followed:

> The Commissioners sent an answer that they were willing to settle the dispute about the boundary line, but a Wyandot Chief [Half King] & Captain Pipe, who had been concerned in the treaty at Fort McIntosh, privately left the Body of Indians, and went to the Commissioners. . . . These Chiefs told the Commissioners that they might not mind Capt. Brant, but attend to the Chiefs of the Western Indians. For (said they) this Brant has parted with all his land; and has no business to meddle with ours. They then told the Commissioners they would stand to the agreement made at Fort McIntosh.

Brant related his own version of the events in a speech to the Western Indians in 1793:

> In consequence [of the series of false treaties], we advised you to attend a Treaty at the Muskingum. . . . [W]e had then agreed on that river as the Boundary . . . [when] the Hurons here present and some Delawares had sent word to the American Commissioners that their Nations would at all events agree to his terms, which afforded General Sinclair [*sic*] an opportunity of taking the advantage of us and making what terms they Pleased with those who attended.

In fact, St. Clair happily reported the treaty as a success to Washington: "I am persuaded their general confederacy is entirely broken: indeed, it would not be very difficult, if circumstances required it, to set them at deadly variance."[27]

According to Aupaumut, after St. Clair sent a message rejecting the Muskingum Compromise, Brant "told the Indians that those people did not desire peace; but were upon bad designs," and the gathered nations decided to leave for home. In his report Aupaumut emphasized Brant's phrase "bad designs," concluding his narrative with a veiled accusation that the commissioners were implicated in a deceitful division of the Common Pot, thus making the American leadership accountable for answering to the whole of the land's inhabitants.[28]

The Muskingum Compromise illustrates Brant's particular conceptualization of native space, which formed the foundation of his peacemaking vision. Although he may have acquiesced control of the east to the United States—by the traditional Fort Stanwix line, the violent land claims of the Revolution, and the continuing boundary negotiations—he was not willing to relinquish the idea that native space could exist independently of American space. Through the Muskingum Compromise he sought to solidify and legalize this conceptualization. The only path to peace, as he saw it, was for the United States to acknowledge the continuing existence of native space and to deal directly with the confederation that represented it.[29]

Yet Brant's conceptualization was problematic for those native people who remained in New York and New England. Apparently, he was willing to concede that native space no longer existed in the east. As his Huron and Delaware adversaries observed, he had released his claim on the Mohawk River lands and occupied a place at Grand River under British protection. In Brant's spatial configuration, the Mahicans and their village were contained by the United States. He even defined them as "Yankees," tying their geographic location to their participation on the side of the United States in the war. In contrast, Aupaumut insisted that New Stockbridge remained native space and that the Mahicans remained an "independent" nation. Even when the Western Indians questioned his claim to sovereignty, saying they had heard "for several years" that the "Yankees" had the Mahicans "surrounded in arms" and "shut up like so many hogs in a pen," he told them this rumor was false, that "we were an independent people, and could go where we pleased."[30]

Aupaumut's sense of the spatial relations between Indians and the United States was more complicated. He believed that native communities needed to secure particular village territories, bound by writing, as he had done for New Stockbridge, because land encroachment, in his experience, was unstoppable. Aupaumut's vision could be interpreted either as pragmatic forethought based on knowledge of the force of colonial settlement or as acquiescence with a nascent colonial policy that claimed "Indian tribes" as part of American space. In either case, this belief made him more supportive of individual treaties. He strived to explain the deceitful and impractical nature of previous agreements, with a view to making legitimate ones to secure land bases that could realistically support communities.[31]

These competing visions were rooted in distinctive cultural constructs of community. Algonquians conceptualized native space as a network of villages connected by rivers and relations. This concept is especially evident in the structure of Aupaumut's journal as a journey through waterways, with the Mahican delegation moving from village to village, encountering friendly kin. In telling his community's history, Aupaumut described "Muhheakunnuk our nativity" as the place where his ancestors "agreed to kindle a fire" and "hang a kettle, whereof they and their children after them might dip out their daily refreshment." Algonquian identity was grounded in the place where you lived, the pot that fed you. For Aupaumut, each village was both a "kettle" unto itself and a part of the larger Common Pot that linked them together.[32]

The Iroquois conceptualization of native space was more complicated and less fluid. The confederacy longhouse consisted of six nations who occupied particular geographic spaces, with clan identity tying each person to maternal relations within the other nations. Land was held in common, by all clans, and more specifically by the clan mothers. Identity was defined by maternity: individuals belonged to the nation and clan of their mother, while membership in the confederacy could only be acquired by birth to an Iroquois woman or formal adoption by a particular family, clan, or nation. The political life of the confederacy was highly structured, with specific roles assigned to individuals based on clan, nation, and aptitude. Entire nations could be absorbed by the confederacy but only through formal incorporation into the longhouse and the complex kinship structure it encompassed. Brant's vision adapted the Algonquian Dish to the Iroquois longhouse, transforming the Ohio's network of rivers and villages into a political space that could be more strictly ordered and a geographic space that could be contained.[33]

Peacemaking protocol was tied to these spatial conceptualizations. As a mediator in the Algonquian network, Aupaumut's most crucial tool was his ancestors' "bag of peace," which contained "all the belts and strings which they received of their allies of different nations," and which the Mahicans used "to establish peace and friendship" between nations. By arriving with the bag of peace and a delegation of Mahican "counselors," Aupaumut wrote, "the western nations may see that we are upon important business." He would use the wampum to recall the binds between Algonquians, to repair the ties broken by war, and to demonstrate the legitimacy of his mission.[34] Brant, however, drew heavily on the traditions of the Iroquois Confederacy in forming the United Indian Confederation, invoking the Peacemaker, in particular, and his vision of a "union of all the nations" who would act as "one head, one body, and one mind." Leaders, according to the Iroquois Great Law, were obliged to "work in unity." They were not to pursue their "own interests but work to benefit the people and for the generations not yet born." Brant's vision rested on communal recognition that the continuance of the whole Dish was threatened, and that the people who shared in its sustenance needed to unite together to work as "one mind," "deliberating" on the best strategy for its preservation.[35]

Two distinct narratives emerged from the shared space of the Ohio Valley that demonstrate these two very different peacemaking traditions in action and elucidate the conflict between the two men who employed them. Hendrick Aupaumut's "Narrative of an Embassy to the Western Indians" and Joseph Brant's "Journal of the Proceedings at the General Council Held at the Foot of the Rapids of the Miamis" stand as the most comprehensive indigenous accounts of the councils that took place in the Ohio Valley in 1792 and 1793, and they provide important counternarratives to colonial versions of events that often misrepresent U.S.-Indian relations.

Aupaumut's "Narrative of an Embassy to the Western Indians" testified to his success in reconstructing the path to his Western relations and renewing the Mahican place in the Algonquian network. After a "stormy" journey west, Aupaumut related, the Mahican delegation arrived in the Ohio Valley in the summer of 1792 and set up camp with their Munsee "brother," and then joined their Delaware grandfather "at the Forks," where they secured their place in council. From there, "the Delawares, Monthees, Wenuhtkowuk, Kuhnauwautheew, five Nations of us called Eastern Nations or Wauponnuhk . . . went together on single file to attend the Council at Shawanny village." He explained, "We went in one body to show that we have been in good friendship this great length of time."[36]

However, both Aupaumut's mission and his position amongst his relations were challenged by the arrival of a message from Brant:

My friends, I now tell you do not believe what Message the Muheconneew brought to you; neither believe what he says, if you do you will be greatly deceived. I have myself seen Washington, and seen his heart and bowels; and he declared that he claims from the mouth of Miamie to the head of it—thence to the land of the Wabash river, and down the same to the mouth of it; and that he did take up dust and did declare that he would not restore so much dust to the Indians, but he is willing to have peace with the Indians.[37]

Aupaumut counteracted the message by directing suspicion away from himself and back toward Brant. He accused Brant's son, who delivered the speech, of spreading lies to foment war. The message, he insisted, was designed "to frustrate peace, and that we may be hated or killed." When the Mahican leader addressed his relations, he put Brant's words in the context of a long history of Mohawk betrayal and evoked the Algonquian Common Pot in his defense:

> Let us consider the meaning of this Brant's Message—by the sound of it, he point[s] at me as a deceiver or roag, that every nation must be warned. But let us now look back in the path of our forefathers, and see whether you can find one single instance wherein, or how my ancestors or myself have deceived you, or led you one step astray. . . . But you look back and see heaps of your bones, wherein the Maquas have deceived you repeatedly. I think I could have good reason to tell you not to believe the message or words of the Mohawks, for they will deceive you greatly as Usual.[38]

According to Aupaumut, the Algonquians frequently discussed their distrust of the Iroquois in council. In particular, leaders recalled the Iroquois' role in drawing them into the American war. Aupaumut reported that the Algonquian "body" concluded, "the English and the Five Nations [Iroquois] did lay a foundation for our ruin . . . [so they] must settle all this difficulties with the Big knifes. But we must retain all our lands just as much as before the war. Let the English and Five Nations lose their lands." From this council at the Shawnee village, he related, "we set out about five hundred of us, on a single file, to the camp of the Senacas" to "have a council with them, and drive away their minds." There could be no greater symbol for a renewed alliance than five hundred Algonquians marching, "on a single file," to chastise the once powerful Iroquois Confederacy. According to Aupaumut, "the head warrior, Puckoncheluh" told the Senecas, "In our publick council you tell us, we who are one [color], now have one heart and one head. If any Nation strikes us, we must all feel it. Now you must consider whether this is true what you told us."[39]

Aupaumut placed himself and Brant in a historical narrative that posed a longstanding Algonquian network against a domineering Iroquois Confederacy, effectively exploiting his relations' suspicions and the rhetoric of the Common Pot to reinforce his position in the network. Brant's main concern, however, was maintaining the unity of the Dish with One Spoon, which rested on a precarious Iroquois-Algonquian alliance. Aupaumut, despite his claims to independence, represented a certain acquiescence to the invaders and a solution that came from the Americans rather than from the councils of the United Indian Nations. Furthermore, Aupaumut's attempts to forge a stronger Algonquian alliance counteracted Brant's own efforts to maintain the confederation. As Aupaumut himself reported, Brant told him "that perhaps the Western Indians thought I had come to divide them; as that had always been the aim and practice of the White People. I answered him I had come with no such intention."[40]

While Brant accused him of dividing the Dish with One Spoon, Aupaumut charged the Mohawk leader with blocking the paths of the Algonquian network. According to Aupaumut's report, when Brant finally arrived at the 1792 council, the Western Algonquians chastised him:

> The Western Indians had heard that I had been stopped by the British at Niagara, & by Brants orders at Grand River the year before, when I was going to the Westward. . . . To the Five Nations [Iroquois] they said, "You Five Nations must open the path between us and the Eastern nations, you must make it wide, and let no stumbling blocks be again thrown in the way, but keep it smooth and clear, thus our friends the Muhekonnucks and others may pass and repass freely."[41]

Aupaumut described this encounter in response to Pickering's query, "What passed between Brant & the Indians at the Rapids?" The Mahican leader may have chosen to privilege this moment to bolster his own position, but he may have also been covering for the larger story. In his reports to Pickering, Aupaumut failed to mention the numerous council discussions about the need to renew the union and the threat Americans posed to it. According to British records of the proceedings, Red Jacket explained, "The white people are now looking at us and know what we are about, they were always the instigators of our quarrels," while the speaker for the Western Indians, Messquakenoe, reminded the Iroquois that the Americans only wanted "to divide us, that we might not act as one Man." Neither did Aupaumut reveal that the Iroquois made pains to describe the difficult situation that they all faced in the wake of the Revolution. Seneca leader Farmer's Brother explained, "From that moment our lands were torn to pieces and the Americans triumphed as the greatest people on this island." Upon his belated arrival in the Ohio Valley, Brant warned them all that Washington's words were full of "cunning," and that the American leadership was intent on dividing the Dish. He advised that when the Americans "send out a flag [of peace] . . . it will not do for one man to turn about and listen to that flag—We must all be at it, as we are all united as one man."[42]

Aupaumut found it difficult to dismiss Brant's words, even as he endeavored to persuade his Western relations of Washington's good intentions. He devoted three pages of his "Narrative" to explaining the lengths to which he went to advocate for the new American government as the Western Indians related their experiences of American land grabbing and deceitfulness, their apprehensions about American desire for domination, and their doubts about the inability of the American leadership to control its settlers on the frontiers. At the end of this account, a frustrated Aupaumut declared:

> In all my arguments with these Indians, I have as it were oblige to say noth-
> ing with regard of the conduct of the Yorkers, how they cheat my fathers,
> how they taken our lands Unjustly, and how my fathers were groaning as it
> were in their graves, in losing their lands for nothing, although they were
> faithful friends to the Whites, and how the white people artfully got their
> Deeds confirmed in their Laws. I say had I mention these things to the In-
> dians, it would aggravate their prejudices against white people.[43]

Aupaumut's charged language unmasked his realization that the Western Indians' story was his own. He was not merely a messenger of the narrative of false treaties but a character within it. British accounts of the 1792 councils reveal a part of Aupaumut's story that he deliberately concealed from his own *Narrative*. As Brant himself knew, during the course of their stay in the Ohio Valley, the Mahicans began to envision a new path. Even if Aupaumut remained silent about their current land troubles, the other Mahicans did not. The Western Indians informed Brant that "the Mohickens have told us ... that they find themselves hampered among the white people and wanted to get into a place where they could be more at their liberty." Unbeknownst to the Americans who funded their journey, the Mahicans were also securing their position within the Algonquian network of relations so that they might have a place to move their pot, away from American encroachment and control.[44]

By the summer of 1793 both Aupaumut and Brant were emissaries of a boundary line compromise. Aupaumut traveled once more to the Ohio Valley to ascertain whether his Algonquian relations would agree to a resolution based on his understanding that the American leadership might be willing to "give up a part of the lands southward of the line settled by the treaties of fort McIntosh and fort Harmar," and allow for hunting rights on any of the lands they "retained." Brant desired an open discussion about the location of the boundary "between us & the Americans" and sought to renew the possibility of the Muskingum Compromise. Due to native efforts to explain the problems with previous treaties, positive changes in American policy, the trustworthiness of the new commission (which included Timothy Pickering), and the defeat of American military expeditions against the Western Indians in 1790 and 1791, the Americans, Brant believed, "now seem earnestly inclined for peace."[45]

The American goal remained confirmation of previous treaties and monetary compensation for land, but for the first time a compromise on the boundary line was a real possibility. Secretary of War Knox instructed his Commissioners that "if the relinquishment of any lands, in the said space, should be an ultimatum with the said Indians, and a line could be agreed upon which would be free from dispute, you may, in order to effect a peace, make such a relinquishment." Still, the United States continued in its attempts to divide the Indian Union. Knox instructed the commissioners to strive "to form separate contracts" with the tribes and to avoid "as much as possible, to confirm the idea of union," to which, he acknowledged, "the said Indians are much attached." Aupaumut, whether he fully realized it or not, was being utilized as an instrument of this divisive policy, and Brant was especially aware of the tightrope on which Aupaumut was walking. In council, the Mohawk leader warned the Western Indians: "There are bad Birds amongst us or there soon will be, whom it is our business to guard against. They will say that they know the Minds of the Commissioners but we must not listen to Spies, who we ought to Banish, as we mean to Meet these Commissioners we will hear from them what they have to say."[46]

In his journal Brant added, "At this time I was informed that Capt. Hendrick was at Detroit & to whom I alluded." He also took further steps to banish the Mahican leader from councils. As Aupaumut reported to Pickering: "Brant brought & deliver[ed] a Message to me which was said from Wyondots Shawanese & Miamis—the substance of it was this—you the Muhheconnuk nation came from among the big knifes—You must not enter into our councils." Aupaumut insisted that these words did not represent his feelings, but came "from Brant alone." The message angered Aupaumut's Delaware relations, fostering anti-Iroquois sentiment. Meanwhile Aupaumut continued to advocate for the United States' proposals in private meetings, which, of course, angered Brant even more.[47]

Brant's "Journal of the Proceedings at the General Council Held at the Foot of the Rapids of the Miamis" thus began with a Dish in rupture. The Mohawk leader arrived at the Miami Rapids "with the Indians of the Six Nations [Iroquois Confederacy] and Delawares from the Grand River" to confront "evil reports" that he was a "traitor." To Brant's dismay, the nations had neither gathered for council nor begun the condolence ceremonies that would clear their minds for deliberation. The nations were severely divided, with some moving more toward the American peace proposals and others hot for war. According to his journal, Brant organized a council himself, reminding the Western Indians of the critical moment they faced in their maintenance of the Dish: "We have had various meetings with the Americans, but none of such importance as this Will be, it therefore Stands us in need to give it the most serious Attention, and requires the greatest Prudence & Unanimity amongst ourselves." Despite the "friendly council," rumors continued to circulate, while the "Shawanoes, Delawares and Miamis held Private Councils many nights, to which none of the Six Nations [Iroquois] were invited."[48]

A new set of misunderstandings erupted after Brant returned from a brief journey to meet with the American commissioners at Niagara. At Alexander McKee's suggestion, Brant had organized a deputation to ensure that the commissioners were authorized to "make a New Boundary Line." When they answered affirmatively, Brant returned to the valley with a strong incentive to rejuvenate his Muskingum Compromise. Although the Western Indian leadership had authorized the trip, some of them—especially McKee's relations, the Shawnee—accused Brant of negotiating with the commissioners in private and remained wary of any conciliation.[49]

The Lake Indians, from the northwest side of Erie, agreed to mediate on the Iroquois Confederacy's behalf with the Shawnee and "the rest of the Confederate Indians." Brant insisted that his greatest desire was for an open council to discuss the location of the line, so that they might speak "with one Voice" to the commissioners. He continued to emphasize the possibility for peace in his original vision, insisting that the Iroquois had "come here at your request to assist you in making peace for this *our* Country. . . . We assure you before the Great Spirit that we do not mean the least Deviation from the Confederacy, and our hearts are true to their Interest." At this time, Brant wrote, "we placed a Moon of Wampum and a Dish with one Spoon in the Council which Signified that the Country was in Common."[50]

The Western nations invoked the Dish as well, to bolster their argument for a defensive war. They implied that the Iroquois were trying to dominate the councils, and they called on the principles of the Dish to rein them in: "You advised us that . . . the whole Country was in Common [and] whatever was done" in the councils of the "Confederacy would remain firm." The nations had made a decision at the previous year's council to stand firm on "the old boundary line" of "the Ohio," and the Shawnee speaker insisted that if the Iroquois Confederacy were committed to the principles of the Dish, they were bound to defend it.[51]

Brant was unwilling to commit to war without a fair discussion of his compromise, which, he told the Western Indians, had failed to come to fruition largely because of division and jealousy within the union. In his final speech, the Mohawk leader pleaded with his relations:

It is well known that for these many years past, we have exerted ourselves for the Confederacy . . . but after Deliberating & Maturely Weighing in our Minds our Force, Resources, and every local advantage we possess, we declare our sentiments from the bottom of our hearts that the Boundary of the Muskingum, if adopted in General Council, is for the interest of us all and far preferable to an uncertain War. . . . I therefore beg of you not to be rash and consider the consequences of a War in which we are not unanimous.[52]

The next day, according to Brant,

the Chiefs of the Shawanoes and those of the Hurons, Delawares and the Seven Nations of Canada come to the Six Nations [Iroquois Confederacy] and spoke as follows: Brothers, We have since yesterday been thinking seriously of your opinion in the last Council, we know that your knowledge of the White People exceeds ours, and that you are from that enabled to form a better Judgment of our Affairs than we can for which reason we are now come to tell you that we mean to adopt your opinion respecting the Boundary line.[53]

The nations unanimously adopted Brant's Muskingum Compromise and laid down wampum to seal their words. Aupaumut reported happily to Pickering:

I think you will receive invitation from the whole confederate nations to meet them near the mouth of this river this week, where highly probable you will establish a permanent peace—for the greater nations sincerely desire. And for the terms of peace I think with no difficulty a new line will be drawn—and taking yearly rent is very acceptable to all.[54]

However, Brant related, "After this meeting . . . Col McKee had a private meeting with the aforementioned chiefs at twelve o'clock at Night." The next morning, when "we met in General Council," the Shawnee speaker reported their "final Resolution" to "unite our Warriors" to defend the Ohio River boundary. According to Brant, the Delaware leader Buckongehalis pointed to McKee, saying, "that is the Person who advised us to insist on the Ohio River for the line." Brant later blamed the failure of peace on McKee's manipulation of his own relations.[55]

Brant painted the final scene of his journal as a picture of division:

When the Council was over a War feast was prepared, and the Chiefs of the Shawanoes singing the War Song encouraging the Warriors of all the Nations to be active in defending their Country, saying their Father the English would assist them and pointing to Colonel McKee. When we arrived at Detroit a Deputation of the Lake Indians overtook us . . . [and] they gave us a Belt with a Number of Streaks across it and said the tribes which these Streaks represent have made Peace with the Americans, and that they would go to Post Vincent and make Peace also.[56]

Concurrently, Timothy Pickering, writing from Detroit as well, sent the following letter to Aupaumut:

> My Friend & Brother, When I first saw you, about two years ago, I remem-
> ber you proposed to make a visit to the Western Indians, to try to bring
> about a peace between them and the US: and I recollect you mentioned as
> the motive of your attempt to promote peace—"That you were a friend to
> the US, and also a friend to the people of your own color." You will there-
> fore be very sorry, as I am, that peace can not now be made. You know that
> in our speech delivered the 31ˢᵗ of last month to their Deputies, we told
> them that we could not make the Ohio the boundary: and yesterday their
> answer arrived, insisting that the Ohio should be the boundary. The nego-
> tiations for peace are therefore over; and we are going home immediately.[57]

Both Aupaumut and Brant fully understood that making peace was a deli-
cate and complicated endeavor. Bernd Peyer has observed that leaders like
Aupaumut and Brant "consciously followed the paths they sincerely believed
would lead their people out of the colonial situation." Each man legitimately
believed that the other posed a threat to his particular vision of peace. By
blocking his path, Aupaumut maintained that Brant was denying him access
to his relations. In his view, Brant was utilizing his geographic position between Algonquians to prevent Aupaumut from fulfilling his traditional role as
a mediator, because Brant sought to dominate that role himself. Yet Brant initially blocked Aupaumut's way at Niagara to keep the road to the Ohio Valley
clear. He wanted to forge a path to peace that emerged from within the Dish,
on which its inhabitants could unanimously agree, and Aupaumut's divided
loyalties posed a threat to this process. Brant was certain that the American
strategy was to divide the Union, and he regarded Aupaumut as an agent of
this strategy, whether he was complicit or not.[58]

Yet each man understood most keenly Young Peter's original criticism
of the United States for the grave mistake the younger nation was making in
following two paths at once. During that initial meeting at Newtown Point,
Aupaumut told Pickering, "I have said that I would go to the Western Indians,
but there is one difficulty in the way: You have an army assembling in that
quarter. . . . [If] I proceed, the operations of your army must be suspended."
Brant was a frequent participant in the councils and correspondence amongst
the Six Nations [Iroquois Confederacy] and the British where this particular brand of American duplicity was discussed with profound bewilderment,
and he expressed great disappointment that some of his Western relations
were "addicted" to war. Both Brant and Aupaumut had experienced severe
ruptures in their home communities and the larger networks to which they

belonged. They understood all too well the grief that followed participation in war. But each man knew that peace could only develop if all participants were able to clear the paths between them and set their minds to deliberate carefully on the best course for all the land's inhabitants. The United States, in believing that its own expansionist plans outweighed indigenous attempts to share space, and in assuming that its diplomatic traditions were superior to native ones, failed to grasp an opportunity to learn from the elder nations of the continent it claimed.[59]

Although Brant and Aupaumut's visions failed to produce a lasting peace in the Ohio Valley, both made deep contributions to the sustenance of their home communities. Aupaumut secured a place for the "kettle" of New Stockbridge with the United States and, more importantly, within the Algonquian network of relations, opening space in the West in case the brotherhood with the United States or the newly developed relationship with the Oneidas failed. During his journeys, Aupaumut reconstructed the "path of my ancestors," reconnecting his village to the network that would ensure its continuance. Even if Brant did not ultimately achieve union among the Western Indians, his efforts did help to reconstruct the Iroquois Confederacy as a political entity. Developing the Dish with One Spoon enabled him to take lessons learned during the horrific breakdown of the confederacy to reconstruct his ancestors' vision of unity. He wrote to British Indian Commissioner Joseph Chew just months before the historic Treaty of Canandaigua: "[I] am happy to say that there never was greater Unanimity prevailed amongst the Six Nations [Iroquois] than appeared at this Council, being to a man determined in One Opinion."[60]

The two leaders also eventually made peace with each other. Aupaumut wrote a sympathetic letter responding to Brant's land troubles with the Canadian government in 1807 that demonstrated a commonality of vision. He related that he was on his way west "to renew the covenant of friendship" with his relations and advised Brant to continue to work to unify his people. He urged the Mohawk leader to "obtain . . . writing for the land" at Grand River and "to keep good courage." In this message, the only surviving communication between the two men, Aupaumut referred to Brant warmly as "my friend."[61]

NOTES

1. Pickering noted that this Peter "is the son of Good Peter, the great speaker of the Oneida Nation." Timothy Pickering Papers, 1731–1792, Massachusetts Historical Society, Boston, Massachusetts, 60:70, 103 [hereafter cited as TPP]. Newtown Point was a new American settlement midway between Philadelphia, Oneida, and the newly reconfigured

confederacy council fire at Buffalo Creek, in Seneca territory. The site had originally been an Iroquois village and then, during the French and Indian wars, a native middle ground under Iroquois control, inhabited by Delawares, Mahicans, and Tutelos, among others. According to Isabel Thompson Kelsay, some one thousand people attended the council at Newtown Point; Kelsay, *Joseph Brant, 1743–1807: Man of Two Worlds* (Syracuse, N.Y.: Syracuse Univ. Press, 1984), 454.

2. Several works have provided valuable historical context for this essay. They include Kelsay, *Joseph Brant*; Richard White, *The Middle Ground: Indians, Empires, and Republics in the Great Lakes Region, 1650–1815* (New York: Cambridge Univ. Press, 1991); Alan Taylor, "Captain Hendrick Aupaumut: The Dilemmas of an Intercultural Broker," *Ethnohistory* 43 (1996); and James P. Ronda, "As They Were Faithful: Chief Hendrick Aupaumut and the Struggle for Stockbridge Survival, 1757–1830," *American Indian Culture and Research Journal* 3 (1979), 43–55. I would like to express my thanks to these authors for their vital research and analysis. I would also like to extend great thanks to the American Antiquarian Society for an outstanding fellowship experience, and especially to Joanne Chaison, Caroline Sloat, Dennis Laurie, and Marie Lamoureaux for the research support and excellent suggestions they provided while I was developing this essay. Thanks also to the Massachusetts Historical Society for providing access to the Timothy Pickering Papers and the coffee to get me through them. I am grateful to the Newberry Library for early support of this research project, and to the John Carter Brown Library, for providing the space and the sources for the final touches. Special thanks to Alyssa Mount Pleasant for sharing her research on Buffalo Creek, and for offering insightful suggestions on an early draft, and to Dan Usner for his continually supportive guidance, and for helping me to focus this essay in particular. Finally, *kchi wliwni* to my father, Brian Brooks, for many meaningful conversations about the challenges of mediation and making peace.

3. Kelsay, *Joseph Brant*, 444–45; TPP, 60:106. As Iroquois space reconfigured after the Revolution, the confederacy council fire was rekindled at Buffalo Creek, where many Senecas, Onondagas, and Cayugas gathered to reconstruct their villages, and some Delawares and Shawnees sought refuge, while Mohawks established villages northwest of Buffalo Creek, on the north side of Lake Ontario. Note that a previous assault by the army in 1790 on the Western Indians' central council fire gave the Iroquois even more ample grounds for suspicion. Kelsay, *Joseph Brant*, 456; White, *The Middle Ground*, 448–54; and William Stone, *Life of Joseph Brant, Thayendanegea* (New York: George Dearborn, 1838), 294–95.

4. TPP 60:94, 61:222.

5. TPP 59:8A, 10A. Even when Brant continued his journey he assured that others in his community would keep Aupaumut from traveling past Grand River. Aupaumut wrote many reports during his missions to the Western Indian Country. They include June 1791 Speech, October 1791 Report, February 1792 "Narrative," December 1792 Report, and February 1793 "Queries," TPP 59:8–13, 18–21, 26–27, 38–43, 60:70–73. See also Hendrick Aupaumut, "A Narrative of an Embassy to the Western Indians," *Collections of the Massachusetts Historical Society*, 10 ser., 70 vols. (Boston: Massachusetts Historical Society, 1792–1941), 9:61–131.

6. On Hendrick and the elder Aupaumut, see Ted Brasser, *Riding on the Frontier's Crest: Mahican Indian Culture and Culture Change* (Ottawa: National Museums of Canada, 1974), 34–36; Patrick Frazier, *The Mohicans of Stockbridge* (Lincoln: Univ. of Nebraska Press, 1992), 9; Massachusetts Archives, Massachusetts Archives Collection, 328 vols.,

Boston, Mass., 29:187, 31:290, 32:251–57; Mary R. Cabot, *Annals of Brattleboro,* 2 vols. (Brattleboro, Mass.: E. L. Hindreth, 1921), 1:10–12; "A Letter from Rev. Jonathan Edwards . . . Relating to the Indian School at Stockbridge," *Collections of the Massachusetts Historical Society,* 1st ser., 10:143–53; Evan Haefeli and Kevin Sweeney, "Revisiting *The Redeemed Captive:* New Perspectives on the 1704 Attack on Deerfield," in Colin G. Calloway, ed., *After King Phillip's War: Presence and Persistence in Indian New England* (Hanover, N.H.: Univ. Press of New England, 1997), 50–53.

Greylock's War was essentially an Abenaki resistance against British colonial expansion. Although the Mohawks refused to join the British in the war, Hendrick and a few others volunteered to serve as scouts. See Colin G. Calloway, "Gray Lock's War," *Vermont History* 54 (1986): 197–228; and *The Western Abenakis of Vermont, 1600–1800: War, Migration, and the Survival of an Indian People* (Norman: Univ. of Oklahoma Press, 1990), 113–31. On Brant's presence at the battle of Lake George, see Stone, *Life of Brant,* 18.

7. On Mohawk and Mahican participation in the Revolution, see Kelsay, *Joseph Brant;* Ronda, "As They Were Faithful"; Stone, *Life of Brant;* and Colin G. Calloway, *The American Revolution in Indian Country: Crisis and Diversity in Native American Communities* (New York: Cambridge Univ. Press, 1995). Calloway has described "Fort Niagara during the Revolution" as "a military headquarters, a trading post, a supply depot, a diplomatic hub, and a multiethnic, multiclass society" that included a substantial Iroquois population. After the war many of the Iroquois people who had sought refuge at Niagara established reconfigured villages at Grand River and Buffalo Creek. Brant's was among these families; Calloway, *Revolution in Indian Country,* 129. The Oneidas also participated on the American side in the Revolution and subsequently made part of their territory available to the Mahicans and other northeastern Algonquian nations to reconstruct new villages in an area less threatened by colonial encroachment.

8. There has been some debate among historians over Brant's claiming of "King" Hendrick as his grandfather. Non-native historians have sometimes interpreted this comment as a braggart's claim, in mistakenly projecting European structures of kinship onto Joseph Brant's words, but the comment makes a great deal of sense within Iroquois conceptualizations of kinship. As the primary leader of Brant's clan in the village they both inhabited, Hendrick played a strong role as "grandfather" to the younger Mohawk, perhaps even more so than his biological grandfathers.

9. United States Congress, *American State Papers: Indian Affairs,* 2 vols. (Washington, D.C.: Gales and Seaton, 1832–1861), 1:8 [hereafter cited as *ASP-IA*]. William Stone has written that it "has been assumed" that Brant wrote the speech. Stone, *Life of Brant,* 280.

10. *ASP-IA* 1:9.

11. Joseph Brant Papers, Ser. F, 22 vols., Lyman C. Draper Manuscript Collection, Historical Society of Wisconsin, Division of Archives and Manuscripts, University of Wisconsin, Madison, Wisconsin [hereafter cited as DMC], 11:204–5. Isabel Thompson Kelsay was the first historian to call attention to Brant's use of the metaphor of the "Dish with One Spoon." Richard White mentioned it briefly, noting, "To eat from a common dish was a standard Algonquian metaphor of peace, alliance, and friendship." Kelsay, *Joseph Brant,* 410, also chap. 20; White, The *Middle Ground,* 441. On McKee, Aupaumut noted that "Colonel McKee is half Shawanny, and the other British" and that he was an "exceeding good instrument for the British," while historian Richard White has written of McKee: "In [trader and interpreter] George Croghan's words, the Shawnees considered

him 'as one of their own people, his Mother being one of their Nation." Aupaumut, "Narrative," 105; White, *The Middle Ground*, 324.

12. Brant quoted in Kelsay, *Joseph Brant*, 346. Richard White has written that "The principle of common ownership was central to the confederacy" and noted that the "greatest political accomplishment" of the confederation was the "acceptance" among all "that the land belonged equally to all Indians of the *pays d'en haute*, could not be ceded without the consent of the entire confederation, and would be defended by all"; see White, The *Middle Ground*, 435. On the formation of the Union, see Brant Papers, DMC, Ser. F., 11:23; White, *The Middle Ground*, 413–68; Kelsay, *Joseph Brant*, 344–47, 399–405; and Stone, *Life of Brant*, 248–54, 264–72.

13. *ASP-IA* 1:9.

14. Frontier Wars Papers, Ser. U, 24 vols, DMC, 23:31. The leadership's awareness of the American "design" did not stop some Shawnees from signing the "Great Miami Treaty" in early 1786.

15. *ASP-IA* 1:9. These efforts to divide the leadership and the confederation were especially directed toward Brant. While the Mohawk leader was en route to the council at Fort Stanwix in 1784, New York governor George Clinton instructed interpreter Peter Ryckman, "If you find that any Jealousy of, or envy to[ward] Brant, you will try to discover who are most jealous or envious of him and promote it as much as you prudently can." Clinton to Ryckman, August 14, 1784, Franklin B. Hough, ed., *Proceedings of the Commissioners of Indian Affairs, Appointed by the Law for the Extinguishment of Indian Titles in the State of NY* (Albany, N.Y.: Joel Munsell, 1861), 1:25.

16. American "divide-and-conquer" policy continued in parallel to Brant's unifying effort. Knox wrote to New York's Governor Clinton in May 1791: "Your Excellency may remember Captain Brandt's [*sic*] exertions, in the year 1786, to form a grand confederation of all the Indians northwest of the Ohio, the Six Nations included. By a late letter which he has written to Mr. Kirkland, and which I received yesterday, it appears that he still should like that measure, if he could find it practicable. But such an event could not be for the interest of the U.S.: for, although justice, policy, and humanity, dictate a liberal treatment of the Indians, it cannot be for the public interest to consolidate them in one body, which would be liable to a single impulse." *ASP-IA* 1:168.

17. Aupaumut, "Narrative," 76.

18. TPP 59:8. Similarly, Aupaumut's 1792 "Narrative" opened with "a short sketch what friendship and connections, our forefathers, and we, have had with the western tribes." Note that Aupaumut was referring to this welcoming reception by his Western relations when he suggested that Brant was jealous of him in dissuading the Western Indians from listening to his words. Aupaumut, "Narrative," 76, 101.

19. TPP 60:71. In analyzing this speech, Alan Taylor has observed, "the Mohicans felt aggrieved by their [the Americans'] failure to reciprocate." Taylor, "Captain Hendrick Aupaumut," 442.

20. TPP 59:9, 71. Aupaumut noted that he had been "invited last spring" by his Western relations to visit and council with them. Taylor has explored Aupaumut's motivations for the journey, including Aupaumut's desire to get the "United States to pay for the trip that he already intended to take west, as much to renew Mohican ties with the natives there as to broker a peace with the Americans." Taylor, "Captain Hendrick Aupaumut," 443.

21. Aupaumut, "Narrative," 78. For an extremely insightful analysis of Aupaumut's role in renewing the Mahican position in the Algonquian network, see Taylor, "Captain Hendrick Aupaumut," 432–57. See also Ronda, "As They Were Faithful," 47.

22. TPP 59:8. Most of the Western Indians referred to Americans generally as "big knifes." However, Aupaumut often made pains to distinguish between the American leadership and the backcountry settlers, referring most often to the latter as "big knifes." But because in this case he was relaying the Western Indian perspective, he used the term to refer to the commissioners. Aupaumut told Pickering in 1791: "I know that there is a distinction between the bad people on the frontiers, and the great body of the people of the US, and that the latter wish the Indians no harm, but are their friends, and I firmly believe that I can make the Indians sensible of that distinction." TPP 60:72. Richard White has observed, "Both the French and Indians distinguished the federal troops from Sullivan's backcountry people. They called the federal troops the 'real Americans.'" But he also notes that this began eroding by 1789. White, *The Middle Ground*, 429–31.

23. Aupaumut concluded his report with a further explication of this injustice: "The Western Indians (and my Cousin) gave me this account of the treaty at Fort McIntosh. That the Commissioners repeatedly urged them to sell their lands, which they constantly refused. At length the Commissioners cause all their soldiers to be drawn up under arms. That they intimidated the Chiefs: Captain Pipe in particular, could hardly hold his pipe to his mouth. Then the Chiefs agreed to whatever the Commissioners were pleased to dictate." TPP 59:13. On the Fort McIntosh treaty, see Kelsay, *Joseph Brant*, 367–68; and White, *The Middle Ground*, 417, 435–39.

24. TPP 59:12.

25. On the Muskingum Compromise and the Fort Harmar treaties, see Kelsay, *Joseph Brant*, 418–25; Stone, *Life of Brant*, 278; and White, *The Middle Ground*, 443–47. On the 1768 Fort Stanwix treaty, see White, *The Middle Ground*, 351–54.

26. Frontier Wars Papers, DMC, 23:66–69.

27. TPP 59:12; E. A. Cruikshank, ed., *The Correspondence of Lieutenant Governor John Graves Simcoe*, 5 vols. (Toronto, Can.: Society, 1923–31), 2:14–15; *ASP-IA* 1:10. The treaties that St. Clair acquired, however, were invalid in native space. Not only did St. Clair fail to acquiesce from much of the Ohio Valley leadership, but furthermore, he did not have the wampum necessary to seal the agreement. See White, *The Middle Ground*, 446.

28. TPP 59:12A. Aupaumut repeated the phrase twice, adding, "Brant told the whole that they could do nothing—that the Commissioners were on bad designs—and that they had best go back, and the next day they all set out for their homes."

29. Brant also articulated this conceptualization in a speech to the U.S. commissioners at Buffalo Creek in 1794: "We are of the same opinion with the people of the U.S.; you consider yourselves as independent people; we, as the original inhabitants of this country, and sovereigns of the soil, look upon ourselves as equally independent, and free as any other nation or nations. This country was given to us by the Great Spirit above; we wish to enjoy it, and have our passage along the lake, within the line we have pointed out." *ASP-IA* 1:481.

30. TPP 59:8A, 9; Cruikshank, ed., *Correspondence of Simcoe*, 5:34.

31. For example, Aupaumut explained to Pickering that his Western relations "said, all last summer, that they did not choose to sell their lands; because they wanted to get their living out of them. . . . They are anxious to get back to the waters running into the

Ohio. There the country is better watered. There are hills bearing berries and roots & supporting game. The heads of those waters afford the best hunting grounds. The lands are also good for corn. Perhaps a few tracts restored for towns with a right of hunting at large might induce them to confirm in the main the former treaties." TPP 59:54. Knox described the Confederated Indians as "the tribes of Indians within the limits of the United States"; see *ASP-IA* 1:9.

32. "Extract from an Indian History," *Collections of the Massachusetts Historical Society,* 1st ser., 9:101. For an outline of Aupaumut's motivations, especially in relation to his home community of New Stockbridge, see Taylor, "Captain Hendrick Aupaumut," 443. For Northeastern Algonquian identity construction, see Calloway, *Western Abenakis;* Haefeli and Sweeney, "Revisiting," and "Wattanummon's World: Personal and Tribal Identity in the Algonquian Diaspora, c. 1660–1712," *Papers of the 25th Algonquian Conference* (Ottawa, Can.: Carleton University, 1994); William A. Haviland and Marjory W. Powers, *The Original Vermonters: Native Inhabitants, Past and Present* (Hanover, N.H.: Univ. Press of New England, 1994); Daniel R. Mandell, *Behind the Frontier: Indians in Eighteenth-Century Eastern Massachusetts* (Lincoln: Univ. of Nebraska Press, 1996); Kenneth M. Morrison, *The Embattled Northeast: The Elusive Ideal of Alliance in Abenaki-Euramerican Relations* (Berkeley: Univ. of California Press, 1984); and Neal Salisbury, *Manitou and Providence: Indians, Europeans, and the Making of New England, 1500–1643* (New York: Oxford Univ. Press, 1982).

As historian Richard White has demonstrated, Western Algonquian space was organized on similar principles. Identity was located more in the "village," which was often multiethnic, than the "tribe." He has noted that "tribes in the *pays d'en haute* were less meaningful as political than as ethnic units." "The basic political unit" was "the village, which sometimes corresponded to the smaller tribal divisions of phatry and clan but most often did not." White, *The Middle Ground,* 389, 413.

33. Seneca Arthur Parker's recorded version of the Great Law states that all members of the same clan, "irrespective of the Nation," shall "recognize" each other "as relatives" and further that "These clans distributed through their respective Nations, shall be the sole owners and holders of the soil of the country and in them is it vested as a birthright." The "lineal descent . . . shall run in the female line. Women shall be considered the progenitors of the Nation. They shall own the land and the soil. Men and women shall follow the status of their mother." Arthur C. Parker, "The Constitution of the Five Nations," in *Parker on the Iroquois,* ed. William Fenton (Syracuse, N.Y.: Syracuse Univ. Press, 1968), 42.

34. Aupaumut, "Narrative," 78; Electa F. Jones, *Stockbridge: Past and Present* (Springfield, Mass.: S. Bowles, 1854), 20.

Aupaumut was accompanied by his brother Solomon and his brother-in-law John Quinney—both of whom would play a large role in Mahican leadership during future years—as well as Capt. David Neshoonhuk, who had served in the Revolutionary War and was familiar with both American and Algonquian warfare and diplomacy. Lastly, he chose a "young man" named John Wautunhqnaut to serve as a runner. This "young man" may have been the grandson of John Waumwaumpequunaunt, one of the first Mahicans to learn to read and write. The elder John left his village of Kaunaumeek—a small community northwest of Housatonic, near present-day New Lebanon, New York—at 12 or 13 to attend Timothy Woodbridge's school at Stockbridge (apparently "crying" to his parents to let him go) and later taught David Brainerd and Jonathan Edwards the Mahican language and served as company clerk for a company of Stockbridge soldiers in the French and Indian War. John Sargeant described Waumwaumpequunaunt as having "superior abilities," while Edwards remarked on his formidable skills in reading, writing, interpreting, and exegesis, describing him as "an extraordinary man." Such skills in literacy would prove instrumental to the Mahicans in renewing their role as messengers in the Western Indian Country; see Frazier, *Mohicans of Stockbridge*, 45, 94, 120.

35. Parker, "Constitution of the Five Nations," 25, 29. Of course, what becomes difficult to discern here is the degree to which Brant's language was influenced by the oral tradition of the Dakanawida epic, versus the degree to which the Dakanawida epic that Parker edited—based on a version carefully compiled by Seth Newhouse, an Onondaga resident of the Six Nations reserve at Grand River—was influenced by Brant's Dish with One Spoon. However, the rhetoric of union shows up frequently in the Iroquois speeches that preceded Brant's Dish. See Cadwallader Colden, *The History of the Five Nations Depending on the Province of New York in America* (New York: William Bradford, 1727); and Carl Van Doren, ed., *Indian Treaties Printed by Benjamin Franklin, 1736–1762* (Philadelphia: Historical Society of Pennsylvania, 1938). For example, the Seneca speaker Kanickhungo told the governor of Pennsylvania at a 1736 treaty: "it is our Desire that we and you should be as of *one Heart, one Mind, and one Body,* thus becoming one People." "A Treaty of Friendship Held with the Chiefs of the Six Nations at Philadelphia in September and October, 1736," in Van Doren, ed., *Indian Treaties,* 7.

36. Aupaumut, "Narrative," 114–15. These "Eastern Nations" were those who had originally inhabited the region from the Hudson to the Susquehanna. British documents also represented the "Mohikens" as part of the "Western Confederacy" in the grand council held in the Shawnee Village at the "Forks." Cruikshank, ed., *Correspondence of Simcoe,* 1:218. On the 1792 councils, see Kelsay, *Joseph Brant,* 177–82; White, *The Middle Ground,* 456–64. On Aupaumut's "Narrative," see Ronda, "As They Were Faithful," 47–49; and Taylor, "Captain Hendrick Aupaumut," 444–47.

37. Aupaumut, "Narrative," 113. Both Brant and Aupaumut had been to Philadelphia to meet with Washington prior to the 1792 councils in the Ohio Valley. See *ASP-IA* 226–33, 236–37, 242–45; and Kelsay, *Joseph Brant,* 461–73. Note that Aupaumut's relationship with the first American president was forged during the Revolutionary War. Washington had appointed Aupaumut as Captain of his Mahican Company at the young age of 23. Calloway, *American Revolution in Indian Country,* 99. Washington was also well known to the Six Nations for his role in the Revolution; their name for him was "Town Destroyer."

38. Aupaumut, "Narrative," 129. The Mohawk leader had grown ill on his way west and apparently sent his son ahead to carry a message to the Western Indians. Aupaumut's suspicion of the young man may have been valid. A contemporary source reported to an Albany newspaper that "Col. Brandt's [*sic*] son, previous to his father's return from Philadelphia, was gone off with a banditti of Mohawks, to join the hostile Indians; but the Colonel has dispatched a messenger to bring him back." Extract of a letter from a gentleman, at the Springs at Saratoga, to the printers of the *Albany Gazette,* August 23, 1792, Brant Papers, DMC, Ser. F, 11:116.

39. Aupaumut, "Narrative," 115–16. Aupaumut's account of this confrontation is supported by the council record in Cruikshank, ed., *Correspondence of Simcoe,* 1:220. Note that although Aupaumut wrote Brant into his dualistic Algonquian-Iroquois narrative,

in reality, Brant was not so much a target of these admonitions as were the Senecas. When Brant finally arrived at the council in the early fall he joined with the Western Indians in questioning the Senecas' loyalty to the confederation. Ibid., 1:224, 242.

40. TPP 59:41. Alan Taylor has provided an insightful analysis of Aupaumut's relationship with and representation of the Iroquois; Taylor, "Captain Hendrick Aupaumut," 444–45.

41. TPP 59:42.

42. Cruikshank, ed., *Correspondence of Simcoe*, 1:221, 225–26, 242.

43. Aupaumut, "Narrative," 128; TPP 59:43.

44. Cruikshank, ed., *Correspondence of Simcoe*, 1:242. Aupaumut did report that he received invitations from the Mohawk and Delaware villages at Grand River, as well as from the Western Indians, for the Mahicans to come live with them, but he presented this as evidence of the Mahicans' good-standing relations. He only revealed that he planned to bring their invitations back to the Mahican council for deliberation; see TPP 59:19.

The Mahicans had a longstanding tradition of "moving the kettle" along the waterways that connected communities when social or geographic pressures necessitated it. Aupaumut's grandfather had originally moved to the village of Stockbridge with a group of Hudson River Mahicans when land encroachment on the Hudson forced him to seek an alternative home in his network of relations. In parallel with his grandson, the older Aupaumut learned that assistance to the colonial military did not ensure that his native village would be protected from colonial settlement. On "moving the kettle," see Aupaumut's "Extract from an Indian History," *Collections of the Massachusetts Historical Society*, 1st ser., 9:101; John W. Quinney's "Memorial to Congress," quoted in J. N. Davidson, *Muh-he-ka-ne-ok: A History of the Stockbridge Nation* (Milwaukee, Wis.: Silas Chapman, 1893). On the elder Aupaumut's move to Stockbridge, see Brasser, *Riding on the Frontier*, 34–36.

45. *ASP-IA* 1:346–47; Cruikshank, ed., *Correspondence of Simcoe*, 2:7, 5:37; White, *The Middle Ground*, 495–96.

46. *ASP-IA* 1:341; Cruikshank, ed., *Correspondence of Simcoe*, 2:6. Washington was prepared to offer the Western Indians $50,000 "in goods" up front, as well as an additional $10,000 worth of goods annually. The documents that traveled between the American leadership and Aupaumut during 1793 demonstrate that both Aupaumut and Brant had made headway in their negotiations with the United States but that Aupaumut was being coerced into increasing complicity with divisive American policy. The Americans instructed Aupaumut not just to carry a message for them, or to mediate, but to present arguments to the Western Indians on behalf of the American compromise "as of yourself, in order to discover how far they may be persuaded to depart from their rigid demands." *ASP-IA* 1:346.

Aupaumut expressed growing concern that he would be perceived as a spy. From his camp at the Miami Rapids Aupaumut wrote to Pickering: "The Shawanese, Wyandots, & Miamis and part of the Delawares have deep prejudice against the Whites, also to us. They expect that I will inform you everything in writing for which I did not sent letters to you before—had they knew that I have sent every necessary intelligence to you they would condemn me." TPP 59:203.

47. TPP 59:203.

48. Cruikshank, ed., *Correspondence of Simcoe*, 2:5–7. For the context of the 1793 councils, see Kelsay, *Joseph Brant*, 491; and White, *The Middle Ground*, 464–68.

49. Cruikshank, ed., *Correspondence of Simcoe,* 2:7.

50. Ibid., 2:11–12.

51. Ibid., 2:13.

52. Ibid., 2:15.

53. Ibid., 2:16.

54. TPP 59:403.

55. Cruikshank, ed., *Correspondence of Simcoe,* 2:16, 102, 193, 3:314. Kelsay has noted, "Some Indians who signed [the statement to the U.S. commissioners] claimed later that this was not their doing and that on hearing of it their women wept. But McKee had told them that they would not get so much as a needleful of thread from the Americans if they gave in to them, and they believed him." Kelsay, *Joseph Brant,* 498, 505 (her source is Halliday Jackson, *Civilization of the Indian Natives* [Philadelphia, Pa.: M. T. C. Gould, 1830], 24–25). The British wanted to maintain an Indian "buffer zone" between their territory in Canada and the United States; see Cruikshank, ed., *Correspondence of Simcoe,* 1:208, 308, 5:317; Kelsay, *Joseph Brant,* 441, 483–91; Stone, *Life of Brant,* 270. Brant had initially insisted that the confederation councils should be an exclusively native space because he feared this kind of colonial interference. The British, however, feared Indian independence. As Governor Simcoe wrote in a letter to his deputy, he did not like Brant's insistence on Indian-only councils: "I am not without suspicion that both this previous meeting and that of the 6 Nations is of Brant's suggestion. The independence of the Indians is his primary object; his views are extensive, and he speaks most contemptuously of the Superintendent General and his Deputies, and indeed, of every body"; see Cruikshank, ed., *Correspondence of Simcoe,* 1:309. Ironically, the British-Shawnee association may have done more to divide the Dish than the Mahican-U.S. partnership, and Brant may have had more to fear from McKee than Aupaumut.

56. Cruikshank, ed., *Correspondence of Simcoe,* 2:17.

57. TPP 59:209.

58. Bernd Peyer, *The Tutor'd Mind: Indian Missionary-Writers in Antebellum America* (Amherst: Univ. of Massachusetts Press, 1997), 19. Aupaumut's own "Narrative" suggests that he was not complicit. When Brant accused him of being an agent of division, he insisted that "I had come with no such intention" and then proceeded to ponder the meaning of Brant's comment in his official report. Perhaps, Aupaumut reflected, Brant referred to the division between those who wanted peace and those who wanted war, which Brant's son may have accused Aupaumut of fomenting. Yet Aupaumut seems to have begun to wonder whether he was being used as an unknowing tool, frequently utilizing the words of Brant and his other relations to raise questions about U.S. duplicity. As Aupaumut reported to Pickering, Brant's message warned: "I have seen the great men of the U.S.—they speak good words to the Muhheconnuck, but they did not speak so well to the Five Nations, and they speak contrary to the Big knifes, that the Big knifes may prepare for war." See TPP 59:41; and Aupaumut, "Narrative," 124. Aupaumut was especially anxious because, by advocating for the Americans, he was risking his own position in the network of relations. If he could not persuade his relations that the new colonial government was sincere, he risked not only the failure of his peacemaking mission but also the loss of the Mahicans' newly secured place in the Algonquian network.

59. TPP 60:72A; Stone, *Life of Brant,* 278. The Mahican leader expressed great disappointment while he was waiting at Niagara in 1791 when he heard that the "army tis gone

across the Indian Country, for which I was very sorry." TPP 60:10–10A. In 1793 he told Pickering, "the Operations of the army was a great obstacle." TPP 59:203.

60. Taylor, "Captain Hendrick Aupaumut," 451; Cruikshank, ed., *Correspondence of Simcoe*, 2:217. One of Aupaumut's achievements was securing an annual appropriation for the Mahicans for their service in the Revolution. Before taking on the role of mediator with the Western Indians, his nation had been "forgotten." During the councils in 1793 he told the Western Indians: "last winter was the first time I had invitation from the great man of the United States to attend Council in Philadelphia"; see Aupaumut, "Narrative," 92. In Philadelphia Washington guaranteed "the yearly appropriation of the sum of one thousand five hundred dollars, for the use and benefit of the Five Nations—the Stockbridge Indians included" in return for their promise to continue to mediate a peace; see *ASP-IA* 1:231.

The "Five Nations" (on the American side) included "the Senecas, Oneidas, and Stockbridge Indians, incorporated with them the Tuscaroras, Cayugas, and Onondogas." In fact, because of Aupaumut's abilities as a mediator, he secured a larger piece of the pot than the Oneidas, causing some resentment among their Iroquois hosts; see Calloway, *American Revolution in Indian Country*, 105. On the Treaty of Canandaigua, see G. Peter Jemison and Anna M. Schein, eds., *Treaty of Canandaigua, 1794* (Santa Fe, N.M.: Clear Light, 2000).

61. Brant Papers, DMC, Ser. F, 12:78–79.

6

"A Superior Civilization"

Appropriation, Negotiation, and Interaction in the
Northwest Territory, 1787–1795

Frazer Dorian McGlinchey

This Strange Monument unquestionably proves that the continent was once inhabited by a superior civilization.[1]

What though the Heathen rage, and savage nations roar and yell in midnight hellish herds. Our feet shall nevertheless stand fast, for our bow is bent in strength, and our arm made strong by the mighty God of Jacob. Through his strength we have laid the foundations of our city, thither shall the tribes go to worship, to worship the mighty God of Israel.[2]

The members of the Ohio Company of Associates who settled the town of Marietta had high hopes for their enterprise as they discussed their plans at Brackett's tavern in Boston on November 21, 1786. They resolved to send out "four surveyors and twenty-two men, six Boat builders, four House carpenters and men, with the Surveyors, [to] be the proprietors of the Company" and ordered that "their tools, one axe and one hoe to each man, and thirty pounds weight of Baggage, be carried in the Companies' Waggons, and their subsistence on the Journey be furnished by the Company." Their New England background and self-image were reflected upon departure west, as the associates changed the name of their boat from the "Adventure Galley" to the "Mayflower." Through judicious planning and selective appropriation of their heritage they believed much was to be achieved in the Northwest.[3]

The lands settled by the Ohio Company of Associates were the first authorized American settlements in the Northwest Territory, having been secured in 1787. Congress had passed an ordinance for organizing survey and sale of western lands on May 20, 1785, which later came to fruition in the Northwest

Ordinance of 1787.[4] It is true, as some historians have asserted, that "the expansion of the Union represented the ultimate test of American sovereignty," yet there was, in addition, a hope that the eventual settlements would not fall prey to the decadence and corruption it was feared may riddle the east: "The Western States will probably retain their primeval simplicity of manners and incorruptible love of liberty." The extended domain of the nation was theoretical, however. In reality the western lands belonged to the United States only in the paperwork and rhetoric of the day. The cession of lands to the Ohio Company was undertaken as much through necessity as ideology. By late 1787 Congress had only sold 73,934 acres of land, raising a paltry $117,108.22 in revenue, quite at odds with the flood of virtuous settlers it had hoped for.[5] This demonstrates the disparity between the myth of settlement as it had been envisaged by legislators and the inability of the government to control American incursions into the land that the nation had claimed control over. More pointedly, such a stance singularly failed to appreciate the hardships inherent in developing the land or in convincing its current indigenous inhabitants of their irrelevance in the future to be mapped out in the Northwest. Indeed, at Marietta the early white settlers of the Old Northwest would find that Indians—both past and present—would impact their visions of a perfect American landscape more than they could rightly imagine.[6]

Following the cession of the lands, the associates settled the main company town of Marietta at the confluence of the Ohio and Muskingum rivers. From its inception the settlement was influenced by Indians. The location of the town was in itself a response to the threat of the tribes, despite the assumed control of the United States over the land. Marietta was built across the Ohio River from the American Fort Harmar, to offer greater protection to the settlers from the neighbors they wished to supplant in the region. As it was, though, the spirit of emigration was apparent in those "banditti" and squatters moving to claim illegal ownership of lands they now considered open. According to accounts from troops at the fort, some 731 boats had passed down the Ohio River between October 1786 and June 1788. The justifiable fear of frontier chaos would certainly serve as a spur for organized action, to combat "the nightmarish prospect of counterrevolution," where "the worst of both worlds would meet: the savagery of sovereign states would unleash the savagery of licentious settlers in their natural state."[7]

The associates believed that this fear alone would reveal the value of the apparently atypical virtue and standing of the Ohio Company members. The vast majority of settlers in Adelphi (as Marietta was originally to be called) were from Massachusetts, Connecticut, and Rhode Island and carried a degree of cultural baggage with them. Significantly, military service had influenced the attitudes of the associates fundamentally and had given them a greater feeling of identity than had their shared New England heritage. Their connection to and affinity with the hierarchy of the new nation was a defining characteristic of the associates as they chose to perceive themselves. Said connections in themselves reaffirmed their own status as gentlemen soldiers. The west provided the chance to prove this point. But their perceived status and rank were at odds with the inability to reach the highest echelons of eastern society, which in itself prompted the move to the Northwest Territory.[8]

This allegiance to government and notion of shared interests helped immeasurably in the securing of lands. Washington wrote to Lafayette that

> A spirit of emigration to the western country is very predominant. Congress has sold in the year past a pretty large quantity of lands on the Ohio for public securities, and thereby diminished the public debt considerably. Many of your military acquaintances, such as Generals Parsons, Varnum and Putnam, Colonels Tupper, Sproat and Sherman, with many more, propose settling there. From such beginnings much may be expected.

Mariettans saw themselves as fundamentally superior to the other settlers arriving in the Northwest Territory, and certainly they considered themselves vastly above the American Indian nations who still lived on the land. They felt no affinity with the "wild Men, either red or white" already in the region; their deference was to the government of Washington and the governorship of St. Clair, and their role was that of standard bearers for the administration in the west. This meant frequent public statements of loyalty and happiness with the government, as in an early letter from the "Inhabitants on the Muskingum" to Governor St. Clair:

> We are fully satisfied with the system of our temporary government: and while gentlemen of the abilities and rectitude of your Excellency and their honors promulgate our laws; we promise ourselves, not with a flattering hope, but with a sure expectation, that we shall be governed by laws, mild in their operation yet efficient for their purposes; such as are founded in wisdom and justice.

Connections to government, exploited for personal gain and publicly displayed, served as a clear vindication of the character of those in the west, both for their self-image and their standing in their community. The settlements they were to oversee would reflect said virtue and ensure a controlling influence on subsequent emigrants to the western lands. Indeed, the members of the Ohio Company were dismissive of the caliber and nature of the other towns springing up in the Northwest. The founders aspired to be atypical from the manners, morals, and customs of the other settlers who moved westward. Moreover, they hoped to influence subsequent settlers by the very nature of the town they had made in the wilderness; the transformation of the landscape was to inspire those who came in their wake and inspire deference and civilization. However, the constraints the founders of the town placed on inhabitants meant that ordinary settlers passed by the town altogether.

Marietta was to simultaneously be a reward for the years of service they had offered the republic and define the expanding nation in tone and character, as the leading lights of the settlement sought to define a meaning of the nation following revolution. The associates hoped that, by systematic planning and development of their town, it would be the first in a string of "Cities of the Confederation" to signal the western expansion of the republic. Inherent in such planning was a significant belief by the settlers in their abilities to determine the future of the nation at a time when its very meaning was still being debated. There was, in addition, a curious overlap between service and self-interest, which seemed in many ways appropriate to attempts at both nation-building and personal advancement on behalf of the Ohio Company of Associates and the government, which ceded them the land.

From the outset, order and discipline were to be imposed on Marietta and the surrounding settlements. The goals of the Ohio Company were to remove their settlements as quickly as possible from a state of nature to one of civilization. Within this there was no perceived tension between the bounty of nature and the development of the city in the west, despite the members' professed love of agrarian bliss and the exaltation of husbandry in the Cincinnatian pantheon. The city was to grow in the wilderness under the watchful eye of the leading members of the company through the transformation and mastery of nature by man.[11]

Yet the relationship between nature and the city was fraught even in theory. "The groves were God's first temples, and the shade and solemn stillness of those vast forests caused a feeling of awe and veneration to steal over the settlers." Despite this, the forest also represented the chaos of nature, which the advent of European Christianity had effectively removed from the faith of the people. The biblical wilderness was the place "where men strayed from the holy path and slid into temptation and blasphemy." There was a duality in meaning of the wilderness as a place of chaos but also "sometimes a place of punitive preparation for salvation."[12]

The land the Ohio Company purchased could offer the chance to fulfill their own vision of nation in the years after the Revolution. "There," proclaimed settler Manasseh Cutler, "in order to begin right, there will be no wrong habits to combat, and no inveterate systems to overturn—there is no rubbish to remove, before you can lay the foundation." Some historians assert that Cutler was referring only to the lack of other white encroachment in the area for the town, thereby leaving the path clear for the unifying vision of the Ohio Company. It can also be seen as unwillingness to acknowledge the importance of the continued presence of native tribes in the west to avoid slowing the sale of lands by raising fears of the savage. Perhaps, though, Cutler was incapable of seeing any "system" or logic in the lives of the "savages" to rival that of those moving west. This stance assumed the west as a blank slate and ignored the human changes in the landscape that had already taken place, from the Adena and Hopewell cultures onward. Land was the means to an end and would simultaneously allow both the imposition of national order and the scope for personal advancement. Importantly, these strands were not viewed as incompatible in the new nation; indeed, the ability of individuals to develop their own interests on the land was to simultaneously enhance their allegiance to government.[13]

Upon their arrival in the Northwest Territory the Ohio Company was immediately confronted with an intriguing challenge to their beliefs and ideology. When the first settlers reached their lands they came across a number of large, complex mounds of earth, including a conical mound surrounded by a parapet, with a ditch within it, complemented by "two truncated pyramids, or elevated squares." The nature and origin of these mounds prompted discussion about the relationship of the settlers with their environment and the history of the area previous to their arrival. Despite their often-professed love of nature, the environment was there to be exploited and changed as best the settlers saw fit. The mounds and earthworks were used as focal points for the city, which was to spring up around them. This was seen in a practical, as well as an ideological light; these strange formations were to be transformed: "These appear to have been the formations of some spacious publick buildings; but however that may be, they are very convenient, and now reserved for that purpose; for the rest of the works can remain, when the city is built, on paper only."[14]

More interesting, though, is the logic the associates applied to the origin of the structures they were confronted with. Instead of acknowledging the indigenous culture of the area (and the continent), a more elaborate and appropriate explanation was concocted:

Solomon Drowne, interested in attaching some kind of classical virtue to them, suggested that they were not unlike the burial mounds of the ancient Trojans, the ancestors of the Roman republicans. Certainly there had been an elaborate civilization on the spot of the Ohio Company settlement and the Mariettans felt a primitive nobility exuding from its remnants.

This is significant in two ways. First, it shows the desire to establish a classical lineage for the American experiment in republicanism. By harking back to antiquity, Americans could distance themselves from the corruption and decadence of contemporary Europeans, despite their shared heritage. Secondly, the stance shows an unwillingness or inability to acknowledge the potential sophistication of the American Indian population at any time, past or present. By creating parameters of savagism and civilization for their current situation, it would be entirely contradictory to acknowledge any lineage between the supposedly heathen Indians and the sophisticated creators of the earthworks.[15]

Early historians of Marietta further perpetuated the notion of the mound builders as some mysterious race, unrelated to the American Indian. Thomas Summers had viewed the tribes as possessing no traditions similar to the mound builders, as did Talbot. Intrigue at the earthworks stretched through many contemporaries of the associates, and the discussion reached important figures in the east. Even European travelers and commentators got in on the act. Jean Pierre Brissot de Warville, while on his travels in the United States, took the same line as early Americans. Speculation even stretched to the president. The conclusion, if slightly more muted, was essentially the same: "These works which are found upon the Ohio . . . traces of the country's having been once inhabited by a people more ingenious, at least, if not more civilized than those who at present dwell there, have excited the enquiries of the curious to learn from whence they came, whither they are gone, and something of their history."[16]

The lack of thought as to the sanctity of the works is also striking. No idea of preserving them intact was given, despite conjecture as to their being some kind of burial mounds. Indeed the great mound in Marietta was leased to the town as a graveyard, despite the fact that it was believed to have already contained the remains of a previous culture on the land. According to Samuel P. Hildreth, "This ancient relic has thus far been carefully preserved, a monument of the good taste of its builders, and an ornament to the city." Instead, the changes were to be incorporated into a new, valid environment. From the outset, they were exploited practically as the basis of the emergent town, as they were discussed in more abstract terms:

> As they ascended from the riverbank to those ruins, they found it easy to trundle their wagons up a graded ramp, one hundred forty feet wide and seven hundred feet in length, while their apprehensions of Indian attack were alleviated by its high protective embankments. This broad ceremonial ascent they rightly called the "Sacra Via."

The mythology ascribed to by the new settlers negated the reality of the very land upon which they settled. The mounds, though, clearly demonstrated that another American civilization had existed on the land long before the grandiose visions of the Ohio Company. It was in itself an advanced culture, and the legacy it left behind on the land rivaled the great Egyptian pyramids.[17]

Still, having seemingly overcome the contradictions inherent in their relationship to the mounds, the associates set about planning the city they would develop in the west. As the focal point of the purchase, Marietta was laid out in such a way as to promote republican virtue throughout the town. Individual purchases had to be "improved" according to a set of guidelines, within a specified time. The conditions for the leasing and ornamenting of public squares, meanwhile, sought to guarantee as pleasant and sophisticated an environment as possible. The squares of Mound Square, Capitolium, Cecilia, and Quadrano were to be identically developed and decorated by those who had leased them. In effect, the Ohio Company was superimposing its identity and beliefs onto the ancient, indigenous culture, which had previously inhabited the area and changed its landscape according to their social structure and beliefs.

Certainly the company was methodical and exact in spelling out what was to be done. Mound Square was leased to General Putnam for twelve years, with clear detail of the improvements to be made. Even indigenous trees and plants were to be supplanted by those that had been deemed appropriate by the new settlers. Aside from the fact that the lands had to be cleared in the region for agriculture and "judicious settlement," the settlers brought trees with them, both for orchards and decoration. Personally, Putnam laid out a nursery for trees with the help of Moravian missionary John Heckewelder. In this manner the Ohio Company was trying to create a sanitized and acceptable version of what had preceded them that was in line with their ideals. The utopia of the landscape, as well as its practical transformation, was not to be left to the vision of the individual on the land. Ownership would not allow a deviation from the overall tone set by the Ohio Company.[18]

However, not all arriving had the same vision of the future. Therefore the associates developed a set of guidelines for the development and upkeep of the donation lands within the purchase. These lands, often on the outskirts of the settlement, were given as a reward for service or offered to those prepared to defend the fringes of the town against the encroachment of the wilderness. Significantly, the company could lay out a plan for altering the previously unchanged environment, just as they could for the native mounds. The specifics for the donation lands were also designed over time as well as space, once again controlling the future to be developed. As these lands were on the edges of the company purchase, it was hoped that their development in such a way would also offer an added degree of military protection. They would be the most troublesome lands to sell, and giving them to enhance the security of the settlements was deemed the most beneficial option. Moreover, the prescribed changes would remove the unordered "wilderness," which would inevitably surround the fledgling town.[19]

Transforming the landscape in such a regimented way would further set the tone of the settlement as a whole, as the individual succumbed to the primacy of the community. Meanwhile all house lots not built upon were forfeited, with the grants made to individuals deemed invalid. The initial responsibility of the settlers to the community included the clearing of the land and the introduction of agriculture. For example, the "Grate Cornfield on the Plain," containing some seventy acres, was "fenced, grubbed, girdled and fit for planting." In this the planning of the Ohio Company revealed their New England heritage, as well as the common experience of transforming wilderness land, making explicit again the wilderness at the edges of the "garden" they were developing. This field was itself a sign of the appropriation of native changes by the settlers on the company lands; the annual fires of the Indians had changed the soil as they had adapted the lands to their own purposes.

Despite the judicious planning and rhetoric of the Ohio Company, the reality of their settlement was quite at odds with the plans they had developed for their city in the west. If the mounds they appropriated pointed to the legacy of the prior inhabitants on the land, the situation in the Northwest Territory would make explicit the gulf between their assumptions of ownership and the reality of the tribes still living in the region. The myths of the land as either "garden" or "wilderness" impacted against the reality that settlers, soldiers, surveyors, and legislators discovered in the journey west. All histories of the region, be they focused on white expansion or on cultural interaction, must acknowledge the fundamental underlying relationship between all inhabitants of the region to the lands they lived on. This relationship relates both to the tangible changes made in terms of a human, or cultural landscape, and to the meanings given to said changes. All relationships and rivalries in the Northwest Territory, whether defined as political, cultural, or economic, were themselves contingent upon the ownership and adaptation of the landscape, both in local and national terms. After all, there remained a gulf between the theoretical possession the United States had of the land and the ability to turn theory into reality. It seems that this fraught transition to reality is taken as a given with the benefit of hindsight. Similarly, the eventual removal of the American Indian nations from a central role in the development of the continent seems inevitable and is therefore removed from many histories, save for the most cursory mention of battles and white expansion.

In this vein, the work of Richard Slotkin provides a foundation for an examination of an American ideology, which allowed the separation of the wilderness land as a resource base from its human inhabitants: "This divisibility of the native and the land permitted the formulation of a myth and ideology in which racial warfare complements the process of agrarian development. The story of American progress and expansion thus took the form of a fable of race war, pitting the symbolic opposites of savagery and civilization, primitivism and progress, paganism and Christianity against each other." Early attempts at expansion in the Northwest Territory served to illuminate the fundamental insecurity of the American position in the region in the present, let alone their visions for the future. Certainly the vision of a future landscape held by the Ohio Company and endorsed by the government (who sold the lands) was effectively one for white, Christian men of suitable moral fiber. Indeed, the regulation imposed on the layout and development of the town was to ensure that the landscape itself communicated the desired virtue and order.[21]

The temporal meanings of landscape, myth, and reality hold a central role in the history of the period as a whole. Each meaning implies a vision of a future landscape, which remained a myth in the present. The legitimacy of this vision as opposed to any others (be they tribes or squatters) was in itself the imposition of a mythology. Indeed, the Americans failed in this period to assert the primacy of their vision through military force, despite often-professed assumptions of superiority and dominance. For the United States to achieve its future, the landscape of the west was to embody all the best virtues, which white, republican, landowning gentlemen bestowed upon themselves. It was believed that this, in turn, would awe the "savages" to either change or vanish and prevent the savagery of the land (as wilderness) from corrupting the lesser members of the new republic who chose to seek self-advancement in the west. Yet to make this mythological future landscape a reality, they had to appropriate a meaning of the past and negate the present in real as well as ideological terms. This related not only to the landscape (and its inhabitants) they discovered in the west, but in a highly selective understanding of their own past.

While the Ohio Company settlers and the government that had endorsed their efforts felt able to negate the legacy of the tribes on the land as they prepared to remove the current inhabitants from the future, they ensured that the negotiation of a shared future between the United States and the American Indian Nations would not occur. For the republic to reach its mythological destiny, the native had to be marginalized and dispossessed. Two such opposing visions and lifestyles were incompatible; there was to be no "middle ground" culturally or literally on the future landscape to develop in the Northwest Territory. As historian Alan Taylor has noted, "One people's freedom came at another's expense. Convinced of the superiority of their race, the citizens of the Early Republic felt that only white men warranted independence. Whites saw Indians as inevitable, and probably deserving, victims of progress, by which they meant the American conquest of the continent and its adaptation to their economic purposes."[22]

These opinions reveal a truth at odds with the aspirations of the Ohio Company and its government. They had not moved onto "virgin land," as the mounds they discovered made explicit. More significant, though, was the fact that the control of the land they assumed was to be contingent upon their relations with the American Indian nations who still called the Northwest Territory home, despite national aspirations of empire.[23]

On July 15, 1788, Arthur St. Clair, governor of the territory, gave a speech at Marietta that urged the settlers to "Endeavour to cultivate a good Understanding with the Natives, without much Familiarity—Treat them on all occasions with Kindness and the strictest Regard to Justice—Run not into their Customs and Habits, which is but too frequent with those who settle near them; but endeavour to induce them to adopt yours." Kindness and justice, then, were to be administered with the fundamental understanding that the culture of the natives was flawed and inferior. This was in part prompted by the very real fear of frontier settlers adopting native customs and thereby becoming white savages in their own right. If, however, advances were made in the quality (and therefore virtue) of life in developed parts of the west, it was believed that this would awe the savages to aspire to similar goals. Such a view is in no way surprising given previous experience with squatters and banditti on the frontier.[24]

Similarly unremarkable was the notion that religion and virtue could prompt the tribes to realize the error of their ways, as St. Clair's words appealed directly to the Puritan heritage of the Ohio Company settlers. In this stance, benevolence and good conduct

will produce on their Parts the utmost Confidence—They will soon become sensible of the superior advantages of a state of Civilization—they will gradually lose their Present Manners, and a Way be opened for introducing amongst them the Gospel of Peace; and you be the happy Instruments in the Hands of Providence of bringing forward that Time which shall surely arrive, when all the Nations of the Earth shall become the Kingdom of JESUS CHRIST.[25]

Significant is the fact that Indian culture in this time was not viewed as a different form of civilization; rather it was simply not civilized at all. Despite the

fact that St. Clair himself was familiar with the beliefs of the tribes, the religious overtones in the governor's exhortations were clear enough, but of
equal importance are the shared social and political goals between the settlers
and the national government.[26]

The early Mariettans' understanding of this issue, as in many others, had
a notion of deference and loyalty to government as fundamental and was referred to explicitly: "We have endeavoured to sow the seeds of peace and harmony in the breasts of the natives. We have treated them like friends, like
brothers and your Excellency's well timed advice has strengthened our resolution, to lead them, if possible by mild and gentle means, to Civilization,
Virtue and Happiness." Aside from the assumption that the Indians were unhappy (with anything other than the repeated and gradually more significant
incursions onto their land), it is clear that the friendship and brotherhood
professed was far from unconditional. Settlers and government alike appeared more inclined to adopt the role of the stern parent, pulling the ignorant child up by his bootstraps. Furthermore, there is the clear implication
that other means, aside from the mild and gentle, would be employed, as became the case in the early 1790s. The outlook of the new Americans from the
outset did not take a favorable view of the native population to be transformed. The religious zeal of many Ohio Company members added to this
perspective and made peaceful cohabitation of the area unlikely from the outset. "I cannot say I am fond of them, for they are frightfully ugly, and a pack of
thieves and beggars," wrote John May. "One of their chiefs died a day before
yesterday, and I am thankful another is just a going to his black master. These
Indians are of an evil nature."[27]

This mentality, though, had little bearing on the reality of the early inhabitants of the Northwest Territory. At the outset of the organized American
settlement, the tribes there already had experience of expansion in the incursions onto the land by frontier banditti and unauthorized settlers. This weakened the credibility of government, but the complexity of the situation
muddied the waters further. Historians have rightly depicted "Indian country" at this time as "the home of a multi-cultural society, in which Indian
societies often included members of several tribes as well as individuals of European descent." By the late 1780s a Confederacy of Tribes had come into
being, as a direct response to American encroachment in the region. Originally advocated in 1783 by Mohawk chief Joseph Brant, the confederacy was
dominated by the Shawnees and the Miamis, who refused to accept American
demands for their land. While divisions were rife, the native stance was in part
dictated by United States policy in the area following the Treaty of Paris in
1783. According to the Americans, the tribes, through their allegiance to the

British in the Revolutionary War, had forfeited their lands. Apparently abandoned by their British allies, the Indians now faced an American policy that outlined unacceptable and non-negotiable terms: "All lands south of the international boundary line belonged to the United States. Tribes in these lands were a conquered and subdued people and subject to the wishes of the United States. Congress could move these Indians, either to Canada, or towards the Mississippi."[28]

This stance softened somewhat in light of later events, but United States government policy continued to focus on the apparently inevitable acquisition of Indian land. Indeed, the petition of the Continental army officers for land in the Northwest Territory states as much in the assertion from the petitioners that "whenever the honorable Congress shall be pleased to procure the aforesaid lands of the natives, they will make a provision for the location and survey of the lands." The rhetoric of the United States for brotherhood and cohabitation thus had a largely hollow ring to it in the 1780s. Still, an apparent respect for the rights of the Indians had been written into the Northwest Ordinance itself:

The utmost good faith shall always be observed towards the Indians; their lands and property, rights and liberty shall never be taken without their consent; and in their property, rights and liberty, they shall never be invaded or disturbed, unless in just and lawful wars authorised by Congress; but laws founded in justice and humanity shall from time to time be made, for preventing wrongs being done to them, and for preserving peace and friendship with them.

Yet the new, apparently benevolent stance of the United States had another aspect to it: it allowed for a "purchase" policy of land by the new nation, eager to extend its dominion and reap much needed financial rewards. The respect for native land rights was little more than a charade.[29]

Indian allegiance thus eventually stayed with the British, in no small part because of the markedly different relations that the two governments had with the nations. Once organized, the Indian tribes of the Northwest Territory refused to accept the land cessions made by the treaties at Fort Stanwix, Fort McIntosh, and the Mouth of the Great Miami. These, they contended, had not been ratified by all the tribes and were therefore invalid. There was also anger that those signing the treaties (particularly Stanwix) did not have the status to grant the cessions and the subsequent boundaries being pressed by the United States as a matter of law. However, the American response seemed to threaten genocide for the nations concerned: "You mention your design of going to the

Miami Indians, to endeavour to persuade them to peace. By this humane measure you will render these mistaken people a great service, and, probably, prevent them from being swept off the face of the earth."

The company settlers were to be made further aware of relations between the Americans and the tribes at the 1789 Treaty of Fort Harmar, but the military actions undertaken by the United States against the Confederacy of Tribes were removed from the immediate vicinity of the Ohio Company lands. Still, the outbreak of the Northwest Indian wars fundamentally affected all aspects of development, despite aspirations to the contrary. In particular, the inability of American troops under Josiah Harmar to check the "haughty savages" in 1791 threatened the stability and security of the Marietta community. Early that year, some of the Ohio Company settlers had left the existing accommodation in the purchase and formed another settlement some forty miles up the river from Marietta, called Big Bottom. Thirty-six men had commenced the improvement of the land, building a blockhouse with cabins nearby, but a joint Delaware and Wyandot war party, intent on destroying the neighboring settlement of Waterford, attacked when they came across the new incursion onto what they still saw as their land. Joseph Barker, in his *Recollections of the First Settlement of Ohio,* saw the failings in finishing the blockhouses in a somewhat grander light:

> They put up a large Blockhouse, which might accommodate the whole in an immergancy [*sic*], Covered it, & laid pinchen floors, & the House was laid up of large Beech logs and rather Open, & it was not Chinked—this Job being left for a rainy day or some more Convenient season. Here was the first greate error, here their building of Babel stop'd and the general interest was lost in that of the convenience of each individual, & with this, all was lost.

And naturally Barker believed the changes in the land because of winter contributed to the success of the Indians in addition to any human failing: "The Indians from the opposite hill had watched their Motions—the ground was froze, the River was froze Over & strong covered with snow. When it began to grow dusk, the Indian[s] slipped across the River, surrounded the Blockhouse, and each had a deliberate ame [*sic*] at the inmates through the Door & cracks between the Logs."[31]

During the attack twelve settlers were killed and two others taken captive. Two settlers in a camp near to the blockhouse rushed to Waterford to raise the alarm. The Indians made it clear that this attack signaled war in the region: "Before departing, they left a war club in a conspicuous place, which is their mode of letting their enemies know that war is begun, and is equivalent to a written declaration among civilized powers."[32]

The attack at Big Bottom had a clear effect on the aspirations of the Ohio Company settlers toward their landscape. Their immediate priority became survival rather than personal advancement. Following the attack, the leaders of Marietta, the most conspicuously loyal of settlements in the Northwest Territory, voiced concern about the intentions of the federal government in the region. Rufus Putnam told Secretary of War Henry Knox:

> I hope that the government will not be long in deciding what part to take, for if we are not to be protected, the sooner we know it the better; better that we withdraw ourselves at once than to be destroyed piecemeal by the savages; better that the government disband their troops now in the country and give it up altogether, than to be wasting public money in supporting a few troops, totally inadequate to the purpose of giving peace to the territory.

Putnam also wrote to President Washington to voice his concerns and describe the events at Big Bottom:

> On the evening of the 2d instant, between sunset and daylight-in, the Indians surprised a new settlement of our people, at a place on the Muskingum, called the Big-bottom . . . in which disaster eleven men, one woman, and two children, were killed: three men are missing, and four others made their escape. Thus, sir, the war which was partial before the campaign of last year, is, in all probability, become general: for I think there is no reason to suppose that we are the only people on whom the savages will wreak their vengeance.[33]

In his communications with the federal government, Putnam highlighted the relative isolation of the settlements and noted that there were few troops at Fort Harmar to offer protection for Marietta. This made the Mariettans very uneasy. As settler Dudley Woodbridge remarked, "The defeat of our army has thrown us into some consternation, [but] we are making ourselves as defendable as possible." Thus plans for the creation of a sophisticated society in the long term had to be put aside simply to ensure the continued presence of the settlers on the land, despite their previous assumptions of dominance. Moreover, the infrastructure of the very system of government they had subscribed to appeared to have abandoned its most loyal subjects in the west during their time of need. Putnam declared that "our situation is truly critical; the governor and secretary both being absent, no aid from Virginia or Pennsylvania can be had." Under such perceived duress, the Ohio Company's grand vision for an altered landscape was clouded by the settlers' need to secure their immediate safety. In a letter to Washington, Putnam highlighted the extent of the Company's accomplishments to date, but lamented that "before the late disaster, we had several other settlements, which are already broken up." Moreover, he feared that war might bring the destruction of the settler's "corn, forage and cattle," making life in the west untenable and preventing the sale of lands, leaving the poorer members of the community isolated, fearful, and destitute.[34]

Warfare in the Northwest Territory had a fundamental effect on the Ohio Company lands. Long-term plans for an elaborate and thriving landscape were replaced by the short-term necessity of securing the lands they had already assumed ownership of and subsequently settled. The inhabitants also resorted to diplomacy in an effort to secure their place in the west. Despite the attack at Big Bottom, in March 1791 the settlers found themselves playing host to "twelve or thirteen Indian Chiefts in a perogue, from the low country going on to the seat of government." The military background of the settlers was much evident during the meeting, as was a gulf between the settlers in Marietta proper and an area known simply as "the Point," the main center on company lands for trade with the tribes as well as passing travelers. The rivalry between the settlers outweighed the disdain for the Indians in this case, and the leading members of the Ohio Company displayed their love of ceremony for their native guests as well as stressing their vision of the military order they intended to impose on both Indians and settlers in that part of the Northwest Territory:

> The Inhabitents were all under Arms, the Guard, in Uniform, drawn up near where the Indians came in. On their entering, the drum struck up a salute, the Guard presented arms, The Cannon was fired in the Northeast bastion; the Indians dodged at the report and looked surprised. Here Genl. Putnam and Doct. Story received them, and marched to Major Putnam's to dine. After dinner they looked round a little and marched as they came. Colonel Sproat was not invited; as the Point folks did not invite Campus Martius, they did not invite the Point.[35]

As it was, however, the Ohio Company undertook changes to the lands in an effort for greater security, trying to sustain their very presence in the west. The outlying settlements were largely abandoned, and the settlers moved into blockhouses for greater protection in case of attack. The settlers may have remained optimistic about the chances to transform their own lands for profit, but the reality was that the Company defenses had to be organized and the lands farmed for the subsistence of all. The spaces between houses were shored up with "pickets and pallisades" to better secure the outlying lands. Of the blockhouses that soon dotted the landscape, Campus Martius at Marietta was still the main settlement on the company lands. However, the ability of the leading associates as distinguished ex-soldiers did not prevent some mistakes in the changes undertaken, despite their apparently unwavering self-belief.[36]

If the main focus of the lands was the blockhouse of Campus Martius, it was not the only change in the landscape around Marietta. One contemporary stated that

Twenty very comfortable houses, made of round logs, for families, and covered with long shingles, are already erected in the town. Nor is this all the labour we have done. Large quantities of land have been cut over and fitted for wheat and rye; besides which, several persons have begun to prepare land for planting next spring, and what is very extraordinary, very few of us have been able to work on our own land.

Aside from Campus Martius, the settlers elsewhere on the company lands had to transform the landscape to ensure their safety rather than express their goals for the future. The settlers at the Point had "No Blockhouse or picketts for defence." Therefore, it was resolved to build an enclosure for the settlers. A large blockhouse with a sentry box was erected at Front Street. For greater security, a line of pickets was erected to the bank of the Muskingum River, and a small blockhouse with a sentry box was erected. Elsewhere, the Belpre settlers showed their love of symbolism on the land with the choice of name for their enclosure. Reflecting their Cincinnatian heritage and professed love of agriculture, they named the fortification "Farmer's Castle." As with the other blockhouses throughout the war, the corner blockhouses were provided with sentry posts to keep guard. But this was far from an ideal scenario for the settlers forced to move, as it made their crops and animals more distant; hardly the realization of the Cincinnatian dream.

Life remained relatively peaceful on the Ohio Company purchase in the months following Arthur St. Clair's defeat. Despite limited attacks, the dreaded wholesale onslaught by the Indian Confederacy throughout the settlements did not materialize. Troops had been stationed around the settlements, providing the settlers with greater protection as well as a market for the goods they managed to cultivate, but their presence eventually proved unnecessary. Still, the changes made to the landscape around Marietta were to have a lasting use for the settlers. Tillinghast had overseen the erection of a blockhouse for the troops stationed at the Point, "built by the United States troops, super-intended by a Carpenter from the Citizens, paid by the U.S." After the war it was used as a courthouse and jail. This example illustrates how the mean-ing of a landscape created out of necessity changed after the war, rather than demonstrating how the Ohio Company succeeded in designing and molding the landscape to fit its own aspirations.[38]

The lull in alarms from the tribes was largely the result of the focus of the warfare having been so far removed from the company settlements. While the long-term fortunes of settlers were directly related to the pretensions of the United States, day-to-day life became more relaxed as the settlers tried to transform more of the lands. Certainly, more settlers were venturing be-yond the confines of the blockhouses to cultivate the lands for their own ben-efit. But this resulted in a degree of conflict between the soldiers and settlers, as the gates of the garrisons were closed at night. Around Campus Martius procedure was changed as well as the landscape:

> A number of families who had houses, stock & outside the garrison, re-sided out by day and returned in by Night. This made it difficult to con-form to the strict policies of the garrison, as the Citizen had to provide his own rations while the soldiers were fed by the public. Many necessary cir-cumstances prevented the Citizen from so arranging his business as to be in the garrison before sunset. Several families moved out into houses in the vicinity of the garrison, and staid out at the risk of the Indians. A consid-erable [amount] of Land was cultivated about the Court House and round by Mr. Slocum's, and out on Hart Street. People who were out here and about Campus Martius were not disturbed by the Indians, and staid out until peace.[39]

Joseph Barker, writing with the benefit of hindsight, saw the regimented control of the Ohio Company lands as the main deterrent to the tribes, par-ticularly when compared to the caliber of the other settlers on the western lands:

> The Indians, finding themselves so closely watched by Men who were their compeers in their own arts of Warfare, and more Vigilent [sic] and untir-ing Soldiers, they (the Indians) became indifferent to enterprises where they were more likely to meet with kicks than coppers, and probably might result in loss and disasters far exceeding any disasters to be obtained.

Like the other settlements in the area, the Indian wars fundamentally affected Marietta. The goals the settlers brought with them for the rapid transforma-tion of the "wilderness" into the garden of the nation were not realized, and the most tangible changes to the landscape were the cramped blockhouses and defenses needed to sustain their very presence on the lands.[40]

The appropriation and adaptation of the mounds can be seen as fundamental in the development of Marietta and offers an insight into the perception of the age, even if it does strike us at odds with the reality of the Northwest Territory in the 1780s and 1790s. Regardless of how American legislators and settlers sought to define the savage as distinct from themselves, they could not so easily theorize away the tangible presence of Indians in the region. Moreover, the inability of the Ohio Company to realize their elaborate vision for the town during the Northwest Indian wars of the 1790s serves as a reminder of how tenuous a grasp the United States had on the lands they had assumed premature ownership of. The Ohio Company lands remained atypical of the rest of the region, much as the associates had planned. However, they never realized the glorious vision of their founders following the eventual removal of the Indians from Ohio.

Their failure to realize their utopian vision for the landscape was inevitable, as was their own exalted place in the expansion of the republic throughout the west. Despite the distance of the Ohio Company settlements from the main military campaigns in the region, the settlers failed to make significant advances toward the city they originally envisaged, showing explicitly the gulf between the mythology they subscribed to and the fraught reality of the early expansion of the United States in the Northwest Territory. It is the disparity between the aspirations for an expanding republic (legitimized by the subsequent scope of the United States far beyond the Old Northwest), and the myriad problems faced in realizing that goal, which helps us better grasp the intricacies of the struggle for preeminence at such a critical juncture for the Early Republic. While atypical, the attitudes and experiences of those who settled the Ohio Company lands offer a unique insight into the early stages of the transition toward an American landscape, and the passing of what it was to replace.

NOTES

1. Brissot de Warville, *New Travels in the United States of America* (Cambridge, Mass.: Harvard Univ. Press, 1964), 416.

2. John May, "Journal of a Journey from Boston Massachusetts to the Mouth of the Muskingum," Ohio Company Records, Marietta Collection, Ohio Historical Society, Columbus, Ohio.

3. Joseph Barker, *Recollections of the First Settlement of Ohio*, ed. George Jordan Blazer (Marietta, Ohio: Richardson Printing Company, 1958), 3. Rufus Putnam and Benjamin Tupper had advertised for "adventurers" to move to lands "of a much better quality than

any known to New England people." They appointed agents throughout Massachusetts, Connecticut, Rhode Island, and New Hampshire to organize settlement, and a committee drew up a plan of settlement. By March 8, 1787, 250 shares had been "subscribed," and Cutler was employed to make a contract with the Continental Congress. Thus the plan for settlement had been formulated before the lands were secured. See Samuel P. Hildreth, *Pioneer History: Being an Account of the First Examinations of the Ohio Valley and the Early Settlement of the Northwest Territory* (Cincinnati, Ohio: Derby, 1848), 194–96.

4. For the 1785 Ordinance, Clarence Edwin Carter, ed., *The Territorial Papers of the United States,* 28 vols. (Washington, D.C.: GPO, 1934–75), 2:12–18. In 1784 Thomas Jefferson led a committee to establish the basis of government in the west. With his grid system Jefferson simplified the geography of the west by the imposition of theory, and originally proposed the land be divided into states. The new territories would, though, have to be settled properly. Jefferson proposed that the west be settled in "hundreds," ten geographical mile square townships bounded by lines running north-south and east-west and divided into lots of 850 acres each. The plan for hundreds was amended before the 1787 Ordinance, since the grid system adopted under Jefferson showed in itself the gulf between myth and reality; "As of 1785, the national grid was a statement of intent rather than a description of reality," since the land was to be surveyed, not "located."

See Gregory H. Nobles, *American Frontiers: Cultural Encounters and Continental Conquest* (New York: Hill and Wang, 1997), 93; John R. Stilgoe, *Common Landscape of America, 1580–1845* (New Haven, Conn.: Yale Univ. Press, 1982), 103; and Edward Countryman, *Americans: A Collision of Histories* (New York: Hill and Wang, 1996), 78. For an overview of the Northwest Ordinance and its implementation, see Peter S. Onuf, *Statehood and Union: A History of the Northwest Ordinance* (Bloomington: Indiana Univ. Press, 1987), *The Origins of the Federal Republic* (Philadelphia: University of Pennsylvania Press, 1983), 42–172, and "From Constitution to Higher Law: The Reinterpretation of the Northwest Ordinance," *Ohio History* 94 (1985): 5–33.

For more on the process leading to the 1787 Ordinance, including the cessions of the states and the drafting of the 1784 version, see C. B. Galbreath, "The Ordinance of 1787: Its Origin and Authorship," *Ohio Archaeological and Historical Society Quarterly* 33 (1924): 111–75; and Andrew R. L. Cayton, *The Frontier Republic: Ideology and Politics in the Ohio Country, 1780–1825* (Kent, Ohio: Kent State Univ. Press, 1986), 1–32. Madison advocated expansion over space, while Jefferson's concept of an Empire of Liberty would allow the nation to expand without the inherent damage it was feared affected all republics; see Eric Hinderaker, *Elusive Empires: Constructing Colonialism in the Ohio Valley, 1673–1800* (New York: Cambridge Univ. Press, 1997), 185; and R. Douglas Hurt, *The Ohio Frontier: Crucible of the Old Northwest, 1720–1830* (Bloomington: Indiana Univ. Press, 1996), 143–78.

5. Cathy D. Matson and Peter S. Onuf, *A Union of Interests: Political and Economic Thought in Revolutionary America* (Lawrence: Univ. of Kansas Press, 1990), 60; Proposed Address to Congress, April 1789, John Fitzpatrick, ed., *Writings of George Washington,* 39 vols. (Washington, D.C.: GPO, 1931–44), 113. This was in effect the test of the reality of American sovereignty, as the theory had already been established with the passing of the Treaty of Paris and the Northwest Ordinance. Certainly colonial governments in the period prior to revolution had been interested in the possibility of western expansion; Simon Newman has argued that the original colonial charters can be viewed in the light

of future expansion. As it was, though, the Northwest Ordinance offered a vision for the nation as it attempted to expand. The hopes and fears of Americans were projected onto the western lands. See Roger Kennedy, *Hidden Cities: The Discovery and Loss of Ancient North American Civilization* (New York: Free, 1994), 109.

6. Onuf, *Statehood and Union*, 42. As one historian has put it, "On paper these ordinances seemed just and reasonable. The problem is that they had nothing to do with reality." Daniel Friedenberg, *Life, Liberty and the Pursuit of Land: The Plunder of Early America* (Buffalo, N.Y.: Prometheus, 1992), 276. The United States found itself in the paradox of 1783: the domain of the country existed only on paper. See Hinderaker, *Elusive Empires*, 225; Nobles, *American Frontiers*, 91–92; Matson and Onuf, *A Union of Interests*, 63–66.

7. Matson and Onuf, *A Union of Interests*, 66; citation from Richard White, *The Middle Ground: Indians, Empires, and Republics in the Great Lakes Region, 1650–1815* (New York: Cambridge Univ. Press, 1991). Marietta was to be built across the river from the fort to offer greater protection from the tribes. The placing of the fort in 1785 reflected attempts by the nation to establish their ascendancy over the land and its inhabitants. See Kim Gruenwald, "Marietta's Example of a Settlement Pattern in the Ohio Country: A Reinterpretation," *Ohio History* 105 (1996): 126–44. The fort was at the forefront of relations with the tribes in the years prior to the arrival of the Ohio Company settlers. It was thirty miles from the falls of the Muskingum, where the Indian nations would convene prior to treaties. Indeed, the fort was a bone of contention between the tribes and the governor of the Northwest Territory, Arthur St. Clair. He wanted treaties to take place at Fort Harmar rather than the falls, where Joseph Brant, the de facto leader and initiator of the Confederacy of Tribes, had insisted. The fort became the site of a graphic display of the gulf between the pretensions of the United States toward the tribes for the future of the lands and the reality of the years to follow for settlers and government alike. The Treaty of Fort Harmar, signed on January 9, 1789, convinced Harmar and St. Clair that the confederacy had capitulated. It was not the case; the Shawnees rejected the Treaty of Fort Harmar out of hand and reminded the Americans that the Senecas, Wyandots, and Delawares did not speak for the confederacy and that its lands were "not in the power of one or two nations to dispose of." The confederacy believed that it had little choice but to face the "encroachers." Runners carried war pipes to the various tribes and a delegation went to Detroit for ammunition from the British. Hurt, *Ohio Frontier*, 104.

8. Andrew R. L. Cayton and Peter S. Onuf, eds., *The Midwest and the Nation: Rethinking the History of an American Region* (Bloomington: Indiana Univ. Press, 1990), 50.

9. *History of Washington County, Ohio, 1788–1881* (Salem, W.Va.: Don Mills, 1989), 44; Ichabod Nye journal, quoted in Andrew R. L. Cayton, "Marietta and the Ohio Company," Robert D. Mitchell, ed., *Appalachian Frontiers: Settlement, Society, and Development in the Pre-Industrial Era* (Lexington: Univ. Press of Kentucky, 1991), 189; July 16, 1788, *Territorial Papers*; Hurt, *Ohio Frontier*, 156–60.

10. Settler Winthrop Sargent reflected such an attitude. In 1792 he moved from his beloved Marietta to Cincinnati for his role as secretary of the territory. The gulf between the two towns was, in his eyes, glaring: He despaired that the people of Cincinnati and Marietta "seem to never have been intended to live under the same government—the latter are very like our Forefathers and the former (generally) very licentious and too great a proportion indolent and extremely debauched." Andrew R. L. Cayton, "A Quiet

Independence: The Western Vision of the Ohio Company," *Ohio History* 90 (1981): 5–32. For more on the contrast between the towns, see Hurt, *Ohio Frontier,* 179–89.

11. This relates to the attitudes of the Cincinnati who were ceded the lands on which Marietta was to be built: "At Valley Forge, around their campfires, Washington had spoken to them all . . . of a world to be won beyond the mountains, a new, purged, open chance. Won and then to be organized. The Cincinnatian dream he offered in their encampment was of a hierarchic, deferential, Roman colony—differing from those of the Romans in being without the abomination of slavery. Life with old comrades still called to George Washington at the end of the 1780s." Kennedy, *Hidden Cities,* 113.

12. S. Talbot, "Benjamin Tupper and His Times," MSS 210, Ohio Company Records, Marietta Collection; Stilgoe, *Common Landscape of America,* 7. The desire was to oversee the building of a City of the Confederation, civilized and advanced in the sciences and arts but still primarily agrarian. This overlaps the ambivalence many Ohio Company members felt toward trade and commerce and their dependence on it to reach their goals. Early in the settlement public worship was held in the hall of Campus Martius, as such removed from the nature around the settlemen, and reaffirming the common faith and solidarity of the settlers in their goal to transform the land. However, there was not a church specifically built early on that would symbolize the changes in the landscape made by a devout and God-fearing people. The underlying intent and belief of the settlers would have to suffice in the present before the landscape itself could embody their character in the future.

13. Manasseh Cutler cited in P. Lee Phillips, ed., *First Map and Description of Ohio, 1787, by Mannasseh Cutler* (Washington, D.C.: W. H. Lowdermilk, 1917), 36; Kennedy, *Hidden Cities,* 115–19. For utopian visions see James E. Vance, "Democratic Utopia and the American Landscape," in Michael P. Cozen, ed., *The Making of the American Landscape* (London: Harper Collins, 1990). For more on the Adena and Hopewell periods, see ibid., 243–87; and Jesse D. Jennings, *Prehistory of North America* (New York: McGraw-Hill, 1968), 212–65.

14. Hildreth, *Pioneer History,* 213; News from the Ohio, letter to Massachusetts Spy, Ohio Historical Society. Certainly the mounds at Marietta had their equivalent throughout the western lands and witnessed the appropriation of the original changes to the land once before, as has been discussed by Kennedy: "The precise relationship between the Adena cone builders and the Hopewellian geometers is an enigma, but to me it is arresting to observe how often the latter built their monuments close to those of the former, integrating their predecessors' work into the grand schemes of their own devising. This was true at Chillicothe, where the Hopewell structures at Dunlap and Ginther were placed on the same north-south axis as the Adena mound. Adena conical mounds were also brought into Hopewell schemes at Marietta and Portsmouth, by rectangles and lengthy parallels." Kennedy, *Hidden Cities,* 265. Moreover, the changes in the landscape were far from haphazard, as borne out by the comparisons first made by William Romain: "He has discovered that the great square which so astounded the Cincinnati at Marietta could precisely contain four of the smaller circles, equal in size to each other, to be found along Paint Creek, and, also, four of the smaller squares to be found, also in equal size to each other, in the same complexes along Paint Creek." Ibid., 268.

15. Cayton, *Frontier Republic,* 29.

16. Thomas J. Summers, *History of Marietta* (Marietta, Ohio: Leader, 1903); S. Talbot, "Benjamin Tupper and His Times," MSS 210, Ohio Company Records, Marietta Collection; de Warville, *New Travels*, 416; Fitzpatrick, *Writings of George Washington*, 370.

17. Hildreth, *Pioneer History*, 242; Kennedy, *Hidden Cities*, 114. It seems likely that the mounds served a ceremonial and cultural role in the society that built them rather than the aesthetics Hildreth seems concerned with.

18. Mandated improvements included the following: (1) Surround squares with mulberry trees; (2) Elm tree at each corner; (3) Base of mound to be encircled by weeping willows; (4) Evergreens on the mound; (5) Circular parapet outside to be encircled with trees; and (6) All to be enclosed with a fence. Capitolium and Mound Square were to be decorated in an identical manner. The squares were to have a different meaning than the rest of the land, to "remain undisturbed by the plow." Putnam was put in charge of Sacra Via for its preservation, and it was seeded with grass. Meanwhile Putnam, Jabez True, and Paul Fearing were made trustees of the squares, to carry out the intentions of the Ohio Company. The rents to be made were "to be appropriated to the education of indigent orphan children of Marietta." Hildreth, *Pioneer History*, 281. For more on the land in the region prior to the arrival of the Ohio Company, see Hurt, *Ohio Frontier*, 4.

19. Military improvements mandated by the Ohio Company included: (1) Settlers to furnish land for highways when needed; (2) Build dwelling house within five years, twenty-four by eighteen feet, eight feet between floors, cellar ten feet square, stone or brick chimney; (3) Put out no less than fifty apple trees and twenty peach within three years; (4) Clear or put into meadow or pasture fifteen acres and into tillage not less than five acres, within five years; (5) To be constantly provided with arms, and subject to militia laws; and (6) Proper defenses or blockhouses to be kept on donation of lands, of such strength as approved by committee. Hildreth, *Pioneer History*, 282.

20. Stilgoe, *Common Landscape of America*, 51; Archer Butler Hulbert, ed., *Records of the Original Proceedings of the Ohio Company* (Marietta, Ohio: Marietta Historical Commission, 1917), 109; Barker, *Recollections*, 64. Despite the New England background of the settlers, it seems that girdling was primarily the southern method of clearing the land and in itself owed much to the technique used by the Indians. This had the advantage of allowing crops to be planted immediately on the land—clearly a benefit for early settlers. The traditional New England technique involved cutting the trees down and burning them, a laborious process by which to clear personal plots. See Robert L. Jones, *A History of Agriculture in Ohio to 1880* (Kent, Ohio: Kent State Univ. Press, 1983), 27–28.

21. Richard Slotkin, *The Fatal Environment: The Myth of the Frontier in the Age of Industrialization, 1800–1890* (New York: Atheneum, 1985), 53.

22. Alan Taylor, "Land and Liberty on the Post-Revolutionary Frontier," in David Thomas Konig, ed., *Devising Liberty: Preserving and Creating Freedom in the New American Republic* (Stanford, Calif.: Stanford Univ. Press, 1995), 86.

23. Again for potentially loaded terminology in terms of historiography, see Henry Nash Smith, *Virgin Land: The American West as Symbol and Myth*, 2nd ed. (Cambridge, Mass.: Harvard Univ. Press, 1970).

24. Richard C. Knopf, ed., *Executive Journals of the Northwest Territory* (Columbus, Ohio: Anthony Wayne Parkway Board, 1957), 4.

25. Ibid. This idea is in itself contradictory when used in relation to the expansion of a specific nation (the United States) rather than the Kingdom of Jesus Christ, which would not differentiate between nations. The nations of the earth, which do not succumb to Christianity, though, are in themselves damned.

26. This can be seen from the journals of the Moravian missionary John Heckewelder, who dined with St. Clair at the Ohio Company blockade Campus Martius in October 1788: "While I was dining with the Governor, the first part of the dinner conversation was about the Turtle and how it carried up the island (the earth) out of the depths of the sea on its back and out of it made this land for the Indians." See the entry for October 13, 1788, in Paul A. W. Wallace, ed., *The Travels of John Heckewelder in Frontier America* (Pittsburgh, Pa.: Univ. of Pittsburgh Press, 1958), 226. This creation story made explicit in itself the relationship of the natives and the land on which they lived.

27. Knopf, ed., *Executive Journals of the Northwest Territory*, 4; John May, "Journal of a Journey from Boston Massachusetts to the Mouth of the Muskingum Ohio," Marietta Collection, Ohio Historical Society. The negative caricaturing of the natives based on belief, and the violence that went hand-in-hand with it, were nothing new; however, the region in which the Ohio Company was expanding saw a chance for cohabitation vanish. Of course, this cohabitation was in part based on expediency and necessity, but it still fostered a language and behavior that promoted a higher degree of understanding between the inhabitants.

28. Colin G. Calloway, "Beyond the Vortex of Violence: Indian-White Relations in the Ohio Country, 1784–1795," *Northwest Ohio Quarterly* 64 (1992): 19. In particular, the Miami chief Little Turtle and the Shawnee Blue Jacket became the dominant figures in the confederacy militarily, as they met the American troops under Harmar, St. Clair, and Wayne. The assertion that the tribes were conquered and subdued related to relations between Britain and the United States rather than with the tribes themselves. See Robert S. Allen, *His Majesty's Indian Allies: British Indian Policy in the Defence of Canada, 1774–1815* (Toronto: Dundurn, 1992), 61.

29. "Report of a committee of Congress on ability of the Ohio Company to fulfill their contract with the Government," Ohio Company Papers, Marietta Collection, Ohio Historical Society; Article III, Northwest Ordinance, in Michael D. Gambone, ed., *Documents of American Diplomacy: From the American Revolution to the Present* (Westport, Conn.: Greenhaven, 2002), 20–24; Wiley Sword, *President Washington's Indian War: The Struggle for the Old Northwest, 1790–1795* (Norman: Univ. of Oklahoma Press, 1985), 50.

30. *American State Papers: Documents, Legislative and Executive, of the Congress of the United States of America*, 38 vols. (Washington, D.C.: Gales and Seaton, 1832–1861), 143. For more on the Fort McIntosh and Mouth of the Great Miami treaties, see Hurt, *Ohio Frontier*, 95–97; for those and Stanwix, see Hinderaker, *Elusive Empires*, 232. Richard White sees the gulf between the aspirations of the new nation and the reality of their inability to control the frontier as the impetus for the problems they were to encounter in the early 1790s: "The American republic that claimed to have conquered most of the pays d'en haut was in fact but one of a group of powers competing for control of the region.... [T]hese treaties, the product of American illusions, launched the republic into a conflict with the western Indian confederation and the British"; see White, *The Middle Ground*, 417. The Americans chose to manifest their supposed dominance by the overt use of force and threats against the tribes.

31. Barker, *Recollections*, 67–69. The second error was the failure to post sentries as the inhabitants had their guns strewn around the blockhouse. Significantly, Marienstras deals with the attack on settlers as a construct: "In every story, the pioneer hut is encircled by savagery. . . . [T]he two territories are visibly separated: the door of the cabin is the vulnerable spot through which barbarism threatens to invade the civilized space. On one side of the door is the intimacy of the home, the warm relations among the family, the innocence of the children, the courage of the women, and the technical aspects of civilization—comfortable furniture, protective guns, or else useful knives and axes; on the other disorganized wild gangs who are united only by their greed and sadism." See Elise Marienstras, "The Common Man's Indian: The Image of the Indian as a Promoter of National Identity in the Early National Era," in Fredrick N. Hoxie, Ronald Hoffman, and Peter J. Albert, eds., *Native Americans and the Early Republic* (Charlottesville: The Univ. Press of Virginia, 1999), 282. Blockhouses were the common way to ensure the protection of the settlers throughout the Indian war, offering greater protection from attacks. Campus Martius was the main center in the company settlements, with Farmer's Castle built by the inhabitants at Belpre.

32. The prisoners were treated well by their captors. Isaac Choate, one of those taken, was nearly killed to avenge the life of an Indian injured in the attack, but he made a full recovery. Most were released, with James Patten adopted into a native family until the conclusion of hostilities with the tribes in 1795. See Hildreth, *Pioneer History*, 438–39. The warning given by the two settlers near Waterford was in itself significant, bearing in mind the disdain that lawful settlers of the company lands held for squatters in the West. It was settlers occupying homes erected by squatters who went to Waterford to raise the alarm. See H. E. Frye, *Waterford and Fort Frye on the Muskingum in the Old Northwest Territory during Indian War* (Lowell, Ohio: Spencer Kile, 1938).

33. Rufus Putnam to Henry Knox, January 8, 1791, United States Congress, *American State Papers: Indian Affairs*, 2 vols. (Washington, D.C.: Gales and Seaton, 1832–1861), 1:105 [hereafter cited as *ASP-IA*]; Putnam to George Washington, January 8, 1791, ibid., 107.

34. Dudley Woodbridge Diary, January 7, 1791, Backus-Woodbridge Collection, Box 1, Fol. 3; Putnam to Washington, January 8, 1791, *ASP-IA*, 1:107. Wolf Creek Mills had been established in the summer of 1790 and as such was a tangible move toward the development of a viable landscape on the company lands. Col. Robert Oliver, Maj. Hatfield White, and Capt. John Dodge owned them. See Frye, *Waterford and Fort Frye*.

35. Frye, *Waterford and Fort Frye*, 31; Barker, *Recollections*, 32. William Dawson Cotton also recounts the visit of the chiefs stopping on the way to Philadelphia, accompanied by an American officer; see Cotton, "Life in Campus Martius, 1788–95," Marietta Collection, Ohio Historical Society.

Ichabod Nye noted the bizarre nature of the feast in the context of Indian warfare: "That, under all the circumstances, the entertainment was very novel, and the scene peculiarly striking. Shut up in the garrison, at war with the other tribes of the forest, shaking hands with our red guests, and the appellation of 'brother' passing from one to the other. It seemed to renew the scenes of the first years' settlement, in 1788, and make us almost forget that war was on our borders." Quoted in Hildreth, *Pioneer History*, 309. For a list of the settlers at Campus Martius, the Point, and Fort Harmar throughout the Indian wars, see Summers, *History of Marietta*. Hurt differentiates between the two places as being the gulf between New Englanders and the frontier people, with the majority of settlers at the Point "back-country Virginians and Pennsylvanians"; see Hurt, *Ohio Frontier*, 182–83.

Certainly there were frontier people at the Point, such as Hamilton Kerr. However, many New Englanders and ex-soldiers also lived there, including Return J. Meigs. The main gulf seems to have been the focus on trade and the unruly influence of taverns, which the Ohio Company struggled to successfully regulate. As such, the landscape emerging at the Point failed to embody the virtue of the settlers and would not induce suitably deferential behavior on those arriving.

36. Hildreth, *Pioneer History*, 362. According to Hildreth, "it was found that the watch towers on the roofs of the block houses were at such an elevation as to render it inconvenient ascending and descending from them at night, in changing the guards." Ibid., 226. Another example of this was the discovery of a large number of moccasin tracks near Campus Martius in March 1791. Combined with the siege mentality of the settlers, this led to the false conviction that there was a British cannon aimed at the fort. "All hands were set to work, soldiers and citizens, to cover the roofs with mud to prevent the fire. They split White oak lath one inch square and ten or twelve feet long, and nailed them within one foot of each other over all the roofs, and then carried up Mud and covered all the Roofs about one Inch thick." As it was, these defenses lasted only as long as the first rainfall. See Barker, *Recollections*, 79.

37. Hildreth, *Pioneer History*, 231; Barker, *Recollections*, 71, 83. Barker recalls that they "found it very difficult to move their stock and feed for them to the vicinity of the Garrison. Those living nigh, left all and went and fed them occasionally; those from a distance had to haul their feed and make the best shift they could til summer." Other Belpre settlers stayed in Stone's garrison during the Indian wars.

38. Barker, *Recollections*, 74. Walter Curtis tells of the massacre of the Brown family on March 15, 1792, which resulted in the abandonment of the lower garrison beside what was to become Blennerhassett Island; see Walter Curtis, "Recollections of Pioneer Life," MSS 210, Ohio Historical Society. Moreover, Fort Frye was attacked by Indians in a two-day siege on March 11 and 12 of the same year; see Frye, *Waterford and Fort Frye*. Once more the movements of the main American force were to affect the numbers garrisoned on the Ohio Company lands: "This house was occupied by the U.S. Troops who kept a sentry and assisted in guarding the Garrison until ordered down the River with Genl. Wayne." Barker, *Recollections*, 74.

39. Barker, *Recollections*, 75. This was despite the fact that the first custom-built courthouse on the company lands was not completed until 1799.

40. Barker, *Recollections*, 13.

7

Three Men from Three Rivers

Navigating between Native and American Identity in the Old Northwest Territory

DONALD H. GAFF

Competition and conflict between Indians and Euro-American settlers on the North American continent tend to be caricatured as a struggle between two utterly separate peoples. Through the years, this dichotomy has manifested itself in the public consciousness in a variety of (often pejorative) ways: red versus white, cowboys and Indians, civilization opposed to savagery. Scholars have frequently been no better, for even the thesis of Richard White's landmark work, *The Middle Ground,* is based on the notion that Indians and settlers facilitated exchange by creating and fostering a zone of interaction between the polar extremes of their respective cultures.[1] Yet, as this essay will show, if such ethnic boundaries did indeed exist, they often were of such porosity as to be essentially nonexistent, especially at the level of individuals rather than communities or tribes.

A critical comparison of the biographies of Little Turtle, Jean Baptiste Richardville, and William Wells serves as a means for examining these boundaries. The lives of these three men were intertwined, and each occupied a significant role in the history of the region and the history of a young nation. Their roles ranged from bringing about one of the largest defeats suffered by the United States military to participating on both sides of the dismantling of Indian hegemony in the western Great Lakes. A careful examination of their lives reveals that they engaged in behavior suggesting a fluency in the cultural vernacular of both Indian and Euro-American worlds. Their case illustrates that ethnic identity and affiliation were remarkably fluid on the frontier, because, while they are generally regarded as belonging to a particular ethnic or racial group, in reality they were intimately familiar with both Indian and

Euro-American cultures and readily switched between them. Instead of doing so out of necessity, these three men actively switched roles as it satisfied any given purpose such as consolidating political power or increasing economic advantage. This is akin to one of the connotations of the word "navigate"— to control or direct one's course.

Interconnections between a variety of ethnicities and individuals in the Northwest Territory argue for a more sophisticated appreciation of the intricate exercise of identity creation in early American history. Even though poles of ethnic identity did exist, these poles were linked in a complex network of fluctuating sociocultural identity by cultural brokers and other intermediaries so as to be indistinguishable as such. This approach addresses one of the points raised by Kent Lightfoot and Antoinette Martinez, who suggest that a multi-scalar approach to the study of boundaries more readily accommodates individual intentionality and individual manipulation of identity than traditional approaches, which have emphasized the study of macroscale phenomena. Consequently, Indians and settlers should not be perceived as staring at each other from opposite shores, but as individuals tacking between the banks of identities in the stream of history.[2]

The geographical locus for these three men is the region in and around what today is Fort Wayne, Indiana. At this location three rivers meet: the St. Marys and St. Joseph come together to form the Maumee. This intersection of rivers became one of the critical nodes in the transportation network of rivers and portages linking the Great Lakes (via the Maumee, which flows into Lake Erie) to the Mississippi River (via a short portage to the Wabash and Ohio rivers), and it was essential for the French and subsequently the English and Americans to solidify political and economic control of Three Rivers in order to secure supremacy over the interior of the continent. The area thus hosted a series of French, English, and American forts and settlements.[3]

It was to this region of vast wetlands and woodlands of oak-hickory forests and stands of beech and maple that the Miami Indians moved from their original homeland at the southern end of Lake Michigan in the early 1700s. They made this move to relieve population pressure in the western Great Lakes created by the large number of refugee tribes pushed westward by the Iroquois wars and, more importantly, to claim land in the southern Great Lakes that these wars left vacant. In terms of European politics, the British had gained ascendancy in the region by the middle of the eighteenth century, and the United States then came to dominance in the region at the end of the century. Yet since the Miamis controlled the portage at what would become Fort Wayne, they still possessed a great amount of economic and political control in the region.[4]

Of the three men, Little Turtle and William Wells are perhaps the best known, as their stories are an integral part of the folk history of northeastern Indiana. In fact, given the paucity of primary documents about these men and the Miamis in general, it might be said that, even to historians, they are better known for their near-mythical exploits than as actual historical figures. Richardville, despite being quite prominent in his time, is little known today except to a handful of scholars and Miami descendants. Regardless, all three were contemporaries and important figures in Miami society.[5]

Little Turtle (Mishikinakwa) was born in 1752 to Ciquenackqua, a Miami leader, and a Mohican woman. At the time, social status in the Miami nation was achieved, which meant that Little Turtle likely began his rise to power before his first noteworthy accomplishment—the successful organization and leadership in the attack on Augustin Mottin de La Balme's party in 1780. This was in retaliation for La Balme's having destroyed the Miami villages at Kekionga, the Miami settlement at Three Rivers. Afterward, in the role of war chief, Little Turtle demolished two American military expeditions, those of Gen. Josiah Harmar in 1790 and Gen. Arthur St. Clair in 1791. After Gen. Anthony Wayne defeated the Miamis in 1794, Little Turtle became a diplomat who labored to bring about normalized and peaceful relations with the United States. Little Turtle continued his diplomatic work until his death in July 1812.[6]

Jean Baptiste Richardville (Pechewa or Wild Cat) was born to a French trader, Antoine Joseph Drouet de Richerville, and a prominent Miami woman, Tacumwah (Marie Louise), in 1761. Tacumwah was the sister of the Miami civil chief Pecanne, and conflicting sources suggest that Jean Richardville shared a familial relationship with Little Turtle. Tacumwah's high status resulted not only from her family but also from her control of all trade at the portage linking the Maumee and Wabash rivers. As her son, Richardville profited from her prosperity. After a long political maturation under his mother, he succeeded to the position of civil chief in 1816 upon Pecanne's death, and Richardville served in this capacity until his own death in 1841.[7]

Around 1777 William Wells was born in Kentucky. At the age of twelve or thirteen Indians captured Wells, and he eventually arrived at Little Turtle's village wherein he was adopted, a common occurrence for Euro-American captives. He was named Apekonit (Wild Carrot), and, by all accounts, Wells became an aggressive and extraordinarily effective warrior for his new family. As with Little Turtle, the campaign of General Wayne signaled a significant change, and Wells sided with Wayne against his adopted nation. Immediately following this conflict, Wells swiftly developed a position of immense influence as a mediator between the United States government and the Indians in his role as an Indian agent. Wells's position was also reinforced by an intimacy with Little Turtle and his role as the Miami leader's personal interpreter. Wells enjoyed the benefits of these roles until he died during the evacuation of Fort Dearborn in 1812, only a few months after Little Turtle's death.[8]

These three men provide a unique microcosm through which to observe how flexible identity was in the Northwest Territory. Conveniently, all three were contemporaries and affiliated with the same tribe. In terms of the Miamis, they each occupied distinct sociopolitical niches—Little Turtle as a war chief, Wells as a warrior, and Richardville as a civil chief. Each also represented a primary racial classification in currency at the time: Wells was white, Little Turtle was full-blood Indian, and Richardville was a multiracial métis. In a similar fashion, their most commonly used names represent this tripartite division: William Wells for the Euro-American, Little Turtle for the Indian, Jean Baptiste Richardville for the progeny of French and Indian admixture. These three men thus offer an alluring sample by which to test conceptualizations of the stereotypical, bounded ethnic groups allegedly operating on the frontier.

The early Little Turtle, of course, conforms to the traditional view of Indians being constantly in conflict with the encroaching settlers. Born to a Miami leader, there were high expectations of him. La Balme's massacre, when Little Turtle and his men slaughtered a party of Frenchmen who were retreating after destroying Kekionga, served as the foundation for the view of Little Turtle as a warrior violently opposed to white incursion. After a seemingly quiet decade, Little Turtle appeared again in 1790 at the head of a Pan-Indian army that ambushed Gen. Josiah Harmar's American expedition with devastating consequences at Kekionga. Outraged with Harmar's failure, President George Washington sent Gen. St. Clair to pacify the Indian nations. Employing a strategy that maximized his Indian army's strengths and exploited St. Clair's weaknesses, Little Turtle destroyed the American army and destabilized the entire border between the United States and Indian Country. At this point in his life, Little Turtle epitomized the prototypical Indian warrior, defending his homeland against invasion.[9]

As Gen. Anthony Wayne began preparations for his assault against the Indian confederation, Little Turtle underwent a shift in thought concerning the Indian effort to resist colonization and removal. He came to appreciate that Wayne was building a larger and better armed force and utilizing tactics that eliminated many of the weaknesses that hampered Harmar and St. Clair. In a speech attributed to Little Turtle before Indian defeat at the hands of Wayne at Fallen Timbers, the Miami leader commented that "We can not expect the same good fortune always to attend us. . . . There is something that whispers to me, it would be prudent to listen to his [Wayne's] offers of peace." Whether this depiction is historically accurate or not is debatable, but what is clear is that by the time of the battle of Fallen Timbers, Little Turtle's orientation toward American culture and his role in Miami society were changing. Although he was no longer in charge, he still participated in the action at Fallen Timbers, and failure to have the most accomplished leader in command at one of the most critical junctures in the long history of Indian resistance to settlement led to a military debacle that delivered the entire Northwest Territory to the Americans.[10]

Little Turtle again emerged as a leader at the subsequent Treaty of Greenville in 1795. Here he counseled the gathered tribes as the shrewdest and most difficult negotiator present. The pivotal point came at the conclusion of these proceedings when Little Turtle finally acquiesced to American demands and informed Wayne he would always uphold the treaty. Throughout these deliberations and later, the government lauded Little Turtle, showering him with riches that included tracts of land, a house, and annuities.[11]

Following the end of hostilities, Little Turtle began to exhibit evidence of a marked shift in cultural values. He cultivated mannerisms of white society while developing the civilized tastes of the elite in the United States, essentially living as a rich white man on the frontier. This is strikingly inconsistent with his advice to other Miamis that they not become beguiled by the American way of life. Little Turtle's behavior reflects a crucial dimension of Indian leadership—the possession of status and wealth that allowed for the redistribution of resources within a tribe and to facilitate coalition building with other nations. In adopting Euro-American tastes, Little Turtle revealed his expectations about what an Indian leader should possess and how he should behave. For example, on one of his visits to Philadelphia, Little Turtle wore a blue suit with pants and a round hat, typical American attire. When asked about this mode of dress, he replied, "At first, they seemed to confine my limbs unpleasantly, but, I have got used to them; and as they defend me against *the heat* and the cold, I now like them well enough." Yet in the course of the same visit, William Wells remarked that Little Turtle, when at home, had to sublimate personal preferences and revert to Indian modes of dress so as not to arouse the jealousy of his people. These comments alone hint at Little Turtle's ability to move between Miami and American cultures with ease, but they also reflect the tenuous nature of Indian leadership. Leadership positions among the Great Lakes tribes often came about through a combination of heredity, persuasion, and demonstrated ability. A chief who was thought to be pretentious or aloof often lost followers and power, which directly influenced Little Turtle's concerns about his perceived status among the Miamis.[12]

At home, Little Turtle possessed many items of American origin, such as his wardrobe and food items like tea and coffee. His wife was known to make

butter, and Little Turtle owned a cow for this purpose. Despite a hunger for
these things, he did not consume them conspicuously due to his deference to
other Miamis. However, he most certainly enjoyed these things, for it is often
noted in descriptions of Little Turtle that he suffered from gout related to his
gluttony. At his home, near present-day Columbia City, Little Turtle owned a
black slave. As in the American South, slave possession denoted a particular
status. He also indulged in the Indian tendency of polygyny when at a late age
he took a seventeen-year-old as his second wife. Little Turtle thus selected elements of both American and Indian cultures from which he could derive
maximum benefit.[13]

Even more indicative of familiarity with American culture, if not his preference for it, is the number of trips Little Turtle undertook to the Eastern
States to secure political and economic favors for the Miamis. These trips
brought Little Turtle into the homes of some of the most famous people of
the age, where he gathered acclaim and notoriety for himself. Little Turtle
always had a propensity for travel. Prior to Wayne's victory at Fallen Timbers,
he had met with the Spanish in Louisiana and met the Creek in Georgia.
While these ventures were in the context of resisting westward expansion
of the Americans, his later trips east reveal much about his ability to operate
within the realm of Euro-American culture. Many Indian leaders had opportunities to visit with an American president on occasion, but Little Turtle visited the capital repeatedly and met three presidents, Washington, John Adams,
and Thomas Jefferson. This is doubly impressive given the exertion required
for a single trip.[14]

As proof of Little Turtle's stature in American society, George Washington
invited him to visit his home in the winter of 1796–97. This is especially worth
noting because Washington was then suffering the debilitating effects of old
age—arthritis, deafness, and poor eyesight—but he was also embittered for
a perceived underappreciation of accomplishments. Washington's meeting
with Little Turtle was one of his last public functions as president. At the time,
Washington presented him with a sword, a gun, and a medal bearing the like-
nesses of both men.[15]

Besides meeting the presidents, Little Turtle consorted with other important figures. He met with the Revolutionary War hero Thaddeus Kosciusko,
who gave him a matching set of pistols. He also sat for a portrait by the renowned artist Gilbert Stuart. Little Turtle, with Wells as his interpreter, spent
many days in discussion with the Comte de Volney, a French traveler, writer,
and polymath. These associations illustrate how esteemed he was in American
society, but these were no mere diplomatic exchanges, for as demonstrated
earlier, Little Turtle had a taste for these things. In fact, Little Turtle seems to
have expressed some regret at having to leave for home. In one of his discus-

sions with Volney, he extolled the virtues of American culture, specifically mentioning clothing, houses, and the markets, but cited old age, unfamiliarity with the language, and the lack of a salable job skill as reasons for returning to the Northwest Territory.[16]

One story related how Little Turtle was vaccinated for smallpox by Doctor Benjamin Rush during a visit to Philadelphia. This is revealing because it precisely shows that Little Turtle, if not thinking like a Euro-American, was conversant enough in the concepts of Euro-American science and thought to appreciate the significance of vaccination. In other words, when exposed to the idea, it was neither foreign nor irrational to Little Turtle. Even more so, this illustrates how Little Turtle operated between the two cultures, because when he returned to the Miamis he personally saw that many of them were vaccinated.[17]

Little Turtle's biography testifies to a shift from a purely Indian identity to one, that if not entirely American, definitely contained many American components. His facility with American customs permitted him to acquire rewards for himself and for his nation, such as assistance in the establishment of an agricultural program. Even more proof for the Americanization of Little Turtle may be found in his treatment by fellow members of the Miamis, such as when his first cow, a flagrantly Euro-American symbol, was maliciously killed. Publicly, Little Turtle expressed a belief that the cow had been diseased, but the message sent by its death was as clear then as it is today. History suggests that many of the Miamis resented Little Turtle, and his stalwart support of the Treaty of Greenville came to be seen as complicity with the Americans. Continual gifts from the government reinforced this view, and Little Turtle's drift toward American culture paralleled his waning influence among the Miamis.[18]

At his death Little Turtle was firmly ensconced in the American cultural tradition. He died at the house of William Wells, where he had moved in order to obtain white medicine from the fort doctors at Fort Wayne. American military honors comprised his funeral, many settlers and military men paid their respects, and he was interred with a large number of grave goods containing a mix of cultural symbols. These included his gun and sword from President Washington, medals, and silver crosses displaying his affinity for American culture, alongside a copper kettle filled with corn and beans, red pigment, and tomahawk pipe, signaling his affinity to the Miamis.[19]

Jean Baptiste Richardville followed an almost opposite path from Little Turtle. In his youth Richardville enjoyed a life of leisure participating in Euro-American pastimes, and in his later years came into a position of leadership where he garnered the respect of the Miamis through his negotiations on their behalf. The literature strongly supports such a bifurcated view of him;

many records detail the high society activities of the youthful Richardville, while the remainder pertain to his business, legal, and political affairs as a businessman and Miami leader. Clearly Richardville navigated between different ethnic identities in his dealings with others. Though it is now recognized that métis were indeed capable of operating within two cultures, Richardville was particularly adept at it, embodying the very fluidity being argued for here.[20]

Richardville's status as a métis afforded him an uncommon advantage. Through his father's connections, Richardville obtained exposure to the French-Canadian trade and a Catholic education. His mother carefully groomed Richardville for a position of leadership within the tribe, initiating his political career when she urged him to rescue a white captive whom the Miamis were intent on killing. Throughout his early life, Richardville assisted Tacumwah with the trade at the portage, where he furthered his alliance-building and acquired knowledge of regional and world politics. His heritage provided him with language abilities that facilitated interactions with traders and agents, among the many others who traveled the rivers.[21]

Until his succession in 1816, Richardville enjoyed a genteel life in the Old Northwest. While many faced a harsh existence, Richardville wore fine European clothing and dined with what would have been the high society of the frontier. One contemporary described days filled with drinking, card playing, and concerts. If that were not European enough, Richardville joined a newly formed society named "Most Light Honorable Society of Monks," known later as "Friars of St. Andrew." He also threw parties at his house, including one for Mardi Gras. All of these activities enhanced his business dealings with Europeans and Americans.[22]

Richardville derived much pleasure from this life. He rarely fought alongside the Miamis in their battles and raids. Instead, he thrived on the social life found among Euro-American company. Nowhere is this more evident than in the house he created in the middle of the Northwest Territory. Treaty houses were provided for nine chiefs in the Treaty at Paradise Springs in 1826. One of these was for Richardville, who accepted the government's offer but added his own funds and converted the original plan for a modest treaty house into an extravagant two-story Greek revival home. It had luxuries such as glass windows, fireplaces with interior chimneys, and a finished staircase with a walnut handrail. The sumptuous interior included imported carpets, silk curtains, French wallpaper, chandeliers, figurines, and a gold clock displayed prominently in the parlor. The house came complete with a wharf on the St. Marys River, barn, and racetrack that provided the most popular entertainment in the Three Rivers area. What makes this house even more impressive is that at the time, many of the white residents of Fort Wayne were still living in one-room cabins. Such an ostentatious display reflected that Richardville was the richest Indian in America at the time. In an ironic twist, this atypically wealthy Indian paid soldiers from the fort to work on his farm. Upon his death, in addition to extensive land holdings, Richardville passed on to his children nearly $200,000.[23]

Much of Richardville's large fortune resulted from a variety of treaties, which he signed as a Miami leader. His involvement in the treaty process tended to be viewed pessimistically because not only did he secure a vast amount of acreage for himself, he also negotiated his family's right to live in Indiana forever. While this might be true, throughout all of the negotiations with which he was associated, Richardville worked exceptionally hard on behalf of the Miamis, beginning with the Treaty of Greenville, where he went in Pecanne's stead. From that treaty onward Richardville was well known for his oratory and maneuvering in negotiations. John Tipton, Indian agent and later a United States senator, described Richardville as "the ablest diplomat of whom I have any knowledge. If he had been born and educated in France, he would have been the equal of Talleyrand." Tipton also wrote, "The Miamies are reduced to a small number, but well organized in their kind of government with one of the most shrewd men in North America at their head." Many of the Miamis also held Richardville in high regard: "They have repeatedly declared to the Chief Richardville that they will never abandon him while he lives. . . . The utmost confidence is reposed in him." Throughout successive treaties, he was able to stave off removal, and by gaining titles to individual plots of land for many of his people (as opposed to a collective reservation), he delayed the breakup of the Miami land base. This effort to retain land for individual tribal members accounts for why Richardville, despite his great wealth, was held in much higher esteem than Little Turtle, who only sought to secure benefits for himself and the tribe collectively. Because of Richardville's skillful negotiations, the Miamis did not begin to undergo removal until the late 1840s, much later than other tribes from the southern Great Lakes.[24]

Richardville's ability to navigate between a variety of ethnic groups is well established. In his capacity as an exceptionally gifted trader and leader, he interacted with French, British, métis, Americans, and a variety of Indian tribes quite successfully, as evidenced by the wealth he established during the course of his life. Confirmation of Richardville's ability to tack between the poles of Indian and Euro-American cultures can be found in his behavior when he became principal chief of the tribe. Richardville could have performed ably as chief had he continued in the tradition of a rich Euro-American, but he chose to become the epitome of an Indian chief. Even though he was a métis, essentially raised as a white man, he became an Indian. Whether it enhanced his standing among the Miamis or benefited him in negotiation with the Americans, Richardville began to wear traditional Miami dress. Even more interestingly, at treaty sessions, he would speak only in Miami and demand interpreters always be available to him and the other leaders even though he spoke several languages. Completing this picture, instead of signing his name to the treaties, he made his mark. He also went about bargaining in the style of the Miamis with extreme delays and eloquent speeches. His switch to Miami culture enhanced his negotiating position by reassuring and securing Miami confidence and exploiting Euro-American apprehensions of dealing with Indians.[25]

When Richardville died on August 13, 1841, he was the wealthiest man in Indiana. Befitting his status as both a rich man and a métis, his family buried him in the burial ground outside Fort Wayne's Catholic church. Later, his daughters had a memorial for him placed in the Catholic cemetery. After his death, both his estate and the Indian land that Richardville worked diligently to retain eventually fell out of Miami control.[26]

The case of William Wells differs from that of Little Turtle and Richardville in that his first shift in ethnicity came when he was captured and adopted by the Miamis. Apparently, Wells was predisposed to life as an Indian because he took to Miami culture with relish and soon joined raids against American settlements. During these attacks, Wells claimed that he "tomahawked and scalped the wounded, dying and dead, until he was unable to raise his arm." He became notorious for acting as a lost white child only to lure unsuspecting and helpful settlers to their deaths. It is commonly believed that Little Turtle adopted Wells shortly after his kidnapping, but it was actually Gaviahatte (Porcupine) who adopted him. After adoption, Wells had many opportunities to escape, but he chose to stay with the Miamis. Wells did not even recognize his brother Carty when he journeyed into the heart of Miami territory to implore William to return to his family. When his brother Samuel finally persuaded him to return home, William rejoined the Indians after only a few days in Kentucky.[27]

It would be the capture of his wife and adopted mother that prompted Wells' return to American society. Wells married Little Turtle's daughter, Sweet Breeze (Manwangopath), who was captured by Col. James Wilkinson's Kentucky militia in 1791. After St. Clair's defeat, Wells went to Vincennes to seek the return of his wife. Major John Hamtramck told him his wife was being held in Cincinnati and he would have to await the arrival of Gen. Rufus Putnam. Wells spent the interim in Louisville where his brother Samuel's second appeal to leave the Miamis was accepted. In one of the interviews with Volney, Wells claimed he left due to the insecurity of their way of life and that he desired a peaceful life and a farm. These statements were somewhat at odds with the remainder of his life.[28]

It seems that Wells did not abandon the Indian life altogether. After joining with the Americans, Wells became a scout for Wayne's Legion with the rank of captain. In this position, Wells continued in the ways inculcated by the Miamis. Wells dressed and painted himself as an Indian. It might be thought that this had more to do with being a scout, but it went much further than that. During this time, a missionary accompanied Wells on a hunt in which he had wounded a bear. The man observed Wells stroking the bear and admonishing it for not dying in a matter befitting such a powerful adversary—behavior at odds with the claim that Wells had supposedly given up Indian ways. Evidence for his having given up Indian ways might be found in his aggressive actions as an American at the head of Wayne's scouts that led several tribes to complain of his outrages to the British Indian agent at Detroit.[29]

After the battle of Fallen Timbers, Wells took on the assignment as interpreter for General Wayne at the treaty sessions at Greenville. During these negotiations, William Henry Harrison took time to school Wells in white cultural mores, as well as reading and writing. Following the conclusion of this treaty, Wells settled at Three Rivers. In addition to establishing his farm, the American cultural ideal, Wells also accepted the position of Indian agent. Once an advocate of Wells, Harrison eventually came to dislike and distrust Wells for his alliance with Little Turtle and dedication to the Miami cause. Over the years, Wells' stance would make him a number of enemies among the politicians and administrators in the Northwest Territory. Ironically, Wells' sense of obligation arose from promises he had made to the nation on behalf of the very government that later so wearied of his convictions. Wells, along with Little Turtle, decided that if the Miamis began to practice agriculture they would acculturate and thus be saved from removal. This reflects the ambiguities of Wells' ethnicity. He advocated a clearly white means of production, which he, with the assistance of several slaves, was implementing on his own property. But he should have known that the Miamis would never embrace agriculture, given that it was antithetical to their traditional way of life. When a Quaker came to demonstrate farming techniques, Miami men sat around and watched in fascination, but did no labor. The Quaker left after one season, exasperated at their unwillingness to farm. This is only one example of how Wells' misjudgment poorly situated him among his bureaucratic peers within the complex arena of frontier politics.[30]

Serving as Little Turtle's interpreter and friend maintained his reputation among his adopted nation, but he continually found himself in many political machinations that led American administrators and bureaucrats to distrust him. Oftentimes Wells was found to be a greater obstacle to the government's agenda than the Miamis themselves. While he continued his political intrigues, which drew the ire of so many, following the death of Sweet

Breeze he married into an eminent white family from Kentucky. In fact, it would be Wells' white kin that would lead to his death.[31]

In the early days of the War of 1812, Wells received word that his niece, Rebecca Heald, and her husband, Capt. Nathan Heald, commander at Fort Dearborn, were facing an impending assault on the fort by a contingent of the Indian confederation. Upon arriving at the fort, Wells saw a hopeless situation. He met with leaders of the Indian force and offered them all of the goods in the fort in exchange for safe passage for the fort's inhabitants. The Indians agreed, but then the American officers chose to destroy the extra arms and munitions. When the Indians discovered that the goods they especially desired had been destroyed they became furious. Without the arms that had been destroyed, Wells and Heald determined they could not hold the fort and opted to leave. Wells deliberately took on a specific identity once the command to abandon the fort had been given, adorning himself in Indian garb and painting his face black according to a Miami tradition invoked when facing death. After evacuating the fort, the American column, headed by Wells, fell under attack by a much larger Indian force. After noticing a wagonload of children being threatened, Wells moved to defend it. Having already been shot once, his horse was shot and fell on him. In front of his niece, whom Wells had come to rescue, an Indian decapitated Wells and thrust his head on a staff. Another ripped open his chest and ripped out the heart. These warriors honored Wells, whom they easily identified, by eating it, a fitting tribute for one who had probably always been a Miami at heart.[32]

These brief biographies provide a glimpse into the complicated nature of ethnicity and identity in the Northwest Territory. They again remind us of the great flaw inherent in the once commonly held notion that the frontier was characterized by little more than violent conflict between two discrete cultural traditions. That view had long been a part of American heritage and for a long time permeated almost every interpretation of the era, but as numerous historians have demonstrated, it is insufficient to explain the forms of cultural transition so often found along the American frontier. Here the metaphor of tacking between shores of ethnicity is exhibited by the different patterns seen in the lives of these three men. Little Turtle went from the position of an anti-white, successful war chief to that of a pro-American statesman and proponent of American ways. Richardville, however, began life firmly rooted in the Euro-American tradition, enjoying a leisurely life as a businessman who in his final days claimed a very traditional orientation, wearing indigenous clothing and speaking in the Miami tongue. Wells provides yet another example; having started life as an American, he adopted Miami culture after his capture, later reentered the white world, and eventually went into his last battle as a Miami would.

At a more abstract level the metaphor continues to stand. Little Turtle's shift in identity was both the most natural of the three men and also the most superficial. He did not navigate, per se, but instead drifted from the Indian world toward the white one. In essence he was accustomed to occupying a position of respect among the Indians and transferred these elite attitudes as he encountered American society. As General Wayne progressed into the heart of the Northwest Territory, Little Turtle realized that, ultimately, the Indian confederation could not stop the advance of white settlers. In the course of treaty signings and meeting whites, Little Turtle became acquainted with the high-class Euro-American lifestyle and began to thirst for it. Thus, with the passing of time, Little Turtle slipped away from his Miami identity and began collecting material symbols like clothing and operating a farm. Most importantly, he came to think like an American too.

Richardville truly did navigate between the shores of ethnicity and he did so expertly and often. With the circumstances of his birth, he was accustomed to seeing and participating in different ethnicities at an early age. His earliest days were spent in the company of the French, British, and Miamis, and he actively partook in each from the very beginning. He would have also been introduced to the many different nations other than the Miamis that visited trading posts and forts with which he was familiar. Richardville's approach to identity was much like an algebraic variable. In any given situation, he chose the particular ethnicity that would benefit him most. When trading along the river, he was métis. When entertaining, he was French, British, or American. When dealing with the government, he was Miami. Consequently, Richardville likely had no core ethnicity but instead tacked between several as suited him.

Wells navigated between extremes of identity as well, but in his particular case, his path can be seen as filled with obstacles around which he navigated. This differs from Richardville, who chose at will, because Wells often chose in reaction to some external condition. When captured by the Miamis, he changed. When his wife was captured by Americans, he changed again. When he went to rescue his niece, he changed yet again. The historical record documents that Wells was the most complex of these three men, at least psychologically. The paradoxical behavior at his death, where he died as an Indian, defending Americans, exemplifies the contradiction of his life.

All this taken together illustrates the porosity of the social and ethnic boundaries in the Old Northwest. These three men alone demonstrate that identifiers such as "Indian" or "White" often have lesser meanings when viewed at the scale of individuals. Boundaries between settlers and Indians did not exist given a métis dressed as an Indian living in a palatial mansion and a white man from Kentucky dressed as an Indian talking to a bear. Traffic across boundaries flowed both ways. Little Turtle brought white vaccinations to the Miamis; Richardville used his knowledge of business to delay Miami removal and loss of lands; and William Wells brought his intimate knowledge of Indians to the service of Wayne and the United States government. Even timeworn words like "acculturation" take on a lesser connotation when the past is seen in terms of individuals making individual choices that yield a spectrum of behaviors.

Perhaps these men were unique in their transgressions of social boundaries; perhaps they were so unique that they were not representative of the population. This criticism contains some validity. Little Turtle, and more so Richardville, were extremely rich Miami leaders. All three men enriched themselves through trade and in their roles as cultural brokers. Another approach is to ask why this is navigation through a fluid stream of ethnicity and not just a byproduct of living at the top economic and social stratum of the day. The answer to this is that the biographies of these men unequivocally prove that they were not just adopting the regalia of different cultures, but that they were intimately familiar with the very values and ideas of those cultures. It was more than slipping into clothes; it was slipping into a culture and an identity.

While history of this era focuses on the leaders and the upper social classes, tantalizing hints suggest that many of the Miamis blurred the boundaries as well. By the early 1700s the Miamis were already intimate with French traders and well versed in French language and culture. In the case of the Miamis at Three Rivers, they were considered to be white by the mid-1800s, suggesting that the common Miamis had been familiar with Euro-American culture for a long period of time. This phenomenon was not just limited to the Miamis. Many Indian adoptions, just like Wells', resulted in many whites staying with their adopted tribes. Another good example is the well-known case of the *Berdache,* whose rapid disappearance upon sustained European contact indicates the early acceptance of European gender roles into tribes like the Illinois. Finally, recent scholarship uses religion to argue the same idea proposed here, that individuals made choices that defy collective categorization. In particular, Christianized Indians were not docile and domesticated as commonly thought, but instead were able to retain their fundamental Indian identity while practicing European religion, unequivocally demonstrating that the average Indian participated in both worlds in much the same way as their better-documented leaders. It is not hard to imagine that these small things— multilingualism, changing dress, affecting mannerisms, religion, adoption, altering attitudes—were constantly navigated during even the most routine encounters between those in the trading houses, homes, council houses, and lodges of the Old Northwest.[33]

If in life, Little Turtle, Richardville, and Wells agilely navigated between extremes of ethnic identity, it is unfortunate that in death their memories are employed in the perpetuation of stereotypes. William Wells, who survived capture by Indians, served as a scout and agent, and died saving children in an Indian attack, lives on in names throughout the region: Streets named for Wells run through Fort Wayne and Chicago; Spy Run Creek in the former city memorializes his reconnaissance for Wayne; and of course, there is Wells County, Indiana. Surely these designations were not meant to honor his years leading brutal attacks against soldiers of the United States or luring white settlers to their deaths.

Similar to Wells, Little Turtle is more a stereotypical Indian today than he ever was in life. While his memory is commemorated nominally, such as the Little Turtle branch library in Fort Wayne, Little Turtle's visage can be found throughout the area on plaques, paintings, and at least one full-sized statue. His likeness was even a candidate for the U.S. Mint's Indiana state quarter. In all of these instances, his portrayal is that of the Noble Savage. None depict him living as a fat, rich man with his slaves and cows or dining with notable Americans in the largest cities of the United States. Most stereotypical of all for an Indian is that in the early twentieth century his remains were disinterred and his grave goods put on display in the Allen County Historical Museum. Even though he did not necessarily die an Indian, the inhabitants of northeastern Indiana have made him one.

Perhaps most tragic of all remains the case of Richardville. It is ironic that a man, who in his day amassed a fortune and had the respect of even the most powerful, should have befallen the same fate as many other métis—forgotten because their histories were written in a society with a dichotomized view of race. Richardville was arguably one of the most well known persons in the Old Northwest due to his wealth and ostentatious lifestyle. Richardville's parties and gatherings were famous and he was respected by his peers, but today almost no one knows who he is. The few things his name graces like Wildcat Creek pale in both number and size when compared to those of Little Turtle and Wells. No Richardville statues are to be found. His ornate house still stands, but remains empty, its place and importance in the local landscape uncertain.[34]

One example of how the métis Richardville has had his name erased can be found in the cadastral history. Whereas Wells has a county named for him, Richardville does not. This was not always the case, for shortly after his death, a Richardville County was formed, but less than two years later it was renamed Howard County, for Gen. T. A. Howard, an Indiana politician. One can only speculate why the name was changed, but the result is only one of the many ways that this important and influential man has been removed from the public consciousness. As stereotypical as it may be, Richardville is likely less remembered for the very reason that he was neither Indian nor white.

Selective representation of these three men in the twentieth century has resulted in the creation and perpetuation of stereotypes that simplify and polarize their ethnic identities. Maybe this comes from a tendency to perceive groups as singular wholes composed of homogeneous members instead of as a collection of individuals. Future research into the social processes that produced such caricatured portraits of them would make an interesting study. The fact remains, however, that the way these three are depicted in the present obscures the complexity of their lives in the past. In attempting to publicly honor them, such treatment fails to recognize how these three men from Three Rivers navigated through racial and ethnic boundaries in the Old Northwest.

NOTES

1. Richard White, *The Middle Ground: Indians, Empires, and Republics in the Great Lakes Region, 1650–1815* (New York: Cambridge Univ. Press, 1991). White does recognize that sociocultural borders are porous, but his central thesis hinges on the notion that cultural groups are separate, thereby necessitating a middle ground for interaction.

2. Kent G. Lightfoot and Antoinette Martinez, "Frontiers and Boundaries in Archaeological Perspective," *Annual Review of Anthropology* 24 (1995): 471–92.

3. White, *Middle Ground,* 448.

4. R. O. Petty and M. T. Jackson, "Plant Communities," in Alton A. Lindsey, ed., *Natural Features of Indiana* (Indianapolis: Indiana Academy of Science, 1966), 280; Charles Callender, "Miami," in Bruce G. Trigger, ed., *Handbook of North American Indians,* vol. 15: *Northeast* (Washington, D.C.: Smithsonian Institution, 1978), 681–82, 686–88.

5. Callender, "Miami," 689.

6. Rex Potterf, "Little Turtle," *Old Fort News* 21 (1958), 1–11. Callender, "Miami," 684–85, discusses the role of ascribed and achieved status in Miami leadership.

7. Lois Shepard Headings, "The Distinguished and Extraordinary Man: Chief J. B. Richardville," *Old Fort News* 61 (1998): 1–22.

8. Bessie Keeran Roberts, "William Wells: A Legend in the Councils of Two Nations," *Old Fort News* 17 (1954): 5–10.

9. Calvin M. Young, *Little Turtle (Me-She-Kin-No-Quah): The Great Chief of the Miami Nation* (Indianapolis, Ind.: Sentinel, 1917; repr., Fort Wayne, Ind.: Public Library of Fort Wayne and Allen County, 1956), 31–67 (page citations are to the reprint edition).

10. "Little Turtle's Oration before the Battle of Fallen Timbers," *Old Fort News* 2 (1937): 7.

11. Young, *Little Turtle,* 103–24.

12. C. F. Volney, *A View of the Soil and Climate of the United States of America,* in George W. White, ed., *Contributions to the History of Geology,* vol. 2 (Philadelphia, Pa.,

1804; repr., New York: Hafner, 1968), 360–61, 378 (page citations are to the reprint edition).

13. Kathryn Troxel, "A Frenchman's View of Little Turtle," *Old Fort News* 6, no. 2 (1941): 10; Clifford H. Richards, "Little Turtle: The Man and His Land," *Old Fort Bulletin* (Nov.–Dec. 1974): 7; Potterf, "Little Turtle," 7, 9.

14. Volney, *View*, 362; Potterf, "Little Turtle," 2; Otho Winger, *Little Turtle: The Great Chief of Eel River* (North Manchester, Ind.: News-Journal, 1942), 8–9; Potterf, "Little Turtle," 2.

15. Potterf, "Little Turtle," 1–2.

16. Young, *Little Turtle*, 145–47; Willis Richardson, ed., "Little Turtle Pictures," *Old Fort News* 2 (1937): 3–4; Volney, *View*, 375.

17. Potterf, "Little Turtle," 2–3.

18. Young, *Little Turtle*, 150–54; Richards, "Little Turtle Land," 7; Otho Winger, "Me-She-Kin-No-Quah (Little Turtle)," *Old Fort News* 2, no. 1 (1937): 5.

19. Young, *Little Turtle*, 161–62, 169–77.

20. Headings, "Richardville," 4–5; D. M. Perry, "The Richardville House," *Old Fort News* 53 (1990): 1–2.

21. Headings, "Richardville," 1–3.

22. Headings, "Richardville," 4–5.

23. Headings, "Richardville," 13–14, 16, 17; Perry, "The Richardville House," 2–3.

24. Charles R. Poinsatte, *Fort Wayne during the Canal Era, 1828–1855: A Study of a Western Community in the Middle Period of American History* (Indianapolis: Indiana Historical Bureau, 1969), 96; quoted in Headings, "Richardville," 11; Nellie Armstrong Robertson and Dorothy Riker, eds., *The John Tipton Papers*, 3 vols. (Indianapolis: Indiana Historical Society, 1942), 2:400; From a report of treaty negotiations quoted in Carole M. Allen et al., eds., "The Man in the Middle—Chief J. B. Richardville," *The Indiana Historian: Exploring Indiana History* (Nov. 1993): 13; Headings, "Richardville," 6–17.

25. Headings, "Richardville," 16.

26. Perry, "The Richardville House," 3–7.

27. Henry Howe, *Historical Collections of Ohio*, 3 vols. (Columbus, Ohio: Henry Howe, 1889), 231; Paul A. Hutton, "William Wells: Frontier Scout and Indian Agent," *Old Fort News* 43 (1980): 63–67.

28. Hutton, "Frontier Scout," 66, 69–70; Volney, *View*, 373–74.

29. Donald B. Grissom, "William Wells, Indian Agent," *Old Fort News* 42 (1979): 53–54; Hutton, "Frontier Scout," 71, 76.

30. Grissom, "Indian Agent," 54, 56–58; Hutton, "Frontier Scout," 81, 85; R. David Edmunds, "Evil Men Who Add to Our Difficulties: Shawnees, Quakers, and William Wells, 1807–1808," *American Indian Culture and Research Journal* 14 (1990): 1–14.

31. Hutton, "Frontier Scout," 81–92; Roberts, "Wells," 6.

32. Hutton, "Frontier Scout," 95–97; Allan H. Dougall, *The Death of Captain Wells* (Fort Wayne, Ind.: Public Library of Fort Wayne and Allen County, 1958).

33. For early Miami history, see Bert Anson, *The Miami Indians* (Norman: Univ. of Oklahoma Press, 1970). For adoption, see James Axtell, "The White Indians of Colonial America," *William and Mary Quarterly* 32 (1975): 55–88. For *Berdache*, see Raymond Hauser, "The *Berdache* and the Illinois Indian Tribes during the Last Half of the

Seventeenth Century," *Ethnohistory* 37 (Winter 1990): 45–65. For religion, see Neal Salisbury, "Embracing Ambiguity: Native Peoples and Christianity in Seventeenth-Century North America," *Ethnohistory* 50 (2003): 247–59.

34. The significance of and interest in Richardville's house has increased and the past decade has seen the beginning of an effort to recognize this. It was listed in the National Register of Historic Places in 1997, and plans to make it a historic landmark open to the public are being considered.

8

Negotiating Law on the Frontier

Responses to Cross-Cultural Homicide in Illinois, 1810–1825

BRUCE P. SMITH

On Sunday June 2, 1811, at approximately 5 o'clock at night, three Potawatomi Indians came to the house of the Cox family on Shoal Creek in St. Clair County, Illinois Territory. The Potawatomis killed the Coxes' son, Elijah, "broke a Chest open [and] took out its contents," and departed with two mares, some colts, "one stud horse," and "two rifle guns." The attackers also took with them Rebecca, Elijah's sister. After leaving the scene of the raid, Rebecca's captors joined up with two other Indians and allegedly entertained them by "mocking" and "imitating" Elijah's actions "when in the agencies of death." Two days later, a search party of white "rangers"—settlers in the Illinois Territory authorized by Congress to counteract "hostile" Indians— discovered the Potawatomis and their young captive. Detecting the approach of the search party, the Indians "made an attempt to kill" Rebecca by striking her "[on] the head and twice on the small of the back with a spear Tomahawk." Although one Potawatomi was killed and a settler injured in the ensuing melee, Rebecca managed to survive, to elude her captors, and to relate the details of the raid, captivity, and escape to Uel Whitesides, a justice of the peace for St. Clair County.[1]

Contemporary chronicles of the Cox incident, focusing as they do on the lurid details of the attack and the swiftness of the settlers' armed response, typically consider the affair to be representative of the violent nature of settler-Indian interactions on the Illinois frontier—as, in many respects, it surely was. More recent treatments, including, most notably, James Davis's 1998 survey *Frontier Illinois*, treat the events as a precursor to the more sustained, aggravated, and well-documented violence that embroiled the Old Northwest during the War of 1812. This, too, is undeniable. But while these historical accounts, like other narratives of frontier "massacres" and "depredations," discuss the violent reaction of white settlers to civilian killings, they say little about the settlers' resort to law. This is a surprising omission, since the only surviving testimony of the events—Rebecca Cox's deposition—is a distinctly legal document, created by a person who resorted to formal legal procedures to tell her story and to seek justice.[2]

Unfortunately, we know surprisingly little about the ways that settlers (and Indians, for that matter) resorted to—and, at times, evaded—legal concepts, procedures, and institutions in resolving cases of homicide. By seeking to understand the ways that settlers and Indians in early-nineteenth-century Illinois used law to respond to occasions of cross-cultural homicide, this chapter takes up—if only in a preliminary way—an invitation issued over fifteen years ago by historian Fred Hoxie, who urged that legal historians write what he termed a "'New' North American Indian Legal History"—a history, based on local legal records, that would portray "Indian people as positive historical actors" capable of using "legal institutions and doctrines for their own ends." In turn, by focusing on the strategies used by native peoples and Euro-American settlers to resolve cross-cultural homicides, the chapter seeks to build on the incisive and suggestive studies of Richard White and John Phillip Reid, who have both explored the differing "cultural formulas" brought to bear by settlers and indigenous persons in resolving disputes arising from cross-cultural killings.[3]

At the threshold, any effort to assess the ways that settlers and Indians in early-nineteenth-century Illinois employed legal concepts, procedures, and institutions to resolve disputes arising from cross-cultural homicides must confront considerable gaps in the existing historiography. On the one hand, although studies of the Old Northwest provide numerous accounts of battles and military campaigns, none devotes sustained attention to the specific phenomenon of murder—that subset of homicides committed against noncombatants and considered by contemporary observers to violate either formal laws or informal norms.[4] On the other hand, despite a recent surge in regional studies in the field of American legal history, legal historians have yet to devote sustained attention to the legal institutions and legal culture of the Old Northwest, either in its territorial phase or during the decades of early statehood.[5]

Accordingly, we are left with little more than unsatisfying generalizations about the role of law in resolving cases of cross-cultural violence. Recent studies depict the residents of early-nineteenth-century Illinois as viewing the law with "great respect," "awe," and "acquiescence," attitudes that helped render the region "amazingly tranquil" during the decades of territorial governance and early statehood. Law awe functions consistently, effectively, and in a manner that ensures civil peace: "[s]ettlers' faith in frontier justice, in its legitimacy and equity, minimized violence"; "frontier courts provided equity, order, and structure for [a] fluid, transient society"; "jurors took their responsibilities seriously and were not rubber stamps for prosecutors"; and "[c]onsensus and common sense guided judicial proceedings." But this interpretation exhibits little understanding of the ways that formal law was negotiated, manipulated, resisted, and circumvented by either settlers or Indians. Settlers on the early-nineteenth-century Illinois frontier—far from exhibiting deference to law—easily lost faith in formal legal procedures and institutions and, instead, resorted to extra-legal violence; frontier courts—far from operating in ordered and structured ways—exhibited, at least in their early years, little regard for formal legal procedure; jurors—far from observing their duties diligently—drank to excess, wandered from the courtroom, and occasionally expressed open animus for Indian defendants; and judicial proceedings—far from being consensual affairs—proved to be hotly contested, generating strong disagreement not only between the litigating parties (as might be expected) but also between trial and appellate courts.[6]

Yet if our perceived understanding of law's operation and legitimacy in frontier Illinois appears unduly simplistic and optimistic, scholarship that has adopted a more avowedly theoretical approach to the problem of violence in frontier societies has proven no more satisfying. Much of this scholarship seeks to explain the legal attitudes of Indians and settlers in frontier settings by positing a set of stark dichotomies—for example, between native notions of "collective responsibility" for wrongdoing and Euro-American notions of "individualized responsibility," or between native desires to "cover the dead" through compensation and Western preferences for retribution or deterrence.[7] Although such constructs possess an element of truth, they also imply that Indians and settlers acted within "static" legal cultures that were both resistant to cultural borrowing and unchanging over time. In short, these theoretical treatments overlook the "concrete experience" of historical actors—including the ways that individuals used, shaped, and borrowed law and the ways that they adopted (and frequently adapted) the concepts and institutions of the opposing culture to pursue their particular goals.[8]

By examining two case studies that illustrate how Potawatomis and Euro-American settlers in Illinois responded to homicides during the 1810s and 1820s, this essay seeks to tell a more complicated story about both human agency and the power (and limits) of law in frontier settings. The first case study discusses a complex series of negotiations between representatives of the territorial government of Illinois and various Potawatomi chiefs from 1810 to 1812, relating to the "delivery" to territorial representatives of several Potawatomis suspected of killing Euro-American settlers, including Elijah

Cox. After local Potawatomi chiefs effectively frustrated the territorial government's processes of arrest, Illinois settlers ultimately resorted to physical violence—destroying the Potawatomis' village on Lake Peoria and dispersing its inhabitants. The second case study concerns a set of legal proceedings involving a Potawatomi named Nomaque, who was tried in 1824 for the murder of a French settler near Peoria, at a time when Potawatomi influence in the Illinois River region had declined considerably. Yet, despite the precipitous decline in Potawatomi influence in the region, Nomaque shrewdly deployed American legal procedures to defend himself, securing a ringing— if relatively fleeting—legal victory in the Illinois Supreme Court. Although both examples demonstrate the ways that Potawatomis in the 1810s and 1820s sought to employ Western legal concepts and Western law to achieve their own goals, both examples also reveal the critical limits of law as a mechanism of dispute resolution in early-nineteenth-century Illinois.

On the evening of July 20, 1810, a party of Indians took horses and goods from a group of white settlers near Portage des Sioux on the Missouri River in the Louisiana Territory, roughly one hundred miles north of St. Louis. The Indians were pursued by the victims, who forced them the following day to jettison deerskins, a saddle, and a quantity of dried venison. Unable to capture the suspects during the initial pursuit, the settlers set up a temporary camp with the intention of continuing to the house of Victor Lagotiere, a local man believed to be in a position to act as an intermediary between the parties and to exercise influence over the alleged perpetrators. Around 2:00 A.M., however, the Indians preempted the settlers' plans by attacking the camp and killing four of the pursuing men: Cornelius Gooch, Abraham Patten, William Cole, and Sarshal Brown. Stephen Cole (who had been tomahawked but remained alive) and James Moredaugh (who had hidden in a thicket during the attack) survived the encounter. When a second contingent of settlers reached the camp the next day, they discovered the bodies of the four dead men.[9]

Representatives of the United States and Louisiana territorial governments responded promptly to the killings. In a letter to Secretary of War William Eustis in September 1810, William Clark, United States Indian Agent in St. Louis, reported that he had contacted Indian agents as far away as Prairie du Chien and had employed "Spies in the Indian Towns . . . where [Clark] had some reasons to suspect improper Conduct," instructing them to determine who had committed the "hor[r]id murder[s]." While in St. Louis, Clark had also hosted delegations of "large parties of Ioways, Sacs, and Kickapoos," who had all strongly protested their innocence. After considering the various possible wrongdoers, Clark had "fix[ed] the murder without much doubt on the Pattawatomie Nation"—a loosely structured group of Algonquian-speaking peoples who resided in villages ranging in a broad arc from the area around

Detroit, through northern Indiana, northern Illinois, and southern Wisconsin. Among this broadly dispersed group of Potawatomis, Clark focused his attention on Gomo, "the principal Chief" of a group of Potawatomis located on the Illinois River in the vicinity of Peoria. On September 10 Clark convened a "Council" with Gomo, several of his "Village Chiefs," and "40 of his Wariours," who assured Clark that "the portion of the Pottowatomies under [Gomo's] authority did not Commit the late murder . . . of the White people." Instead, Gomo implicated certain Potawatomis then believed to be under the influence of Tecumseh's brother, The Prophet. Recognizing that he had "no power given [him] to make a demand of [the] Murderers," Clark prevailed on Gomo to "deliver up" the suspects to the proper territorial authorities. Much to Clark's dismay, however, Gomo returned to his village without delivering up the suspects to the Americans.[10]

Two months after Clark's abortive meeting with Gomo in St. Louis, Gov. Benjamin Howard of the Louisiana Territory wrote Ninian Edwards, governor of the Illinois Territory, to express concern that the suspected killers still remained at large. By mid-autumn, Howard, like Clark, had "used every means in [his] power to ascertain [the identities of] the Indians" who had "murdered [the] four white men." Like Clark, Howard had "collected circumstantial proof sufficient to convince [him] that the party was composed of Potawatomies, one of whom called Catfish, resides within the Territory of Illinois." Noting that his "duty" (as well as his "inclination") compelled him to seek Catfish's arrest, but observing that he had "no authority to arrest him out[side]" the Louisiana Territory, Howard "demand[ed]" that Edwards bring about the arrest of the wrongdoers in Illinois. Justice, if it would be done, would require the cooperation and capacity of Illinois's territorial authorities.[11]

Edwards, who had been appointed governor of the Illinois Territory in 1809, does not appear to have devoted immediate attention to Howard's request. By the summer of 1811, however, the sensational killing of Elijah Cox, the death of another Illinois settler named Price, and a spate of other acts of Indian-settler violence had forced Edwards' hand. On June 7, a few days after the Cox killing, Edwards wrote Secretary of War Eustis to express his mounting concern and frustration with the Indian groups living on the Illinois River. Edwards observed that he had "good reason to believe that no less than forty horses [had] been recently stolen from this territory by some of those Indians, the most lawless of whom is a small tribe calling themselves Pottawottomies, but principally composed of outcasts and vagabonds of the neighbour tribes[,] who seem to live by their depredations and whose audacity in them is unequalled." Although eager to bring a cessation to the violence through negotiations with the Potawatomi leaders, Edwards expressed concern that he lacked the resources to convince them to cooperate. Although he had "*applied* to send a belt of wampum & a talk to the cheifs [*sic*]of some of the tribes for the purpose of obtaining restitution of some horses," he was "not supplied with wampum or any other article usual & necessary in inter-course with Indians—nor [could he] procure any of them here." Thus, al-though Edwards claimed to possess the will to resolve the issue peaceably, he feared that he lacked the economic and political capital to do so.[12]

Doubtful about his ability to secure cooperation from the Potawatomis, Edwards put into action another plan. The following day he wrote a letter to a commander of a company of Illinois Rangers authorizing him to "pre-pare to march at a moments warning" and to "be ready should any depreda-tions be committed . . . to repel the attacks or to follow and take those Indians, who may commit those outrages." Frustrated both with the rising level of vi-olence and his limited ability to apprehend the suspects through legal chan-nels, Edwards authorized the commander to engage in more direct measures:

> Should immediate persuit be made after any Indians who may have stolen horses, or committed murders &c. and they be over-taken with the prop-erty in their possession, or be otherwise clearly ascertained to be the iden-tical persons who committed those offences—your orders must be for the men to take them peacably if possible that they may be brought to trial in a legal way, and be made examples of—but if they cannot otherwise be taken, to let not a single man escape alive.[13]

Quite simply, if the suspects could not be brought successfully into custody, they would have to be eliminated on the spot.

Given the large territorial range of the Potawatomis and the settlers' limited resources and knowledge of Potawatomi political and social organization, Edwards likely also understood that search parties of Illinois-based Rangers—no matter how vigilant—would face considerable challenges in identify-ing and capturing the suspects. Thus, he continued to prevail on Gomo and other Potawatomi chiefs in the region of Peoria to relinquish the suspects. To this end, in late July 1811, Edwards directed Capt. Samuel Levering to pro-ceed up the Illinois River to Gomo's village with, among others, a company of eight oarsmen, a Potawatomi, and a French interpreter. Levering's delegation traveled from Kaskaskia through Cahokia and Portage des Sioux, finally reaching Peoria on August 3. There Levering met with the local Indian agent Thomas Forsyth, who reported that, based on his intelligence, Gomo felt that he lacked sufficient authority among his fellow chiefs to produce the sus-pects. For his part, a local trader named Jacques Mette provided Levering with equally disheartening news, explaining that the persons suspected of the killings in the Louisiana Territory had by now ventured far afield—one to a

distant village, another to a town called White Pigeon in the direction of Detroit, and a third to a location even farther east. Levering also assessed reports
suggesting that opinion amongst the Potawatomis was divided as to whether
they should even attempt to furnish the suspects to the Americans: "One
party were of [the] opinion that it would be [good] policy to send a mission to
those chiefs who afforded shelter to the murderers, make a demand of them,
and surrender them to the Americans. Another party were opposed to making
any attempt to deliver up the offenders, but proposed to collect much of the
stolen property . . . , with representations that the offenders could not be
found."[14]

Levering, Gomo, and other Potawatomi chiefs located on the Illinois River
engaged in a complex set of negotiations concerning the "delivery" of the
suspected killers. On August 15 Levering presented Governor Edwards' "demand" that the "bad men, and all others [who] were of the party" involved
in the murders in July 1810 be "delivered up" to Levering, "together with the
property they stole." For good measure, Edwards also demanded "delivery" of
the persons responsible for the June 1811 killing of Elijah Cox, as well as those
involved in the murder of the settler Price. The next day Gomo responded.
After noting that he had "listened with attention" to the visitors' entreaties, he
presented his own perspective on the injustices that Indians had suffered at
the hands of American settlers. He acknowledged that Gen. Anthony Wayne
had "told us that the tomahawk must be buried, and even thrown into the
great lake" during the negotiations leading to the Treaty of Greenville in 1795.
But he also articulated his view that the treaty required that the "delivery"
of suspected murderers be observed reciprocally. According to Gomo, if "any
white man [should] murder an Indian, he should be delivered up to the Indians; and we, on our part, should deliver up the red men, who murdered a
white person, to the Americans." Little Chief, another Potawatomi leader, set
forth a similar view, arguing that under the treaty "[o]ne of the promises of
the Americans to the Indians . . . was that whenever murders should be committed on either side, the murderers should be delivered up to the opposite
party."[15]

After advancing his interpretation of the treaty Gomo observed that "[t]he
red skins [had] delivered up their offenders" to the Americans—whereas the
Americans, without exception, had failed to reciprocate. In response to one
American demand, the Potawatomis had even killed a tribesman named
Turkey Foot "in satisfaction for his [alleged] murders" of white settlers. Gomo
then outlined a litany of complaints relating to the treatment of Indians
suspected of criminal wrongdoing, including the killing of a Potawatomi in
St. Louis, the murder of "an innocent Kickapoo" suspected of stealing a horse,
and the beating and shooting of a Wyandot who had set fire to an area of

prairie while engaged in hunting. Gomo even took issue with the ways that American law defined wrongdoing in cases of homicide, recounting the case of a Chippewa who, while "looking at a gun," had the misfortune of having the gun discharge "accidentally," whereby it "shot an American." According to Gomo, "[w]henever an instance of this kind happens, it is usual for the red skins to regard it as an accident"; by contrast, the Americans demanded that the unfortunate Chippewa be "demanded, delivered up, and executed."[16]

By advancing a Potawatomi interpretation of the Treaty of Greenville, by arguing that American authorities had not produced white suspects to face Indian justice, by stressing the frequent resort of white settlers to extra-legal measures, and by criticizing the treatment of accidental killings under American law, Gomo and the other Potawatomi chiefs in the vicinity of Peoria articulated a sustained critique of frontier justice in Illinois. Levering, not surprisingly, took a very different view. He strenuously argued that the "ideas" set forth by Gomo and Little Chief about the Treaty of Greenville were "inaccurate" because they presumed that white suspects could be "delivered up" to Indian justice. Although the Potawatomis "supposed that our fathers promised that all murderers, on either side, should be delivered up to the opposite party," that surely "[could not] be the case," because American law "would not allow the Great Father, or Gen[eral] Wayne with him, to make such a stipulation in a treaty." Because "[a]ll offenders against [American] laws must be tried by [American] laws and by a jury of twelve men of our citizens," the Treaty of Greenville merely required that "each of our Governors . . . catch a murderer of an Indian, . . . have him tried for murder, and if found guilty, . . . see that he was hung." Notwithstanding these claims, Levering apparently failed to convince the Potawatomi chiefs and departed Peoria without the suspects in hand.[17]

Throughout 1812 the territorial government of Illinois continued its efforts to secure the Indian murder suspects. In an address to Gomo delivered at a council in Cahokia in April 1812, Edwards observed bitterly that "[i]njuries have been done, anger has been produced, and war . . . [is now] almost unavoidable." In this dangerous climate, made more perilous by the machinations of the British, the Potawatomis had opted to "protect" suspected killers, thus encouraging those individuals "to do more mischief," denying the Americans appropriate "satisfaction" for the deaths. With "the blood of . . . innocent persons . . . [crying] aloud . . . for vengeance," Edwards threatened that the "thirst for revenge" among white settlers in Illinois had become virtually unquenchable. In response, Gomo now claimed that he lacked the political and legal authority to accomplish Edwards' desired ends. Although the American territorial authorities had "troops and laws" to enforce their will

on white settlers, enforcement of law among the Potawatomis required negotiation, compromise, and coordinated agreement. According to Gomo, although he "could very easily secure or kill the murderers" sought by Edwards,
he "would be killed in the process" unless "the whole of [his] chiefs and young
men [were] consenting."[18]

Stymied by Gomo's continued resistance, Edwards reiterated his demand
for the suspects, threatening that Gomo "[could not] suppose that we are
people who can suffer our brethren to be murdered without having revenge."
Increasingly aware of the limited reach of the settlers' legal authority, and increasingly doubtful that the Potawatomis would produce the suspects, Edwards urged them to punish the suspects themselves in the presence of one
of Edwards' representatives: "My Children, you objected to give up those bad
men to be hung, like dogs, as you call it, and I now agree to permit you to *kill
them yourselves* [emphasis mine]; and, if you will consent to do it, I will send a
man with you to see it done, and we shall then have peace." If the Potawatomis
failed to execute the suspects themselves, Edwards vowed that dire results
awaited them:

> If twenty of your men murders a hundred of our people, what are we to
> do? We cannot find them and you will not punish them; what are we to do?
> You surely do not expect that we will let our people be murdered, without
> revenge. If you will not give up your bad men, who kill us, we must kill as
> many of yours—and then we may kill the innocent, which we do not wish
> to do.

Although Gomo agreed to "pay attention" to Edwards' words and follow his
recommendations, he declined to enter into any agreements, stating that Edwards would hear what he had done "when [he had got] home." As the summer of 1812 passed into autumn, Edwards continued to wait.[19]

By late 1812, however, conflict between settlers and Indians in Illinois had
expanded well beyond formal legal channels. In the fall of 1811 a prominent
comet had appeared in the Illinois skies that "was believed by many to be a
true harbinger of war." That fall white settlers attacked Indians across the Illinois and Indiana territories, precipitating a full-scale conflict. In what John
Mack Faragher has styled a "war of extirpation," Governor Edwards and the
Illinois volunteers under his command from 1811 to 1812 destroyed Indian
towns, burned fields of maize, and established a bounty of $50 "for the scalp
of any Indian—man, woman, or child—who entered an American settlement
with 'murderous intent.'" In 1812 a contingent of roughly 350 rangers and
other volunteers "broke up the Indian towns" on the bluffs near the head of

Lake Peoria, "destroyed their crops, killed a number, [and] took some prisoners." Unable to secure the suspected killers through resort to law, frustrated by
the recurring conflicts between whites and Indians in the vicinity of Peoria,
and distrustful that some of the white inhabitants of Peoria had become too
"intimate and friendly" with the Potawatomi chiefs, the territorial militia
destroyed the town and drove all of Peoria's inhabitants—both Indian and
white—from its environs.[20]

The authority of Gomo and other Potawatomi chiefs in the area around
Peoria waned in the wake of the War of 1812. By the early 1820s Anglo-
American settlers had begun to trickle into the area, a region that a decade
earlier had been the domain of the Potawatomis and a few French traders. In
a climate of diminished Potawatomi influence and heightened American
power, the ability of Indians to negotiate over the law (or to evade its grasp altogether) appeared to have decreased considerably. Nonetheless, Indians continued to find ways to use formal law in ways that suited their purposes.

On November 16–17, 1825, Nomaque, a Potawatomi, was tried in the Peoria
County circuit court for the murder of Pierre Londri, a French trader. The
proceedings in the trial court were marked by a series of curious events. In its
first term of existence, the court met in the home of Joseph Ogee, a multiracial interpreter who lived in Peoria's only hewn-wood home. After insufficient persons were identified in the Peoria area to serve on the grand jury,
individuals from a neighboring county were called on to sit on the jury.
According to a contemporary account the grand jurors arrived at Peoria with
considerable stocks of whiskey, which they consumed liberally during the
proceedings. After impaneling nine trial jurors, Sawyer permitted them to
wander outside the courtroom before the final three were impaneled. The
judge then swore Ogee and the trader Mette as interpreters, who "read" and
"explained" the indictment to Nomaque. The charge in any language was
grave: Nomaque, "not having the fear of God before his ey[es] but being
moved and secured by the instigation of th[e] Devil," had struck Londri in the
belly with "a certain knife common[ly] called a scalping knife," from which
Londri died.[21]

At trial Nomaque was represented by William Hamilton, the son of
Alexander Hamilton—who, like his father, was a lawyer, though a fledgling
one. After the indictment had been read, Hamilton moved to dismiss the action on the grounds that jurisdiction was improper, ostensibly under treaties
entered into between the Potawatomis and the United States. After Sawyer
overruled this jurisdictional motion, Nomaque entered a plea of not guilty
and put himself "on the country"—requesting a trial by jury. Hamilton next
attempted to prevent a prospective juror from being sworn, arguing that the
individual was not a "taxable inhabitant" of the county. This argument, too,

was rejected by Sawyer. Efforts by Hamilton to introduce an almanac to rebut the testimony of one of the witnesses and to read from various treaties between the Potawatomis and the United States appear to have been similarly thwarted by the trial judge. After Hamilton's legal maneuvers proved unavailing, the jury of twelve men returned a verdict of guilty.[22]

Hamilton, however, was far from finished. After the jury returned their verdict, he continued to press his client's case in the trial court by filing a motion for arrest of judgment. In support of the motion, Hamilton submitted an affidavit claiming that several of the grand jurors were not "good and lawful men" of the stature qualified to serve. After hearing argument on this point, Sawyer rejected this effort as well. Not finished, Hamilton then moved for a new trial on the basis that "one of the jurors was partial and not a fit person to sit." According to supporting affidavits, a juror named Peter Dumont had referred to Nomaque as a "rascal" and had expressed a "passion against the Indians previous to his being sw[orn]" as a juror. This effort was also rejected by Sawyer, who ordered that Nomaque "[be] [con]fined in some safe jail or place of safe keeping until the thir[d] Saturday in the month of January next between the hours of twelve and three . . . at which time the said Nomaque is to be taken to some convenient place of execution and be hanged by the neck until he is DEAD." So ended the eventful first term of the Peoria County circuit court.[23]

But Nomaque's legal saga did not end there. Nomaque's counsel then moved for leave to file a bill of exceptions to prepare the case for an appeal. In late 1825 Nomaque's appellate counsel filed a writ of error in the Supreme Court of Illinois. The writ alleged several types of "manifest error" in the proceedings below. Nomaque's counsel first alleged that the trial court had erred in overruling the motion for a new trial because the jurors had failed to render their verdict in open court but had instead submitted their verdict to the trial judge pursuant to an agreement between Hamilton and the state attorney general. Second, the writ revived Hamilton's claim that Dumont "was not an impartial juror" and had irretrievably tainted the jury's deliberations. Finally, the writ argued that the judgment against Nomaque was void because the record of the proceedings below did not reveal that the grand jury had ever found the indictment to be a "true bill," a precondition for placing a suspect on his defense at trial.[24]

In an opinion issued in 1825, the Illinois Supreme Court reversed Nomaque's conviction. Writing for the court, Justice Theophilus Smith agreed with Nomaque's argument that a conviction secured on an indictment that had not been endorsed by a grand jury as a "true bill" was a legal "nullity." In turn, the court concluded that the presence on the trial jury of Dumont— "one who, so far from standing perfectly indifferent between the parties, as the law emphatically requires, was in a condition the very opposite"—warranted a new trial. Reversal was also proper because the jury had failed to deliver its verdict in open court, thus depriving Nomaque of the opportunity to have the jurors polled individually to confirm the existence of unanimity. Although the court declined to give a "positive opinion" about the trial judge's curious decision to let nine of the jurors "go at large" before the trial had begun, it did express concern that this practice—if permitted to continue—might allow jurors to gain "other impressions in regard to the prisoner, than those . . . made by the testimony given [at] the trial" itself.[25]

At first blush, Nomaque had secured a ringing victory in the state's highest court. In practice, however, his victory proved hollow. In its opinion, the Illinois Supreme Court ordered that Nomaque be held in custody for thirty days "to enable the local authorities [in Peoria] to take measures to bring him again to trial." According to the court, Nomaque should remain in custody because "a flagrant crime [had] no doubt been committed, and possibly by the prisoner." In the court's view, maintaining the suspect in custody was proper so that "public justice [would] not be evaded." After facilities in Peoria proved too rudimentary to ensure Nomaque's safe confinement, he was transferred to Springfield and Edwardsville before facing a second indictment for the same offense. After additional legal skirmishes, including an argument by defense counsel that he could not be tried on the grounds of double jeopardy, the attorney general entered a *nolle prosequi* in 1828, effectively ending the prosecution of the Potawatomi Nomaque.[26]

Nomaque's life after his brush with the law remains shrouded in mystery. Some accounts suggest that he ultimately fought on the side of Black Hawk during the Black Hawk Wars from 1831 to 1832. Another contemporary report suggests that he suffered injury at the battle of Stillman's Run and was killed on the battlefield by militia raised from the area of Peoria.[27] If true, force of arms had once again prevailed where law had failed to secure a conviction for murder.

What conclusions should we draw from the experiences of Gomo and Nomaque? To begin, their stories—and others like them—suggest that the resolution of cases of homicide was an important and recurring concern of both Indians and settlers in early-nineteenth-century Illinois. In Illinois, in the generation after the Treaty of Greenville, Indians killed white settlers and white settlers killed Indians, both within the context of warfare and outside the murky boundaries of military conflict. Thus, as in White's Great Lakes region or Reid's Pacific Northwest, homicides and efforts to resolve them proved to be a problematic and persistent concern. In this respect, Davis's recent portrait of early-nineteenth-century Illinois as a land of tranquility and non-violent "exceptionalism" (as compared to other portions of the Old Northwest) must be seriously questioned.

So too law in frontier Illinois—contrary to Davis's claims—does not emerge as a well-ordered system whose equitable rulings garnered widespread legitimacy and effectively deterred violence. Rather the evidence suggests that the criminal law—at least with respect to allegations of murder brought against Indians—operated fitfully in the 1810s and 1820s. On the one hand, a series of institutional weaknesses—including defects in policing, in the mechanism of extradition, in pretrial detention, and in the conduct of trial proceedings—provided opportunities for Indians suspected of murder to evade and, occasionally, to escape justice. On the other hand, Euro-American settlers, who might have been expected to benefit from the existence of formal law, exercised considerable latitude to resort to coercive violence when recourse to formal law proved frustrating or unavailing.[28]

In turn, as Hoxie no doubt expected when he issued his invitation for a "'New' North American Indian Legal History" nearly twenty years ago, Indians in early-nineteenth-century Illinois emerge from the primary sources not as lawless evaders or law-dominated victims but as individuals who, at times, actively used legal arguments, legal procedures, and legal institutions to pursue their own ends. Because territorial authorities seeking to apprehend Indian suspects in the 1810s felt the need to negotiate with Indian leaders to produce the suspected killers, Indians could "talk back" with arguments based on the parties' practices, notions of fairness, and legal principle. A decade later lax procedures that helped secure convictions favorable to settler interests at the trial level also exposed those same convictions to successful challenges in the higher courts.[29]

We must be careful not to draw overly strong conclusions from the evidence of two micro-historical case studies. To be sure, further research is needed to chart the shifting role of law in early-nineteenth-century Illinois and the shifting uses to which it was made over time. The history of Indian-settler relations in Illinois, in certain respects, supports the dour assessment of White, who argues that the "middle ground" forged between Algonquian and European interests "withered and died" with the decline of Indian political power after the War of 1812 and the unleashing of American settler ambitions. In White's view, whereas practices designed to resolve disputes arising from cross-cultural homicides had once proved a "centerpiece" of "the middle ground," relations between Indians and settlers by the 1810s and 1820s increasingly involved parties with widely differing bargaining power who increasingly had little interest in negotiation.[30] With that said, the *legal* empire that white settlers in the Old Northwest sought to construct remained fragile, exposed, contingent, and susceptible to skillful negotiation by its participants throughout the 1820s.[31] In short, criminal law on the early-nineteenth-century Illinois frontier did not so much manifest the state's monopoly over violence as demonstrate the limits of that monopoly—limits imposed both by the willingness of individuals to evade the grasp of formal law and by the efforts of individuals whom the law ensnared to negotiate its turns and its terms.

NOTES

1. My reconstruction draws on the following sources: Deposition of Rebecca Cox, June 13, 1811, Ohio Valley, Great Lakes Ethnohistory Archive, Glenn A. Black Laboratory of Archaeology, Indiana University, South Bend, Indiana [hereafter cited as GBL], Potawatomi File, Jan.–June 1811 Binder (describing attack and discovery of raiding party); William Clark to William Eustis, July 3, 1811, GBL Potawatomi File, July–Dec. 1811 Binder (referring to Potawatomis who "killed a Young Man on the Northern frontiers of the Illinois Territory, and took a young woman Prisoner" and later sought "to kill the woman who received three wounds before she was retaken"); and Ninian Edwards to Eustis, June 7, 1811, GBL Potawatomi File, Jan.–June 1811 Binder ("Yesterday I was informed by respectable authority that one young man on the frontier . . . in the county of St[.] Clair had been killed and his sister carried off by some Indians who also stole some horses"). On the activities of Rangers in Illinois, see James E. Davis, *Frontier Illinois* (Bloomington: Indiana Univ. Press, 1998), 135–36. In preparing this essay, I have benefited from the assistance of the staffs at the Glenn A. Black Laboratory of Archaeology, the Illinois State Archives, the Illinois Historical Survey at the University of Illinois at Urbana-Champaign, and from the encouragement and advice of Fred Hoxie, Elizabeth Robischon, and Stephen Ross.

2. For a typical early treatment, see, for example, David McCulloch, ed., *History of Peoria County Illinois* (Chicago: Munsell, 1902). For Davis's recent study, part of a multivolume history of the trans-Appalachian frontier, see Davis, *Frontier Illinois*, 138–39. For another modern retelling of the Cox episode, see R. David Edmunds, *The Potawatomis: Keepers of the Fire* (Norman: Univ. of Oklahoma Press, 1978), 174.

3. Frederick E. Hoxie, "Towards a 'New' North American Indian Legal History," *American Journal of Legal History* 30 (1986): 356–57; Richard White, *The Middle Ground: Indians, Empires, and Republics in the Great Lakes Region, 1650–1815* (New York: Cambridge Univ. Press, 1991), esp. 76; John Phillip Reid, *Patterns of Vengeance: Crosscultural Homicide in the North American Fur Trade* (Sacramento, Calif.: Ninth Judicial Circuit Historical Society, 1999). By "cross-cultural homicide" or "cross-cultural killings," I refer to homicides in which the perpetrators and victims are from different cultural backgrounds. For examinations of cross-cultural violence on the frontier, see, for example, John R. Wunder, "Anti-Chinese Violence in the American West, 1850–1910," in John McLaren, Hamar Foster, and Chet Orloff, eds., *Law for the Elephant, Law for the Beaver: Essays in the Legal History of the North American West* (Regina, Sask.: Canadian Plains Research Center, 1992), 212–36; and "Chinese in Trouble: Criminal Law and Race on the Trans–Mississippi West Frontier," *Western Historical Quarterly* 17 (1986): 25–41.

4. By "murder," I seek to distinguish killings of non-combatants perceived by Indians or settlers as unlawful or improper from killings of combatants. Admittedly, the distinction was often blurred in practice. On the important difference between "homicide" and "murder," see Reid, *Patterns of Vengeance*, 19. For historical treatments of Indians accused of murder, see John Howard Payne, *Indian Justice: A Cherokee Murder Trial at Tahlequah in 1840*, ed. Grant Foreman (Norman: Univ. of Oklahoma Press, 2002); Carol Chomsky, "The United States–Dakota War Trials: A Study in Military Injustice," *Stanford Law Review* 43 (1990): 13–98; Yasuhide Kawashima, "Forced Conformity: Criminal Justice and Indians," *University of Kansas Law Review* 25 (1977): 361–73; Louis Pfaller, "The Brave Bear Murder Case," *North Dakota History* 36 (1969): 121–40; and Henry Brackenridge, "The Trial of Mamachtaga, a Delaware Indian, the First Person Convicted of Murder West of the Allegheny Mountains and Hanged for His Crime," *Western Pennsylvania History Magazine* 1 (1918): 27–36.

5. In recent years legal historians have devoted considerable attention to the South, the West, and even the Great Plains, but far less to the Midwest. For example, the most comprehensive multivolume bibliography of American legal history contains entries for "the South," "the West," and "New England," but none for "the Midwest." See Kermit L. Hall, *A Comprehensive Bibliography of American Constitutional and Legal History, 1896–1979* (Millwood, N.Y.: Kraus International, 1984). For examples of regional approaches to American legal history, see, for example, John Phillip Reid, "The Layers of Western Legal History," in *Law for the Elephant*, 23–73; *Law and the Great Plains: Essays on the Legal History of the Heartland*, ed. John R. Wunder (Westport, Conn.: Greenwood, 1996); and Kermit L. Hall, "The Legal Culture of the Great Plains," *Great Plains Quarterly* 12 (1992): 86–98.

Legal studies of the Old Northwest and other territories are similarly underdeveloped. As Reid and others have properly noted, "[t]he territories are . . . a subject of study too much neglected." Reid, "Layers," 64n102 (citing Harry N. Scheiber, "Western Legal History: Where Are We and Where Do We Go from Here," *Western Legal History* 3 [1990]: 127, 128). One classic exception, as Reid notes, remains the pioneering study by Francis S. Philbrick, ed., *The Laws of Illinois Territory, 1809–1818*, vol. 25, *Collections of the Illinois State Historical Library* (Springfield: Illinois State Historical Library, 1950). For other treatments of law in the territories, see William Wirt Blume, "Criminal Procedure on the American Frontier: A Study of the Statutes and Court Records of Michigan Territory, 1805–1825," *Michigan Law Review* 57 (1958): 195–256; Gordon Morris Bakken, "Judicial Review in the Rocky Mountain Territorial Courts," *American Journal of Legal History* 15 (1971): 56–65; Elizabeth Gaspar Brown, "The Views of a Michigan Territorial Jurist on the Common Law," *American Journal of Legal History* 15 (1971): 307–16; and David D. Banta, "The Criminal Code of the Northwest Territory," *Indiana Magazine of History* 9 (1913): 234–46.

6. See, for example, Davis, *Frontier Illinois*, 7, 331–33. According to Davis, "Although dangers lurked and tensions flared, frontier Illinois was amazingly tranquil, a highly significant fact. Settlers and visitors—people on the scene—rarely wrote about conflict, violence, and homicide" and "few Illinoisans died violent deaths." Ibid., 287.

7. For studies of pre-modern legal systems that stress "collective responsibility," see Richard A. Posner, "An Economic Theory of Criminal Law," *Columbia Law Review* 85 (1985): 1,195; and James Lindgren, "Why the Ancients May Not Have Needed a System of

Criminal Law," *Boston University Law Review* 76 (1996): 29. On aboriginal approaches to criminal justice, see Kathleen Joan Bragdon, "Crime and Punishment among the Indians of Massachusetts, 1675–1750," *Ethnohistory* 28 (Winter 1981): 23–32.

8. On these themes, see Hoxie, "Towards a 'New' Indian Legal History," 357.

9. For descriptions of the incident, see E. B. Washburne, ed., *The Edwards Papers: Being a Portion of the Collection of the Letters, Papers, and Manuscripts of Ninian Edwards* (Chicago: Fergus, 1884), 37–38; Deposition of James Moredaugh, August 17, 1810, and Deposition of Stephen Cole, September 21, 1810, Ninian Edwards Papers, Chicago Historical Society, Chicago, Illinois; Clark to Eustis, September 12, 1810, Clarence Edwin Carter, ed., *The Territorial Papers of the United States*, 28 vols. (Washington, D.C.: GPO, 1934–75), 14:412–14; and Edmunds, *Potawatomis*, 173. Volume 14 of the *Territorial Papers of the United States* is available through the University of Missouri Digital Library at http://digital.library.umsystem.edu.

10. Clark to Eustis, September 12, 1810, *Territorial Papers*, 14: 412–14. On the Potawatomis, see *Encyclopedia of North American Indians*, ed. Frederick E. Hoxie (Boston, Mass.: Houghton Mifflin, 1996), 506; James A. Clifton, *The Prairie People: Change and Continuity in Potawatomi Indian Culture, 1665–1965* (Lawrence: Regents' Press of Kansas, 1977); and Edmunds, *Potawatomis*. On the Prophet, see R. David Edmunds, *The Shawnee Prophet* (Lincoln: Univ. of Nebraska Press, 1983); and Milo Milton Quaife, *Chicago and the Old Northwest, 1763–1835: A Study of the Evolution of the Northwestern Frontier* (Urbana: Univ. of Illinois Press, 2001), 185–90.

11. Howard to Edwards, November 15, 1810, Washburne, ed., *Edwards Papers*, 56–57.

12. Edwards to Eustis, June 7, 1811, GBL Potawatomi File, Jan.–June 1811 Binder.

13. Edwards to Colonel Whiteside, June 8, 1811, GBL Potawatomi File, Jan.–June 1811 Binder. Both William and Samuel Whiteside served as commanders of regiments of rangers. See Davis, *Frontier Illinois*, 136.

14. Details of the delegation to Gomo are set forth in Ninian W. Edwards, *History of Illinois from 1778 to 1833; and Life and Times of Ninian Edwards* (Springfield: Illinois State Journal, 1870), 37–72.

15. Ibid. For discussion of the Treaty of Greenville (1795), see Quaife, *Chicago and the Old Northwest*, 122–25. Article 6 of the treaty provided that any citizen of the United States who settled on lands relinquished to the signatories by the United States "shall be out of the protection of the United States" and punishable by the Indians "as they shall think fit." Article 9 stated that "no private revenge or retaliation shall take place" for "injuries done by individuals on either side." Neither article referred specifically to the delivery of persons suspected of murders. The treaty is available through the Yale Law School Avalon Project at www.yale.edu/lawweb/avalon/greenvil.htm.

16. Edwards, *History of Illinois*, 37–72.

17. Ibid.

18. Address of Edwards, ibid., 56–60; Answer of Gomo, ibid., 61–63; Reply of Edwards, ibid., 64–65; and Answer of Gomo, ibid., 65.

19. Ibid.

20. John Mack Faragher, *Sugar Creek: Life on the Illinois Prairie* (New Haven, Conn.: Yale Univ. Press, 1986), 31–32 (quoting future Illinois Gov. John Reynolds); Edwards, *Life and Times*, 69.

21. The following account is reconstructed from the case files in *People v. Nomaque,* Case No. 81, in the Illinois State Archives [ISA], Springfield, Illinois, Record Group 901.001 [hereafter cited as *People v. Nomaque,* ISA Case Files]. On Ogee, see Edmunds, *Potawatomis,* 228. Ogee received payment of $1 and one ration per day to serve as an interpreter in 1822. See James Latham, Estimate of Expenses of Peoria Sub Agency, St. Louis, October 24, 1822, GBL Potawatomi Files, 1822 Binder.

22. *People v. Nomaque,* ISA Case Files. Although a trial transcript of the proceedings does not exist, Hamilton's legal tactics can be reconstructed—at least in part—from the materials in the files of the Illinois Supreme Court. On Hamilton and his representation of Nomaque, see Sylvan Joseph Muldoon, *Alexander Hamilton's Pioneer Son: The Life and Times of Colonel William Stephen Hamilton* (Harrisburg, Pa.: Aurand, 1930), 43–44.

23. Ibid.

24. Ibid.

25. *Nomaque v. People,* Case No. 81, Record Group 901.001, Illinois State Archives, Springfield, Illinois.

26. See Bill Moon, "The Story of Noma-a-Que: Court Records Tell Interesting Story of Peoria County's First Murder Trial," *Journal of the Illinois State Historical Society* 5 (1913): 246–55.

27. Ibid.

28. Moreover, in considering the nature of law on the Illinois frontier, it is important to contrast the limited legal experience and knowledge of the trial court with the relative sophistication of the appellate body. There were, in short, two types of criminal law at work—one at the trial level and one on appeal. On the nature of law on the frontier, including the personnel of trial and appellate courts, see Kermit L. Hall, "Constitutional Machinery and Judicial Professionalism: The Careers of Midwestern State Appellate Court Judges, 1861–1899," in Gerard W. Gawalt, ed., *The New High Priests: Lawyers in Post–Civil War America* (Westport, Conn.: Greenwood, 1984), 29–49; Larry A. Bakken, *Justice in the Wilderness: A Study of Frontier Courts in Canada and the United States, 1670–1870* (Littleton, Colo.: Fred B. Rothman, 1986); and David J. Bodenhamer, "Law and Disorder on the Early Frontier: Marion County, Indiana, 1823–1850," *Western History Quarterly* 10 (1979): 323–36. On the particular difficulties of trying cases of murder on the nineteenth-century American frontier, see Avery N. Beebe, "Judge Theophilus L. Dickey and the First Murder Trial in Kendall County," *Journal of the Illinois State Historical Society* 3 (1911): 49–58; Harry L. McGuirk, "A Pioneer Indiana County Circuit Court," *American Journal of Legal History* 15 (1971): 278–87; Raymond M. Momboisse, "Early California Justice: First Murder Trial," *California Bar Journal* 37 (1962): 736–42; Joel Samaha, "A Case of Murder: Criminal Justice in Early Minnesota," *Minnesota Law Review* 60 (1976): 1,219–32; and John R. Wunder, *Inferior Courts, Superior Justice: A History of the Justices of the Peace on the Northwest Frontier, 1853–1889* (Westport, Conn.: Greenwood, 1979).

29. On the phenomenon of "talking back," see Frederick E. Hoxie, Preface to *Talking Back to Civilization: Indian Voices from the Progressive Era* (Boston, Mass.: Bedford/St. Martin's, 2001), vii–viii.

30. See White, *Middle Ground,* 523.

31. For a perceptive revisionist discussion of the constraints and weaknesses of British imperialism, see Linda Colley, *Captives: Britain, Empire and the World, 1600–1850* (New York: Pantheon, 2002).

9

"Justice and Public Policy"

*Indian Trade, Treaties, and Removal from
Northern Indiana, 1826–1846*

PHYLLIS GERNHARDT

In 1833 the United States federal government attempted to negotiate two separate treaties with the Potawatomi and Miami Indian nations of northern
Indiana. In both instances the negotiations failed. Triumphantly claiming responsibility were the Indian traders of the region. By this year, the patronage
granted traders at the negotiations had become an expected income for these
frontier entrepreneurs. When the government bypassed them in both the
Potawatomi and then the Miami negotiations later in the year, northern Indiana traders used their influence to sabotage successful outcomes. One trader
complained that both he and his brother had been "unjustly neglected in the
division of contracts and the allowance of claims." This, he warned, would
not repeat itself. Either the government would provide him with a written
contract confirming the amount of patronage he would be given and the provisions the government could guarantee to him, "or no treaty could or should
be made." Although the treaty commissioner refused to be intimidated by the
threats, the Potawatomis and Miamis were more easily influenced. The merchants had successfully discouraged the Indians from agreeing to any terms
with the United States unless the traders' conditions were met, "keep[ing]
those damn politicians back from furnishing one cent" of goods. If the traders could not benefit from the profits of providing goods for the native nations, then no one would.[1]

What had seemed to be the perfect opportunity for the government to negotiate two successful treaties in 1833 was thus thwarted. The Miami leaders
previously had assured government officials that their nation would negotiate
for at least part of their lands as well as discuss the possibilities of removal.

They ultimately proposed to sell only a small percentage of their land, how-ever, an amount that the commissioners "couldn't for a moment have thought of accepting . . . for it would not have provided the views of the government nor have satisfied the citizens of Indiana." Terms of removal were not even considered. Frustrated with this turn of events, the commissioners recognized the merchants' influence with the Indians. Seemingly working in the Miamis' best interest, the traders had persuaded this nation "that the Government must and would buy the land at any price," and, if the Miamis remained firm in their demands, they would get the amount of money they desired from the government. But the governing officials saw the situation much differently. They blamed the failed treaty on the "deep laid plan by some artful and de-signing persons whose interest it was to defeat the treaty at present and it suc-ceeded but too well."[2]

By the early 1830s those engaged in the Indian trade on the Indiana fron-tier and the federal government of the United States had become inextricably linked in implementing Indian affairs. On the one hand, the trade with the native population on the frontier had become a highly profitable venture. The Indians had come to rely on these merchants for the goods they provided and, to a certain extent their advice, as well. On the other hand, the gov-ernment relied on the traders to help affect their Indian policies, namely the policy of removal hallmarked by the passage of the 1830 Indian Removal Act. Recognizing the traders' familiarity with the Indians, they relied on these merchants' abilities to influence the native nations of the region to bring them to treaty negotiations and particularly took advantage of the Indians' debts to these merchants in order to procure land cessions. From this central place of influence the Indian traders of northern Indiana played the needs of their na-tive customers against the desires of the federal government, manipulating both so that they might reap the highest profits possible.

While both state and federal governments desired the removal of the native inhabitants of the region, the traders wanted to keep the Indians in Indiana as long as they could profit from them, and they worked to ensure that the removal, when it did happen, proved beneficial for them as well. Lobbying to postpone removal, they argued that the Indians' removal from the state was impractical. Most of the individuals involved would benefit, they argued, if the government could "suffer them to occupy back & un-important situations for a while, as their increased annuity will be of material benefit in the first settling of our country." Besides, they said, "there is yet room for all."[3]

In the very earliest years of the new nation, the government did, indeed, consider the country large enough for both United States citizens and the na-tive inhabitants. However, in order to ensure lasting peace on the frontier, the federal government needed to control American settlement as it progressed westward. Its first regulations thus called for distinct boundary lines and forbade Anglo-Americans from hunting or settling within the Indian Country, allowing them to enter only if engaged in government-approved business. Settlers were strictly prohibited from buying or trading for Indian lands. Unscrupulous traders, who would "aggrandize a few avaricious Men to the prejudice of many, and the embarrassment of Government," were especially feared.[4]

In order to prevent private citizens from trading on the frontier, and to provide the Indians with goods at the same time, a formal system of trade, the factory system, was established. Its primary purpose of keeping peace on the frontier was a mostly successful policy before the War of 1812. It created "ties of interest" between the Indians and the federal government that would simultaneously undermine "alien [British] traders and their anti-American influences," as well as undersell any private traders. Thus the factory system would protect the natives from dishonest merchants and regulate trade to maintain a peaceful frontier.[5]

But the factory system also provided the United States government with the increased opportunity for land acquisitions. Its secondary effect was to allow the Indians of the Old Northwest to run up large debts as means of forcing them to sell their land. While the factory system was not to be created as a money-making venture for the United States, it was not to operate at a deficit. If the Indians put themselves in debt, it would be to the American government, not to the British or private traders. The goods the Indians received from the factory would accustom the native nations to the domestic comforts the American government could provide, becoming even more desirable to them than "the possession of extensive but uncultivated wilds." Dependent on American goods and becoming indebted as they purchased them on credit, Indians would be forced to sell their only asset—their land. This "disposition to exchange lands . . . for necessaries" would be strongly encouraged by the government.[6]

The factory at Fort Wayne engaged in a large trade with the Indians of the Great Lakes until the War of 1812, exchanging manufactured goods for pelts and furs. Great care was taken to have goods appropriated for the Indian trade. The Fort Wayne factor, John Johnston, assumed responsibility for gauging the Indians' needs and providing that information to the factory's government suppliers. He supplied the eastern administrators of the system with descriptions of necessary articles, examples of Indian blankets, and other "such specimens of articles as will lend to the perfection of the system." "Dead articles," or those that did not satisfy Indian needs or desires, were sent back east if possible.[7]

Up to the time of the war the factory at Fort Wayne operated quite well. Larger transactions such as that completed in 1806 by Black Raccoon, a Miami, consisted of an exchange of $32.50 worth of furs (63 doeskins and 3 bucks) for $35.50 worth of goods. The hunt for furs was profitable for the Indians of northern Indiana in this early frontier period. In the decade prior to the War of 1812, the Fort Wayne factory brought in more furs than any other in the Great Lakes region. Exchanges such as Black Raccoon's were very common. To the extent that it provided a regulated means of trade, the factory system thus achieved the government's goals and allowed the United States administrators to compete with the British traders who attempted to gain the economic benefits and the political and military loyalties of Great Lakes Indians. Just as important, the Fort Wayne factory successfully staved off large numbers of private traders who wished to engage in business with Indians of the area. In this way the factory limited American access to the frontier region prior to 1812 and thereby maintained peace with the original inhabitants.[8]

The history of the trading factory at Fort Wayne illustrated the brevity and overall effectiveness of this policy of the United States government. The factory at Fort Wayne was one of the twenty-eight government trading stores that operated between the years 1796 to 1822, and like the rest it suffered economically during the War of 1812. The system as a whole was abandoned in 1822, although the factory no longer operated in northern Indiana after the war. British defeat meant the loss of British competition and influence through trade and lessened the threat of Indian uprisings. The reliance on the hunt for furs was declining as well, as the abundance of wildlife diminished. The decline of the factories changed the relationship between the native nations on the frontier and the federal government. Where the Indians had traded primarily with the government factor due to the strict limitations of trade, private citizens, backed with government licenses, now had increased contact with the merchants who dominated the trading system.[9]

By the time that the factory system was no longer in operation, the northern third of the state, in which Fort Wayne was the only white settlement of any notable size, remained an Indian territory. A small number of Americans had found protection at the garrison that had been built at the headwaters of the Maumee River in 1794 after Anthony Wayne's victory at the decisive battle of Fallen Timbers. But until 1818 the post and its inhabitants lived far within the frontier. Land was not to be opened for settlement in its vicinity until that year, when the Delaware and Wea nations forfeited all of their land within Indiana to the United States government.[10]

The half-decade following this treaty was an important period for northern Indiana. One year after the 1818 treaty, the troops that had been posted at Fort Wayne in 1794 were removed. Three years later, in the same year the factory system was abandoned, a land office was opened and operated out of the now-abandoned fort to handle land sales for the nearby regions. The Miami and Potawatomi nations, who together totaled 2,441, claimed over 6 million acres of land in northern Indiana. No longer restricted by the factory system, private traders moved to the area and, though licensed and monitored by the government, they began to dramatically transform the system of trade. By the mid-1820s, with furs less plentiful, trade based on credit had evolved, forcing the remaining native nations of northern Indiana in an economic system that they clearly did not understand. While selling goods on credit was not unfamiliar to the Indian traders on the frontier, when it came to trading with their white neighbors they allowed this privilege "only with those whome they supposed to be perfectly good." Hesitant to extend credit to their fellow settlers, the merchants of northern Indiana happily engaged in a liberal and open trade with the Potawatomis and Miamis. With the federal government backing their debts, profits were assured.[11]

In 1826 treaties hastened this economic transition for the remaining Indians in northern Indiana. As a result of pressure from settlers and accrued debts, the Miamis ceded most of their land north and west of the Wabash and Miami rivers, about one million acres. They were now entirely restricted to reservations in northern Indiana. The Potawatomis gave up a strip of land along the northern banks of the Wabash. Even more significantly for the Indian trade, the treaties of 1826 allowed for specific payments of debts that the Indians had accumulated in the eight-year period following the 1818 treaties—$9,573 for the Potawatomis and $7,727 for the Miamis. These debts were to be paid by the federal government, using the purchase monies for the Potawatomis and Miami lands.[12]

This course of action set a precedent for the treaties that followed, in which the Potawatomis and Miamis found themselves caught in a system of economic entrapment, relying on the purchase of goods on credit from the region's merchants for which the sale of their lands would be required in order to pay their debts. This system gave to these entrepreneurs an incredible amount of influence over both Indian affairs and the government's interactions with the natives on the frontier. While the native nations relied on the traders for goods, the federal government allowed the merchants to encourage this indebtedness with the final transactions of land cessions as the desired end. With the establishment of this mutually beneficial trade merchants began stocking goods in anticipation of the forthcoming treaties and the government looked forward to achieving removal. Four years later Congress passed the Indian Removal Act and with this added emphasis on moving the Indian natives west of the Mississippi River, the constant debts of the Indians provided a useful tool to achieve this policy objective.[13]

Despite this congressional push for removal in 1830, government officials did not let the interference of the traders and the subsequent failure of the negotiations of 1833 concern them too deeply. They were convinced that the ever increasing debts that the Indians had incurred and the failure to pay the traders' claims by treaties in 1833 would make the native nations even more desperate. This would bring them to the point of removal even more quickly, one commissioner reported, for the "principal men are now greatly in debt, and they must soon have a treaty or they are ruined, as to their property and influence."[14]

The Miamis and Potawatomis did sign a treaty the following year in 1834. Both nations forfeited a number of their reservations to the United States in that year. As in 1826, the treaty set aside money to repay the traders. One trader thankfully declared that "the debts of the Indians have been provided for and will be paid. Ours are very large and we hope that justice will be extended to us." A delay in the ratification of the 1834 Miami treaty until the end of 1837, however, was a cause of great consternation for the merchants of northern Indiana. One protested that the wait would be "a serious injury" to his finances. Moreover, failure to ratify this treaty in a timely fashion, which threatened the livelihood of the traders, might delay the possibilities of treaties in the near future.[15]

In 1836, while the Miami treaty of 1834 awaited ratification, the Potawatomis were once again negotiating terms with the United States government. By that year only 441 Potawatomis had willingly emigrated from Indiana, leaving three thousand others still within the state's boundaries. While the traders were waiting for the 1834 Miami treaty to be ratified, the Potawatomis agreed to cede their remaining lands and to move west of the Mississippi River within two years. Final removal of the Potawatomis from Indiana came in 1838, when the last 850 went west, escorted by a military guard. The Potawatomis joined 45,690 eastern United States Indians that had already made the trek west of the Mississippi River. Nearly another 49,000 Indians, including the Potawatomis of northern Indiana, had agreed to removal. The removal policy was achieving success; little more than 8,000 Indians remained east of the Mississippi River.[16]

Nearly 1,100 Miamis in northern Indiana were among those natives that had not yet agreed to removal, making them the only native inhabitants left in Indiana by 1838. Hoping that this nation would soon follow the others, the government worked diligently to secure their removal. Determined to remain, the Miamis found support from the merchants involved in the Indian trade who desired to maintain their lucrative business with the natives and to use the remaining Miamis as leverage to force the federal government to cover the Indians' unpaid debts. The traders' claims from 1834 had not been paid until 1837, and then the traders received only half of the total amount of $91,561.42 that they declared the Indians owed them. This difference frustrated the merchants, who continued to press the Indians for payments of their debts as well as put pressure on the government officials to negotiate a further cession of lands in order to pay the outstanding claims.[17]

Thus the Miamis were once again pressured to negotiate a treaty by 1838. Federal commissioners noted a "sudden excitement amongst the whole nation, originating from the unexpected information, that they were again much involved in debt." The excitement was not surprising; within the previous decade dramatic changes had occurred. The Miami land base was greatly reduced, their debts continued to mount, and their culture was quickly fading as the contact with the encroaching whites changed even the means by which they supported themselves. They no longer relied on the hunt but rather purchased goods on credit. Their tribe was also divided over the issue of the rising debts and the resulting loss of lands. Individuals whose "extravagance" had involved the whole tribe in debts were encouraged to deny any of the traders' claims. These extravagant individuals not only feared the disapproval of their nation but also the "knife of the more economical" members of the Miamis, as well. Emotions ran high. Despite the tension, in 1838 the Miamis were forced to cede all but a portion of the remaining reservation on the Wabash River. Although the Miamis did not agree to emigrate, the government promised to set aside land for them west of the Mississippi River and to pay for their removal expenses, when they did decide to move. It also provided for a commission that would investigate the traders' claims against the Miami since the treaty of 1834. The treaty designated that $150,000 be set aside for those debts.[18]

Once again the traders did not receive the payments they claimed they were owed. Angered, they protested vehemently. One merchant declared that both the traders and the Indians had believed that the federal government would pay the Miamis' debts "up to the time of the investigation" according to the last treaty, and "labouring under this belief the doors of all stores were thrown open to the people of said Tribe and they were almost unlimited in their purchases." The commissioner's findings created "dismay and consternation with[in] every wig-wam as well as trading establishment." The traders warned they would continue to pressure the Indians for the payments as well as liberally supply merchandise on credit regardless of the current financial problems of the Miamis. Under these conditions, both traders and the Indians called for yet another treaty in 1840 in order to see that these outstanding claims were paid.[19]

By this time many government officials had begun to question the policy of permitting the Indians to access goods on credit. They were becoming convinced that, in spite of the number of honest traders who had honorably represented their claims against the Miamis, many traders were using the treaty system as an opportunity for financial gain. Dishonorable traders, policy makers began to see, thought "the property of the Indian a fair prize" and brought nothing but devastation to the native nations. Nonetheless, the government was well aware that the traders were proving to be very effective in achieving the government's goals of removal. It even appeared that removal would take place earlier than federal officials had anticipated. This consideration proved very important, as removal was becoming an urgent necessity from the federal point of view. Northern Indiana had developed rapidly between the passage of the Indian Removal Act and the treaty of 1840. During that decade white settlers north of the Wabash River increased from 3,380 to 65,897, and the westward push of pioneers increased the pressures on the Miamis to move and the government to remove them. By 1840 the Miamis finally gave in. At the treaty they forfeited their claim to their remaining lands in Indiana and agreed to move west of the Mississippi within five years. Yet, while the traders were pleased that this treaty allowed for the payments of Indian debt, they were now faced with the fact that with the region's loss of the Miamis came their own loss of an assured profitable income.[20]

Nonetheless, immediate promises of profits were at hand. To pay the newly accrued debts, a commission was once again created to investigate new claims. An unprecedented amount of $250,000 was designated to cover the debts of the Miamis incurred within just the previous two years. Yet even this large amount of repayment funds would not be sufficient. By the time the debts were totaled, it was discovered that the Miamis owed $550,000. Then, in the months that followed, merchants completely sold out their stores in an effort to increase the Miamis' indebtedness to unbelievable proportions. However, the 1840 commission discovered the rising debts and questioned their legitimacy. The commissioners had established two terms of investigation: The first was to assess debts that had been created from the payments of the 1838 treaty up to November of 1840—the time of the treaty negotiations; the second term was to cover debts that the Miamis had accrued from treaty negotiations to the date of ratification in 1841, a period of just over two months. The commissioners totaled the debts in the latter time period alone at a staggering $292,871.20 for an Indian nation who, the United States government reported, "counting men woman and children do not exceed six hundred persons in number." The commissioners thus logically concluded that these claims "were evidently created not with any view of supplying the wants of the Indians real or supposed; but in a spirit of speculation."[21]

Part of these outrageous debts incurred by the Miamis came as a result of traders desperately seeking to get out from under the burden of their goods.

Knowing that the Miamis would soon leave the region and their best customers would thus be gone, and tempted by the almost effortless profits promised by government reimbursements, many traders looked for individual
Indians to whom they could sell their goods. For example, Fort Wayne Indian
merchants Francis Comparet and John Stapleford sold their entire stores
shortly after the treaty was negotiated. Comparet turned in a claim against a
Miami Indian, Bill Shappeen, for a sale that occurred less than a month after
the 1840 removal treaty. Shappeen's debt to Comparet totaled $8,057.62, the
sum of two separate purchases, made on the same day in December of 1840.
Comparet, in fact, turned over the key of his store to the Miamis. The claims
investigators found that Shappeen had a reputation, according to all who
knew him, of being "an utterly drunken and reckless Indian," and that Comparet sold the goods to the unsuspecting Miamis at highly inflated prices. Interestingly, the personnel of the store could neither "tell how, or by whom the
goods were taken away," and Shappeen more than likely did not get the majority of the goods for which he was billed. Nonetheless, the commissioners
allowed Comparet to be reimbursed for more than $6,000. Bill Shappeen was
indebted to other traders, as well, incurring a total of $16,600 worth of debts,
which the Miami nation was beholden to pay.[22]

Shortly following Comparet's sale to Shappeen, another Fort Wayne merchant, John D. Stapleford, like Comparet and other merchants in town, wanted
to sell his store of goods. Subsequently, he requested that a friend locate an
Indian who would likely purchase his remaining merchandise. Stapleford sold
out completely to Pigeon, a Miami, for the price of $6,200, although the
commissioners calculated that only $2,000 worth of goods were actually in
the store. Still, out of his claim against Pigeon, the commissioners allowed
Stapleford to be paid $3,000. After closing the deal, Stapleford congratulated
Pigeon on his purchase. "Well, my friend," exclaimed Pigeon, "I am glad of
it. Now I am rich. I have got plenty of goods." What Pigeon failed to realize
was that his short-lived wealth helped to impoverish his nation as a whole.
Shappeen and Pigeon were not the only Miamis to have made such extravagant purchases; individual Miami Indians Paul Longlois and Kilsonsah, for
example, had debts of $13,974 and $14,894, respectively.[23]

The investigators found that prominent among those who engaged in
suspicious trade with the Indians of northern Indiana were the merchants
George W. and William G. Ewing, brothers who had been involved in the
trade in northern Indiana since 1822. They led many of the protests regarding
the presumed injustices the federal government dealt the traders in the payment of their claims. As did the other traders in the region, they dealt almost
exclusively with the Miamis and the Potawatomis, although they differed
from their competitors in that their trade network extended throughout the

region. Encouraged by the treaties of 1838 and particularly the removal treaty of 1840, they bought between $130,000 and $160,000 worth of goods for trade with the Miamis between 1839 and early 1841. Many of these goods were purchased from England. Overall, in the twenty years they traded in northern Indiana, the Ewing brothers tallied the Indian merchandise they had purchased from New York, England, and elsewhere for northern Indiana at anywhere between $500,000 and $1,000,000. The Ewings boasted of the quality of goods they brought into northern Indiana for the Indian trade. They had "the most splendid kinds of qualities, far superior to & of much greater cost, than those ordinarily brought into this country," they claimed, even for trade with the settlers in the region. They believed that they were unusually attuned to the "wants and tastes" of the Miamis, and the Ewings prided themselves that they had "dealt fairly liberally with their Miami friends," having "indulged them & waited on them for years."[24]

Overall, the investigators concluded that the close proximity of the Indians with whites such as the Ewings, coupled with federal policies that allowed such economic abuses against the native peoples, dramatically altered the Indian way of life. For example, the Miamis had become "greatly relaxed in their accustomed Hunt, & collected but very few Furs and Skins" now. They had developed an increasing reliance on goods acquired on credit, and merchants engaged in the Indian trade continued to extend this credit based on government reimbursement through treaties.[25]

Disturbed by the investigations as a whole, the commissioners reported regarding one trader's claim that the

> whole transaction is so connected with suspicious circumstances attending the sale, that we feel almost constrained to disallow it. But in reality there is in all the claims so little to commend them, that if we should select this for disallowance, from among them, it might seem an arbitrary judgement. For the most that could be said in favour of any of the large claims of their class, would be, that they were only a little less suspicious than the others.

Commissioners were increasingly convinced that "the policy of the government in permitting the Indian tribes to assume for payment the debts of individuals [was] fraught with evils to the Indians." Ignorant of the ways of the white man, they had

> no other knowledge of dates, than the division of the year into seasons. Most of them are either ignorant of prices or are entirely careless of the amount with which they are charged. They have but little knowledge of the

legal effect of notes, and accounts and may be induced to sign almost any sort of written obligation. They are ignorant of our laws and language entirely regardless of the future and ready to do any thing that ministers to their present gratification.

This situation brought out the worst elements of greed and corruption in the traders. These merchants, "foreseeing that the government will provide for the payment of his debts when a treaty is made," did not care about the individual to whom he provided credit, or his ability to pay.[26]

Therefore, while the merchants profited, the Miamis experienced "utter corruption and degradation." Impoverished and fearful of the impending removal, which by now was only three years away, the tribe quickly split over the issue of debt and payments. The majority of the Miamis suffered as a result of those few who were extravagant in their purchases on credit. Overall, the tribe's sense of integrity called for payment of those debts. Individuals such as Pigeon and Bill Shappeen, who were described as "intemperate to a proverb" and "utterly incapable of exercising any providence or forethought," had become easy targets of the merchants and contributed to the ultimate destruction of the traditional Miami way of life, including the loss of their lands.[27]

The claims investigation, completed in 1842, ended a decade of cultural and economic disruption for the Indians of northern Indiana. In its efforts to implement its policy of removal, United States federal officials had allowed them to incur debts of extraordinary amounts. These debts were encouraged in order to press for treaty negotiations and their subsequent land cessions, which ultimately would force the Indians to move west of the Mississippi River. While the federal government succeeded in implementing its policy of removal and the Indian traders on the frontier prospered economically, the Indians lost the basis of their subsistence, many of their cultural traditions, and ultimately their land.[28]

Recognizing the devastating input this had on the Indians, the commissioners concluded that it was in the best interest of all parties

> to remove the temptation which is held out, to the traders and others in the vicinity of these unfortunate and ignorant people to involve them in unnecessary debts, we must earnestly recommend that, the whole system of investigations be abolished. We believe they will not only prove destructive to the Indians, but become very expensive to the government.

Unfortunately, in spite of the growing distaste for current policy and its negative impact, their recommendations came far too late for the Potawatomis and Miamis. Nonetheless, the policy of arranging for the removal of the final Indian nations from northern Indiana had been implemented. This fact did not escape the commissioners who declared that the traders had brought about total land cession and removal much earlier than government officials ever thought possible.[29]

Yet despite the success of the federal government in the unexpected timing of removal, the traders would have to fight for their payments once again. And, once again, they would threaten to thwart policy goals until they received what they felt was their just pay. To the traders' dismay, in September of 1842 the federal government reassessed the commissioners' reports and readjusted the claims allowed to the traders under the 1840 investigation. This revision "reduced the allowence of the commissioners on claims after the treaty some $80,000 without Law or authority," complained one of the Ewings. This action by the government created "an evident distrust in this political outrage upon the rights of the claimants." With removal having been "affected by the Means of the Business Men of the Country," the merchants argued, they believed "that Justice to them requires a speedy adjustment and payment of all the just claims"—claims that had been "created in furtherance of the just and humane policy of the government in removing [the Miami] Indians."[30]

Led by the Ewings, the traders of northern Indiana warned that removal could be postponed indefinitely should their claims not be paid. Recalling that the natives' "principal inducement" to sell and move west resulted from their need to pay their debts, the traders claimed that "Justice and Public Policy" required that an adequate amount of money should be put toward the Miami debts. This action would in all probability "secure a speedy emigration" of the Miamis. However, should "a prolonged or doubtful payment of these debts" occur, they warned, such an action might hinder this greatly desired political end. Anything less than the original agreement of payment "would be gross ingratitude in the Government," they protested, particularly "after having availed itself of [the traders'] influence to purchase the country."[31]

The citizens of northern Indiana entered into the debate, petitioning the federal government in support of the merchants. They reminded their national officials that the Miamis had refused to go west when the United States administrators had requested they do so, but "when credited liberally by the merchants of the country," Indiana's native inhabitants had sold their land. Traders, not government officials, had achieved the government's policy goals. They also warned their federal officials that delaying the payments of the Indians' debts might lead to war. The three to four hundred families that had settled in the lands recently purchased by the late treaty might be caught up in "controversies" that could "terminate in bloodshed" with the Indians who still lived in the region. But should the debts be paid, and the government fulfill its responsibilities as promised, the Indians just might be induced to move west as a result of the traders' influence.[32]

The residents of northern Indiana also argued that the government was responsible for paying the debts and, in essence, repaying the traders for their role in achieving federal policies. They viewed their central administration as obligated to expend its vast resources on the frontier. In their estimation, the government engaged in "but very few Expenditures of Public Moneys in northern Indiana," and should the government fail to make this final payment and remove this source of income from those who relied on it, the present administration "would be denounced with great unanimity by the People: Political feelings can not but mix with this subject!" The goods, after all, had been sold to the Indians "in good faith . . . in legitimate Indian Trade" sanctioned by the federal government, which had promised to pay for said property. As such, the government had become their "Trustee" and only held the "money for the benefit of their claimants."[33]

Nonetheless, in 1845, the year the Miamis had agreed to move west, the government continued to be indebted to the traders, who in turn increased their protests. Aware of their administrators' great desire to see the final removal of Indiana's natives to the West, they reminded their officials of the situation that had occurred with the Potawatomi payments and removal and the role the traders had played in that event. Like the Miamis, the Potawatomis had agreed to pay their debts through treaty negotiations, but the traders were dissatisfied with the amount of claims allowed them. Likewise, as with the Miamis, United States officers had failed to remove the Potawatomis. Once the federal government had agreed that the Potawatomis' debts should be paid to the traders' satisfaction, "all parties were reconciled" and it was a mere ten days before the process of removal began. Once the government agreed to pay the Miami debts as requested, "the serious individuals" to whom this nation was indebted would remove their opposition toward removal.[34]

Thus, the Miamis, supported by the traders, albeit for self-interested reasons, managed to postpone their westward move. But once the federal government relented to the traders' demands for restitution, the Miamis lost their allies and were forced to remove in 1846. By that time the Ewings, the most persistent protesters, had been guaranteed the payment of their debts, had received one-third of the removal contract, and had decided to move west with the Indians in order to continue their trade there. Once these powerful traders joined the push for immediate removal, the Miamis lost the necessary support to change their fate.[35]

The final move was an emotional event for all involved. One Fort Wayne resident observed:

> With the exception of a few of their chiefs the Miamis were removed to what is now Kansas, in 1846, and I recollect the doleful descriptions which came from them of that country. To them it was a desert over which the fierce winds were constantly sweeping, without trees, and without game. The change from a country like Northern Indiana, its lakes and rivers abounding with fish, and its splendid forests alive with game of nearly all descriptions, to a nearly treeless plain, was indeed disheartening. Said one of the traders who went with them to me on his return: "I am, as you know, unused to the melting mood; but when the young braves at my parting with them burst into tears and begged like children to be taken back to their old home, I could not help crying also."[36]

The last Indian removal from northern Indiana had finally taken place. In a little more than half a century since Anthony Wayne had established the fort at the headwaters of the Maumee, the native inhabitants had experienced a complete economic transformation and a reduction in their land base that resulted in the final loss of their beloved home in northern Indiana. They had successfully negotiated with the United States agents on the frontier, but with the arrival of the licensed, private traders, and the introduction of an economy based on credit, they found themselves caught in a system with which they were unfamiliar. Yet for the Indian traders in northern Indiana, this era provided an economic boon for them, and in their financial dealings with the Potawatomis and the Miamis, they found a place of profit. They also made possible the achievement of the government's Indian policy of removal. As one commissioner of the 1840 claims investigation stated, removal would have occurred anyway, but with the traders' work it came "some years sooner" than it would have otherwise.[37]

The removal of the Miamis and Potawatomis was part of a pattern that appears unique to the Indian nations of the Old Northwest. The Ottawas, Chippewas, Winnebagos, Menominees, Sioux, Sacs, and Foxes of Ohio, Indiana, and Illinois, as well as the Wisconsin and Michigan territories, all experienced a similar dynamic between traders and removal. Indeed, during the sixteen years from 1826 to 1842, the majority of the treaties the United States government concluded with these native nations to set aside money to pay traders' claims. Until 1832 the amounts ranged from $4,000 to $25,000. But beginning in 1833 the average total dramatically increased, ranging from $70,000 to $250,000 as the debts brought against Indian nations rose in response to the Indian Removal Act. Still, the largest claim made by the region's merchant traders came as a result of the 1840 Miami treaty, totaling a whopping $550,000.[38]

With the United States government paying their hefty debt demands, traders became more aggressive, and ultimately they positioned themselves in increasingly precarious positions. In 1842 events focused the government's attention on the problems the traders created in the treaty process during negotiations with the Sacs and Foxes, who had been removed to Kansas. The government's treaty with the tribes included a provision for the payment of over $258,000 worth of Indian debts to traders, most of who, not coincidentally, once hailed from northern Indiana. When the Great Lakes tribes had been removed to this location, these entrepreneurs had followed and quickly set about replicating the system that had worked so favorably for them in the Midwest. The government, however, seized on this treaty to remove the traders from the treaty-making process, as federal officials no longer saw placating the merchants as necessary to secure Indian removal. Consequently, in 1843 the Senate passed a resolution declaring that "in the future negotiations of Indian treaties no reservations of lands should be made in favor of any person, nor the payment of any debts provided for," thus ending the inclusion of traders' claims against the Indians in treaty negotiations.[39]

The events in northern Indiana leading to the removal of the Potawatomis and Miamis tell an important story, revealing the influence that the Indian trade allowed these civilian merchants on the northern Indiana frontier. The role of traders' claims in Indian affairs in the Great Lakes region played a large part in the federal government's achievement of its removal policy. Significantly, the pattern of claims for debts established by the traders of the Great Lakes, many of whom had trading houses throughout the region, made the treaty process and achievement of removal in the Great Lakes different than that in any other region. To what extent the government could have successfully carried out its policy of removal of the Great Lakes Indians without the frontier merchants is unknown. What is more certain is that in the Old Northwest, and northern Indiana in particular, Indian removal often occurred within a pattern of economic decline, forced by the unique dealings of the private, licensed traders who occupied a unique "middle ground" between Indian nations and the United States government.

NOTES

1. J. T. Schermerhorn, Treaty Ground, Forks of the Wabash, October 31, 1833; Schermerhorn to Elbert Herring, January 24, 1834; J. G. Godfroy, Addendum to Schermerhorn

to Elbert Herring, January 30, 1835, Letters Received by the Office of Indian Affairs, 1824–1881, Records of the Bureau of Indian Affairs, Record Group 75, National Archives and Records Administration, Washington, D.C. [hereafter cited as BIA Records].

2. Schermerhorn to Elbert Herring, Commissioner, January 24, 1834, ibid.

3. William G. Ewing to Tipton, Feb. 3, 1830, Nellie Armstrong Robertson and Dorothy Riker, eds., *The John Tipton Papers*, 3 vols. (Indianapolis: Indiana Historical Society, 1942), 2:244 [hereafter cited as *JTP*].

4. George Washington to James Duane, September 7, 1783; Report of Henry Knox on the Northwestern Indians, June 15, 1789; President Washington on Government Trading Houses, December 3, 1793, Francis Paul Prucha, ed., *Documents of the United States Indian Policy* (Lincoln: Univ. of Nebraska Press, 1990), 1–2, 12, 16.

5. Clarence Edwin Carter, ed., *The Territorial Papers of the United States*, 28 vols. (Washington, D.C.: GPO, 1934–75), 7:86–87; President Washington on Government Trading Houses, December 3, 1793, Prucha, *Documents*, 16; An Act for Establishing Trading Houses with the Indian Tribes, April 18, 1796, ibid., 16–17; President Jefferson on Indian Trading Houses, January 18, 1803, ibid., 21–22; Gayle Thornbrough, ed., *Letter Book of the Indian Agency at Fort Wayne, 1809–1815* (Indianapolis: Indiana Historical Society, 1961), 11–12; Stewart Rafert, *The Miami Indians of Indiana: A Persistent People, 1654–1994* (Indianapolis: Indiana Historical Society, 1996), 66–69.

6. President Jefferson on Indian Trading Houses, January 18, 1803; Jefferson to William Henry Harrison, February 27, 1803, Prucha, *Documents*, 21–23.

7. Indent Books, vol. 8, BIA Records; John Johnston to John Mason, November 29, 1808, Letters Received by the Superintendent of Indian Trade, 1806–1824, BIA Records; "Articles unsaleable, damaged and lost on the route to Fort Wayne at Fort Wayne Trading House," enclosed in John Johnston to Gen. John Shee, September 10, 1807, Daybooks, 1807–1809, Factory Records, Fort Wayne Factory, Entry 57, Records of the Office of Indian Trade, BIA Records.

8. Black Raccoon traded his furs for two shirts, a hat, a pair of leggings, two yards of muslin, six yards of calico, powder, lead, eight quarts of salt, one box of flints, two strouds, twenty skeins of thread, five dozen needles, tea, a padlock, two blankets, and a bridle; Purchase of Aug. 23, 1806, Daybooks, 1804–1806, Factory Records, Fort Wayne Factory, Records of the Office of Indian Trade, BIA Records. See also Robert A. Trennert Jr., *Indian Traders on the Middle Border: The House of Ewing, 1826–54* (Lincoln: Univ. of Nebraska Press, 1981), 3.

9. Paul Woehrmann, *At the Headwaters of the Maumee: A History of the Forts of Fort Wayne* (Indianapolis: Indiana Historical Society, 1971), 86–87; Prucha, *Documents*, 33.

10. Charles J. Kappler, *Indian Affairs: Laws and Treaties*, 2 vols. (Washington, D.C.: GPO, 1904), 2:169–72; Rafert, *Miami Indians of Indiana*, 85.

11. Rafert, *Miami Indians of Indiana*, 88; Population Figures, 1800–1853, Records of the Civilization Division, 92, 107, BIA Records; John Tipton to Thomas L. McKenney, November 13, 1824, *JTP*, 1:408.

12. Indianapolis *Gazette*, October 26, 1826; Kappler, *Indian Affairs*, 2:278; Rafert, *Miami Indians of Indiana*, 91.

13. Kappler, *Indian Affairs*, 2:275–80; David H. Colerick to John Tipton, July 18, 1832, *JTP*, 2:660; William Rockhill to Tipton, August 1, 1832, ibid., 2:670–71; David Burr to Tipton, July 26, 1832, ibid., 2:663–64; David H. Colerick to Tipton, August 8, 1832, ibid.,

2:677–79; Willian G. Ewing to Tipton, September 4, 1832, ibid., 2:700; and Allen Hamilton to Tipton, January 14, 1835, ibid., 3:104–6.

14. Allen Hamilton to John Tipton, January 14, 1835, *JTP,* 3:104–6.

15. Kappler, *Indian Affairs,* 2:425–35; W. G. Ewing to Lewis Cass, February 21, 1835, Letters Received by the Office of Indian Affairs, Roll 355, BIA Records; Rafert, *Miami Indians of Indiana,* 96; Allen Hamilton to John Tipton, January 15, 1835, *JTP,* 3:106.

16. Miscellaneous Records, 1836–37, vol. 1, 1830–1836, Office of Indian Affairs, BIA Records; Statement showing the number of Indians now east of the Mississippi, Miscellaneous Records, No. 2, July 1836–Dec. 1837, BIA Records; R. David Edmunds, *The Potawatomis: Keepers of the Fire* (Norman: Univ. of Oklahoma Press, 1978), 267–68.

17. Report of Nathaniel West, United States' Commissioner, on the Claims against the Miami Indians, Presented under the Treaty of October 23, 1834, made with said Indians, Indianapolis, 1838; Report of Nathaniel West to T. Hartley Crawford; and, A Register of Claims against the Miami Indians, Journals of Commissions, 1824–39, Box 1, PI-163, Entry 106, BIA Records.

18. Report of Nathaniel West, United States' Commissioner, on the Claims against the Miami Indians, Journals of Commissions, 1824–39, Box 1, PI-163, Entry 106, BIA Records; Rafert, *Miami Indians of Indiana,* 97; Kappler, *Indian Affairs,* 2:519–21.

19. Allen Hamilton to T. Hartley Crawford, Nov. 10, 1840, Letters Received by the Office of Indian Affairs, 1824–81, Roll 357, BIA Records; D. Colerick (Confidential) to J. R. Poinsette, September 12, 1838, ibid., Roll 356; Rafert, *Miami Indians of Indiana,* 99.

20. Report of Nathaniel West, United States' Commissioner, on the Claims against the Miami Indians, Journals of Commissions, 1824–39, Box 1, PI-163, Entry 106, BIA Records.

21. Rafert, *Miami Indians of Indiana,* 95; Kappler, *Indian Affairs,* 2:531–32, Miami Investigation, vol. 2, November 1840–41, Finance Division, Box 14, BIA Records; Records Concerning Traders' Claims, Miami, ibid., Box 11; Report of Commissioners to T. Hartley Crawford, Indianapolis, Feb. 25, 1842, Miami Investigations, vol. 1, November 1838 to November 1840, ibid., Box 14.

22. Claim of Francis Comparet, Records Concerning Traders' Claims, ca. 1819–64, Miami, Box No. 11, Finance Division, BIA Records; Miami Investigation, vol. 2, Finance Records, ibid., Box 14.

23. Miami Investigation, vol. 2, Finance Records, Box 14, BIA Records; Claim of John D. Stapleford, Records Concerning Traders' Claims, ca. 1819–64, Miami, ibid., Box 11.

24. W. G. and G. W. Ewing to O. L. Clark and L. Bloomfield, Commissioners, Records Concerning Traders' Claims, ca. 1819–64, Miami, Box 11, Finance Division, BIA Records.

25. Ibid.

26. Ibid.; Report of Commissioners to T. Hartley Crawford, Indianapolis, February 25, 1842, Miami Investigations, vol. 1, Finance Division, Box 14, BIA Records; Report of O. L. Clark and L. Bloomfield, ibid.

27. Report of Commissioners to T. Hartley Crawford, Indianapolis, February 25, 1842, Miami Investigations, vol. 1, Finance Division, Box 14, BIA Records.

28. United States Commissioners on the Claims of Creditors of the Miami Indians of the Wabash, February 25, 1842, Miami Investigations, vol. 1, Finance Division, Box 14, BIA Records.

29. Ibid.

30. W. G. Ewing to William L. Marcy, August 8, 1845, Letters Received by the Office of Indian Affairs, Roll 360, BIA Records.

31. Citizens of Northern Indiana to John C. Spencer, February 12, 1842, Letters Received by the Office of Indian Affairs, Roll 359, BIA Records; W. G. Ewing to William L. Marcy, August 8, 1845, ibid., Roll 360.

32. Citizens of Northern Part of State of Indiana to John Bell, April 15, 1841, enclosed in O. H. Smith to John Bell, April 28, 1841, Letters Received by the Office of Indian Affairs, Roll 358, BIA Records; Citizens of the County of Allen (Fort Wayne) and State of Indiana to John Bell (forwarded by A. W. White), July 7, 1841, ibid.

33. W. G. Ewing to William L. Marcy, August 8, 1845, Letters Received by the Office of Indian Affairs, Roll 360, BIA Records; Citizens of the State of Indiana to His Excellency, John Tyler, President of the United States, August 23, 1842, ibid., Roll 359.

34. George W. Ewing to William Wilkins, February 11, 1845, Letters Received by the Office of Indian Affairs, Roll 360, BIA Records; Memorandum Submitted by the Commissioner of Indian Affairs for the Consideration of the Secretary of War, Miscellaneous Records, No. 3, January 1838 to April 1839, BIA Records.

35. Rafert, *Miami Indians of Indiana*, 100–113.

36. Hugh McCulloch, *Men and Measures of Half a Century: Sketches and Comments* (New York: Scribner's, 1888), 110.

37. United States Commissioners on the Claims of Creditors of the Miami Indians of the Wabash, February 25, 1842, Miami Investigations, vol. 1, Finance Division, Box 14, BIA Records.

38. For specific treaties and terms, see Kappler, *Indian Affairs*, 2:220–549.

39. U.S. Congress, 27th Congress, 3rd Session, *Senate Executive Journal* (Washington, D.C.: J. Allen, 1843), February 15, 1843.

10

Bringing About the Dawn

Agriculture, Internal Improvements,
Indian Policy, and Euro-American Hegemony in
the Old Northwest, 1800–1846

GINETTE ALEY

I was inclined to be poetical about the Grand Canal. . . . I pictured the
surprise of the sleepy Dutchmen when the new river first glittered by
their doors, bringing them hard cash or foreign commodities, in exchange for their hitherto unmarketable produce. Surely, the water of
this canal must be the most fertilizing of all fluids.
—*Nathaniel Hawthorne, 1835*[1]

In June of 1843 Charles Titus, a young Methodist schoolteacher and minister
from Kennebec County, Maine, traveled on Indiana's Wabash and Erie Canal
as the first leg of a two-month journey that would take him to Toledo, on to
Detroit, and from there to explore the Indian lands around Lakes Huron and
Superior, before returning permanently to the East. Titus's aspirations of su-
perintending a Methodist-sponsored seminary school in Madison, Indiana,
had recently been crushed when financial support did not come through.
However, his own failed endeavor did not blind him to the positive spirit of
enterprise and industry that dotted his route through Indiana. His critical observations and vivid depictions of fertile farms and development along the
recently built canal system reveal an awareness of the "Great West" as a region
and society in transition. Transplanted eastern farmers, with whom he identified, displayed an impressive inclination toward industry and stood to prosper on land that matched their productive energy. "Such farmers on such
land," he noted, "can never want." The new canal system stretched ultimately
from New York's Erie Canal to the Mississippi River. It not only created water-

connected communities and market access in the interior region but also shifted the flow of trade from a cumbersome and costly mode of wagon-to-flatboat transportation to the New Orleans market toward an easier and certainly more remunerative, canal-dominated easterly one, generating changes of considerable consequence for the West's settler-farmers. Titus noted that as a result, "A new day has now dawned upon the agriculturist of this region."[2]

The eagerly anticipated new era of improved travel, transportation, and market access had been decades-long in the making, and Titus arrived on the Indiana scene as portions of the artificial waterway were opening up for general use. The state had endured much in the way of financial strain, mismanagement, localist rivalries, and even bankruptcy in the course of implementing its internal improvement system, and in the end it could claim little of the financial redemption that New York accrued through its canal system. According to Titus, though, farmers could now enjoy "a convenient & never failing market"; he noted that the corn he had seen selling for ten cents a bushel "went quick" on the canal, "without any parleying, for 37 [cents] a bushel." His 1843 travel route along the Wabash and Erie Canal on the way to Toledo followed an important new 175-mile canal interstate connection with Ohio. A few weeks later, on July 4, the opening was the cause of a great patriotic celebration held in Fort Wayne during which neither pomp nor circumstance was spared. As if to signify the beginning of a new day for the region, the Lafayette *Journal and Free-Press* reported that a twenty-six-gun salute commenced the canal festivities at dawn, joined later by flag-draped boats lining the canal, rounds of commemorative and congratulatory toasting, the attendance of "more than fifteen hundred ladies," and a parade that included three bands and an array of farmers, townspeople, Miami Indians, and notable figures such as Ohio's governor Ethan Allen Brown and Gen. Lewis Cass. Cass, whose grand entrance was marred by an unfortunate misstep into the canal, spoke grandly and eloquently about the past, present, and future, encouraging the crowd to consider that at one time the "line of your canal was a bloody path, which has seen many a deed of horror." With this canal, this "peaceful victory over the natural impediments," he reflected, it was "better to look forward to prosperity than back to glory."[3]

The nascent market and transportation revolution in the West, which began in earnest in the 1820s and continued through the 1840s, is fraught with under-explored meaning in terms of its emergence, complexities, and consequences for the people of early Midwest societies. Much has been written about the social and economic permutations in the East following the opening of the Erie Canal in 1825; in fact, the story of the nation's canal era is often told only from the perspective of the fantastic success of the Erie Canal, with little mention or analysis of the more complicated way in which it played out in the states arising from the Old Northwest. Here, in relationship to Euro-American settlement, American Indian displacement, and regional development, the elements of the story appear to be the same but are weighted somewhat differently in their meanings and consequences. We have not explored, for example, what influence the internal improvement movement had in shaping Indian policy in the region, including removal, or in promoting and furthering the establishment of an American commercial agricultural system.[4]

More broadly, it begs the question: What role did the Midwest's canal and road building era play in the American settler-farmers' transformation of the region from a place of raw wilderness into a landscape dominated by cultivated fields and commercial agriculture activities (a makeover that was at once visual, cultural, economic, and physical)? On one level this metamorphosis sprang from the widespread participation in settled agriculture, which in itself represented a diffusion of traditional practices and beliefs, ideologies, behaviors, and, typically, a commercial orientation within the area. On another level, the altered landscape and corresponding resettling of inhabitants, old and new, reflected an enduring swing in the dynamics of power between the natives and the newcomers in which the latter assumed dominance and in which the former participated. The evolution of these changes, its relationship to the convergence of internal improvement and Indian policy interests in the Old Northwest, and the multilevel consequences that followed deserve stronger consideration than they have received until now. If, as Titus, Hawthorne, and others believed, the canal era represented a new day for the settler-farmers, then how and under what assumptions was that day secured? If the construction of western canals inaugurated the dawn of an era then, by implication, it superceded another. This suggests some degree of finality in the ongoing struggle for dominance and control over resources, especially land, between the region's Euro-Americans and American Indians. What emerges in Indiana and elsewhere in the Old Northwest is that the movement for canals, along with other internal improvements, represents a dividing channel, a symbolic and at times ironic boundary between natives and newcomers in the region; metaphorically speaking, once built they signified a *fait accompli* in the spread of a Euro-American cultural and economic hegemony in the region that was instrumental in promoting commercial agriculture, "progress" and improvement, and participation in a national market economy.[5]

There is still much to be learned about the process by which Euro-Americans assumed hegemony over the native peoples in other areas beside the battlefield. The narrative of the transformation of the Old Northwest into a "place" with Euro-American designs describes a complex event that was fre-

quently intersected by counter narratives of American Indian "displacement,"
participation, and resistance. How this comes about is discernible through
an examination of the vision of agrarianism for the West and its influence on
policymakers, farmers' perspectives, local patterns of the internal improvement movement, and the immediate consequences for some of the region's
Indians. While tracing the spread of Euro-American hegemony, this study
also identifies the often understated role of settler-farmers in shaping policy,
altering the landscape in their farm building, and ultimately making it possible for five states to emerge from the Old Northwest and form the heart of
the region now known as the Midwest. Scholars have tended to view agriculture, internal improvements, and Indian policy as disparate strands instead of
seeing them as tightly woven into the same fabric that constitutes the early
American history of the region and the core of its identity. In other words, the
internal improvement movement and market development in the Old Northwest cannot fully be understood apart from their relationship to contemporary federal Indian policy, to the consequences for the American Indians, and
to the difficulties facing the settler-farmers in their aspirations to become not
only landowners but also prosperous producers for a market.[6]

Early federal Indian policy and the securing of cession treaties to obtain titles to Indian lands has received little scholarly attention within the context of
an early national commitment to agricultural development and the push to
build a strong agricultural economy, a commitment that remained apparent
for much of the nineteenth century. Yet the internal improvement movement,
as an articulation of both local and national aspirations for better transportation and market access, also came to inform Indian-white relations and Indian policy objectives. This is apparent at the federal, state, and local levels,
in the records of federal and state officials, and the writings of farm people
as well as Indian agents such as John Tipton. In the case of Indiana, some Indian lands were highly coveted when it became evident that a number of the
roads and canal routes desired by the settlers ran through them. To the Euro-
Americans there, the contest for the land had less to do with ownership than
it did with controlling economic opportunity, ensuring prosperity, and shor-
ing up their power and authority—all at the expense of American Indians.
Canal and road lands represented potential profits to the newcomers as well
as progress in the region's development of its agricultural promise.[7]

Indiana was uniquely situated in place and time to afford insight into these
complexities. In 1800 it represented the first U.S. territorial division of the
Northwest Territory, later attaining statehood in 1816. As a territory it was of
particular importance to officials inasmuch as it comprised most of the desirable Indian lands for speculative and military ventures north of the Ohio
River. In 1803 Indiana's territorial governor, William Henry Harrison, received

an expressly stated (though privately communicated) official policy briefing from President Thomas Jefferson that, aside from urging speedy land acquisition from the Indians, also connected Indian policy to agriculture and the vision for the West. In following policy, Harrison initiated the process of formally dispossessing the territory's Indians of their land to accommodate the advance not only of the settler-farmers but also of an American commercial agricultural system. Tellingly, just a few decades later, by 1830, Indian cession treaties would be linked to formal removal policies, although the first one to include an emigration clause was concluded at St. Mary's, Ohio, in 1818, involving the Delaware Indians of Indiana and Ohio; more soon followed. Subsequent removal or emigration treaties not only resulted in the loss of tribal lands and removal to Indian Country west of the Mississippi River but also symbolized the ascendance of American cultural and economic hegemony in the region. An event that pulls together these tensions is the tragic removal of a Miami band west to Indian Country in 1846, a journey that was compelled by way of Indiana and Ohio canal systems, portions of which traversed land only recently held by the American Indians.[8]

Dawn for the region's agriculturists had its origins and "first light" in a widely held though contested vision for the nation, the West, and for Indiana. The agrarian vision, which was often voiced, motivated Americans as they developed Indian, land, and internal improvement policies, expanded westward after the Revolution, determined their activities and livelihood, manipulated a landscape and its resources, and succeeded in establishing a cultural and economic hegemony over the natives, although not without their resistance. In a paper he read before the Society for Political Enquiries then meeting at the Philadelphia home of Benjamin Franklin on May 11, 1787, former Revolutionary official and future government appointee Tench Coxe underscored the importance of agriculture, "the great leading interest" of the new nation, and its relationship to industrial development. Considering that emigration added to the numbers of planters and farmers, that states possess millions of "vacant acres" that "court[ed] the cultivator's hand," and that settling these vast tracts would greatly increase the taxables, resources, and powers of the country, Coxe cautioned: "Let us be careful to do nothing that can interrupt this happy progress of our affairs." Fundamentally, he surmised, "agriculture appears to be the spring of our commerce, and the parent of our manufactures."[9]

Thomas Jefferson, a key source of western policy formulation spanning more than a decade preceding his first term as president in 1800 and throughout his second term, was of course in many ways the author and chief proponent of this vision for Euro-Americans, American Indians, the West, and the United States. Although Jefferson is most commonly associated with a localist view of agrarianism (that of the independent yeoman farmer), Joyce Appleby points out that he early advocated the commercialization of agriculture, particularly for the Old Northwest. Indeed among some leading thinkers of the new republic, contends Peter Onuf, the vision for America was one in which the West would be developed to promote agriculture, and agriculture in turn would provide the means of future national growth. With this crucial end in mind, devising an official land disposal policy that would put farmland into the hands of Euro-American settlers who were headed west, as well as determine settlement and town-building patterns in a manner that was orderly and that generated revenue came to resemble, was a national preoccupation according to one scholar. Jefferson chaired the congressional committee charged with this responsibility in 1784, and the resulting proposal became in essence the Land Ordinance of 1785. The grid surveys required by the ordinance would impose a ubiquitous geometric pattern of land use on the Old Northwest, still quite visible today, and signify a blueprint-like materialization of this early national agricultural vision. That the new nation would be predicated on the strength of agriculture and its practitioners is not surprising in one tangible sense. In 1790 the first federal census recorded that 94 percent of Americans were living on farms and in rural villages.[10]

Disregarding whatever American Indians envisioned for themselves, policymakers, beginning in 1789 with the first secretary of war, Henry Knox, embedded federal Indian policy with agrarian aspirations for both groups. In his desire to inculcate "civilization" and an attachment to the United States through farming activities, Knox sought the molding of a native culture compatible with Euro-American interests. It was clear to Knox, and from Jefferson more explicitly later, that given the developing agricultural economy, the Euro-American population growth, the rate of westward expansion toward Indian boundaries, and the depletion of game—"the inevitable consequence of cultivations"—the preservation of the natives' hunting culture neither would not nor could not be maintained. However painful it was to consider, it was obvious, Knox wrote, that "all the Indian tribes, once existing in those States now the best cultivated and most populous[,] have become extinct." Fortuitously for the Americans, under those circumstances Indian lands could thus be acquired "for small considerations," and future purchases could similarly be made once American Indians could be persuaded to adopt small-scale farming (what Jefferson later referred to as "the culture of a small piece of land") and leave behind the extensive-land-use and hunting lifestyle.[11]

To thwart the perceived imminent extermination and encourage acculturation, Knox's policy authorized missionaries to go and live with the natives and teach the ways of settled husbandry, principally to the men. The government would supply the missionaries with farm tools and livestock. Yet this was representative of numerous cultural misunderstandings and insensitivities that transpired between the groups in that Knox and others failed to recognize the implications of their own assumptions. Agriculture, for example, represented a set of tasks within a cultural context, the responsibilities for which were often determined by gender, as was basically true among both Indian and Euro-American societies. In the case of the former, farming had historically fallen under the purview of women, and the men were reluctant if not staunchly resistant to supplant them in the way that Knox and others laid out. While some missionaries could eventually point to successes in encouraging settled agriculture and other evidences of Euro-American civilization among the natives, others such as the Moravians, who established an Indian mission among the Delawares on the White River in the Indiana Territory in 1800, counted only "difficulties, dangers, and sorrows" in return for their efforts.[12]

The Moravians, whose missionary work among the natives predates Knox's policies, made little headway in their agonizing six-year attempt to carry out civilizing and christianizing objectives in the territory. Their failure was largely due to a number of variables beyond their control including the ease with which natives were able to get whiskey and their apparent widespread addiction to it, recent memories of Indian massacres and white encroachment, and disinterest in adopting wholesale the newcomers' cultural and economic practices. "We white brethren," as the Moravians referred to themselves, found the agricultural labor "bitter" as "we have to do the fence making and planting all alone." To their surprise, the natives had their own expectations, and the missionaries came to believe that all they really wanted from them was unreciprocated labor and assistance. Observing the "white" custom of building fences around the corn fields, the natives insisted that the missionaries build some for them, wielding threats not to plant without them. Quaker missionaries among the territory's Miami and Potawatomi tribes would encounter a similar disinterest. In an 1803 dispatch, Indian leaders Little Turtle and Five Medals expressed appreciation for the farm implements sent to them but were sorry to report that "the minds of our people are not so much inclined towards the cultivation of the earth as we would wish," though they hoped that the Great Spirit would tell them that this would be better than for them to drink the whiskey.[13]

In reality the natives could take or leave the whites' agricultural practices, but they asked to have what intrigued them, namely, in the case of the Moravians, the fences. Rather than risk alienation and failure, the missionaries relented. And while this first Protestant missionary effort in Indiana did ultimately fail, and its effect on the natives was negligible, the Moravians left an emblem of the advancing American agricultural system on the landscape in the form of their fences. These fairly quickly became less of a novelty and increasingly common considering that the territorial census taken four years after their departure in 1806 revealed that with the opening up of former Indian lands, the population of free whites and a relatively small number of slaves and "negroes" had grown from 5,641 in 1800 to 24,520 in 1810, reaching 63,897 in 1815, one year before statehood. American Indians were not included in the census, but one source estimated that about 100,000 natives lived in the expansive territory as of 1800.[14]

Knox was succeeded by Henry Dearborn in 1801 as secretary of war, but it would be Jefferson, then president, who would have the strongest influence on determining the formal way in which the natives and newcomers would relate to each other in the Indiana Territory. In particular, Jefferson's policies and Governor Harrison's actions in carrying them out reveal how Euro-American agrarianism continued to expand at the expense of the American Indians and the lands they held. Concerning his policy objectives for the territory, Jefferson expressed in a private letter to Harrison in 1803 the belief that in order for the two groups to live in "perpetual peace," the Indians must be encouraged to take up settled agriculture as well as spinning and weaving on the part of the women. The diminishing supply of game made this switch away from a hunting culture imperative for their survival. He presumed that this would also make them more agreeable "to exchange lands, which they have to spare and we want," for "necessaries" they need "for their farms and families" through trading. Westward expansion would inevitably result in one of two possible outcomes: either American settlements would overtake those of the Indians, at which time they might become United States citizens, or they would remove beyond the Mississippi. The latter proved to be a prophetic statement. Jefferson concluded his letter by urging Harrison to move quickly in securing land cessions since the French, who were favored by the Indians, were about to occupy New Orleans. This, he predicted, would cause them to "immediately stiffen" against such transactions in the interior region in hopes of French protection. In this ironic scheme, convincing natives to give up both their hunting and their "spare" lands in favor of farming meant that more land would be available for the newcomers to venture into the territory and in this way expedite their transformation of the heavily forested, game-stocked Old Northwest into a widely cultivated agricultural landscape.[15]

As governor, Harrison needed to accede not only to federal policy but also to the wishes of the citizens who sought access to Indian lands. In one 1802 petition the residents beseeched officials to extinguish the Indian titles in the vicinity, believing it would aid in "the speedy [white] population of the country." Harrison wasted little time once he was officially granted the authority to negotiate on behalf of the government in 1803 and proved highly adept at concluding numerous treaties with the various tribes residing in the territory. Between 1803 and 1814 he formalized twelve treaties that dispossessed American Indians of about 75,000 square miles of land (adding that much to the side of the U.S. government). Much of this land lay west of the Wabash River in what is now the state of Illinois, and when this became a separate territory in 1809, the remaining cessions in Indiana loosely blanketed the southern third of the state. Harrison had assumed his responsibilities with an almost insatiable zeal that exacerbated tensions between natives and newcomers.[16]

With a covetous eye toward the obviously agriculturally rich Indian lands, he advised the legislature in 1810 that while much had been accomplished in extinguishing Indian titles in the territory, much was yet left undone. "We do not yet have a sufficient space to form a tolerable state," he contended. Furthermore, "the most fertile tracts within our territorial bounds are still their property. . . . Is one of the fairest portions of the globe to remain in a state of nature, the haunt of a few wretched savages?" The trend in alienating Indian lands thus continued, with the next major Indian cession occurring in 1818 (as a consequence of the War of 1812) under Jonathan Jennings, Indiana's first state governor. The land cession involved the middle portion of the state, afterward commonly referred to as the New Purchase. With this cession and more that followed, Jefferson's 1803 policy statement to Harrison regarding the immediate acquisition of the Indian land in Indiana was all but met by the middle of the 1830s. Noting the cumulative population shift, Secretary of War John C. Calhoun told Congress in 1825 that a combined total of just over 11,500 Indians was all that remained in the states of Indiana and Illinois.[17]

The Euro-American settlers steadily pushed on into the region in waves, especially after the War of 1812, with a rapacious land hunger that threatened to overwhelm the American Indians. During a treaty council in Chicago in 1821, Potawatomi chief Metea protested that in the newcomers' haste to create farms from Indian lands, "the plowshare is driven through our tents before we have time to carry out our goods and seek another habitation." This eager and intrusive class of newcomers was made up of squatters who were trying to anticipate government land sales, if not altogether force them by virtue of their presence. They were common to frontier areas and not only formed the vanguard of each wave of westward migration but also functioned as the preliminary emissaries of Euro-American agriculture. Exemplifying this pattern, Robert Duncan's family began squatting within the area of an Indian village comprised mostly of Delawares in central Indiana in the spring of 1820. Other families squatted close by. Duncan recalled that "all newcomers were then called squatters," in reference to the large numbers of illegal farmer-settlers who had been arriving in the region. In this instance, the government had only recently acquired this land from the natives, and it was still unsurveyed and off the market.[18]

For nearly three years the two cultures coexisted in opposing degrees of rootedness. In a scene that would become increasingly familiar in the decades to come, the central Indiana natives were in the process of uprooting themselves and severing their attachment to a habitat that had sustained their culture, as they now prepared to emigrate west of the Mississippi River by the terms of the 1818 Treaty of St. Mary's (Ohio). The newcomers, from that first year, began widely transplanting Euro-American culture as they consciously altered the landscape to support their agricultural system by clearing, breaking up, planting, and enclosing the land as well as constructing physical structures such as barns, cabins, and mills. In the meantime, the two cultures did not isolate themselves from the other. Duncan relates that on one level, agricultural pursuits provided a small but useful intersection of economic activities. That the settlers enjoyed an adequate supply of livestock and ample pork "to start with," for example, was due to their ability to add to their own supply by procuring hogs from the natives, "a few of whom followed farming rather than the chase." These interactions reveal that nineteenth-century American frontiers were not simply zones of encounter but also places in transition—demographically, culturally, physically, and in terms of power—as the Euro-Americans moved to assert hegemony over the American Indians and the regions they inhabited.[19]

The farm people that migrated to the early Midwest in search of farmsteads were the principal actors in the western agricultural drama scripted by visionaries, policymakers, and officials. At times, both natives and newcomers shared the stage, but the latter upstaged the former with their entrance and came to dominate most of the scenes. Although lines were written and spoken to the contrary, the natives would not be permitted to share the spotlight. The Euro-Americans were ambitious, land hungry, and, according to agricultural historian Doug Hurt, overall a "profit-minded people." In the land's abundance and obvious fertility, they saw productivity, prosperity, and progress for themselves, their region, and a nation; and this cultural and economic vision they pursued, predicated as it was on control of the land base, would render Indian autonomy and compatibility tenuous at best. Israel Ludlow, a land surveyor in the Miami Country along the Ohio River in 1788, was excited by the land's natural fecundity and potential for wealth. "The fertility of the country is such," he recorded, "as will afford an easy and wholesome sustenance to the inhabitants & the prospects of future opulence, perhaps as great as any country in the world that depends upon the cultivation of the land for its source of wealth." Similarly, William Johnston traveled from Fort Wayne to Fort Dearborn (Chicago) in 1809 and wrote that the area in between was "of the greatest importance to the United States to have it settled" in large part because he believed that the prairies therein "would support immense herds of cattle at very little cost."[20]

Clearly, American farmers and their supporters during the early national period intended for agriculture to develop along commercial lines. In ways that suggest regional distinctiveness, this incipient commercial impulse anchored the Old Northwest's, and future Midwest's, identity by delineating the activity in which the majority of its citizens would participate and through which it was widely believed the region would prosper. But it was one thing to take up farms and build settlements in a frontier environment and yet another to transport surplus produce to a market when neither serviceable roads nor other means existed to make that market connection. This dilemma affected Indiana farm people in a number of ways and more than anything else served to demonstrate the need for internal improvements in the region. As early as 1805 the Indiana Territory inhabitants petitioned Congress to complain about how poor market and transportation access (as well as the recent loss of the army market and the appearance of the "Insect. Fly, & weaval") left them indebted and unable to make payments on their land. Initially their prospects "were flattering, from the growth of our country, the increase of Citizens, & our commerce with the City of [New] Orleans, the fertility of soil, our industerous intentions . . . [and] our wishes for the Prosperity of our common Country." The land's great abundance in produce, however, especially flour, had begun to glut the market; worse than this were the freight charges that not only "swallowed up" the profits but also indebted the producers.[21]

The situation had not improved a decade and a half later. One pioneer farmer recalled that even when they "produced something to sell, there was no market place, no demand and no price." Conversely, lack of market access kept prices high on items that were needed and desired by the settlers, often at a great inconvenience. "Even with money," another farmer remembered, "wheat flour, which had to be hauled seventy miles over a mud road, could rarely be bought, as little was offered for sale." Many were in the position of knowing which commodities would fare well at the market, but they were also aware that to try to transport them was not feasible under the current conditions. In 1836 Jacob Schramm, a German immigrant farmer, wrote to relatives across the ocean that while he knew that rye and wheat "are well paid for in Indianapolis, and sell well, it is difficult to deliver them, since the roads in that direction are so terribly bad that you can't take a wagon over them."[22]

Indiana had become a state in 1816, and from the outset state officials understood the impediment that kept their commercial prospects and regional development in the dark. Successive administrations grappled with the internal improvement issue, keeping it at the fore of political discussions in the early Midwest from the 1820s through the 1840s. Fairly quickly, however, settlers and officials alike argued that the bigger impediment lay in the fact that the proposed routes for a number of the roads and canals traversed land that was still in the hands of American Indians. This thread of commercial impetus and the drive for internal improvements and market development has not yet been fully teased out of our study of Indian policy objectives during the early period of westward expansion. What becomes evident is that additional motivations aside from simple land hunger suffused the rationale behind the policy of Indian removal at the state level; here the demands that the commercial needs of the settlers for transportation be met became imperative for political leaders to push for additional Indian land cessions from the government, especially during the 1820s. Without these concessions the commercial agricultural system that Euro-American farmers were trying to build in the region would continue to falter in terms of market participation, and the prosperity and progress most sought would elude them.[23]

Indiana's earliest state effort toward internal improvement is found in Gov. Jonathan Jennings' first annual message in 1817 and is representative of the initial view that equated canals with prosperity. In it, Jennings related New York governor DeWitt Clinton's vision of a great "navigable communication" between the Atlantic coast and the western waterways. For Indiana the emphasis at this stage was on opening up a canal at the falls of the Ohio River near Louisville to improve navigation and transport of the already vast and growing amount of commerce moving on the water. In his next annual message, Jennings identified internal improvement as "a subject of the greatest importance [that] deserves the most serious attention." Roads and canals, he proffered, "enhance the value of the soil by affording to the agriculturist the means of deriving greater gain from its cultivation" in the form of transportation to a market. The region's commitment to promoting profitable agriculture could not be understated, as Jennings pointed out to his fellow legislators, inasmuch as these "products of our soil . . . form the basis of our public and private wealth." The 1819 annual message maintained that the opening and improving of public roads remained an essential consideration for the increasing populace. And in 1820, Jennings linked the canal work with the "commercial enterprise" of the majority of the state's citizens and with notions of progress; its completion, he said, "cannot be separated from the reputation of the state."[24]

By the mid-1820s the complex of settlement and development issues in Indiana had changed, and state political leaders now believed that federal Indian policy must be brought to bear on that singular issue, true or not, which would encourage commercial prosperity—internal improvements. In other words, while prosperity continued to appear connected to the development of internal improvements, the complicated relationship that existed between western states, the lands therein, and the press of settlement now turned on the issue of Indian policy. Indiana's formal settlement process followed behind the favorable conclusion of land cession treaties and proceeded upward from the southern tier of the state. By this time settlement of the New Purchase had revealed more clearly the agriculturists' dilemma of market access. It also revealed the critical role that an internal canal linking the Great Lakes to the Ohio River along the Wabash and Maumee rivers would play. A portion of this route, however, cut across land held by the Miamis and Potawatomis, and this would require remediation through treaty. In 1825, when New York's Erie Canal officially began its operations, Gov. James Brown Ray remarked to the General Assembly that "some of our sister states" (Ohio) had effectively remedied their transportation problems. Indianans, however, still labored under the difficulties and expenses "in reaching their only approachable market." Now was the time to seek grants of land from Congress for this purpose, Ray urged the legislative body, and it passed a joint resolution asking that Indian title to land along the proposed canal routes be extinguished.[25]

Like many of his contemporaries, Ray was awed by the transformations occurring in his state and described their consequences in his next message to the General Assembly. The picture about them constituted "one busy scene of bustle and preparation." He noted that the tides of emigration still rolled on: the forests were "daily yielding to the axemen"; tracts of "wild land" were constantly being brought under cultivation; even water sources had to be "imprisoned in new channels, and made to subserve the essential purposes of agriculture." Of the 37,000 square miles that comprised the state, nine-tenths were judged to be "susceptible of cultivation," and "[a]n industrious and virtuous race of people are rapidly preparing these extensive domains for the plough." They must have had a way of selling their produce, however, or agriculture as a livelihood would lose its appeal, "so soon as it fails to be profitable." But for the American Indians, their future would be bound up somewhere else. "The children of nature," he said, "fly still further towards the setting sun." To Ray this outcome seemed inevitable whenever the culture of ambitious agriculturist met that of the hunter. The natives knew too well "that their game will fly from the approach of that bustle, which accompanies the location of white man."[26]

That Ray and his fellow legislators were constrained to seek the title to land that lay within the state's boundaries—and as such they presumed to be "theirs"—in order to proceed with internal improvements demonstrates how and why federal Indian policy came to matter in building a commercial infrastructure in Indiana and in the West. Their initiatives reveal a degree of influence over the direction of Indian policy in promoting the development of commercial agriculture in the West. Simply stated, the foundation for internal improvements was land, and securing uninterrupted access to that land became the challenge facing statesmen during this period. But as Indiana senator William Hendricks made plain to his Senate colleagues in 1826, this was only half the battle for Indiana; because the acquired Indian lands reverted to the government, the state had to seek grants of land for its own needs from the government. In fact, Hendricks was at that point seeking a grant of land in his state to aid in the construction of the Wabash and Erie Canal. A May 13, 1826, circular to his constituents made several references to forward progress on canal work being predicated on the continued extinguishment of Indian titles.[27]

The strength and influence of the internal improvement movement on the conduct of Indian policy in Indiana and her "sister states" in the region is discernible in an examination of the treaty process that resulted in the conclusion of the two October 1826 treaties near the mouth of the Mississinewa River with the Potawatomis and the Miamis. On February 11, 1825, a letter coauthored by Fort Wayne Indian agent John Tipton affirming the practicality of building a twenty-five-mile canal connecting the Wabash and Maumee rivers was attached to a committee report written by Sen. John Ewing and brought before the Indiana Senate. Ewing's committee recommended that favorable action be taken, including the seeking of a grant of land from the federal government of the sections through which the proposed canal would be built, as well as the request that the Indian title to lands along the Wabash be extinguished to enable this public work. The following December Governor Ray wrote to Ewing that progress was being made with regards to obtaining the Indians' approval. In May of 1826 Tipton, along with Ray and Michigan territory governor Lewis Cass, was appointed treaty commissioner charged with securing an exchange of Potawatomi and Miami land in Indiana, acre for acre, for land west of the Mississippi, and west and north of Missouri and Arkansas. Secretary of War James Barbour informed them of their appropriation of $15,000, which was intended to cover all treaty expenses including the provision for "the necessary supplies incident to the emigration."[28]

Although nearly stymied by the tribes' initial refusal to sell and leave their lands, the commissioners achieved most of their objectives. They and leaders from the two nations, along with a number of Weas and Ottowas, encamped at Paradise Spring near the mouth of the Mississinewa River and met from September 20 through October 23. Lewis Cass opened the council on October 5 with a lengthy discourse on why the natives could not stay and must yield to the agricultural needs of the newcomers. "Your Great Father," he told them, "whose eyes survey the whole country, sees, that you have a large tract of land here, which is of no service to you [since] you do not cultivate it, and there is but little game upon it." The white children, however, "would be glad to live upon this land. They would build houses, raise corn, and cattle and hogs." After promising to pay what appeared from the Euro-American perspective to be "much more than it is worth to you," Cass added that the Great Father was also desirous that "you should remove far from his white children." The natives could not live in the same neighborhood as the newcomers for several reasons, but especially because their presence separated white settlements, making it so that "we cannot have roads and taverns and ferries, nor can we communicate together, as you know it is necessary we should do." Moreover, their game "flies before our improvements, and when that goes you must follow it." But the Potawatomis and the Miamis were reluctant to sell more land to the whites and move west of the Mississippi. In response to Cass, Miami chief Legro insisted that his people wanted to "live like neighbors, and barter and trade" with them. As for the game retreating from sight, he blamed the whites who "trampled our soil, and drove it away."[29]

After a "long, tedious negotiation" (also described as "semi-barbarous"), the Potawatomis and Miamis capitulated and the two treaties were concluded on October 16 and October 23, respectively. The commissioners obtained some but not all of the land cessions they sought, and, they wrote Secretary of War Barbour later, "It was impossible to procure the assent" of the Indians to removal at that time. More importantly for the internal improvement movement, the Potawatomis ceded the strip of land needed to allow the building of the Michigan road, a route that would begin at a point near Lake Michigan, run through Indianapolis, and terminate at some point at the Ohio River. The Miamis drove a harder bargain with the commissioners largely due to the fact that they knew the land they held was considered "essential to the interests of Indiana; for, without it, her citizens can have no access to that important outlet." The commissioners justified spending beyond the initial appropriation to acquire the tribal lands to Barbour by explaining that Miami-held lands not only broke up the "continuity" of the Euro-American settlements but also prevented Indiana "from entering upon that system of internal improvements to which she is invited by nature, policy, and interest." The additional expenditure was thus rationalized as necessary and critical for Indiana's development.[30]

The commissioners' assumption that "nature, policy, and interest" privileged Indiana citizens with power reflected the larger belief that Euro-Americans were well on their way to establishing an economic and cultural hegemony based on commercial agriculture. As the internal improvement movement picked up in intensity in the region, particularly by the mid-1830s, so too did calls for Indian removal. Between 1829 and 1831, a mere two-year period, Indiana's legislature petitioned Congress on six occasions, seeking the extinguishing of remaining Potawatomi and Miami titles. In one of these, state officials claimed that the persistence of a "few" natives "who claim so large a space of the best soil" worked to "materially impede a system of internal improvements essential to the prosperity of our citizens." In the natives' hands, the land was neither profitable to them nor allowed Euro-Americans access to the portion that was contiguous to the Wabash Canal. In step with federal Indian removal sentiment and policies, Indianans supported the major Potawatomi removal to Indian Country that occurred in 1838, involving some 850 natives, many of whom were ill or disease ridden, in a process that can only be characterized as pathetic, violent, and humiliating.[31]

As they did in the 1826 Mississinewa treaty proceedings, the Miamis resisted removal until finally agreeing to cede the remainder of their Indiana lands (numerous reserves excepted) in a treaty they signed in 1840. According to the terms, the natives had five years to remove from the state. After repeated delays amidst increasing tension, the Miami removal began on October 6, 1846, when they gathered at the designated collection point on the Wabash and Erie Canal in Peru, Indiana. There, accompanied by a small military force, the Miamis boarded three canal boats and were transported via the newly constructed waterway to Fort Wayne, where they were joined by two additional canal boats of their countrymen and women. What Charles Titus had recorded three years earlier of his enthusiasm for the dawn of profitable possibilities for the region's agriculturists because of this very canal, the Miamis knew to be the twilight of life as they had known it east of the Mississippi River. The somber procession of natives moved on in a northeasterly direction toward Toledo, tracing land they knew in their heart, which had only recently belonged to them on paper but by now was springing up with the newcomers' farms and towns. When the boats reached the juncture with Ohio's Miami and Erie Canal, they turned and headed down toward Cincinnati where the natives boarded the steamboat *Colorado* that would follow the Ohio River to the Mississippi, and from there westward to the final destination in Indian Country.[32]

In 1850, looking back on his family's migration first to Fort Miami in 1789 and then later to Indiana, Ezra Ferris marveled at the "improvement of the country," remarking that "the face of the country has been changed from what I then saw it to what it is now." He, like many Euro-Americans, came west as a newcomer and engaged in a struggle with the natives over land use and dominance in the early Midwest. Immediately, however, the newcomers transplanted both their agrarian ideologies and their agricultural system and in the process began transforming the landscape into a place that would support commercial agriculture on a broad scale. Newly cleared, fenced, and cultivated fields were accompanied by cabins, barns, mills, and, later, canals. These changes were far more than symbolic; they indicated a shift in power and authority and the ascension of Euro-American hegemony over the region. Here, the histories of internal improvement and Indian policy are threaded together in places with the force of a Euro-American commercial impulse that ultimately excluded—and removed—the native peoples from a role in developing the region along mutually acceptable circumstances. More importantly for this study, acknowledging the early commercial aims of the Old Northwest's farm people, and the subsequent tailoring of Indian policy to support the development of a transportation and market infrastructure, encourages a reconsideration of this area of Indian-white relations while discouraging the predominant, obviously reductionist conclusion that Euro-Americans were simply land hungry. Evidently, they sought, dreamt about, and labored over considerably more.[33]

To both Euro-Americans and American Indians, the land has historically been suggestive of cultural and economic opportunity; distinctive to the former are countless comments linking its fertility and productivity with economic prosperity and cultural progress. Early-twentieth-century novelist Willa Cather captured this ethos and linkage to the past on a later "frontier" in the character of Jim Burden who, on seeing Nebraska's open plains for the first time, understood it as something more than land: it was, he contemplated, "not a country at all, but the material out of which countries are made."[34]

NOTES

1. "Sketches from Memory, By a Pedestrian, No. II," *New England Magazine* 9 (1835): 398. Hawthorne first published this travel sketch anonymously and then included it as part of one of his later works. See Alfred Weber, Beth L. Lueck, and Dennis Berthold, eds., *Hawthorne's American Travel Sketches* (Hanover, N.H.: Univ. Press of New England, 1989), 34–35.

2. The original 1843 travel journal is housed in the Huntington Library, San Marino, California, as manuscript HM 29181. Otherwise, see George P. Clark, ed., "Through Indiana by Stagecoach and Canal Boat: the 1843 Travel Journal of Charles H. Titus," *Indiana Magazine of History* 85 (1989): 193–201, 215–17, 234; Louis C. Hunter, *Steamboats on the Western Rivers: An Economic and Technological History* (New York: Octagon, 1969), 482–84; Erik F. Haites, James Mak, and Gary M. Walton, *Western River Transportation: The Era of Early Internal Development, 1810–1860* (Baltimore, Md.: Johns Hopkins Univ. Press, 1975), 9–11; Ronald E. Shaw, "The Canal Era in the Old Northwest," in *Transportation and the Early Nation: Papers Presented at an Indiana American Revolution Bicentennial Symposium* (Indianapolis: Indiana Historical Society, 1982), 89–112.

In this essay, "dawn" is not meant to imply that the assertion of American hegemony over American Indians was somehow the beginning of a "better day"; rather, it is simply meant to mark a turning point in the struggle for regional dominance in which the Euro-Americans come out ahead, permanently.

3. Clark, "1843 Travel Journal," 234; (Lafayette) *Journal and Free-Press,* July 29, 1843. Paul Fatout describes this event within the context of Indiana's canal-building era; see Fatout, *Indiana Canals* (West Lafayette: Purdue University Studies, 1972), 109–10.

4. George Rogers Taylor, *The Transportation Revolution, 1815–1860,* vol. 4: *The Economic History of the United States* (New York: Harper and Row, 1951), 45–55. Two of the more recent studies of the Erie Canal are by Laurence M. Hauptman, *Conspiracy of Interests: Iroquois Dispossession and the Rise of New York State* (New York: Syracuse Univ. Press, 1999); and Carol Sheriff, *The Artificial River: The Erie Canal and the Paradox of Progress, 1817–1862* (New York: Hill and Wang, 1996). A good study of the nation's canal era is by Ronald E. Shaw, *Canals for a Nation: The Canal Era in the United States, 1790–1860* (Lexington: Univ. Press of Kentucky, 1990). The definitive economic study of Ohio's canal system is by Harry N. Scheiber, *Ohio Canal Era: A Case Study of Government and the Economy, 1820–1861* (Athens: Ohio Univ. Press, 1969). From Paul Fatout we learn about Indiana's canal politics but not about what the canal meant to those it would serve; see Fatout, *Indiana Canals.* An engaging study of the national politics surrounding the internal improvement movement is by John Lauritz Larson, *Internal Improvement: National Public Works and the Promise of Popular Government in the Early United States* (Chapel Hill: Univ. of North Carolina Press, 2001). The emerging states of the Old Northwest, along with the year they attained statehood, were as follows: Ohio (1803), Indiana (1816), Illinois (1818), Michigan (1837), and Wisconsin (1848).

5. William Cronon's discussion of the parallel relationship between eighteenth-century New England's economic transformation and the ecological one as it pertained to the lives of the region's American Indians and Euro-Americans is instructive and suggestive about the Midwest as well. Although he emphasizes ecological change where I emphasize changes in the landscape, his argument that the "New England ecology was transformed as the region became integrated into the emerging capitalist economy of the North Atlantic" can to some degree be applied in this instance as well. Here, too, was interest in turning wilderness into a "mart." See William Cronon, *Changes in the Land: Indians, Colonists, and the Ecology of New England* (New York: Hill and Wang, 1983), 159, 161.

As social and physical constructions, landscapes and landscape changes should be considered within a framework that blends "natural" and cultural history while also exploring the influence of ideologies and struggles for power on the land itself; together they reveal a human story. "The reorganization of a landscape," contend Alan Baker and Gideon Biger, "signifies a realignment of authority." See Alan Baker's introductory essay in Alan R. H. Baker and Gideon Biger, eds., *Ideology and Landscape: Essays on the Meanings of Some Places in the Past* (Cambridge, U.K.: Cambridge Univ. Press, 1992), 2–5, 6.

Along with power and hegemony, the predominance of earning a livelihood as a producer of food or fiber, and the attendant agricultural system, plays an obviously significant part in shaping and altering the landscape. See John Fraser Hart, *The Rural Landscape* (Baltimore, Md.: Johns Hopkins Univ. Press, 1998), chap. 1, esp. p. 4; John R. Stilgoe, *Common Landscape of America, 1580 to 1845* (New Haven, Conn.: Yale Univ. Press,

1982), offers additional insight on the meanings of landscape in history, with particular relevance to rural America. A suggestive article that examines how an agricultural region originates by identifying "the intrinsic processes by which dominance and change take place" is by J. E. Spencer and Ronald J. Horvath, "How Does an Agricultural Region Originate?" *Annals of the Association of American Geographers* 53 (1963): 74–92 (quote is on page 74). An early commercial orientation is overwhelmingly apparent in the primary sources and as noted by scholars of the Midwest and the frontier. See, for example, R. Douglas Hurt, *The Ohio Frontier: Crucible of the Old Northwest* (Bloomington: Indiana Univ. Press, 1996), chap. 8. Midwesterners' historical subscription to the ideology of "progress" is described in several places in an excellent introductory essay in Andrew R. L. Cayton and Susan E. Gray, eds., *The American Midwest: Essays on Regional History* (Bloomington: Indiana Univ. Press, 2001), 1–26.

6. R. David Edmunds, *The Potawatomis: Keepers of the Fire* (Norman: Univ. of Oklahoma Press, 1978), illustrates the struggle for control—and the consequences for native peoples—leading ultimately to removal from the Midwest; an excellent study of the multiple zones, or frontiers, of contact including in the area now known as the Midwest is by R. Douglas Hurt, *The Indian Frontier, 1763–1846* (Albuquerque: Univ. of New Mexico Press, 2002), see especially chaps. 5 and 7. My research disputes the notion that to any significant degree Midwestern settlers harbored "ambivalence" toward the market, a contention that is yet found, for example, in Andrew R. L. Cayton and Peter S. Onuf, *The Midwest and the Nation: Rethinking the History of an American Region* (Bloomington: Indiana Univ. Press, 1990), chap. 2.

7. Prominent agricultural historian R. Douglas Hurt does address this nexus of agriculture and Indian policy although the emphasis is on the broad policy outcomes as they pertain to American Indians, not "white" Americans, transportation, or regional development; in R. Douglas Hurt, *Indian Agriculture: Prehistory to the Present* (Lawrence: Univ. Press of Kansas, 1987), chaps. 6 and 7.

More immediately, Laurence Hauptman has noted a connection in New York between Iroquois land dispossession and the transportation revolution in the building-up of that state. He argues that the loss of Indian lands "was not merely an unfortunate consequence or unexpected result of state transportation, land settlement, or defense policies, but an integral part of those policies." See Hauptman, *Conspiracy of Interests*, xvii, 1–23; John Larson explains that during the 1780s the phrase "internal improvement" referred to various programs that encouraged security, prosperity, and enlightenment following the Revolution, coming later to particularly signify public works projects aimed at improving transportation. His study traces Americans' use of government power at the state and federal levels to carry out these projects as expressed emanations of the people in Larson, *Internal Improvement*, 1–7; William Collins concludes that Indiana Indian agent John Tipton saw the link between internal improvements, Indian removal, and the interests of the state's legislators, but he does not develop the broader significance to regional and agricultural development. See William Frederick Collins, "John Tipton and the Indians of the Old Northwest" (Ph.D. diss., Purdue Univ., 1997), 345. For more on the relationship of John Tipton to the internal improvement movement in the Midwest, see Ginette M. Aley, "Westward Expansion, John Tipton, and the Emergence of the American Midwest, 1800–1839" (Ph.D. diss., Iowa State Univ., 2005).

8. Clarence Edwin Carter, ed., *The Territorial Papers of the United States,* 28 vols. (Washington, D.C.: GPO, 1934–75), 7:7–10; Anthony F. C. Wallace, *Jefferson and the Indians: The Tragic Fate of the First Americans* (Cambridge, Mass.: Harvard Univ. Press, 1999), 208; for Indian policy relevant to the period see Francis Paul Prucha, *American Indian Policy in the Formative Years: The Indian Trade and Intercourse Acts* (Lincoln: Univ. of Nebraska Press, 1970) and George Dewey Harmon, *Sixty Years of Indian Affairs* (Chapel Hill: Univ. of North Carolina Press, 1941), chaps. 4, 6, and 19; Bert Anson offers a useful and informative overview of the policy of Indian removal in "Variations of the Indian Conflict: The Effects of the Emigrant Indian Removal Policy, 1830–1854," *Missouri Historical Review* 59 (1964–65): 64–89 (reference to the St. Mary's treaty is found on page 72).

9. T[ench] C[oxe], "An Enquiry into the Principles on which a Commercial System for the United States should be founded," *American Museum* 1 (1787): 498–500.

10. Joyce Appleby, "What Is Still American in the Political Philosophy of Thomas Jefferson?" *William and Mary Quarterly* 39 (1982): 295–96, 304; John Opie, *The Law of the Land: Two Hundred Years of American Farmland Policy* (Lincoln: Univ. of Nebraska Press, 1994), 4, 8–11. Peter Onuf describes how officials saw the West in the post-Revolutionary era and the role of the West in creating the American nation in Peter S. Onuf, "Liberty, Development, and Union: Visions of the West in the 1780s," *William and Mary Quarterly* 43 (1986): 179–203. The 94 percent farm and rural population designation was derived from the 1940 census that adopted "urban" and "rural" area definitions, applied these retrospectively to the 1790–1930 censuses, and then published the results in the sixteenth Census of the United States, 1940, Population, vol. 1, Number of Inhabitants, 10.

11. Henry Knox's Civilization policy is communicated in General Knox, Secretary of War, to the President of the United States, May 23, 1789, United States Congress, *American State Papers: Indian Affairs,* 2 vols. (Washington, D.C.: Gales and Seaton, 1832–1861), 1:53–54 [hereafter cited as *ASP-IA*]; see Wallace, *Jefferson and the Indians,* chap. 6, for a discussion of the Civilization policies; Thomas Jefferson's quote is from Thomas Jefferson to Gov. William H. Harrison, February 27, 1803, and is reprinted in Albert Ellery Bergh, *The Writings of Thomas Jefferson,* 20 vols. (Washington, D.C.: Thomas Jefferson Memorial Assoc., 1903), 10:368–73; quote is on page 370.

12. Regarding the relationship between native women and agriculture, the effects of Euro-American interference and pressure for change, policy results, and both native resistance to and achievement in American agriculture, see Hurt, *Indian Agriculture,* chap. 7; J[ohn] P[eter] Kluge to Brother Loskiel, August 5, 1806, reprinted in Lawrence Henry Gipson, ed., *The Moravian Indian Mission on White River: Diaries and Letters, May 5, 1799 to November 12, 1806* (Indianapolis: Indiana Historical Bureau, 1938), 571–74.

13. See introductory essay in Gipson, ed., *Moravian Indian Mission,* 1–19; Diary entry for May 17, 1803, is reprinted ibid., 229–30; Little Turtle, Five Medals, and Others to Evan Thomas, George Ellicott, and Others, September 18, 1803, Gerard T. Hopkins, *A Mission to the Indians, from the Indian Committee of the Baltimore Yearly Meeting* (Philadelphia, Pa.: T. Ellwood Zell, 1862), 4–5. See also Joseph A. Parsons Jr., "Civilizing the Indians of the Old Northwest, 1800–1810," *Indiana Magazine of History* 56 (1960): 195–216.

14. William Wesley Woollen, ed., *Executive Journal of the Indiana Territory, 1800–1816* (Indianapolis, Ind.: Bowen-Merrill, 1900), 82–85. The population change in the Indiana Territory between 1800 and 1810 is particularly impressive considering that in the

meantime Michigan and Illinois emerged as separate territories in 1805 and 1809, respectively; thus the census takers in the Indiana Territory recorded a dramatic population increase for a land area that had at the same time been drastically reduced. The American Indian population estimate for 1800 is cited in Homer J. Webster, "William Henry Harrison's Administration of Indiana Territory," *Indiana Historical Society Publications* 4 (1907): 189.

15. Thomas Jefferson to Gov. William H. Harrison, February 27, 1803, Bergh, *Writings of Jefferson*, 368–73. Anthony Wallace gives an in-depth explanation of Jefferson's letter to Harrison (and others) in the context of the era and presidential policy; see Wallace, *Jefferson and the Indians*, chap. 7.

16. Petition of the Vincennes Convention, December 28, 1802, reprinted in Logan Esarey, ed., *Messages and Letters of William Henry Harrison*, 2 vols. (Indianapolis: Indiana Historical Commission, 1922), 1:62–67; Commission of Governor Harrison to Treat with the Indians, February 8, 1803, *ASP-IA*, 1:84. The texts of these cession treaties are found in *ASP-IA*, 1:687–90, 693–97, 704–5, 761–63. For maps outlining the cessions in relation to the state of Indiana see Charles C. Royce, *Indian Land Cessions in the United States* (Washington, D.C.: GPO, 1900; rep., New York: Arno, 1971), plate 126.

Webster notes that the tribes with whom Harrison treated included the Delaware, Shawnee, Miami, Eel River, Wea, Kickapoo, Piankashaw, Kaskaskia, Sauk and Fox, and the Potawatomi; see Webster, "William Henry Harrison's Administration," chap. 9.

17. Annual Message, November 12, 1810, Esarey, ed., *Messages and Letters of Harrison*, 487–96. Jennings was involved in the series of treaties conducted at St. Mary's, Ohio, in October of 1818 with the Weas, Potawatomis, Delawares, and the Miamis in which the Delawares and the Weas gave up their land claims in Indiana; see *ASP-IA*, 2:168–70. See also Royce, *Indian Land Cessions*, 692. The Calhoun reference is noted in Andrew R. L. Cayton, *Frontier Indiana* (Bloomington: Indiana Univ. Press, 1996), 263–64.

18. Chief Metea's comments are quoted in Edmunds, *The Potawatomis*, 220; Hurt, *Ohio Frontier*, 144–48; Francis S. Philbrick, *The Rise of the West, 1754–1830* (New York: Harper and Row, 1965), chap. 12, particularly 309; Robert B. Duncan, "Old Settlers," (Indianapolis) *Herald*, January 11, 1879. This represents the first of four articles penned by Duncan that were later collected and reprinted as Robert B. Duncan, "Old Settlers," *Indiana Historical Society Publications* 2 (1894): 376–402; quote is on page 377.

19. Duncan, "Old Settlers," 385.

20. Hurt, *Ohio Frontier*, 211; Beverley W. Bond Jr., ed., "Dr. Drake's Memoir of the Miami Country, 1779–1794," *Quarterly Publication of the Historical and Philosophical Society of Ohio* 18 (1923): 56. William Johnston's journal is excerpted in Shirley S. McCord, ed., *Travel Accounts of Indiana, 1679–1961* (Indianapolis: Indiana Historical Bureau, 1970), 53–57; the accuracy of Johnston's assessment of the potential for cattle kingdoms in the Kankakee and Wabash valleys in Indiana is born out in Paul W. Gates, "Hoosier Cattle Kings," *Indiana Magazine of History* 44 (1948): 1–24.

21. Petition to Congress by Inhabitants of the Territory, October 1, 1805, *Territorial Papers*, 307–11; see also memorial dated December 12, 1804, ibid., 243–45. Charles Sellers argues that as of 1815 the market revolution was in the process of establishing a "capitalist hegemony over economy, politics, and culture" such that it "created ourselves and most of the world we know;" see Sellers, *The Market Revolution: Jacksonian America, 1815–1846* (New York: Oxford Univ. Press, 1991), 5. Yet it is important to distinguish that

conceding a "market revolution"—in this case, the building of canals as well as roads in the early American Midwest that yielded profitable new byways involving producers, consumers, processors, and merchants—is not the same as to imply that agriculturists experienced a corresponding sudden impulse or "epiphany" to participate in regional and national markets. In fact, it was there all along. Allan Kulikoff (and others) postulates that Colonial and post-Revolutionary American farm people in general operated within a changing and growing capitalist world economy that incorporated the North Atlantic rim and also participated semi-regularly in commodity markets to try to secure money to pay taxes or to buy manufactured goods. Farmer-settlers' demands and expectations for market access are also evidenced in the contemporary writings of officials and settlers alike; see Allan Kulikoff, *The Agrarian Origins of American Capitalism* (Charlottesville: Univ. Press of Virginia, 1992), 20, and chaps. 1 and 2. Richard Hofstadter's analysis of the agrarian myth and commercial realities still rings true; historically the farmer, "in most cases, was in fact inspired to make money, and such self-sufficiency as he actually had was usually forced upon him by a lack of transportation or markets;" see Hofstadter, *The Age of Reform: From Bryan to F.D.R.* (New York: Knopf, 1955), chap. 1.

22. J. S. Clark, *Life in the Middle West* (Chicago: Advance, 1916), 25; Judge Finch's account was originally printed in *Indianapolis Journal,* May 30, 1885, and as "Reminiscences of Judge Finch," *Indiana Magazine of History* 7 (1911): 155–65 (quote is on page 160); Jacob Schramm to Brother-in-Law and Sister-in-Law, April 10, 1836, is reprinted in Jacob Schramm, *The Schramm Letters: Written by Jacob Schramm and Members of His Family from Indiana to Germany in the Year 1836,* trans. and ed. Emma S. Vonnegut (Indianapolis: Indiana Historical Society, 1935), 67.

23. Ralph D. Gray, "The Canal Era in Indiana," in *Transportation and the Early Nation: Papers Presented at an Indiana American Revolution Bicentennial Symposium* (Indianapolis: Indiana Historical Society, 1982), 113–34. A good though dated study with an emphasis on the politics behind the internal improvement remains in Logan Esarey, "Internal Improvements in Early Indiana," *Indiana Historical Society Publications* 5 (1912): 47–158.

24. Annual Message, December 2, 1817, Logan Esarey, ed., *Messages and Papers of Jonathan Jennings, Ratliff Boon, William Hendricks,* vol. 3: 1816–1825 (Indianapolis: Indiana Historical Commission, 1924), 41; Annual Message, December 9, 1818, ibid., 66, 68; Annual Message, December 7, 1819, ibid., 79; Annual Message, November 28, 1820, ibid., 116.

25. Message to the General Assembly, December 8, 1825, Dorothy Riker and Gayle Thornbrough, eds., *Messages and Papers Relating to the Administration of James Brown Ray, Governor of Indiana, 1825–1831* (Indianapolis: Indiana Historical Bureau, 1954), 78–80, 81n7.

26. Message to the General Assembly, December 8, 1826, ibid., 163, 166, 168, 169, 176.

27. Hendricks to His Constituents, May 13, 1826, *Messages and Papers of Jonathan Jennings et al.,* 339–48.

28. John Tipton et al., to John Ewing, January [?], 1825, *JTP,* 1:441–42n66; James Barbour to Lewis Cass, James B. Ray, and John Tipton, May 24, 1826, ibid., 1:536–37.

29. Proceedings, Potawatomi and Miami Treaty Negotiations, October 5, 1826, *JTP,* 1:577–92; *ASP-IA,* 2:679–85.

30. [Lewis] Cass, [John B.] Ray, and [John] Tipton to James Barbour, October 23, 1826, *JTP,* 1:598–606.

31. Two memorials of the General Assembly of the State of Indiana, January 22, 1829, and February [?], 1829, appear as part of a report of the Committee on Indian Affairs, *Senate Document* no. 22, 21–22, serial 203, 1–4; Gray, "Canal Era in Indiana," 113. Another example is *House Document* no. 68, 21–22, serial 208. The 1838 Potawatomi treaty is found in Charles J. Kappler, ed., *Indian Affairs: Laws and Treaties,* 2 vols. (Washington, D.C.: GPO, 1904), 2:519–24. See also Stewart Rafert, *The Miami Indians of Indiana: A Persistent People, 1654–1994* (Indianapolis: Indiana Historical Society, 1996), 95–101; Irving McKee, "The Trail of Death: Letters of Benjamin Marie Petit," *Indiana Historical Society Publications* 14 (1941): 5–141; Bert Anson, "Chief Francis Lafontaine and the Miami Emigration from Indiana," *Indiana Magazine of History* 60 (1964): 242–43; Rafert, *Miami Indians,* 108–13; and Edmunds, *The Potawatomis,* chap. 10.

32. Anson, "Chief Francis Lafontaine," 241–68; Rafert, *Miami Indians,* 108–13. The 1840 Miami treaty is found in Kappler, *Indian Affairs,* 2:531–34.

33. Ezra Ferris, "The Early Settlement of the Miami Country," *Indiana Historical Society Publications* 1 (1897): 251.

34. Willa Cather, *My Antonia* (Boston, Mass.: Houghton Mifflin, 1918), 7.

11

"A Perfect Apollo"

Keokuk and Sac Leadership during the Removal Era

THOMAS J. LAPPAS

At the confluence of the Bad Axe and Mississippi rivers, Black Hawk, a Sac Indian chief, watched as a detachment of Illinois militiamen massacred the women, children, and warriors who had followed him along the Rock River and through the driftless region of southwestern Wisconsin. As the Americans on the gunboat *Warrior* spilled the blood of Black Hawk's band into the Mississippi, the Black Hawk Wars of 1831–32 came to a dramatic close. Although he knew that resisting the United States' command to move west of the Mississippi might result in his dying on the lands of his fathers, the Sac Indian leader could not have anticipated the carnage that occurred on the Wisconsin shores in August 1832. In the summer of 1833, Black Hawk's American captors paraded the defeated warrior through the cities of the East. Eventually Black Hawk came to symbolize both Indian resistance and its ultimate defeat by the United States. Black Hawk fit the image of a fierce Indian brave who preferred to risk death at the hands of the government rather than endure the shame of being torn from his Illinois homeland. He has emerged as a major folk hero in the region, lending his name to a community college, a professional hockey team, a brand of ham, and even a Web site company. However, Black Hawk's influence within the Sac and Fox community was eclipsed by Keokuk, whose impact on Indian-white relations has been overshadowed by Black Hawk and his military ventures.

In August 1832, at the time of Black Hawk's final battle, Keokuk's people remained downstream on the west bank of the Mississippi, removed from the violence occurring to the north. Keokuk and the majority of Sacs and Foxes followed the United States' commands to move west of the Mississippi, solidifying their subordinate relationship to the government. In doing so, they escaped the violence that befell Black Hawk's followers. The dissidents in the Sac tribe, including Neapope and Black Hawk, idealized the path of resistance without giving much credit to the prudence and shrewdness of Keokuk's dealings with whites. In his autobiography Black Hawk later declared, "We were a divided people, forming two parties. Ke-o-kuk being at the head of one, willing to barter our rights merely for the good opinion of the whites; and cowardly enough to desert our village to them." Dismissing Keokuk as a traitor to the Sac people was clearly a result of Black Hawk's unwavering view that overt resistance to the Americans' incursions was the only honorable way to respond to their demands. American memory has consistently honored Black Hawk as another stoic warrior in the pantheon of Tecumseh and Pontiac. Historians such as William T. Hagan and Alvin Josephy have continued this tradition, characterizing Keokuk as a panderer to the Americans while romanticizing Black Hawk's military endeavors. Contrary to the image constructed by many scholars, Keokuk was more successful than Black Hawk within his own tribe because he was able to balance his traditional role as a chief with the realities of the United States' westward expansion.[1]

Like many American Indian leaders in the first half of the nineteenth century, Keokuk faced the question of how to deal with the flood of white American settlers encroaching on their lands. By the 1820s and 1830s the prevailing view among federal officials was that Indians needed to be relocated from their present locations in order to make way for white settlers. Like the Cherokees, Choctaws, Chickasaws, Creeks, and Seminoles to the south, the Sacs and Foxes were being pressured by both local whites and the distant federal government to move west of the Mississippi River. The Sacs and Foxes, although two distinct tribes, had shared a common history since the eighteenth century, when they formed an alliance in response to French aggressions. The Sacs and Foxes had lived in the Rock Island region on the Mississippi for generations, after relocating from the north. The settlement of the Old Northwest, and the establishment of Illinois in 1818, set the stage for the removal of the Indians who lived there. By the 1820s farmers and miners began to outnumber the Indians. The United States employed Indian agents to make treaties with the tribes in order to solidify white claims to the land. Over time, Keokuk realized that the flood of whites was unstoppable through violence. Instead of advocating open resistance, he developed a strategy of dealing peaceably with federal officials while at the same time fulfilling traditional expectations of a Sac leader. This became especially important when removal became the law of the land with the passage of the Indian Removal Act in 1830, which authorized the president to relocate Indians living east of the Mississippi to the western territories. Keokuk's ability to walk the tightrope between violence and acquiescence allowed him to become a successful leader and to keep his supporters alive. This essay discusses Keokuk's upbringing in Sac and Fox society and argues that his rise to power reflected both tribal traditions and the reality of the nineteenth-century Removal Era.[2]

Some of the differences between Keokuk and Black Hawk stemmed from their difference in age as well as their differing roles within Sac society. Black Hawk grew up during the late imperial wars of 1776–1815, when the Sacs and Foxes tended to side with the British against the Americans. One scholar suggests that Americans might have even attacked Black Hawk's village during the eighteenth century, when he was still a child. Thus his earliest experience with the Americans was as their adversary. In the early days of the republic, the Americans persistently tried to put an end to the Sacs' autonomy by preventing them from fighting with their traditional enemies, the Osages, who tended to be pro-American. The Treaty of 1804, signed between the Sacs and Foxes and the United States, was supposed to put an end to war with the Osages in addition to being a cession of almost all the Sac and Fox lands east of the Mississippi. The treaty became a constant point of contention for the Sacs and the Americans throughout the following decades. Many Sacs, especially Black Hawk, argued that the treaty did not force them to relinquish their lands.[3]

The antagonistic relationship between the tribes and the United States continued through the next decades. During the War of 1812 Black Hawk fought on the side of the British. Keokuk, who was younger than Black Hawk, also opposed the Americans. What distinguished the two was that Black Hawk continued to believe in the possibility of an Indian-British alliance. He held on to this vision even after the American defeat of Tecumseh, the Shawnee leader of a Pan-Indian movement, who was killed during the War of 1812. Throughout the 1820s and 1830s Black Hawk made frequent visits to the British, who were relegated to Canada after the war. These sojourns were a constant concern for settlers and frontier officials who referred to Black Hawk and his followers as the "British Band." During this time, Keokuk was developing his leadership skills and modifying his tactics in dealing with the Americans. Conversely, Black Hawk held on to a past when defiance of the Americans was a feasible tactic. One historian put it this way: "Each side in this internal dispute worked to ensure the survival of Sauk identity. Black Hawk and the other traditionalists assumed that in order to keep the heart of the tribe alive, the Indians had to retain Saukenuk [the principal Sac village], with its ancestral graves and the accompanying annual ceremonies that they had shared. Keokuk and his supporters saw a need to accommodate the Americans to prevent them from destroying the people." Accommodation, however, did not necessarily mean abandoning one's past or one's cultural values.[4]

Keokuk's eventual acceptance of the Americans' demands to move across the Mississippi and begin a more sedentary lifestyle unquestionably altered many of the Sac traditions of seasonal hunting and intertribal warfare. His leadership between 1812 and 1831 nonetheless reflected Sac expectations of their chiefs. The tribe valued generosity and elevated to leadership positions those hunters who could provide food for the nation. They also honored the gift of oratory and the ability to lead through persuasion. Keokuk's ability in councils, his persistent support of the Sacs' right to go to war with neighboring tribes, and his astuteness in increasing annuities and obtaining food and other goods from American Indian agents exemplified the type of leadership that the Sac community expected. Keokuk came of age in a conflicted era, when holding on to traditional ways of life often seemed to be at odds with the removal project of the Americans. His success as a leader and as a Sac must be examined in terms of his ability to navigate his tribe through this era of tradition and change. Understanding his place in Sac society requires examining his role as prescribed by Sac customs of kinship.

In Sac kinship organization, individuals born to a certain father were granted membership in alternate moieties, placing the males of the tribe into either the civil branch or the martial branch of the nation. Keokuk was born into the martial side of this bicameral organization and was excluded from becoming a true civil chief. In terms of his birth, Keokuk's opinions on internal civil matters would not have had as much authority as those of an individual born into the civil moiety. Sac society was not organized strictly along these lines of kinship or inheritance. Personal attributes and gifts might allow individuals to play roles that they were not born into. Recognized early for his oratorical skills, Keokuk acquired respect from civil leaders for his ability to speak effectively in councils concerning treaties, removal, and other matters that would usually have been the responsibility of the civil chiefs. As one historian points out, Keokuk's role as speaker gave him a great deal of influence as "a negotiator with white authorities." From 1804 until the conclusion of the Black Hawk Wars, the Sacs and Foxes were involved in frequent negotiations with Americans over the terms of annuity payments and the details of removal, and they were constantly arguing with Indian agents over the right of war parties to retaliate against other tribes. During such an era, the Sacs and Foxes looked to Keokuk to perform outside his inherited function as a warrior, even though he continued to be influential in martial matters as well.[5]

Born into the martial moiety, Keokuk would have been a warrior but customarily would only have earned war chief status through brave actions in battle. During the War of 1812, when the majority of Sac warriors were fighting the Americans on the side of the British, the civil chiefs decided to grant

Keokuk the status of chief. This action was an unconventional one to take, but with an American attack rumored to be imminent, the civil chiefs feared for the safety of the village. They began to discuss a possible response to the American attack, but with few warriors, except for Keokuk and some other young Indians around the village, surrender seemed to be the only option. Though he would not normally be allowed to speak in the war council since he had not proven himself in battle, Keokuk was granted the right to address the elders. He revealed his bravery to the chiefs by offering to lead a group of warriors against the Americans to protect his village. They rewarded Keokuk by allowing him to lead a war party and granting him the title of chief, though these actions would have been outside the usual jurisdiction of the civil chiefs. The threat never materialized in the village of Saukenuk, but this incident shaped the role Keokuk would play throughout his life in the Sac community. Keokuk has often been discounted as a military leader for his eventual acquiescence to the Americans, but Keokuk's first adult role was that of a warrior.[6]

Throughout the early decades of the nineteenth century, Keokuk identified himself as a warrior, and he was referred to as such by United States officials. In 1830 Indian agent to the Sacs and Foxes, Thomas Forsyth, provided a description of the various chiefs to the commissioner of Indian affairs, Col. Thomas McKenney. Forsyth stated that Keokuk was "the hereditary Brave of the Sac Nation of Indians." He continued his description, saying that Keokuk had a "love or fondness for war," which he demonstrated in numerous conflicts with the Sioux and Menominees. On federal annuity documents and treaties, Keokuk placed his mark under the heading of Sac braves or warriors, not under Sac chiefs. As a warrior, Keokuk was not the primary leader with whom whites spoke—this was the role of the civil chiefs. His tribe, however, recognized his value as an orator and supported him as a negotiator. Thus, within the organization of his tribe, he was viewed as a brave and war chief, not as a civil chief, and he was expected to listen to the decisions of the civil chiefs in matters relating to the internal affairs of the tribe.

In many ways, Keokuk and Black Hawk had similar positions within Sac society, though Black Hawk's age earned him a measure of respect. As treaty negotiations with the United States became the defining characteristic of Indian-white relations, the younger warrior's ability to speak in councils and deal peaceably with the Americans distinguished him from Black Hawk. His skill placed him in a difficult position. From one perspective, he was able to see the power of the United States and understand the need to accept their demands to move west and to put an end to tribal wars on the plains. From another vantage point, he had a duty as a warrior to avenge depredations committed on the Sacs by other tribes. This ambivalence often led Keokuk to

have conflicting goals in terms of influencing independent war parties that
acted without support from the whole of Sac society.[7]

If an individual warrior wished to form a war party, he did so by invit-
ing other men to join him in performing certain ceremonies the evening before their departure for war. The authority of civil chiefs to stop a war party
relied almost entirely on persuasion rather than coercion. For instance, the
civil chiefs might confiscate the party's sacred war bundles, leaving the warriors without their spiritual medicine during the battle. Often, appeals by the
women of the tribe could convince a war party to stay at home. Normally,
however, civil chiefs left war parties to make their own decisions in these matters. The United States tended to hold the entire Sac and Fox population accountable for the actions of these independent war parties, creating tensions
between the younger warriors, civil chiefs, and the Americans.[8]

Keokuk showed his diplomatic power in mediating these situations by
giving the whites what they wanted while simultaneously gaining concessions
for his people. Throughout the 1820s and 1830s, Keokuk continued to lead war
parties in attacks against the Sioux and defended his tribe's right to retaliate
against Sioux and Menominee attacks. His ability to fulfill certain expectations of the United States while acting against their other wishes stood in contrast to Black Hawk, whose animosity toward the whites only grew as white
officials began to show their preference for Keokuk's diplomacy. Keokuk
gradually acquiesced to American demands and tried to stop parties of Sacs
from going to war with the Osages, Sioux, and other tribes by the late 1820s.
Even through the Black Hawk Wars, however, he resented the Americans'
intrusion on the Sacs' right to engage in warfare and was often vocal in his
opposition.

Following the War of 1812 the Sacs acquired a reputation for being an
unruly tribe who refused to heed the orders of the United States. During the
war both Keokuk and Black Hawk demonstrated overt animosity toward the
Americans, although Black Hawk was involved more deeply in actual fighting. The Sacs continued, even after signing a treaty in 1816, to attack whites
with some degree of freedom. In June 1820 a small party of Sacs attacked a
group of whites, looting the party and killing two of them. When Thomas
Forsyth's attempts to capture the two prisoners failed, the territorial governor
of Missouri, William Clark, told him, "indeed, the Sacks, by their late conduct, have made very unfavorable impressions on the people." By this time,
Keokuk realized that the Sacs had to accommodate the Americans, but the extent to which the Sacs would have to bend to them was not yet clear.[9]

The following summer Keokuk informed Forsyth that he had detained
the two men accused of murder and apologized because he was not yet able
to deliver them to him. Forsyth trusted that Keokuk "would deliver them at a

proper time." He then relayed to Clark that he had procured an ally in Keo-kuk, who had the respect of his community in addition to being cooperative with whites. When the Sacs finally did visit Clark in St. Louis to surrender the two suspects, Black Hawk failed to accompany them. This meeting not only brought Keokuk to the forefront as a mediator but also precluded Black Hawk from acting as an important player in the imminent Sac-white councils that were to follow. With his prestige based on wartime exploits, Black Hawk had a disadvantage when victories and losses with whites began to be decided at the negotiating table.[10]

Keokuk's ability to remain in the good graces of white officials while con-tinuing to defend his people was exemplified in the intertribal wars of the early 1820s. War parties, and their ability to act independently of the majority of the Sac and Fox community, not only angered the Americans when they at-tacked whites but also frustrated officials with their persistence in continuing the intertribal warfare on the prairie. While the officials in Washington and St. Louis prodded Forsyth to convince the Sacs and Foxes to lay down their weapons, he realized that the conflicts would not stop merely at the urging of an agent. In a letter to Secretary of War John C. Calhoun, Forsyth argued that the United States' commands to the Sacs and Foxes not to retaliate against the Sioux were ludicrous, citing that the chiefs were unable to control their young people's actions in battle. The Americans' influence over the tribe was not yet strong enough to stop them from fighting with their enemies.[11]

That summer the warpath was well worn between Saukenuk and the Sioux camps to the west. On June 24, 1822, five hundred Sac, Fox, and Iowa Indians set out to wage war against the Sioux. After a prolonged battle the Sacs, Foxes, and Sioux suffered casualties, yet Forsyth continued to urge the Sacs to cease warfare on the plains, saying that the Sioux would soon come to make peace with them. This was unlikely, as intertribal warfare tended to consist of nu-merous retaliations for the deaths of kinsmen in a previous battle. Keokuk rejected Forsyth's suggestion, saying, "The Sioux Chiefs will never come for-ward, and as the war has commenced we must not let our guard down." In the fall, Keokuk's brother-in-law experienced a vision that inspired him to lead a war party of two hundred warriors west toward the Sioux, where he was to await a sign as to what to do next. The civil chiefs assured Forsyth that they would come back, while Forsyth was convinced that more Indian blood would be shed on the prairie, making the situation more intimidating for settlers. In fact, the war party fizzled, as they failed to find any Sioux on the plains. Although Keokuk was becoming the primary mediator between the Sacs and Foxes and the whites, he maintained his role within the Sac commu-nity as a warrior. His power within both communities began to feed off each other, as he could support the Sac war effort while explaining the reality of

intertribal warfare to the whites. The agents recognized this important function and treated Keokuk as the most important Sac leader.[12]

Clark wrote a letter to Forsyth in August 1822 explaining that he had informed Keokuk that unofficial visits to St. Louis must cease because he suspected that the voyages were made under pretenses of obtaining free goods.
During this general reduction of the quantity of presents to be given to Indians, Clark listed Keokuk and a few other influential chiefs who were allowed
to receive goods from the agents. Clark recognized Keokuk as a "man of importance" and distributed provisions to his party. The next year the officials
declared that foodstuffs would be given as presents only to widows, orphans,
the old, and the infirm, saying that able-bodied hunters were to receive only
gun powder and tobacco. Keokuk, Peshepaho, Wapelo, and a few others were
listed as exceptions to this restriction. Forsyth explained, "I always found by
giving a present privately to influential chiefs and warriors I always had their
good will, and as a matter of course, the good will of their nation followed."
Throughout the 1820s Keokuk received greater quantities of flour, meat, salt,
and whiskey than any other Sac leader. This flow of goods not only reflected
Keokuk's status among federal officials but also enabled him to become more
influential within the Sac community. In Sac and Fox custom the distribution
of presents represented an important source of power within the tribe. By re-
ceiving the greatest share of Forsyth's presents and distributing them to the
people, Keokuk gained a great deal of respect among his people. One scholar
attributed the exchange of gifts between the Americans and Keokuk as the
result of the Americans having "learned to appeal to his weak points, his cu-
pidity and love of display." But Keokuk's desire for American goods and annuities had more to do with his leadership position in the tribe than with his
personal weakness or greed. It was his responsibility to his people rather than
his hubris that required him to amass presents from the Americans. By using
his position of favor among whites to earn respect within the Sac community
Keokuk secured his place as a leader among his people.[13]

Black Hawk remained conspicuously absent during these and other meetings. In the summer of 1824 Keokuk led a large group of Sacs eastward to visit
with officials in Washington, D.C., and to nurture his relationship with the
United States. The American leaders showed them around Baltimore, Philadelphia, and New York. Ostensibly, the function of the visit was to settle the
business of intertribal warfare. In the long run the most important result
of the conference was the demonstration of American power to the western
Indians who attended. These were the largest settlements of human beings
that Keokuk had ever seen. The cities impressed on Keokuk the image of the
United States as a great power while Black Hawk remained in Illinois. Black
Hawk never visited the eastern cities until after his much-publicized defeat.

Black Hawk was escorted through the cradle of American civilization in his traditional clothing as a spectacle. Alvin Josephy suggested that after his tour "Black Hawk returned to the West, impressed by what he had seen, and filled with gratitude for the warmth with which he had been received." For white Americans living in the East, the image of the defeated but honorable warrior reinforced their faith in the power of the United States. This image, combined with Black Hawk's namesake, persisted in American culture. Keokuk's visit to the East was less dramatic for white observers. However, the timing of his trip allowed the leader to modify his tactics for the greater good of his people.[14]

After his visit to the East, Keokuk began to take the Americans' demands to stop the intertribal warfare more seriously. Motivated by another Sac attack on the Sioux in 1824, Forsyth wrote a letter to Clark in the spring of 1825 requesting a general Indian council. Paying attention to Indian needs, Forsyth also suggested that the council be delayed until August so as not to interfere with the harvest or the hunt. Afraid that tensions might flare into warfare at the council, Forsyth demanded that no liquor be served lest it increase the chance of violence. After the federal officials agreed that a council would take place, Keokuk responded favorably to the restriction of alcohol and complimented Clark for always keeping their best interest at heart. Unfortunately the council failed to resolve the problem of intertribal war, though many other matters were addressed. At the council, which was well attended, Sac annuities were raised to $2,000, from the previous $1,000. This was partially a response to persistent traders who extracted much of the Indians' debt from these annuity payments, leaving the Sacs with little after the debt had been paid. Forsyth, even prior to getting the annuity raised, kept traders at bay who wanted the Sacs and Foxes to pay their outstanding debts. One trader who had lost some cattle to the Sacs demanded remuneration as well as payment for past debts. Forsyth wrote to the trader informing him that although the Sacs wanted to pay their debt, they were awaiting next year's annuity payment in order to do so. Indeed, Forsyth was very clear that the debts ringing up against annuity payments caused much tension on the frontier, and he requested that Clark work out some better system. The increase in annuity payments, while supported by the traders, was almost certainly a response to Keokuk's requests as well.[15]

While Keokuk showed his appreciation of these and other attempts by the agents to assist the Sacs and Foxes, he continued to oppose unfair land purchases of Sac and Fox lands. In their quest to drive the Sacs and other Mississippi Valley Indians from the land, the Americans purchased a section of territory north of the Missouri from the Kansas Indians. Although the Kansas Indians had little claim to the region, it was indeed claimed by the Sacs and Foxes. When Thomas Forsyth used the Kansas purchase as evidence of the

United States' possession of the Sac and Fox lands to the east of the Mississippi, he received a harangue from Keokuk and the Fox leader Strawberry: "I was answered by Strawberry and Kiocuck who said that the Kansa nor any other Indians had any claims to the land in question except themselves, the Sac and Foxes." Even those Indians who were cooperative with the Americans attacked removal policy when it was implemented poorly. In other words, the friendly Sacs continued to fight for fair treatment in the sale of their lands, despite Black Hawk's accusations that these Indians pandered to the whites.[16]

Intertribal warfare continued to anger government officials who attempted to keep the frontier safe for settlers. While the Sacs did make some attempts to improve their relations with the Sioux, their efforts fell short due to unforeseen circumstances. In the summer of 1826 a party traveling west with a pipe and "friendly words" for the Sioux failed to find their old adversaries. Thus peace was never formalized between the two tribes. After the party returned home, Keokuk received word that an alliance of Shawnees, Delawares, and Kickapoos had sent scalps, wampum, and a speech seeking aid in war against the Osages. While Forsyth warned the Sacs of their promises to the United States, Keokuk traveled to St. Louis to hear the "straight story" from Clark concerning intertribal wars. The remaining Sacs assured the agent that nothing would happen until Keokuk's return. Keokuk kept his followers out of this conflict, but other Sacs and Foxes were not as eager to listen to American pleas for moderation.[17]

Despite Keokuk's opposition to warfare with the Osages, the tinderbox on the frontier threatened to ignite again during the next year. In 1827 Keokuk and his supporters called on Forsyth and informed him that "Black Hawk was organising a party of Indians to war" with the Sioux. A number of chiefs attempted to persuade Black Hawk from going to war by offering him three horses and other gifts but the old war chief was still determined to go. Keokuk assured Forsyth that he would do everything in his power to keep Black Hawk off the warpath. If the friendly band was unable to stop Black Hawk, Keokuk said, the rebellious band would have to "take their chances" with the United States. Forsyth implored Keokuk to inform Black Hawk that "if he went to war, I would demand him and party be sent down in irons to St. Louis."

The American threats still failed to pacify Black Hawk, who swore that "nothing but death should prevent him from going to war." As Black Hawk prepared for battle the civil chiefs continued to show their disapproval. In June, after much pleading from other Sacs, Black Hawk changed his mind, a development that Forsyth attributed to the "industry" of the other Sac chiefs and braves. Though Keokuk and the chiefs relieved the immediate problem, the rift between Keokuk and Black Hawk began to grow larger. To Black Hawk, Keokuk seemed to be siding with the whites against a just and rightful act of revenge against their enemies. This was an insult to Black Hawk, who was appalled by the idea of the Sacs becoming cowards in order to conciliate the Americans. As tensions between whites and Indians rose over the next two years, the rivalry between the two grew more intense.[18]

During the summer of 1828 the Sacs sent out peaceful parties to Fort Malden, Canada, to meet with the British, while Keokuk traveled to the Otoes to receive some horses. During the absence of much of the warrior population, rumors began circulating of a growing anti-American faction among the Sacs. Clark received questionable information from two Sac and Fox warriors that a group of followers were listening to their British father's plans to attack the Americans. Aware that Sacs had visited the British in Canada, Clark and other officials demanded answers. Forsyth assured Clark that the villagers at Rock Island were seeking out perpetrators of these rumors in order to kill them. "Kiocuck very properly observed to all the Indians present yesterday that he was satisfied that you did not believe the story because you are too well acquainted with Indians to suppose that the Sac Indians intended to war against the U.S." Keokuk, though, showed some concern that these stories would be believed by the settlers, causing white animosity toward the Sacs to increase. If this happened Keokuk would lose the fruits of his diplomatic ventures over the past decade. Such a loss would come at an especially bad time, because the Sacs were unable to remove west until the following year. Meanwhile, some Sacs, including Black Hawk, continued to deny the American claim that the Sacs had ceded their lands in the treaty of 1804. The Americans called more vehemently for the Sacs and Foxes to move west, while resistance to these efforts grew within the Sac and Fox community.[19]

In 1829, as Sac opposition to removal mounted, Forsyth received a visit from all the Indians who had not yet moved west. Declaring that they would defend their land and had formed an alliance with the Potawatomis, Kickapoos, and Menominees, this party opposed Keokuk's efforts to move the tribe gradually westward. In response, Keokuk assured Forsyth that these opponents were a minority and that they spoke without understanding the situation. Black Hawk and other warriors at Rock Island viewed the situation differently. The anger of the British Band toward whites was growing as the settlers acted violently toward the remaining Sacs and Foxes. One of Black Hawk's warriors watched as a settler ploughed up his land. When he protested, the settler beat him with a beanpole. Both sides were growing hostile. Keokuk was forced to admit that some of the Indians at Rock Island, primarily those who opposed removal, had shown their outward disdain for him and his more moderate stance toward whites. Other Sacs supported his efforts. Although Keokuk wished to travel west and be among his relatives, the civil chiefs had asked him to stay as a mediator in the Black Hawk situation.

Keokuk had been successful at preventing the British Band from going to war, and the civil chiefs hoped that he could use his influence for peace.[20]

Keokuk entertained the idea of remaining at Saukenuk even though he believed that negotiation was a more prudent course of action than warfare. In one instance, Black Hawk left a council with Forsyth after complaining of the acts committed by whites on the remaining Sacs. After Black Hawk was gone Keokuk entered and asked secretly "if he and some friends could remain at Rocky River to raise the corn they had planted." Keokuk assured Forsyth that "most of the principal chiefs had gone to reside at a place within a few miles of the Iowa River, and that more than half of those now at Rocky River would also go shortly to the same place." Forsyth responded that he did not have the power to agree to such a request. Evidently, Keokuk hoped his shrewdness would gain him some privileges from Forsyth. Black Hawk, conversely, had come to disregard mediation as an option. Although Keokuk realized that the final push for removal was imminent, he tried to use his power to remain on his homeland as long as possible.[21]

In 1829 Forsyth called the Sacs, Potawatomis, and Chippewas together for a treaty to be held in early August. The treaty made American claims to Sac lands concrete. Keokuk and the other chiefs agreed to the conditions, which gave the Winnebagos control over the lands north of the Wisconsin and Fox rivers, while the region south of the Wisconsin belonged to the United States. Keokuk assured Forsyth that his relatives would not return to Rock Island but would remain along the Des Moines and Iowa rivers, west of the Mississippi. In declaring his people's loyalty to American demands, Keokuk made some requests and asked Forsyth to relate to William Clark a message: "[Keokuk] asks that in the Spring, they send up a small two horse plow with gears and for his own use, he would be thankful to you if you would send him by return of Wm. Davenport's boat, two iron kettles, each to contain four or five gallons and as light as possible, with bales to them."

While Keokuk was acting in accordance with American wishes, he hoped to reap some benefits from dealing cordially with them. This skillfulness did not preclude him from fulfilling his duties to the tribe. If they were to be successful in their new homeland, the Sacs would need a plow to till the hard prairie sod—such a device that would have been shared by the whole tribe. Miscellaneous domestic goods, such as kettles that would be for "his own use," were simply small perquisites. As removal time approached Keokuk grasped the reality of the situation while trying to assure that his people would have the necessary tools to survive the coming years.[22]

During the late 1820s and early 1830s Keokuk was not as obsequious as Black Hawk's characterization made him appear. Despite a willingness to move across the Mississippi permanently, Keokuk fought with William Clark over the distribution of annuities. As the possibility of remaining east of the river waned, he made it clear that he would negotiate the best terms for payments for their tribal lands. When Clark paid a portion of their annuities to a group of Sacs who had been living on the Missouri and had little claim to the annuity payments of the northern Sacs and Foxes, Keokuk registered a protest with Thomas Forsyth. The agent agreed with Keokuk's claim and suggested that Clark remedy the situation.[23]

Not all of the Indian agents of the western tribes appreciated Keokuk's persistence in negotiating for fair payment of annuities. Lawrence Taliaferro, agent to the Sioux and longtime opponent of the Sacs, accused them of wanting "to be paid twice for the Illinois purchase." He let his wrath fly, declaring that "our lenient government will indulge them." To Taliaferro it would have been "[b]etter far to exterminate them at once for permit me to assure you that year after year similar occurrences will take place not only with these tribes but their example will be followed by others." Taliaferro was especially biased against Keokuk's tribe because the Sacs had been a thorn in the side of the Eastern Sioux since his tenure at the agency. What stands out is that Keokuk's effectiveness as an advocate for his tribe earned him a bad reputation among some American officials who thought that he was too successful on behalf of his people.[24]

Even as the United States prepared to use force in removing the British Band from Rock Island, most officials, with the notable exception of Taliaferro, continually praised Keokuk, Wapelo, and Stabbing Chief for their cooperative efforts with the government. Lt. George A. McCall referred to Keokuk as "a perfect Apollo in figure, and [he] is one of the most graceful and eloquent speakers I have seen among the Indians of any tribe." Clark declared that the trio had "consistently and zealously cooperated with the Government Agents in furtherance of its views, and in their endeavors to effect the removal of all their people from the ceded lands." Despite Keokuk's complaints regarding annuity payments and his defense of numerous raids on rival Indian tribes, he remained a leader respected by the Americans.[25]

While Keokuk remained at Rock Island he and the civil chiefs tried to convince all the remaining Sacs to move west before the situation escalated into violence. Keokuk, fearing that the Americans were ready to unleash the militia on the Rock Island Sacs, requested that the officers refrain from using violence until all of Keokuk's friends and relations moved across the Mississippi. The civil chiefs of the Sac and Fox, most of whom had moved to Iowa, expected Keokuk to remain at Rock Island to convince Black Hawk and his followers to move west.

As a result Keokuk and other Sac leaders attempted to smooth relationships between the Sacs and the whites. Conversely, Black Hawk angered many settlers with attempts to reclaim his homeland. The white trader, Rinah Wells, supported by settlers upset at Black Hawk's intrusion on their lands, wrote to officials in Washington requesting aid in the removal of the Indians. When the trader and others at Rock Island advised him to move with Keokuk to the Iowa River, he angrily snapped, "I would not" and added that Keokuk had "accomplished nothing towards making arrangements for us to remain, or to exchange other lands for our village. There was no more friendship existing between us. I looked upon him as a coward, and no brave, to abandon his village to be occupied by strangers." Their relationship, which once had been characterized only by a divergence of views, had evolved into a bitter, personal rivalry.[26]

Seeking council, Black Hawk traveled north along the Rock River to visit Wabioshek (White Cloud), the Winnebago prophet, for advice and support in his opposition to the whites. Black Hawk declared to the commander of the western department of the army, Gen. Edmund P. Gaines, that he was merely occupying the land and did not intend violence. However, the general began to distrust Black Hawk's supposedly non-violent intentions. Gaines also believed that Keokuk and his followers "were not much to be relied upon," since they too seemed to be reluctant to break their ties with Rock Island. Other settlers were able to recognize the differences between Black Hawk's and Keokuk's factions. William Deniston assured the authorities that Keokuk and his followers had always maintained a friendly relationship with him and other settlers but that some individuals from Keokuk's band were planning to join the Black Hawk band the next day. According to Deniston, "The despondant heard the Indians speak of Keokuk in a rough manner. They called him a rascall and assigned as the reason for calling him so, that he talked too much with whites." Yet while the British Band criticized Keokuk as a panderer to whites, he continually defended Sac actions against white criticisms. Although Keokuk urged the stragglers at Rock Island to move west, he vocally justified Sac retaliatory acts against the Menominee. The United States began to doubt the ability of the friendly band to influence the British Band when they heard of Sac attacks on the Menominees in July. The "Articles of Agreement and Capitulation," signed on June 30, 1831, between the Sacs and Foxes and the Americans, stipulated that the intertribal warfare must stop and that the friendly chiefs of the Sac and Fox were responsible for controlling the British Band. Black Hawk came to the meeting only after Keokuk convinced him to attend. When he placed his mark on the paper, Black Hawk thrust the nib into the paper with such force that he broke the pen. He then returned to his seat.[27]

Although this agreement suggested that all the factions were to listen to Keokuk, direct power over another Indian was an uncomfortable concept for the Sac leaders. The articles required these "peace chiefs" to perform functions that contradicted their traditional organization. Even some whites understood the flaws behind the terms of the agreement. Atkinson responded to Joseph Street's memo describing the death of twenty-five Menominees at the hands of the Sacs with the following statement: "I doubt very much whether the principal men of the nation could have prevented such a strike. . . . There is a point of honor (if it may be called such a sentiment) felt by all Indians to retaliate in Blood for similar wrongs. If they fail to do so, they fall under the ridicule of their neighbors and even their own women."

At a September 5 council, Maj. John Bliss and agent Felix St. Vrain reprimanded the Sacs for their actions. Keokuk rose to oppose their criticisms, citing that the Menominees had struck first and that the Sacs continued to be loyal to U.S. demands. "The reason I say so much against you is because our hearts are good. Our chiefs were killed with the pipe of peace and the wampum in their hands. This is all I have to say. As for my chiefs and braves, they will do as they please. . . . Why do you not let us be as the Great Spirit made us and let us settle our differences?"

Intertribal warfare had been an object of some dispute since the Prairie du Chien council where Keokuk and four chiefs asked Clark and Morgan about how the Sacs should react to acts committed against them. Keokuk justified his complacency with the warriors by saying that he had no power to track down and capture the murderers without the consent of their relations and that the perpetrators were on the fall hunt anyway. The Sacs' attacks embittered the Menominees and made them more willing to join the American campaign against Black Hawk the following year. The actions of the British Band had made it impossible for Keokuk or the civil chiefs to prevent the Americans' punishment of Black Hawk.[28]

As Keokuk realized that he would be unable to convince the British Band to move west or to appease white demands to surrender renegade warriors, his life at Rock Island drew to a close. During the Black Hawk War Keokuk began a new life on the shores of the Iowa River, about one hundred miles from Saukenuk. Black Hawk was left to lead his ill-fated party without the influence of Keokuk and the other Sacs and Foxes who had removed according to American demands. In the ensuing decades the Sacs would be confronted with many of the same challenges that they had faced in the 1820s and 1830s. Disputes over land, annuities, and the right to practice long-standing customs did not end when Keokuk made his mark on the 1829 treaty. Despite the persistence of many traditions, Keokuk had begun to define a new type of leadership for the Sac people. The source of his authority had been the Sac value system, which had always honored bravery, generosity, oratorical skill, and inherited roles. Although he recognized the United States as a superior military

force, Keokuk never betrayed the values that were important to so many Sac
people. It is unclear if the Sacs and Foxes who followed Black Hawk had chosen death as a favorable alternative to living away from Saukenuk. But to Keokuk's followers, their chief represented an alternative type of leadership, which
represented an alteration of traditional ways of life but was nonetheless rooted
in Sac custom. In commemorating those valiant warriors who risked their
lives in opposing the United States, it is imperative that we remember those
leaders who fulfilled their duty to their people without creating martyrs for
the American memory.

<h2 style="text-align:center">NOTES</h2>

1. Milo Milton Quaife, ed., *Life of Black Hawk* (New York: Dover, 1994), 47; Wil-
liam T. Hagan, *The Sac and Fox Indians* (Norman: Univ. of Oklahoma Press, 1958), 5;
Alvin Josephy, *The Patriot Chiefs: A Chronicle of American Indian Resistance* (New York:
Penguin, 1993), 213.

2. Indian Removal Act, May 28, 1830, *Documents of United States Indian Policy,* ed.
Francis Paul Prucha (Lincoln: Univ. of Nebraska Press, 1990), 52–53.

3. Roger Nichols, *Black Hawk and the Warrior's Path* (Arlington Heights, Ill.: Harlan Davidson, 1992), 10; Hagan, *Sac and Fox Indians,* 18–20.

4. Nichols, *Black Hawk,* 85.

5. Alanson Skinner, *Observations on the Ethnology of the Sac Indians* (Westport,
Conn.: Greenwood, 1970), 11–13; Anthony F. C. Wallace, "Prelude to Disaster: The Course
of Indian-White Relations which Led to the Black Hawk War of 1832," *Wisconsin Magazine of History* (1982): 247–88.

6. Donald Jackson, ed., *Black Hawk: An Autobiography* (Urbana: Univ. of Illinois
Press, 1990), 72; Nichols, *Black Hawk,* 51.

7. Thomas Forsyth to Col. Thomas McKinney, August 5, 1830, Forsyth Papers,
Ser. T, 9 vols., William Preston Papers, Lyman C. Draper Manuscript Collection, Historical Society of Wisconsin, Division of Archives and Manuscripts, University of Wisconsin,
Madison, Wisconsin, 4T:140 [hereafter cited as DMC]; Wallace, "Prelude to Disaster,"
250.

8. Skinner, *Observations,* 56–57; Wallace, "Prelude to Disaster," 252.

9. William Clark to Thomas Forsyth, June 25, 1820, Forsyth Papers, DMC, 1T:54.

10. Clark to Forsyth, June 29, 1821, Forsyth Papers, DMC, 1T:55.

11. Forsyth to John C. Calhoun, March 11, 1822, Forsyth Papers, DMC, 4T:117. In light
of the fact that civil chiefs could support a war party by simply remaining silent, these
might have had a more broad-based support than the agents understood.

12. Forsyth to Clark, September 19, 1822, Forsyth Papers, DMC, 6T; Forsyth to Clark,
September 16, 1822, ibid., 4T; Clark to Forsyth, August 3, 1822, ibid., 4T:22; Forsyth to
Clark, April 3, 1823, ibid., 4T:159.

13. Abstract of Provisions Issued to Indians by Thomas Forsyth, Indian Agent at
Fort Armstrong, September 1822–29, Forsyth Papers, DMC, 2T; Hagan, *Sac and Fox Indians,* 89.

14. Hagan, *Sac and Fox Indians,* 94; Josephy, *Patriot Chiefs,* 212.

15. Forsyth to Calhoun, Forsyth Papers, DMC, 4T:196; Forsyth to Clark, April 9, 1825, ibid., 4T; Forsyth to Clark, June 25, 1825, ibid., 4T:236–38.

16. Forsyth to Clark, May 29, 1826, Forsyth Papers, DMC, 4T:245.

17. Forsyth to Clark, June 20, 1826, Forsyth Papers, DMC, 4T:250; Forsyth to Clark, July 13, 1826, ibid., 4T:254.

18. Forsyth to Clark, May 24, 1827, Forsyth Papers, DMC, 4T:266–67; Forsyth to Clark, May 30, 1827, 6T:59; Forsyth to Clark, June 15, 1827, ibid., 4T:268.

19. These two warriors were Whish-co-baughm, a Sac, and Naw-te-waig, a Fox. Forsyth to Clark, June 25, 1828, Forsyth Papers, DMC, 6T:89; Forsyth to Clark, June 16, 1828, ibid., 6T:86–87; Forsyth to Clark, June 16, 1828, ibid., 6T:86–87; Forsyth to Clark, May 24, 1828, ibid., 6T:81–82.

20. Forsyth to Clark, May 22, 1829, Forsyth Papers, DMC, 6T:100.

21. Forsyth to Clark, May 17, 1829, Forsyth Papers, DMC, 6T:97.

22. Forsyth to Clark, October 1, 1829, Forsyth Papers, DMC, 6T:113.

23. Forsyth to Clark, April 28, 1830, Forsyth Papers, DMC, 6T:118.

24. Lawrence Taliaferro to Joseph Street, July 6, 1831, Joseph Street Papers, Historical Society of Wisconsin, Division of Archives and Manuscripts, University of Wisconsin, Madison, Wisconsin [hereafter cited as JSP].

25. George McCall to Archibald McCall, June 17, 1831, *Illinois Historical Collections: The Black Hawk War,* vols. 35–38, ed. Ellen Whitney (Springfield: Illinois State Historical Library, 1973), 36:57 [hereafter cited as *BHW*]; Clark to Edmund P. Gaines, May 28, 1831, ibid., 36:16–17.

26. George McCall to Archibald McCall, June 17, 1831, *BHW,* 36:57; Report, June 10, 1831, ibid., 36:40–44; Quaife, ed., *Life of Black Hawk,* 41–42.

27. Deposition of William, William H., and Erastus S. Deniston, November 4, 1831, *BHW* 36:196; Hagan, *Sac and Fox Indians,* 132–33.

28. Memo of Joseph Street, August 1, 1831, *BHW* 36:121; Henry Atkinson to Edmund P. Gaines, August 10, 1831, ibid., 36:130; Council Report, September 5, 1831, in Frank E. Stevens, *The Black Hawk War, Including a Review of Black Hawk's Life* (Chicago: Frank E. Stevens, 1903), 107; Morgan to Street, October 31, 1831, JSP 1:17.

Bibliography

PRIMARY SOURCES

ARCHIVES

Additional Manuscripts. British Library, London, England.

Colonial Office Records, Class 5 Papers. Records Office of Great Britain, Kew, England.

Conrad Weiser Correspondence. Historical Society of Pennsylvania, Special Collections Research Library, Philadelphia, Pennsylvania.

Deposition of Rebecca Cox. June 13, 1811. Ohio Valley, Great Lakes Ethnohistory Archive, Glenn A. Black Laboratory of Archaeology, Indiana University, South Bend, Indiana.

Friendly Association Records, Collection 1250, Quaker Collection. Haverford College, Haverford, Pennsylvania.

Frontier Wars Papers, Ser. U, 24 vols. Lyman C. Draper Manuscript Collection. Historical Society of Wisconsin, Division of Archives and Manuscripts, University of Wisconsin, Madison, Wisconsin.

Huntington Manuscripts. Huntington Library, San Marino, California.

Israel Pemberton Papers, Etting Collection. Historical Society of Pennsylvania, Special Collections Research Library, Philadelphia, Pennsylvania.

Jeffery Amherst Papers. William L. Clements Library, Ann Arbor, Michigan.

Joseph Brant Papers, Ser. F, 22 vols. Lyman C. Draper Manuscript Collection. Historical Society of Wisconsin, Division of Archives and Manuscripts, University of Wisconsin, Madison, Wisconsin.

Joseph Street Papers. Historical Society of Wisconsin, Division of Archives and Manuscripts, University of Wisconsin, Madison, Wisconsin.

Massachusetts Archives Collection, 328 vols. Massachusetts Archives, Boston, Massachusetts.

Ninian Edwards Papers. Chicago Historical Society, Chicago, Illinois.

Nomaque v. People. Case No. 81, Record Group 901.001. Illinois State Archives, Springfield, Illinois.

Ohio Company Records, Marietta Collection. Ohio Historical Society, Columbus, Ohio.

Penn Manuscripts, Official Correspondence. Historical Society of Pennsylvania, Special Collections Research Library, Philadelphia, Pennsylvania.

Potawatomi Files. Ohio Valley Great Lakes Ethnohistory Archive, Glenn A. Black Laboratory of Archaeology, Indiana University, Bloomington, Indiana.

Records of the Bureau of Indian Affairs, Record Group 75. National Archives and Records Administration, Washington, D.C.

Thomas Forsyth Papers, Ser. T, 9 vols. Lyman C. Draper Manuscript Collection. Historical Society of Wisconsin, Division of Archives and Manuscripts, University of Wisconsin, Madison, Wisconsin.

Thomas Gage Papers. William L. Clements Library, Ann Arbor, Michigan.

Timothy Pickering Papers, 1731–1792. Massachusetts Historical Society, Boston, Massachusetts.

War Office Papers. Records Office of Great Britain, Kew, England.

William Preston Papers, Ser. QQ, 6 vols. Lyman C. Draper Manuscript Collection. Historical Society of Wisconsin, Division of Archives and Manuscripts, University of
Wisconsin, Madison, Wisconsin.

ARTICLES AND BOOKS

Abbot, W. W., ed. *The Papers of George Washington, Colonial Series.* 10 vols. Charlottesville: Univ. Press of Virginia, 1983–95.

Adair, James. *Adair's History of the American Indians.* Ed. Samuel Cole Williams. New
York: Argonaut, 1966.

Alden, Timothy, ed. "An Account of the Captivity of Hugh Gibson among the Delaware
Indians." *Collections of the Massachusetts Historical Society.* 3rd Ser. Boston, Mass.:
American Stationer's, 1837.

Alvord, Clarence Walworth, and Clarence Edwin Carter, eds. *The New Régime, 1765–1767.*
Vol. 11. *Collections of the Illinois State Historical Library: British Series.* Springfield: Illinois State Historical Library, 1916.

*American State Papers: Documents, Legislative and Executive, of the Congress of the United
States of America.* 38 vols. Washington, D.C.: Gales and Seaton, 1832–1861.

Armour, David A., ed. *Attack at Michilimackinac: Alexander Henry's Travels and Adventures in Canada and the Indian Territories between the Years 1760 and 1764.* Mackinac
Island, Mich.: Mackinac State Historical Parks, 1971.

Aupaumut, Hendrick. "A Narrative of an Embassy to the Western Indians." *Collections of
the Massachusetts Historical Society.* 1st ser. Boston, Mass.: 1826.

Barker, Joseph. *Recollections of the First Settlement of Ohio.* Ed. George Jordan Blazer.
Marietta, Ohio: Richardson, 1958.

Bergh, Albert Ellery, ed. *The Writings of Thomas Jefferson.* 20 vols. Washington, D.C.:
Thomas Jefferson Memorial Assoc., 1903.

Bond, Beverly W., Jr., ed. "The Captivity of Charles Stuart, 1755–1757." *Mississippi Valley
Historical Review* 13 (1926–1927): 58–81.

———. "Dr. Drake's Memoir of the Miami Country, 1779–1794." *Quarterly Publication of
the Historical and Philosophical Society of Ohio* 18 (1923).

Brasser, Ted. *Riding on the Frontier's Crest: Mahican Indian Culture and Culture Change.*
Ottawa: National Museums of Canada, 1974.

Brock, R. A., ed. *The Official Records of Robert Dinwiddie, Lieutenant-Governor of
the Colony of Virginia, 1751–1758.* 2 vols. Richmond: Virginia Historical Society,
1883–84.

C. T. [Coxe, Tench]. "An Enquiry into the Principles on which a Commercial System for
the United States Should Be Founded." *American Museum* 1 (1787): 498–500.

Calloway, Colin G. "Beyond the Vortex of Violence: Indian-White Relations in the Ohio
Country, 1784–1795." *Northwest Ohio Quarterly* 64 (1992): 16–26.

Carter, Clarence Edwin, ed. *The Correspondence of General Thomas Gage with the Secretaries of State, 1763–1775.* 2 vols. New Haven, Conn.: Yale Univ. Press, 1931.

———. *The Territorial Papers of the United States.* 28 vols. Washington, D.C.: GPO, 1934–75.

Clark, George P., ed. "Through Indiana by Stagecoach and Canal Boat: The 1843 Travel Journal of Charles H. Titus." *Indiana Magazine of History* 85 (1989): 193–234.

Colden, Cadwallader. *The History of the Five Nations Depending on the Province of New York in America.* New York: William Bradford, 1727.

Collections of the Massachusetts Historical Society. 10 ser. 70 vols. Boston: Massachusetts Historical Society, 1792–1941.

Cruikshank, E. A., ed. *The Correspondence of Lieutenant Governor John Graves Simcoe.* 5 vols. Toronto, Can.: Society, 1923–31.

Darlington, William M., ed. *Christopher Gist's Journals.* Pittsburgh, Pa.: J. R. Weldin, 1893.

Dexter, Franklin D., ed. *Diary of David McClure, Doctor of Divinity, 1748–1820.* New York: Knickerbocker, 1899.

Easterby, J. H., ed. *Colonial Records of South Carolina: Journals of the Commons House of Assembly.* 14 vols. Columbia: Historical Commission of South Carolina, 1951–89.

Edwards, Ninian W. *History of Illinois from 1778 to 1833; and Life and Times of Ninian Edwards.* Springfield: Illinois State Journal, 1870.

Esarey, Logan, ed. *Messages and Letters of William Henry Harrison.* 2 vols. Indianapolis: Indiana Historical Commission, 1922.

———. *Messages and Papers of Jonathan Jennings, Ratliff Boon, William Hendricks.* Vol. 3: 1816–1825. Indianapolis: Indiana Historical Commission, 1924.

Finch, Judge. "Reminiscences of Judge Finch." *Indiana Magazine of History* 7 (1911): 155–65.

Finley, James B. *Life among the Indians.* Cincinnati, Ohio: Hitchcock and Walden, 1857.

Fitzpatrick, John, ed. *The Writings of George Washington.* 39 vols. Washington, D.C.: GPO, 1931–44.

Fleming, William. *A Narrative of the Sufferings and Surprizing Deliverances of William and Elizabeth Fleming.* Boston, Mass.: Green and Russell, 1756.

Frazier, Patrick. *The Mohicans of Stockbridge.* Lincoln: Univ. of Nebraska Press, 1992.

Gambone, Michael D., ed. *Documents of American Diplomacy: From the American Revolution to the Present.* Westport, Conn.: Greenhaven, 2002.

Gipson, Lawrence Henry, ed. *The Moravian Indian Mission on White River: Diaries and Letters, May 5, 1799 to November 12, 1806.* Indianapolis: Indiana Historical Bureau, 1938.

Grenier, Fernand, ed. *Papiers Contrecoeur et autres documents concernant le conflit anglo-français sur l'Ohio de 1745 à 1756.* Ottawa, Can.: Presses Universitaires Laval, 1952.

Hamilton, Edward P., ed. *Adventure in the Wilderness: The American Journals of Louis Antoine de Bougainville, 1756–1760.* Norman: Univ. of Oklahoma Press, 1964.

Hazard, Samuel, ed. *Colonial Records of Pennsylvania, 1683–1790.* 16 vols. Philadelphia, Pa.: T. Fenn, 1851–53.

Henning, William Waller, ed. *The Statutes at Large: Being a Collection of All the Laws of Virginia.* 18 vols. Richmond, Va.: Samuel Pleasants, 1809–23.

Hopkins, Gerard T. *A Mission to the Indians, from the Indian Committee of the Baltimore Yearly Meeting.* Philadelphia, Pa.: T. Ellwood Zell, 1862.

Hough, Franklin B., ed. *Diary of the Siege of Detroit in the War with Pontiac.* Albany, N.Y.: Joel Munsell, 1860.

———. *Proceedings of the Commissioners of Indian Affairs, Appointed by the Law for the Extinguishment of Indian Titles in the State of NY.* 2 vols. Albany, N.Y.: Joel Munsell, 1861.

Howe, Henry. *Historical Collections of Ohio.* 3 vols. Columbus, Ohio: Henry Howe, 1889.

Hulbert, Archer Butler, ed. *Records of the Original Proceedings of the Ohio Company.* Marietta, Ohio: Marietta Historical Commission, 1917.

Jackson, Donald, ed. *Black Hawk: An Autobiography.* Urbana: Univ. of Illinois Press, 1990.

Jacobs, Wilber, ed. *The Appalachian Indian Frontier: The Edmund Atkin Report and Plan of 1755.* Lincoln: Univ. of Nebraska Press, 1954.

James, Alfred Proctor, ed. *The Writings of General John Forbes Relating to His Service in North America.* Menasha, Wis.: Collegiate, 1938.

Jemison, G. Peter, and Anna M. Schein, eds. *Treaty of Canandaigua, 1794.* Santa Fe, N.M.: Clear Light, 2000.

Jordan, John W., ed. "Journal of James Kenny, 1761–1763." *Pennsylvania Magazine of History and Biography* 37 (1913): 24, 45.

Kappler, Charles J. *Indian Affairs: Laws and Treaties.* 2 vols. Washington: GPO, 1904.

Kirk, Robert. *The Memoirs and Adventures of Robert Kirk, Late of the Royal Highland Regiment.* Limerick, Ireland: J. Ferrar, 1770.

Knopf, Richard C., ed. *Executive Journals of the Northwest Territory.* Columbus, Ohio: Anthony Wayne Parkway Board, 1957.

Labaree, Leonard W., ed. *The Papers of Benjamin Franklin.* 32 vols. New Haven, Conn.: Yale Univ. Press, 1959–96.

Lambling, A. A., ed. *The Baptismal Register of Fort Duquesne.* Pittsburgh, Pa.: Myers, Shinkle, 1885.

"Little Turtle's Oration before the Battle of Fall Timbers." *Old Fort News* 2 (1937): 7–8.

Louden, Archibald, ed. *A Selection, of Some of the Most Interesting Narratives of Outrages, Committed by the Indians, in Their Wars, with the White People.* 2 vols. Carlisle, Pa.: A. Louden, 1808–11.

McCord, Shirley S., ed. *Travel Accounts of Indiana, 1679–1961.* Indianapolis: Indiana Historical Bureau, 1970.

McDowell, William L., Jr., ed. *Colonial Records of South Carolina: Documents Relating to Indian Affairs, May 21, 1750–August 7, 1754.* Columbia: South Carolina Archives Department, 1958–70.

Minutes of Conferences Held at Lancaster in August 1762. Philadelphia, Pa.: B. Franklin and D. Hall, 1763.

O'Callaghan, E. B., ed. *Documents Relative to the Colonial History of the State of New York, Procured in Holland, England, and France.* 15 vols. Albany, N.Y.: Weed, Parsons, 1857.

Parker, Arthur C. *Parker on the Iroquois.* Ed. William N. Fenton. Syracuse, N.Y.: Syracuse Univ. Press, 1968.

Pease, Theodore C., ed. *Trade and Politics, 1767–1769.* Vol. 16. *Collections of the Illinois State Historical Library: British Series.* Springfield: Illinois State Historical Library, 1921.

Pease, Theodore C., and Ernestine Jenison, eds. *Illinois on the Eve of the Seven Years' War.* Springfield, Ill.: Trustees of the State Historical Library, 1940.

Pennsylvania Archives. 9 ser. 138 vols. Philadelphia: State Printer of Pennsylvania, 1852–56, 1875–1949.

Persinger, Jacob. *The Life of Jacob Persinger.* Sturgeon, Mo.: Moody and McMichael, 1861.

Philbrick, Francis S., ed. *The Laws of Illinois Territory, 1809–1818.* Vol. 25. *Collections of the Illinois State Historical Library.* Springfield: Illinois State Historical Library, 1950.

Phillips, P. Lee, ed. *First Map and Description of Ohio, 1787, by Manasseh Cutler.* Washington, D.C.: W. H. Lowdermilk, 1917.

Prucha, Francis Paul, ed. *Documents of the United States Indian Policy.* Lincoln: Univ. of Nebraska Press, 1990.

Quaife, Milo Milton, ed. "Captivity of Peter Looney." *Mississippi Valley Historical Review* 15 (1928): 95-96.

———. *The Siege of Detroit, 1763.* Chicago: R. R. Donnelley, 1958.

Reese, George, ed. *The Official Papers of Francis Fauquier, Lieutenant Governor of Virginia, 1758–1768.* 3 vols. Charlottesville: Univ. Press of Virginia, 1980–83.

Richards, Clifford H. "Little Turtle: The Man and His Land." *Old Fort Bulletin* (Nov.–Dec. 1974): 7.

Riker, Dorothy, and Gayle Thornbrough, eds. *Messages and Papers Relating to the Administration of James Brown Ray, Governor of Indiana, 1825–1831.* Indianapolis: Indiana Historical Bureau, 1954.

Robertson, Nellie Armstrong, and Dorothy Riker, eds. *The John Tipton Papers.* 3 vols. Indianapolis: Indiana Historical Society, 1942.

Rogers, Robert. *A Concise Account of North America: Containing a Description of the Several British Colonies on that Continent.* London: J. Millan, 1765.

Schramm, Jacob. *The Schramm Letters: Written by Jacob Schramm and Members of His Family from Indiana to Germany in the Year 1836.* Trans. Emma S. Vonnegut. Indianapolis: Indiana Historical Society, 1935.

Seaver, James Everett, ed. *A Narrative of the Life of Mrs. Mary Jemison.* Canandaigua, N.Y.: J. D. Bemis, 1824.

Smith, William. *An Historical Account of the Expedition against the Ohio Indians, in the Year 1764, under the Command of Henry Bouquet Esq.* Philadelphia, Pa.: T. Jefferies, 1766.

Steele, Roberta Ingles, and Andrew Lewis Ingles, eds. *The Story of Mary Draper Ingles and son Thomas Ingles, as Told by John Ingles Sr.* Radford, Va.: Commonwealth, 1969.

Stevens, Sylvester K., and Donald H. Kent, eds. *Wilderness Chronicles of Northwestern Pennsylvania.* Harrisburg: Pennsylvania Historical Commission, 1941.

Stevens, Sylvester K., Donald H. Kent, and Autumn L. Leonard, eds. *The Papers of Henry Bouquet.* 6 vols. Harrisburg: Pennsylvania Museum and Historical Commission, 1951–1994.

Sullivan, John, ed. *The Papers of Sir William Johnson.* 14 vols. Albany, N.Y.: Univ. of the State of New York, 1921–65.

Thomson, Charles. *Hopewell Friends History, 1734–1934, Frederick County, Virginia.* Strasburg, Va.: Shenandoah, 1936.

———. *An Inquiry into the Causes of the Alienation of the Delaware and Shawanese Indians from the British Interest.* London: J. Wilke, 1759.

Thornbrough, Gayle, ed. *Letter Book of the Indian Agency at Fort Wayne, 1809–1815.* Indianapolis: Indiana Historical Society, 1961.

Thwaites, Reuben Gold, ed. *Early Western Travels, 1748–1846.* 32 vols. Cleveland, Ohio: A. H. Clark, 1904–7.

———. *Jesuit Relations and Allied Documents.* 73 vols. Cleveland, Ohio: Burrows, 1896–1901.

Thwaites, Reuben Gold, and Louise Phelps Kellog, eds. *The Revolution on the Upper Ohio, 1775–1777.* Port Washington, N.Y.: Kennikat, 1970.

Troxel, Kathryn. "A Frenchman's View of Little Turtle." *Old Fort News* 6 (1941): 10.

United States Congress. 27th Congress, 3rd Session. *Senate Executive Journal.* Washington, D.C.: J. Allen, 1843.

United States Congress. *American State Papers: Indian Affairs.* 2 vols. Washington, D.C.: Gales and Seaton, 1832–61.

Van Doren, Carl, ed. *Indian Treaties Printed by Benjamin Franklin, 1736–1762.* Philadelphia: Historical Society of Pennsylvania, 1938.

Waddington, Richard. *La Guerre de Sept Ans.* 5 vols. Paris: Firmin, 1899–1914.

Wainwright, Nicholas B., ed. "George Croghan's Journal, 1759–1763." *Pennsylvania Magazine of History and Biography* 71 (Oct. 1947): 393–94.

Wallace, Paul A. W., ed. *The Travels of John Heckewelder in Frontier America.* Pittsburgh, Pa: Univ. of Pittsburgh Press, 1958.

Washburne, E. B., ed. *The Edwards Papers: Being a Portion of the Collection of the Letters, Papers, and Manuscripts of Ninian Edwards.* Chicago: Fergus, 1884.

Weber, Alfred, Beth L. Lueck, and Dennis Berthold, eds. *Hawthorne's American Travel Sketches.* Hanover, N.H.: Univ. Press of New England, 1989.

Whitney, Ellen, ed. *Illinois Historical Collections.* Vols. 35–38: *The Black Hawk War.* Springfield: Illinois State Historical Library, 1973.

Woollen, William Wesley, ed. *Executive Journal of the Indiana Territory, 1800–1816.* Indianapolis, Ind.: Bowen-Merrill, 1900.

NEWSPAPERS

Gazette (Indianapolis, Ind.)
Herald (Indianapolis, Ind.)
Journal and Free-Press (Lafayette, Ind.)
London Chronicle (*Universal Evening Post*)
New York Mercury
Pennsylvania Gazette
South Carolina Gazette

SECONDARY SOURCES

Alford, Thomas Wildcat. *Civilization and the Story of the Absentee Shawnees.* Norman: Univ. of Oklahoma Press, 1979.

Allen, Robert S. *His Majesty's Indian Allies: British Indian Policy in the Defense of Canada, 1774–1815.* Toronto: Dundurn, 1992.

Almon, John. *An Impartial History of the Late War: Deduced from the Committing of Hostilities in 1749, to the Signing of the Definitive Treaty of Peace in 1763.* London, 1763.

Alvord, Clarence Walworth. *The Mississippi Valley in British Politics: A Study of the Trade, Land Speculation, and Experiments in Imperialism Culminating in the American Revolution.* 2 vols. Cleveland, Ohio: Arthur H. Clark, 1917.

Anderson, Fred. *Crucible of War: The Seven Years' War and the Fate of Empire in British North America, 1754–1766.* New York: Knopf, 2000.

Anderson, Gary Clayton. *The Indian Southwest, 1580–1830: Ethnogenesis and Reinvention.* Norman: Univ. of Oklahoma Press, 1999.

Anson, Bert. "Chief Francis Lafontaine and the Miami Emigration from Indiana." *Indiana Magazine of History* 60 (1964): 241–68.

———. *The Miami Indians.* Norman: Univ. of Oklahoma Press, 1970.

———. "Variations of the Indian Conflict: The Effects of the Emigrant Indian Removal Policy, 1830–1854." *Missouri Historical Review* 59 (1964–65): 64–89.

Antrim, Joshua. *The History of Champaign and Logan Counties.* Bellefontaine, Ohio: Press Printing, 1872.

Appleby, Joyce. "What Is Still American in the Political Philosophy of Thomas Jefferson?" *William and Mary Quarterly* 39 (1982): 295–96, 304.

Aron, Stephen. *How the West Was Lost: The Transformation of Kentucky from Daniel Boone to Henry Clay.* Baltimore, Md.: Johns Hopkins Univ. Press, 1996.

Auth, Stephen F. *The Ten Years' War: Indian-White Relations in Pennsylvania, 1755–1765.* New York: Garland, 1989.

Axtell, James. *After Columbus: Essays in the Ethnohistory of Colonial North America.* New York: Oxford Univ. Press, 1989.

———. *Beyond 1492: Cultural Encounters in Colonial North America.* New York: Oxford Univ. Press, 1992.

———. *Natives and Newcomers: The Cultural Origins of North America.* New York: Oxford Univ. Press, 2001.

———. "The White Indians of Colonial America." *William and Mary Quarterly* 32 (1975): 55–88.

Baker, Alan R. H., and Gideon Biger, eds. *Ideology and Landscape: Essays on the Meanings of Some Places in the Past.* Cambridge, U.K.: Cambridge Univ. Press, 1992.

Bakken, Gordon Morris. "Judicial Review in the Rocky Mountain Territorial Courts." *American Journal of Legal History* 15 (1971): 56–65.

Bakken, Larry A. *Justice in the Wilderness: A Study of Frontier Courts in Canada and the United States, 1670–1870.* Littleton, Colo.: Fred B. Rothman, 1986.

Bancroft, George. *History of the United States of America.* Centenary ed. 6 vols. Boston, Mass.: Little, Brown, 1879.

Banta, David D. "The Criminal Code of the Northwest Territory." *Indiana Magazine of History* 9 (1913): 234–46.

Beattie, Daniel J. "The Adaptation of the British Army to Wilderness Warfare." In *Adapting to Conditions: War and Society in the Eighteenth Century,* ed. Maarten Ultee, 56–83. University: Univ. of Alabama Press, 1986.

Beebe, Avery N. "Judge Theophilus L. Dickey and the First Murder Trial in Kendall County." *Journal of the Illinois State Historical Society* 3 (1911): 49–58.

Blume, William Wirt. "Criminal Procedure on the American Frontier: A Study of the Statutes and Court Records of Michigan Territory, 1805–1825." *Michigan Law Review* 57 (1958): 195–256.

Bodenhamer, David J. "Law and Disorder on the Early Frontier: Marion County, Indiana, 1823–1850." *Western History Quarterly* 10 (1979): 323–36.

Brackenridge, Henry. "The Trial of Mamachtaga, a Delaware Indian, the First Person Convicted of Murder West of the Allegheny Mountains and Hanged for His Crime." *Western Pennsylvania History Magazine* 1 (1918): 27–36.

Bragdon, Kathleen Joan. "Crime and Punishment among the Indians of Massachusetts, 1675–1750." *Ethnohistory* 28 (Winter 1981): 23–32.

Brandão, José António. *"Your Fyre Shall Burn No More": Iroquois Policy toward New France and Its Native Allies to 1701.* Lincoln: Univ. of Nebraska Press, 1997.

Brown, Elizabeth Gaspar. "The Views of a Michigan Territorial Jurist on the Common Law." *American Journal of Legal History* 15 (1971): 307–16.

Brumwell, Stephen. *Redcoats: The British Soldier in the Americas, 1755–1763.* New York: Cambridge Univ. Press, 2001.

Cabot, Mary R. *Annals of Brattleboro.* 2 vols. Brattleboro, Mass.: E. L. Hindreth, 1921.

Calloway, Colin G. *The American Revolution in Indian Country: Crisis and Diversity in Native American Communities.* New York: Cambridge Univ. Press, 1995.

———. "Gray Lock's War." *Vermont History* 54 (1986): 197–228.

———. *New Worlds for All: Indians, Europeans, and the Remaking of Early America.* Baltimore, Md.: Johns Hopkins Univ. Press, 1997.

———. *The Western Abenakis of Vermont, 1600–1800: War, Migration, and the Survival of an Indian People.* Norman: Univ. of Oklahoma Press, 1990.

———, ed. *The World Turned Upside Down: Indian Voices from Early America.* Boston, Mass.: Bedford, 1994.

Casgrain, H. R., ed. *Extraits des Archives des Ministères da la Marine et de la Guerre à Paris.* Quebec, Can.: L. J. Demers, 1890.

Cather, Willa. *My Antonia.* Boston, Mass.: Houghton Mifflin, 1918.

Cayton, Andrew R. L. *Frontier Indiana.* Bloomington: Indiana Univ. Press, 1996.

———. *The Frontier Republic: Ideology and Politics in the Ohio Country, 1780–1825.* Kent, Ohio: Kent State Univ. Press, 1986.

———. "A Quiet Independence: The Western Vision of the Ohio Company." *Ohio History* 90 (1981): 5–32.

———, and Fredericka Teute, eds. *Contact Points: American Frontiers from the Mohawk Valley to the Mississippi, 1750–1830.* Chapel Hill: Univ. of North Carolina Press, 1998.

———, and Peter S. Onuf, *The Midwest and the Nation: Rethinking the History of an American Region.* Bloomington: Indiana Univ. Press, 1990.

———, and Susan E. Gray, eds. *The American Midwest: Essays on Regional History.* Bloomington: Indiana Univ. Press, 2001.

Chomsky, Carol. "The United States–Dakota War Trials: A Study in Military Injustice." *Stanford Law Review* 43 (1990): 13–98.

Clark, J. S. *Life in the Middle West.* Chicago: Advance, 1916.

Clifton, James A. *The Prairie People: Change and Continuity in Potawatomi Indian Culture, 1665–1965.* Lawrence: Regents' Press of Kansas, 1977.

Colley, Linda. *Captives: Britain, Empire and the World, 1600–1850.* New York: Pantheon, 2002.

Collins, William Frederick. "John Tipton and the Indians of the Old Northwest." Ph.D. Diss. Purdue Univ., 1997.

Corkran, David H. *The Cherokee Frontier: Conflict and Survival, 1740–1762.* Norman: Univ. of Oklahoma Press, 1962.

Countryman, Edward. *Americans: A Collision of Histories.* New York: Hill and Wang, 1996.

Crass, David Colin, ed. *The Southern Colonial Backcountry: Interdisciplinary Perspective on Frontier Communities.* Knoxville: Univ. of Tennessee Press, 1998.

Cronon, William. *Changes in the Land: Indians, Colonists, and the Ecology of New England.* New York: Hill and Wang, 1983.

Davidson, J. N. *Muh-he-ka-ne-ok: A History of the Stockbridge Nation.* Milwaukee, Wis.: Silas Chapman, 1893.

Davis, James E. *Frontier Illinois.* Bloomington: Indiana Univ. Press, 1998.

Demos, John. *The Unredeemed Captive: A Family Story from Early America.* New York: Knopf, 1994.

Dictionary of Canadian Biography. 14 vols. Toronto: Univ. of Toronto Press, 1966–91.

Dixon, David. *Bushy Run Battlefield.* Mechanicsburg, Pa.: Stackpole, 2003.

Donehoo, George P. *A History of the Indian Villages and Place Names in Pennsylvania.* Harrisburg, Pa.: Telegraph, 1928. Repr., Lewisburg, Pa.: Wennawoods, 1994.

Dougall, Allan H. *The Death of Captain Wells.* Fort Wayne, Ind.: Public Library of Fort Wayne and Allen County, 1958.

Dowd, Gregory E. "The Panic of 1751: The Significance of Rumors on the South Carolina–Cherokee Frontier." *William and Mary Quarterly* 53 (1996): 527–60.

———. *A Spirited Resistance: The North American Indian Struggle for Unity, 1745–1815.* Baltimore, Md.: Johns Hopkins Univ. Press, 1991.

———. "Thinking and Believing: Nativism and Unity in the Ages of Pontiac and Tecumseh." *American Indian Quarterly* 16 (1992): 309–36.

———. *War under Heaven: Pontiac, the Indian Nations & the British Empire.* Baltimore, Md.: Johns Hopkins Univ. Press, 2002.

Downes, Randolph C. *Council Fires on the Upper Ohio.* Pittsburgh, Pa.: Univ. of Pittsburgh Press, 1940.

Duncan, Robert B. "Old Settlers." *Indiana Historical Society Publications* 2 (1894): 376–402.

Dunn, Walter. *Opening New Markets: The British Army and the Old Northwest.* Westport, Conn.: Praeger, 2002.

Dunnigan, Brian Leigh. *Siege—1759: The Campaign against Niagara.* Youngstown, N.Y.: Old Fort Niagara Association, 1996.

Eavenson, Howard N. *Map Maker and Indian Traders: An Account of John Patten, Trader, Arctic Explorer, and Map Maker.* Pittsburgh, Pa.: Univ. of Pittsburgh Press, 1949.

Edmunds, R. David. "Evil Men Who Add to Our Difficulties: Shawnees, Quakers, and William Wells, 1807–1808." *American Indian Culture and Research Journal* 14 (1990): 1–14.

———. *The Potawatomis: Keepers of the Fire.* Norman: Univ. of Oklahoma Press, 1978.

———. *The Shawnee Prophet.* Lincoln: Univ. of Nebraska Press, 1983.

———. *Tecumseh and the Quest for Indian Leadership.* Boston, Mass.: Little, Brown, 1984.

Entick, John. *General History of the Late War, Containing Its Rise, Progress, and Event in Europe, Asia, Africa, and America.* London: E. and C. Dilly, 1764–66.

Esarey, Logan. "Internal Improvements in Early Indiana." *Indiana Historical Society Publications* 5 (1912): 47–158.

Etcheson, Nicole. *The Emerging Midwest: Upland Southerners and the Political Culture of the Old Northwest, 1787–1861.* Bloomington: Indiana Univ. Press, 1996.

Faragher, John Mack. *Sugar Creek: Life on the Illinois Prairie.* New Haven, Conn.: Yale Univ. Press, 1986.

Fatout, Paul. *Indiana Canals.* West Lafayette, Ind.: Purdue University Studies, 1972.

Fenn, Elizabeth A. "Biological Warfare in Eighteenth-Century North America: Beyond Jeffery Amherst." *Journal of American History* 86 (1999–2000): 1,552–80.

Fenton, William N. *The Great Law and the Longhouse: A Political History of the Iroquois Confederacy.* Norman: Univ. of Oklahoma Press, 1998.

Ferling, John. "Soldiers for Virginia: Who Served in the French and Indian War?" *Virginia Magazine of History and Biography* 94 (1986): 307–28.

Ferris, Ezra. "The Early Settlement of the Miami Country." *Indiana Historical Society Publications* 1 (1897): 251.

Flexner, James Thomas. *Mohawk Baronet: Sir William Johnson of New York.* New York: Harper, 1959.

Frégault, Guy. *Canada: The War of the Conquest.* Trans. Margaret M. Cameron. Toronto, Can.: Univ. of Toronto Press, 1969.

Friedenberg, Daniel. *Life, Liberty and the Pursuit of Land: The Plunder of Early America.* Buffalo, N.Y.: Prometheus, 1992.

Frye, H. E. *Waterford and Fort Frye on the Muskingum in the Old Northwest Territory during Indian War.* Lowell, Ohio: Spencer Kile, 1938.

Furbee, Mary Rodd. *Shawnee Captive: The Story of Mary Draper Ingles.* Greensboro, N.C.: Morgan Reynolds, 2001.

Galbreath, C. B. "The Ordinance of 1787: Its Origin and Authorship." *Ohio Archaeological and Historical Society Quarterly* 33 (1924): 111–75.

Gates, Paul W. "Hoosier Cattle Kings." *Indiana Magazine of History* 44 (1948): 1–24.

Gipson, Lawrence Henry. *The British Empire before the American Revolution.* 15 vols. New York: Knopf, 1958–70.

Grabonski, Jan. "French Criminal Justice and Indians in Montreal, 1670–1760." *Ethnohistory* 43 (1996): 405–29.

Gray, Ralph D. "The Canal Era in Indiana." In *Transportation and the Early Nation: Papers Presented at an Indiana American Revolution Bicentennial Symposium,* 113–34. Indianapolis: Indiana Historical Society, 1982.

Gray, Susan E. *The Yankee West: Community Life on the Michigan Frontier.* Chapel Hill: Univ. of North Carolina Press, 1996.

Grissom, Donald B. "William Wells, Indian Agent." *Old Fort News* 42 (1979): 53–58.

Gruenwald, Kim. "Marietta's Example of a Settlement Pattern in the Ohio Country: A Reinterpretation." *Ohio History* 105 (1996): 126–44.

Haefeli, Evan, and Kevin Sweeney. "Revisiting *The Redeemed Captive:* New Perspectives on the 1704 Attack on Deerfield." In *After King Phillip's War: Presence and Persistence in Indian New England,* ed. Colin G. Calloway, 50–53. Hanover, N.H.: Univ. Press of New England, 1997.

Hagan, William T. *The Sac and Fox Indians.* Norman: Univ. of Oklahoma Press, 1958.

Haites, Erik F., James Mak, and Gary M. Walton. *Western River Transportation: The Era of Early Internal Development, 1810–1860*. Baltimore, Md.: Johns Hopkins Univ. Press, 1975.

Hall, Kermit L. *A Comprehensive Bibliography of American Constitutional and Legal History, 1896–1979*. Millwood, N.Y.: Kraus International, 1984.

———. "Constitutional Machinery and Judicial Professionalism: The Careers of Midwestern State Appellate Court Judges, 1861–1899." In *The New High Priests: Lawyers in Post–Civil War America*, ed. Gerard W. Gawalt, 29–49. Westport, Conn.: Greenwood, 1984.

———. "The Legal Culture of the Great Plains." *Great Plains Quarterly* 12 (1992): 86–98.

Hamilton, Milton W. *Sir William Johnson: Colonial American, 1715–1763*. Port Washington, N.Y.: Kennikat, 1976.

Hanna, Charles A. *The Wilderness Trail, or The Ventures and Adventures of the Pennsylvania Traders on the Allegheny Path*. 2 vols. New York: Putnam's, 1911.

Harmon, George Dewey. *Sixty Years of Indian Affairs*. Chapel Hill: Univ. of North Carolina Press, 1941.

Hart, John Fraser. *The Rural Landscape*. Baltimore, Md.: Johns Hopkins Univ. Press, 1998.

Harvey, Henry. *History of the Shawnee Indians from the Years 1681 to 1854, Inclusive*. Cincinnati, Ohio: E. Morgan, 1855.

Hatley, Tom. *Dividing Paths: Cherokees and South Carolinians through the Revolutionary Era*. New York: Oxford Univ. Press, 1995.

Hauptman, Laurence M. *Conspiracy of Interests: Iroquois Dispossession and the Rise of New York State*. New York: Syracuse Univ. Press, 1999.

Hauser, Raymond. "The *Berdache* and the Illinois Indian Tribes during the Last Half of the Seventeenth Century." *Ethnohistory* 37 (1990): 45–65.

Haviland, William A., and Marjory W. Powers. *The Original Vermonters: Native Inhabitants, Past and Present*. Hanover, N.H.: Univ. Press of New England, 1994.

Hawthorne, Nathaniel. "Sketches from Memory, By a Pedestrian, No. II." *New England Magazine* 9 (1835): 398.

Headings, Lois Shepard. "The Distinguished and Extraordinary Man: Chief J. B. Richardville." *Old Fort News* 61 (1998): 1–22.

Heard, Norman J. *White into Red: A Study of the Assimilation of White Persons Captured by Indians*. Metuchen, N.J.: Scarecrow, 1973.

Hickey, Donald. *The War of 1812: A Forgotten Conflict*. Urbana: Univ. of Illinois Press, 1990.

Hildreth, Samuel P. *Pioneer History: Being an Account of the First Examinations of the Ohio Valley and the Early Settlement of the Northwest Territory*. Cincinnati, Ohio: Derby, 1848.

Hinderaker, Eric. *Elusive Empires: Constructing Colonialism in the Ohio Valley, 1673–1800*. New York: Cambridge Univ. Press, 1997.

Hinderaker, Eric, and Peter C. Macall. *At the Edge of Empire: The Backcountry in British North America*. Baltimore, Md.: Johns Hopkins Univ. Press, 2003.

History of Washington County, Ohio, 1788–1881. Salem, W.Va.: Don Mills, 1989.

Hofstadter, Richard. *The Age of Reform: From Bryan to F.D.R.* New York: Knopf, 1955.

Hoxie, Frederick E. *Talking Back to Civilization: Indian Voices from the Progressive Era*. Boston, Mass.: Bedford/St. Martin's, 2001.

————. "Towards a 'New' North American Indian Legal History." *American Journal of Legal History* 30 (1986): 356–57.

————, ed. *Encyclopedia of North American Indians.* Boston, Mass.: Houghton Mifflin, 1996.

Hunter, Charles E. "The Delaware Nativist Revival of the Mid-Eighteenth Century." *Ethnohistory* 18 (1971): 39–49.

Hunter, Louis C. *Steamboats on the Western Rivers: An Economic and Technological History.* New York: Octagon, 1969.

Hunter, William A. *Forts on the Pennsylvania Frontier, 1753–1758.* Harrisburg: Pennsylvania Historical and Museum Commission, 1960.

————. "Traders on the Ohio: 1730." *Western Pennsylvania Historical Magazine* 35 (1972): 85–89.

————. "Victory at Kittanning." *Pennsylvania History* 23 (1956): 376–407.

Hurt, R. Douglas. *Indian Agriculture: Prehistory to the Present.* Lawrence: Univ. Press of Kansas, 1987.

————. *The Indian Frontier, 1763–1846.* Albuquerque: Univ. of New Mexico Press, 2002.

————. *The Ohio Frontier: Crucible of the Old Northwest.* Bloomington: Indiana Univ. Press, 1996.

Hutton, Paul A. "William Wells: Frontier Scout and Indian Agent." *Old Fort News* 43 (1980): 63–67.

Jackson, Halliday. *Civilization of the Indian Natives.* Philadelphia, Pa.: M. T. C. Gould, 1830.

James, Alfred Proctor, and Charles E. Stotz. *Drums in the Forest.* Pittsburgh: Historical Society of Western Pennsylvania, 1958.

Jennings, Francis. *The Ambiguous Iroquois Empire: The Covenant Chain Confederation of Indian Tribes with English Colonies, from Its Beginnings to the Lancaster Treaty of 1744.* New York: Norton, 1984.

————. *Empire of Fortune: Crowns, Colonies and Tribes in the Seven Years' War in America.* New York: Norton, 1988.

————. "A Vanishing Indian: Francis Parkman versus His Sources." *Pennsylvania Magazine of History and Biography* 87 (July 1963): 306–23.

Jennings, Jesse D. *Prehistory of North America.* New York: McGraw-Hill, 1968.

Jones, Electa F. *Stockbridge: Past and Present.* Springfield, Mass.: S. Bowles, 1854.

Jones, Robert L. *A History of Agriculture in Ohio to 1880.* Kent, Ohio: Kent State Univ. Press, 1983.

Josephy, Alvin. *The Patriot Chiefs: A Chronicle of American Indian Resistance.* New York: Penguin, 1993.

Kawashima, Yasuhide. "Forced Conformity: Criminal Justice and Indians." *University of Kansas Law Review* 25 (1977): 361–73.

Keeley, Lawrence H. *War before Civilization.* New York: Oxford Univ. Press, 1996.

Kelsay, Isabel Thompson. *Joseph Brant, 1743–1807: Man of Two Worlds.* Syracuse, N.Y.: Syracuse Univ. Press, 1984.

Kennedy, Roger. *Hidden Cities: The Discovery and Loss of Ancient North American Civilization.* New York: Free, 1994.

Kent, Donald H. *The French Invasion of Western Pennsylvania, 1753.* Harrisburg: Pennsylvania Historical and Museum Commission, 1954.

Kinietz, Vernon, and Erminie W. Voegelin, eds. *Shawnee Traditions: C. C. Trowbridge's Account.* Ann Arbor: Univ. of Michigan Press, 1939.

Kopperman, Paul E. *Braddock at the Monongahela.* Pittsburgh, Pa.: Univ. of Pittsburgh Press, 1977.

Kulikoff, Allan. *The Agrarian Origins of American Capitalism.* Charlottesville: Univ. Press of Virginia, 1992.

Larson, John Lauritz. *Internal Improvement: National Public Works and the Promise of Popular Government in the Early United States.* Chapel Hill: Univ. of North Carolina Press, 2001.

Lightfoot, Kent G., and Antoinette Martinez. "Frontiers and Boundaries in Archaeological Perspective." *Annual Review of Anthropology* 24 (1995): 471–92.

Lindgren, James. "Why the Ancients May Not Have Needed a System of Criminal Law." *Boston University Law Review* 76 (1996): 29.

Mancall, Peter C. *Deadly Medicine: Indians and Alcohol in Early America.* Ithaca, N.Y.: Cornell Univ. Press, 1995.

Mandell, Daniel R. *Behind the Frontier: Indians in Eighteenth-Century Eastern Massachusetts.* Lincoln: Univ. of Nebraska Press, 1996.

"The Man in the Middle: Chief J.B. Richardville." In Carole M. Allen et al., eds., *The Indiana Historian* (Nov. 1992): 1–15.

Mante, Thomas. *The History of the Late War in North America and the Islands of the West Indies.* London: W. Strahan and T. Cadell, 1772.

Marienstras, Elise. "The Common Man's Indian: The Image of the Indian as a Promoter of National Identity in the Early National Era." In *Native Americans and the Early Republic,* ed. Fredrick N. Hoxie, Ronald Hoffman, and Peter J. Albert, 261–96. Charlottesville: The Univ. Press of Virginia, 1999.

Martin, James Kirby. "The Return of the Paxton Boys and the Historical State of the Pennsylvania Frontier." *Pennsylvania History* 38 (1971): 117–33.

Matson, Cathy D., and Peter S. Onuf. *A Union of Interests: Political and Economic Thought in Revolutionary America.* Lawrence: Univ. of Kansas Press, 1990.

McClure, James P. "The Ends of the American Earth: Pittsburgh and the Upper Ohio Valley to 1795." Ph.D. Diss. Univ. of Michigan, 1983.

McConnell, Michael N. *A Country Between: The Upper Ohio Valley and Its Peoples, 1724–1774.* Lincoln: Univ. of Nebraska Press, 1992.

McCulloch, David, ed. *History of Peoria County Illinois.* Chicago: Munsell, 1902.

McCulloch, Hugh. *Men and Measures of Half a Century: Sketches and Comments.* New York: Scribner's, 1888.

McGuirk, Harry L. "A Pioneer Indiana County Circuit Court." *American Journal of Legal History* 15 (1971): 278–87.

McKee, Irving. "The Trail of Death: Letters of Benjamin Marie Petit." *Indiana Historical Society Publications* 14 (1941): 5–141.

Merrell, James H. *The Indians' New World: Catawbas and Their Neighbors from European Contact through the Era of Removal.* Chapel Hill: Univ. of North Carolina Press, 1989.

———. *Into the American Woods: Negotiators on the Pennsylvania Frontier.* New York: Norton, 1999.

Merritt, Jane T. *At the Crossroads: Indians and Empires on a Mid-Atlantic Frontier, 1700–1763.* Chapel Hill: Univ. of North Carolina Press, 2003.

Mitchell, Robert D., ed. *Appalachian Frontiers: Settlement, Society, and Development in the Pre-Industrial Era.* Lexington: Univ. Press of Kentucky, 1991.

Momboisse, Raymond M. "Early California Justice: First Murder Trial." *California Bar Journal* 37 (1962): 736–42.

Moon, Bill. "The Story of Noma-a-Que: Court Records Tell Interesting Story of Peoria County's First Murder Trial." *Journal of the Illinois State Historical Society* 5 (1913): 246–55.

Morrison, Kenneth M. *The Embattled Northeast: The Elusive Ideal of Alliance in Abenaki-Euramerican Relations.* Berkeley: Univ. of California Press, 1984.

Muldoon, Sylvan Joseph. *Alexander Hamilton's Pioneer Son: The Life and Times of Colonel William Stephen Hamilton.* Harrisburg, Pa.: Aurand, 1930.

Myers, James P. "Pennsylvania's Awakening: The Kittanning Raid of 1756." *Pennsylvania History* 66 (1999): 399–420.

Namias, June. *White Captives: Gender and Ethnicity on the American Frontier.* Chapel Hill: Univ. of North Carolina Press, 1992.

Nichols, Roger. *Black Hawk and the Warrior's Path.* Arlington Heights, Ill.: Harlan Davidson, 1992.

Nobles, Gregory H. *American Frontiers: Cultural Encounters and Continental Conquest.* New York: Hill and Wang, 1997.

Olmstead, Earl P. *Blackcoats among the Delaware.* Kent, Ohio: Kent State Univ. Press, 1991.

Onuf, Peter S. "From Constitution to Higher Law: The Reinterpretation of the Northwest Ordinance." *Ohio History* 94 (1985): 5–33.

———. "Liberty, Development, and Union: Visions of the West in the 1780s." *William and Mary Quarterly* 43 (1986): 179–203.

———. *The Origins of the Federal Republic.* Philadelphia: Univ. of Pennsylvania Press, 1983.

———. *Statehood and Union: A History of the Northwest Ordinance.* Bloomington: Indiana Univ. Press, 1987.

Opie, John. *The Law of the Land: Two Hundred Years of American Farmland Policy.* Lincoln: Univ. of Nebraska Press, 1994.

Parkman, Francis. *The Conspiracy of Pontiac and the Indian War after the Conquest of Canada.* 2 vols. Lincoln: Univ. of Nebraska Press, 1994.

———. *Montcalm and Wolfe.* 3 vols. Boston, Mass.: Little, Brown, 1905.

Parmenter, Jon. "At the Woods' Edge: Iroquois Foreign Relations, 1727–1768." Ph.D. Diss. Univ. of Michigan, 1999.

Parsons, Joseph A., Jr. "Civilizing the Indians of the Old Northwest, 1800–1810." *Indiana Magazine of History* 56 (1960): 195–216.

Payne, John Howard. *Indian Justice: A Cherokee Murder Trial at Tahlequah in 1840.* Ed. Grant Foreman. Norman: Univ. of Oklahoma Press, 2002.

Peckham, Howard H. *Pontiac and the Indian Uprising.* Detroit, Mich.: Wayne State Univ. Press, 1994.

———. "The Sources and Revisions of Parkman's *Pontiac.*" *Papers of the Bibliographic Society of America* 37 (1943): 298–99.

Perdue, Theda. *Slavery and the Evolution of Cherokee Society, 1540–1866.* Knoxville: Univ. of Tennessee Press, 1979.

Perry, D. M. "The Richardville House." *Old Fort News* 53 (1990): 1–7.

Petty, R. O., and M. T. Jackson. "Plant Communities." In *Natural Features of Indiana,* ed. Alton A. Lindsey, 280. Indianapolis: Indiana Academy of Science, 1966.

Peyer, Bernd. *The Tutor'd Mind: Indian Missionary-Writers in Antebellum America.* Amherst: Univ. of Massachusetts Press, 1997.

Pfaller, Louis. "The Brave Bear Murder Case." *North Dakota History* 36 (1969): 121–40.

Philbrick, Francis S. *The Rise of the West, 1754–1830.* New York: Harper and Row, 1965.

Poinsatte, Charles R. *Fort Wayne during the Canal Era, 1828–1855: A Study of a Western Community in the Middle Period of American History.* Indianapolis: Indiana Historical Bureau, 1969.

Posner, Richard A. "An Economic Theory of Criminal Law." *Columbia Law Review* 85 (1985): 1,193–231.

Potterf, Rex. "Little Turtle." *Old Fort News* 21 (1958): 1–11.

Prucha, Francis Paul. *American Indian Policy in the Formative Years: The Indian Trade and Intercourse Acts.* Lincoln: Univ. of Nebraska Press, 1970.

Quaife, Milo Milton, ed. *Chicago and the Old Northwest, 1763–1835: A Study of the Evolution of the Northwestern Frontier.* Urbana: Univ. of Illinois Press, 2001.

———. *Life of Black Hawk.* New York: Dover, 1994.

Rafert, Stewart. *The Miami Indians of Indiana: A Persistent People, 1654–1994.* Indianapolis: Indiana Historical Society, 1996.

Reid, John Phillip. *Patterns of Vengeance: Crosscultural Homicide in the North American Fur Trade.* Sacramento, Calif.: Ninth Judicial Circuit Historical Society, 1999.

Richardson, Willis, ed. "Little Turtle Pictures." *Old Fort News* 2 (1937): 3–4.

Richter, Daniel K. *Facing East from Indian Country: A Native History of Early America.* Cambridge, Mass.: Harvard Univ. Press, 2001.

Richter, Daniel K., and James H. Merrell, eds. *Beyond the Covenant Chain: The Iroquois and Their Neighbors in Indian North America, 1600–1800.* New York: Syracuse Univ. Press, 1987.

Roberts, Bessie Keeran. "William Wells: A Legend in the Councils of Two Nations." *Old Fort News* 17 (1954): 5–10.

Robinson, W. Stitt. *James Glen, From Scottish Provost to Royal Governor of South Carolina.* Westport, Conn.: Greenwood, 1996.

Ronda, James P. "As They Were Faithful: Chief Hendrick Aupaumut and the Struggle for Stockbridge Survival, 1757–1830." *American Indian Culture and Research Journal* 3 (1979): 43–55.

Royce, Charles C. *Indian Land Cessions in the United States.* Washington, D.C.: GPO, 1900. Repr., New York: Arno, 1971.

Salisbury, Neal. "Embracing Ambiguity: Native Peoples and Christianity in Seventeenth-Century North America." *Ethnohistory* 50 (2003): 247–59.

———. *Manitou and Providence: Indians, Europeans, and the Making of New England, 1500–1643.* New York: Oxford Univ. Press, 1982.

Samaha, Joel. "A Case of Murder: Criminal Justice in Early Minnesota." *Minnesota Law Review* 60 (1976): 1,219–32.

Scheiber, Harry N. *Ohio Canal Era: A Case Study of Government and the Economy, 1820–1861.* Athens: Ohio Univ. Press, 1969.

Sellers, Charles. *The Market Revolution: Jacksonian America, 1815–1846*. New York: Oxford Univ. Press, 1991.

Shaw, Ronald E. "The Canal Era in the Old Northwest." *Transportation and the Early Nation: Papers Presented at an Indiana American Revolution Bicentennial Symposium*, 89–112. Indianapolis: Indiana Historical Society, 1982.

———. *Canals for a Nation: The Canal Era in the United States, 1790–1860*. Lexington: Univ. Press of Kentucky, 1990.

Sheriff, Carol. *The Artificial River: The Erie Canal and the Paradox of Progress, 1817–1862*. New York: Hill and Wang, 1996.

Sipe, C. Hale. *The Indian Wars of Pennsylvania*. 2nd ed. Harrisburg, Pa.: Telegraph, 1931. Repr., Lewisburg, Pa.: Wennawoods, 1994.

Skaggs, David Curtis, and Larry L. Nelson, eds. *The Sixty Years' War for the Great Lakes, 1754–1814*. East Lansing: Michigan State Univ. Press, 2001.

Skinner, Alanson. *Observations on the Ethnology of the Sac Indians*. Westport, Conn.: Greenwood, 1970.

Slaughter, Thomas. *The Whiskey Rebellion: Frontier Epilogue to the American Revolution*. New York: Oxford Univ. Press, 1986.

Slotkin, Richard. *The Fatal Environment: The Myth of the Frontier in the Age of Industrialization, 1800–1890*. New York: Atheneum, 1985.

———. *Regeneration through Violence: The Mythology of the American Frontier, 1600–1860*. Middletown, Conn.: Wesleyan Univ. Press, 1973.

Smith, Dwight L. "Shawnee Captivity Ethnohistory." *Ethnohistory* 2 (1955): 29–57.

Smith, Henry Nash. *Virgin Land: The American West as Symbol and Myth*. 2nd ed. Cambridge, Mass.: Harvard Univ. Press, 1970.

Smith-Rosenberg, Carroll. "Captured Subjects/Savage Others: Violently Engendering the New American." *Gender and History* 5 (1993): 177–95.

Snapp, J. Russell. *John Stuart and the Struggle for Empire on the Southern Frontier*. Baton Rouge: Univ. of Louisiana Press, 1996.

Sosin, Jack M. *Whitehall and the Wilderness: The Middle West in British Colonial Policy, 1760–1775*. Lincoln: Univ. of Nebraska Press, 1961.

Spencer, J. E., and Ronald J. Horvath. "How Does an Agricultural Region Originate?" *Annals of the Association of American Geographers* 53 (1963): 74–92.

Stephenson, R. S. "Pennsylvania Provincial Soldiers in the Seven Years' War." *Pennsylvania History* 62 (1995): 196–212.

Stevens, Frank E. *The Black Hawk War, Including a Review of Black Hawk's Life*. Chicago: Frank E. Stevens, 1903.

Stilgoe, John R. *Common Landscape of America, 1580–1845*. New Haven, Conn.: Yale Univ. Press, 1982.

Stone, William. *Life of Joseph Brant, Thayendanegea*. New York: George Dearborn, 1838.

Sugden, John. *Blue Jacket, Warrior of the Shawnees*. Lincoln: Univ. of Nebraska Press, 2000.

Summers, Thomas J. *History of Marietta*. Marietta, Ohio: Leader, 1903.

Sword, Wiley. *President Washington's Indian War: The Struggle for the Old Northwest, 1790–1795*. Norman: Univ. of Oklahoma Press, 1985.

Tanner, Helen Hornbeck. *Atlas of Great Lakes Indian History.* Norman: Univ. of Oklahoma Press, 1986.

Taylor, Alan. "Captain Hendrick Aupaumut: The Dilemmas of an Intercultural Broker." *Ethnohistory* 43 (1996).

———. "Land and Liberty on the Post Revolutionary Frontier." In *Devising Liberty: Preserving and Creating Freedom in the New American Republic,* ed. David Thomas Konig, 81–108. Stanford, Calif.: Stanford Univ. Press, 1995.

Taylor, George Rogers. *The Transportation Revolution, 1815–1860.* Vol. 4: *The Economic History of the United States.* New York: Harper and Row, 1951.

Titus, James. *The Old Dominion at War: Society, Politics, and Warfare in Late Colonial Virginia.* Columbia: Univ. of South Carolina Press, 1991.

Trennert, Robert A., Jr. *Indian Traders on the Middle Border: The House of Ewing, 1826–54.* Lincoln: Univ. of Nebraska Press, 1981.

Trigger, Bruce G. *Handbook of North American Indians.* Vol. 15: *Northeast.* Washington, D.C.: Smithsonian Institution, 1978.

Utley, Robert M. *A Life Wild and Perilous: Mountain Men and the Paths to the Pacific.* New York: Henry Holt, 1997.

Vance, James E. "Democratic Utopia and the American Landscape." In *The Making of the American Landscape,* ed. Michael P. Cozen, 204–20. London: Harper Collins, 1990.

Vaughan, Alden T., and Daniel K. Richter. "Crossing the Cultural Divide: Indians and New Englanders, 1605–1763." *American Antiquarian Society Proceedings* 90 (1980): 23–99.

Volney, C. F. *A View of the Soil and Climate of the United States of America.* In *Contributions to the History of Geology,* ed. George W. White, 360–61, 378. Philadelphia, Pa.: 1804. Repr., New York: Hafner, 1968.

Volwiler, Albert Tangeman. *George Croghan and the Westward Movement, 1741–1782.* Cleveland, Ohio: Arthur H. Clark, 1926.

Waddell, Joseph. *Annals of Augusta County, Virginia.* 2 vols. Richmond, Va.: Ellis Jones, 1886.

Waddell, Louis M. "Defending the Long Perimeter: Forts on the Pennsylvania, Maryland, and Virginia Frontier, 1755–1765." *Pennsylvania History* 62 (1995): 185–88.

Waddington, Richard. *La Guerre de Sept Ans.* 5 vols. Paris: Firmin, 1899–1907.

Wainwright, Nicholas B. *George Croghan, Wilderness Diplomat.* Chapel Hill: Univ. of North Carolina Press, 1959.

Wallace, Anthony F. C. *Jefferson and the Indians: The Tragic Fate of the First Americans.* Cambridge, Mass.: Harvard Univ. Press, 1999.

———. "New Religions among the Delaware Indians." *Southwest Journal of Anthropology* 12 (1956): 1–21.

———. "Prelude to Disaster: The Course of Indian-White Relations which Led to the Black Hawk War of 1832." *Wisconsin Magazine of History* (1982): 247–88.

Wallace, Paul A. W. *Indians in Pennsylvania.* Rev. ed. Harrisburg: Pennsylvania Historical and Museum Commission, 1993.

Ward, Matthew C. "An Army of Servants: The Pennsylvania Regiment during the Seven Years' War." *Pennsylvania Magazine of History and Biography* 119 (1995): 75–93.

————. *Breaking the Backcountry: The Seven Years' War in Pennsylvania and Virginia, 1754–1765*. Pittsburgh, Pa.: Univ. of Pittsburgh Press, 2003.

————. "'The European Method of Warring Is Not Practiced Here': The Failure of British Military Policy in the Ohio Valley, 1755–1759." *War in History* 4 (1997): 258–60.

————. "Fighting the Old Women: Indian Strategy on the Virginia and Pennsylvania Frontier, 1754–1758." *Virginia Magazine of History and Biography* 103 (1995): 297–320.

————. "La Guerre Sauvage: The Seven Years' War on the Virginia and Pennsylvania Frontier." Ph.D. Diss. The College of William and Mary, 1992.

————. "Redeeming Captives: Pennsylvania Captives among the Ohio Indians, 1755–1765." *Pennsylvania Magazine of History and Biography* 125 (2001): 161–89.

Warville, Brissot de. *New Travels in the United States of America*. Cambridge, Mass.: Harvard Univ. Press, 1964.

"Wattanummon's World: Personal and Tribal Identity in the Algonquian Diaspora, c. 1660–1712." *Papers of the 25th Algonquian Conference*. Ottawa, Can.: Carleton University, 1994.

Way, Peter. "The Cutting Edge of Culture: British Soldiers Encounter Native Americans in the French and Indian War." In *Empire and Others: British Encounters with Indigenous Peoples, 1600–1850*, ed. Martin Daunton and Rick Halpern, 123–48. Philadelphia: Univ. of Pennsylvania Press, 1999.

Webster, Homer J. "William Henry Harrison's Administration of Indiana Territory." *Indiana Historical Society Publications* 4 (1907): 189.

Weslager, C. A. *The Delaware Indians, a History*. New Brunswick, N.J.: Rutgers Univ. Press, 1972.

White, Richard. *The Middle Ground: Indians, Empires, and Republics in the Great Lakes Region, 1650–1815*. New York: Cambridge Univ. Press, 1991.

Winger, Otho. *Little Turtle: The Great Chief of Eel River*. North Manchester, Ind.: News-Journal, 1942.

————. "Me-She-Kin-No-Quah (Little Turtle)." *Old Fort News* 2 (1937): 5.

Woehrmann, Paul. *At the Headwaters of the Maumee: A History of the Forts of Fort Wayne*. Indianapolis: Indiana Historical Society, 1971.

Wright, J. Leitch. *Britain and the American Frontier, 1783–1815*. Athens: Univ. of Georgia Press, 1975.

Wunder, John R. "Anti-Chinese Violence in the American West, 1850–1910." In *Law for the Elephant, Law for the Beaver: Essays in the Legal History of the North American West*, ed. John McLaren, Hamar Foster, and Chet Orloff, 212–36. Regina, Sask.: Canadian Plains Research Center, 1992.

————. "Chinese in Trouble: Criminal Law and Race on the Trans-Mississippi West Frontier." *Western Historical Quarterly* 17 (1986): 25–41.

————. *Inferior Courts, Superior Justice: A History of the Justices of the Peace on the Northwest Frontier, 1853–1889*. Westport, Conn.: Greenwood, 1979.

————, ed. *Law and the Great Plains: Essays on the Legal History of the Heartland*. Westport, Conn.: Greenwood, 1996.

Wyman, Mark. *The Wisconsin Frontier*. Bloomington: Indiana Univ. Press, 1998.

Young, Calvin M. *Little Turtle (Me-She-Kin-No-Quah): The Great Chief of the Miami Na-tion.* Indianapolis, Ind.: Sentinel, 1917. Repr., Fort Wayne, Ind.: Public Library of Fort Wayne and Allen County, 1956.

Young, Chester Raymond. "The Effects of the French and Indian War on Civilian Life in the Frontier Counties of Virginia, 1754–1763." Ph.D. Diss. Vanderbilt Univ., 1969.

Young, Henry J. "A Note on Scalp Bounties in Pennsylvania." *Pennsylvania History* 24 (1957): 208–11.

Contributors

GINETTE ALEY is assistant professor of history at the University of Southern Indiana. She has published articles and essays in *Agricultural History, The Oxford Companion to United States History,* and *The Encyclopedia of the Midwest.* She is currently revising her dissertation, "Westward Expansion, John Tipton, and the Emergence of the American Midwest, 1800–1839," for publication.

DANIEL P. BARR is assistant professor at Robert Morris University in Pittsburgh, Pennsylvania, where he teaches Early American and American Indian history. He is currently completing two book-length projects: a study of warfare and society on the early Pittsburgh frontier, to be published by the Kent State University Press, and an examination of Iroquois warfare in Colonial America.

LISA BROOKS, a member of the Abenaki Indian nation, received a Ph.D. in English and American studies at Cornell University. She is the past recipient of a Ford Foundation Dissertation Fellowship for 2002–2003 as well as a research fellowship from the John Carter Brown Library and the Newberry Library's Francis C. Allen Fellowship in American Indian studies. She currently teaches in the history and literature program at Harvard University.

DAVID DIXON is professor of history at Slippery Rock University in western Pennsylvania. He is the author of *Never Come to Peace Again: Pontiac's Uprising and the Fate of British Empire in North America* (2005). An earlier book, *Hero at Beecher Island: The Life and Military Career of George A. Forsyth* (1994), won the Spur Award from the Western Writers Association for best book in the history of the American West.

DONALD H. GAFF, a Ph.D. candidate in anthropology at Michigan State University, earned his M.S. in cultural anthropology at the University of Wisconsin-Milwaukee in 1997. He has led or participated in numerous archaeological field projects in Wisconsin, Illinois, and Michigan, as well as authoring essays and technical reports on the historical archaeology and ethnohistory of northwest Indiana.

PHYLLIS GERNHARDT is assistant professor and chairperson of the department of history at the University of Saint Francis in Fort Wayne, Indiana. She earned a Ph.D. in American history from Bowling Green State University in 1999, where she specialized in early America and the American frontier. Professor Gernhardt has presented papers at scholarly conferences concerning the history of the Old Northwest and she is currently completing revisions on a manuscript for publication, entitled "Here Will Arise a Town of Great Importance: The United States Government, Federal Agents, and Frontier Settlement at Fort Wayne, Indiana."

THOMAS J. LAPPAS is assistant professor of history at Nazareth College in Rochester, New York, where he teaches courses in Colonial America, American Indian History, and France in North America. He has presented his research at conferences held by the Great Lakes Historical Society and the Ohio Valley Historical Association, while also publishing numerous essays pertaining to American Indian histories in *The Encyclopedia of American History* (2003).

FRAZER DORIAN McGLINCHEY received his M.A. in American history from the University of Glasgow in Scotland. He is currently a doctoral candidate at Cambridge University, where he is completing his dissertation, "Myth and Reality on the Early American Frontier: Visions of Landscape and Future in the Northwest Territory."

BRUCE P. SMITH is associate professor of law at the University of Illinois College of Law, where he co-directs the Illinois Legal History Program. His primary research interests focus on the history of Anglo-American criminal justice administration in the eighteenth and nineteenth centuries.

IAN K. STEELE, an accomplished historian, is professor emeritus of history and retired chair of graduate studies at Western Ontario University. The author of numerous books, including *Warpaths: Invasions of North America, 1513–1765* (1994), *Betrayals: Fort William Henry and the Massacre* (1990), and *Guerillas and Grenadiers: The Struggle for Canada, 1689–1760* (1969), he is currently working on a study of captivity in North American frontier warfare.

MATTHEW C. WARD is lecturer in American history at the University of Dundee in Scotland. He earned a Ph.D. in early American history from the College of William and Mary in 1992. Professor Ward has published many articles pertaining to the Seven Years' War in the Ohio Valley and is the author of *Breaking the Backcountry: The Seven Years' War in Virginia and Pennsylvania, 1754–1765* (2003).

Index

Ohio Company of Associates: attitudes of,
119–21; and Indians, 126–28, 131–35; plans
for Marietta, xv, 118–19, 121–22, 124–25,
135; theories about origin of Indian
mounds, 122–24
Ohio Company of Virginia, 25, 77
Ohio Country, xii, xiii, 25, 33, 46–47, 53, 58,
80
Ohio Country Indians (Ohio Indians), 68,
72, 78; relations with British, 54–58
Ohio Indians. *See* Ohio Country Indians
Ohio Shawnees. *See* Shawnee Indians
Old Briton. *See* Memeskia
Old Northwest Territory, ix–xiii, 40, 78
Onuf, Peter, ix, 201
Osage Indians, 221, 224, 228
Ottawa Indians, 30, 47, 49–52, 55, 58, 191, 209

Parkman, Francis, 10, 62; *The Conspiracy of
Pontiac*, 44–45
Patten, John, 5–6
Paxton Boys, 75
pays d'en haut (upper country), 50–51
Pecanne (Miami), 145, 151
Peckham, Howard, 45
Pennsylvania, 32, 33; efforts to defend
frontier during Seven Years' War, 33–37;
enacts scalp bounties, 36
Peoria, 165–66, 168, 172; Potawatomi village
destroyed, 164, 169–70
Peters, Richard, 48–49
Pickawillany (Ohio), 27, 51–52
Pickering, Timothy, 92–95, 103, 106–7
Pigeon (Miami), 186, 188
Pisquetomen (Delaware), 38–39
Pontiac (Ottawa), 44–45, 59–62, 78
Pontiac's Rebellion (Pontiac's Uprising), 40,
45, 60, 72, 75
Pontiac's Uprising. *See* Pontiac's Rebellion
Post, Christian Frederick, 38–39
Potawatomi Indians, xvi, 58, 60, 170–71,
229–30; murder of Elijah Cox, 161–62;
Peoria destroyed by Illinois militia, 164,
169–70; relations with the French, 30, 50,
52; removal from Indiana, 183, 191–92,
209–10; treaties, 182; violence in frontier
Illinois, 163–68
Proctor, Thomas, 88
Putnam, Rufus, 124, 131, 152

Quebec Act, 79–80

Ray, James Brown, 208–9
Recollections of the First Settlement of Ohio
(Barker), 130, 134
Red Hawk (Miskapalathy), 14–15
Red Jacket (Seneca), 88, 102
Redstone Creek, 77–78
Richardville, Jean Baptiste, xv–xvi, 143, 152;
advantages as métis, 150; biographical
sketch, 145; cross-cultural characteristics,
154–58; historical treatment of, 157–58;
house of, 150–51, 157; as Miami principal
chief, 151–52; wealth, 150–51, 156
Richter, Daniel, xi
Rogers, Robert, 1, 10, 53

Sac and Fox Indians, 191–92, 219–34
Saukenuk, 222–23, 230, 233
Scarouady (Monacatootha) (Oneida), 4, 5,
48, 51
Seneca Indians, 46–47, 49, 51, 55, 58, 101; plot
uprising against the British, 56–57. *See
also* Mingo Indians
Seven Years' War (French and Indian War),
27, 52, 68, 79
Shappeen, Bill (Miami), 186, 188
Shawnee Indians, 30, 76, 92–93, 105, 128, 228;
attack Virginia frontier during Seven
Years' War, 11–12; captives, 11–13, 14–16;
captivity as motivation for war, xii–xiii,
4, 9–11; escape from Charles Town
prison, 5, 7–8; imprisonment in South
Carolina, xii–xiii, 3–4; Logstown council
(1754), 6–7; migrate to upper Ohio Val-
ley, 25–26, 46; raid Catawbas, 1–2; rela-
tions with British, 7–8, 16–17, 52–53, 58;
relations with French, 8–10; take
Croghan and Montour prisoner, 6
Shingas (Delaware), 29, 31–32, 34, 36–39
Sioux Indians, 73, 191, 224–25, 227–28, 231
Six Nations. *See* Iroquois Confederacy
Slotkin, Richard, 126
Sonajoana (Seneca), 57
Stapleford, John, 186
St. Clair, Arthur, 88, 92, 97, 120, 127–28, 133,
152
Stephen, Adam, 36
St. Louis, 164, 167